The Ship That Held the Line

The Ship That

Lisle A. Rose

Naval Institute Press

Held the Line —————————————

The U.S.S. *Hornet* and the
First Year of the Pacific War

Annapolis, Maryland

Library of Congress Cataloging-in-Publication Data

Rose, Lisle Abbott, 1936–
    The ship that held the line : the USS Hornet and the first year of
the Pacific War / Lisle A. Rose.
        p.   m.
    Includes bibliographical references and index.
    ISBN 1-55750-729-5 (acid-free paper)
    1. Hornet (Aircraft carrier : CV8)   2. World War, 1939–1945—
Naval operations, American.   3. Shipwrecks—Pacific Ocean.
    I. Title.
    PN774.H6R67   1995
    940.54'5973—dc20   95-8693

Printed in the United States of America on acid-free paper ∞

02 01 00 99 98 97 96 95   9 8 7 6 5 4 3 2
First printing

All photos courtesy of the U.S. Naval Institute's
photographic library.

Contents

Introduction

KIDS DREAM. Lonely kids dream more. One night sometime in the late forties I stumbled across a book in the Champaign, Illinois, Public Library titled *A Ship to Remember: The Saga of the* Hornet. Hastily written by Alexander Griffin shortly after the carrier's sinking, on the basis of numerous interviews, the book had a captivating immediacy and color. Griffin took the reader aboard a big, new ship and made the danger, heroism, and excitement of the early Pacific war come alive. I read and reread *A Ship to Remember,* and a lifelong obsession with naval history and World War II in the Pacific began.

Shortly thereafter my father informed me casually that Oscar Dodson, the *Hornet*'s communications officer, was head of the Naval ROTC department at the University of Illinois, and a meeting was soon arranged between a nervous thirteen-year-old and a combat veteran of the Pacific war. Dodson was a wonderful man—quiet, unassuming, and very approachable. His stories about his days on the *Hornet* and his descriptions of the ship were enthralling. (Dodson later came back to Illinois while I was an undergraduate and taught an excellent course on Roman history, based to some extent on his long fascination with ancient coins, some of which unfortunately went down with the *Hornet*.) After pestering the patient admiral on several occasions, I proceeded to read everything I could find about the naval war in the Pacific, and during high school I compiled a formidable library of primary sources about the Pacific war gleaned from a dozen used bookstores in the Chicago area. My fascination with the *Hornet* never departed. It remained throughout my own brief naval service, which did not include carrier duty, and continued through the years.

By the eighties Griffin's book, now unknown to any but the most meticulous scholars of the Pacific war, was outdated. Only two of the prewar carriers had received the book-length attention they deserved. Edward Stafford had written a fine account of the *Enterprise*. The *Yorktown* still awaited a biographer; so did the *Wasp* and the *Saratoga*. Stanley Johnston's *Queen of the Flat-tops*, about the *Lexington*, remained surprisingly pertinent because Johnston learned of and guardedly wrote about the work of Joseph Rochefort and his small band of supersecret cryptanalysts, who were reading Japan's naval messages in the basement of the Fourteenth Naval District Building at Pearl Harbor. When *Queen of the Flat-tops* appeared in 1942, a furious chief of naval operations, Adm. Ernest J. King, tried to have Johnston court-martialed and the book suppressed. Fortunately for history and historians, King never got his way, and the Japanese never caught on to what Johnston was suggesting.

While I was considering the need for a rewriting of the *Hornet*'s story I became aware of the *Hornet* Reunion Committee, run energetically and efficiently by Albert and Connie Massie. I contacted them, and they kindly included me in the 1989 gathering at Norfolk. The majority of those attending were, of course, veterans of CV-12, the second carrier *Hornet*, commissioned in November 1943. But a handful of survivors of the old CV-8 also came and provided me with many hours of reminiscences. Subsequently, the Massies gave me a list of CV-8 veterans throughout the country, which allowed me to broaden substantially my interviewing and my understanding of the ship. Rear Adm. Francis Foley not only spoke to me for an entire afternoon at his Annapolis home, he also gave me a copy of his article "Every Good Ship Has a Heart," only a portion of which was subsequently published in *Naval History* (Winter 1992). From then on I was hooked. The story of CV-8 had to be told again to a new generation and from the perspective of half a century of scholarship and reflection about the first year of the Pacific war.

In addition to the Massies and Admiral Foley, I want to extend my sincere thanks to CV-8 veterans Keith Bancroft, Eugene Blackmer, Glen Dock, William J. Hill, Roger Kimpton, Gerald McAteer, Henry Martin, Jack Medley, Cardon Ruchti, Bob Taylor, and James Walker for taking time to talk to me and, equally important, for providing me with invaluable newspaper clippings that detailed the *Hornet*'s loss and described incidents that had occurred before the sinking. In addition, Keith Bancroft kindly allowed me to examine and to quote from the brief diary that he kept sporadically while on board the carrier.

Dr. Dean C. Allard and his staff at the Naval Historical Center in Washington, D.C., were especially helpful, providing me with about four hundred pages of documents regarding the *Hornet*. These materials—basically ship's reports on the Doolittle mission, Midway, the mid-October fighting around Guadalcanal, and the Battle of Santa Cruz—are cited under the title "U.S.S. *Hornet* (CV-8) War Diary" in the bibliography and notes. Paul Stillwell and his staff in Annapolis directed me to the score or so of pertinent interviews with veterans of the Pacific war and the *Hornet* housed in the U.S. Naval Institute's oral history collection.

Finally, of course, every author must acknowledge with awe and gratitude the work of several hundred historians, biographers, and participants who during the past half-century have investigated every nook and cranny of the Pacific war and have analyzed and reanalyzed every strategic and tactical decision on both sides. Any writer who now comes to the subject has a broad and sure frame of reference from which to work. Nonetheless, the scope and scale of that incredible conflict was so vast that it will never exhaust the interest of either readers or writers. Like the American Civil War, World War II is an event that will live in memory and imagination for generations.

The Ship That Held the Line

I

Birth

By 25 September 1939 World War II was three weeks old and the German army had completed its rush across the sun-baked fields of Poland to surround Warsaw. Waves of Nazi Stukas appeared over the beleaguered city and in screaming dives terror-bombed the tormented inhabitants, who had only days of precarious freedom remaining. A week before, Soviet armies had pushed across Poland's eastern frontiers to help Hitler carve up the hapless nation and to provide Stalin a buffer against German aggression. In the West, Germany's enemies sat uneasily behind Maginot fortifications or squatted apprehensively beneath barrage balloons awaiting tyranny's next blow.

Across the Atlantic that Monday morning, in Virginia, workmen in one of the two large slipways at the Newport News Shipbuilding and Drydock Company began laying the keel of a new aircraft carrier. They were proud men, these shipbuilders. They had plied their trade for decades, and their motto was that they would build a good ship, at a profit if they could, at a loss if they must, but always a good ship.[1] In the coming months, as the eight-hundred-foot hull gradually took form, Hitler became the master of all Europe. The fall of Poland was followed by a long winter of uneasy calm, the "phony war." Then in the spring of 1940 the Wehrmacht suddenly raced north through Denmark and into Norway, then turned on the Low Countries and France. To the collective horror of the West, the French, who had held out heroically against the Germans for four years a generation before, fell apart and sued for peace. Nazi troopers swaggered in serried ranks down the Champs-Elysées, while their comrades took positions on the coast of the Pas de Calais, only twenty miles across the English Channel from Dover.

As the Luftwaffe began to soften up Britain in preparation for a climactic invasion, Americans bitterly debated the wisdom of isolation or intervention. Pundits, politicians, and citizens argued, shouted, and pleaded that Britain could or could not stand alone, could or could not be saved with American aid. On only one point could everyone agree. The nation had to rearm, either to protect its shores or eventually to project its power worldwide in the cause of freedom. The great ship emerging on the slipway at Newport News would be a key element in the fulfillment of whichever policy was eventually pursued.

The vessel had been authorized under the Naval Expansion Act of May 1938, legislation that reflected the world's growing gloom over the probability of renewed conflict. In 1934 Japan had announced that it would no longer adhere to the international armament limitations agreed to at the Washington and London naval conferences; three years later it began a war against China that included reckless attacks against Western gunboats and property. The large, efficient Imperial Japanese Navy continued to expand dramatically, achieving the capability to overwhelm its U.S. counterpart in the Pacific. Congress responded by authorizing a major increase in naval tonnage, including forty thousand tons of new carrier construction.

The first vessel to be built under the act would be a product of compromise both within the navy as a whole and in the smaller carrier community. Admirals and seamen remained deeply divided over the relative merits of the carrier versus the battleship, the warplane versus the big gun. It had been fifteen years since Billy Mitchell had convinced some skeptics that airplanes could sink battleships; no one could deny that planes had an exponentially greater range than did the largest naval gun. Between 1927 and 1938 five carriers entered service in the U.S. Navy, and fleet exercises in the late thirties suggested that these ships could play a dominant—not merely an auxiliary—role in future warfare. But "surface sailors" also seemed to have a good bit of history and technology on their side. While the aircraft carrier had become a promising new weapon of war, the battleship itself had been transformed. Britain's *Dreadnought*, launched in 1905, had revolutionized war at sea. Battleships were now huge vessels carrying many large naval rifles on enormous hulls that could at least theoretically be so minutely subdivided as to make them virtually unsinkable. Thus traditionalists continued to insist that the carrier's role was primarily as a scout platform and secondarily as a supplementary offensive weapon in fleet actions between opposing lines of battleships. The increasingly aggressive naval aviation community insisted just as vociferously that in any coming conflict the carrier would be the major strike weapon, projecting naval power many hundreds of miles farther, much more rapidly, and with much greater collective force than any line of battlewagons could.

But the supremacy of carrier warfare remained unproven. The great naval battle of what was now being referred to as merely a first world war had conformed to custom. Long lines of British and German battleships and battle cruisers had blazed away at one another at Jutland, and Winston Churchill had observed trenchantly that Sir John Jellicoe, the British commander, was the only man who could lose an empire in an afternoon. The debate over the relative merits of guns and planes continued throughout the late thirties both inside and outside of the naval community. By 1938, however, a rough consensus had apparently been reached among moderates on both sides: Carriers would support the battle line, but they would do so offensively by aggressively seeking out and sinking opposing carriers so that the battleships could get at their enemy counterparts unhindered.[2] Under the circumstances Congress and the White House made the expedient decision: The United States would build both battleships and carriers. In 1937 and 1938 Congress authorized six new battleships of the *North Carolina* and *South Dakota* classes, and by 1938 naval designers were developing a new six-ship class of very fast battleships whose lead vessel would be named *Iowa*. Thereafter, Congress allocated the major portion of capital ship spending for dramatic expansion of the modest carrier fleet.

A new class, the *Essex*, would be constructed, incorporating all the lessons learned from operating the *Lexington, Saratoga, Ranger, Yorktown,* and *Enterprise*. But developing this advanced design would take time, and by late 1939 there was no time. The most recent two-ship *Yorktown* class had been developed years before, and although the vessels themselves were still young, they had exhibited some striking deficiencies in size, armor, and design. But if the U.S. Navy was to counter the large Japanese fleet successfully and provide some support in any naval war against

Germany, it had to get as many carriers as possible into the water quickly. A smaller and marginally suitable fleet carrier, the *Wasp*, was due to be commissioned in the spring of 1940, but the first of the *Essex* class was not scheduled to touch water before 1943. The quickest way to get sufficiently large and fast flight decks to sea would be to replicate the *Yorktown* design. The new carrier would be the last of the old, not the first of the new.

Few carriers have been as elegant as the *Yorktown* class. Battleship and cruiser critics derisively condemned the vessels as barn doors laid over bathtubs, but they were actually graceful ships with clean, sharp lines. From the bulbous bow a high forecastle swept back about one hundred feet to even higher forward gun galleries on both the port and starboard sides. Each of these galleries mounted two powerful 5-inch, 38-caliber, dual-purpose surface and antiaircraft guns. The galleries sloped away to a 565-foot enclosed hangar bay that could be opened at many points by steel roller curtains, allowing aircraft to be warmed up without creating a buildup of deadly fumes. When planes were not aboard, the steel deck of this huge cavern gleamed and shone like an immense ballroom. At the after end of the hangar bay rose the rear gun galleries, each of which mounted two 5-inch, 38-caliber guns. The after gallery structures dropped away to the incurving fantail.

Nestled in the hull were the engineering spaces and quarters for nearly three thousand men. Nine immense Babcock and Wilcox boilers provided sufficient steam power to drive the attendant geared turbines at more than 120,000 horsepower, giving the ship a trial speed of slightly more than thirty-three knots, roughly thirty-eight miles an hour. Living conditions were superior to those aboard most U.S. Navy vessels in 1940. Large galleys could turn out hot meals for the crew three times a day; each ship contained a bakery that was possibly better than many found in small American communities at the end of the Depression decade. There was even a "mechanical cow" that turned out gallons of ice cream each day. It was not the best product, since it was made with dehydrated milk. But after long days at sea, any kind of treat was to be treasured.

The hull and hangar deck comprising the "bathtub" were topped by an 809-foot "barn door," the wooden flight deck. It stretched from just aft of the fantail to just short of the bow. The sides of the flight deck were lined with 20-millimeter and 1.1-inch light guns for close-in air defense. The deck itself was more than one hundred feet wide and unbroken except on the starboard side amidships, where an enormous, narrow funnel faired gracefully into an equally narrow island structure nearly forty feet high, which contained the navigation bridge, chart house, captain's sea cabin, admiral's quarters and bridge (flag plot), aviation offices, flight control station, gun director platform, and signal bridge. Unloaded, the *Yorktown* and *Enterprise* each displaced almost twenty thousand tons. The new carrier would displace exactly that figure but would differ in minor ways from her older sisters—most notably in the number of gun directors and the provision of a prominent conning tower forward on the island just below the navigation bridge. Fully loaded for combat, each of the ships displaced more than twenty-five thousand tons.

Because she was a "repeat," the third member of the *Yorktown* class grew quickly in her slipway. She was the eighth aircraft carrier built by the United States, and so she became "CV-8," the "C" standing for carrier, the "V" for heavier-than-air aircraft (that is, planes instead of airships). The thousands of steelworkers, electricians, boilermen, mechanics, and shipwrights knew exactly how to build her, and they moved swiftly and confidently to complete the contract. By mid-December 1940, CV-8 was ready for launching into the midst of a world war whose contours had suddenly become unclear. Hitler had not been able to sweep the Royal Air Force from British skies after all, and the European conflict remained in doubt as England hung on grimly against the onslaughts of both Göring's bombers and Dönitz's U-boats. In the Far East, Germany's new Axis ally, Japan, continued its incessant aggressions, which now threatened to spread from China into the imperial holdings of Nazi-occupied Holland and France. As the long hull of CV-8 slid down the way to touch saltwater for the first time, Annie Reid Knox, the wife of Secretary of the Navy Frank Knox, christened her *Hornet*. Her place on the slip was immediately taken by the keel of the *Essex*. The navy and the country were gearing up for war.

But it was an agonizingly slow process. America had been mired in economic depression for a decade; industrial production and know-how, along with public morale, had slumped badly. As the nation's great factories slowly came back to life, managers and laborers had to deal with novel problems involved in manufacturing goods for war, not peace, while those who contended that Britain was America's first line of defense insisted that most of the new planes, tanks, and ships be sent across the North Atlantic. The *Hornet* was a potentially splendid weapon, but would she be given the right tools to fulfill her mission?

And would she have the right men to do the job? As the big carrier took final shape alongside her fitting-out pier in the summer of 1941, the nucleus of her crew began to report. One of the first was Capt. Marc

Birth: The hull of CV-8 slides into the water at the Newport News Shipbuilding and Drydock Company on 14 December 1940.

Andrew Mitscher, a small, wizened fifty-four-year-old holder of the Navy Cross whom friends called "Pete." He was a natural leader, "the epitome of a Navy man who had been brought up in ships, been brought up in planes," according to Lt. Stephen Jurika, who served under him on the *Hornet.* Mitscher was a doer more than a thinker, a no-nonsense man, soft-spoken, direct, to the point. Detailed planning and logistical strategy bored him. Jurika recalled: "He was a man whom men followed. He was a man who could inspire a shipload of men or a task force of men, and he never used five words where one would do. Sincerity just oozed out of him." Colleagues said he never lied, never evaded, never issued an unnecessary order. His concern for his men was legendary. His attitude toward subordinates was simple: Everyone was an essential part of a big team, all working for the same objective. According to Jurika, the captain's manner proclaimed, "I'm Pete Mitscher and I want to know what goes on."[3] As the *Hornet*'s chief disciplinarian he would be strict with the older petty officers and seamen who got in trouble but lenient with the younger sailors. They were kids in an alien environment. They needed to be trained and trained hard, but Mitscher believed harsh punishment could break their spirits before they became seasoned professionals.

He was nearly a chain smoker, and at sea he wore a little baseball cap with a long brim, which became such a legend that decades later the navy made baseball caps part of the sea uniform. The caps did not keep him from getting sunburned and freckled, however, and he always seemed to be itching.[4]

Mitscher had been a Wisconsin farm boy before going to Annapolis. After serving in World War I, he won his service's highest decoration for piloting the NC-1 on the navy's first transatlantic flight in 1919. He alternated shore and sea duty during the long, dreary years of peace and penury in the interwar navy, gradually climbing the promotional ladder until 1937, when he received command of the aircraft tender *Wright*. By the spring of 1941 Mitscher was assistant chief of the navy's Bureau of Aeronautics. After two years of the steadily mounting paperwork that accompanied the navy's gradual expansion, he was eager to get back to sea. He also had a crusade. The chief of naval operations, Adm. Harold "Betty" Stark, had recently issued a new Operating Force Plan, which Mitscher believed was designed to subtly but unmistakably eliminate· aviation as a distinct component of the U.S. Navy. The best place to defend naval aviation was not behind a desk but on the bridge of a new carrier.

Mitscher was determined to get the finest senior officers and petty officers he could for the *Hornet,* not only men whom he could trust implicitly but those who had "a spectrum of abilities," including naval intelligence.[5] He succeeded brilliantly. Comdr. George Henderson, the executive officer, was a veteran of seaplane service who held nine world records. He had been a test pilot and Mitscher's exec on the *Wright* before moving on to command a patrol wing. He and Mitscher were close friends. While ashore the two men and their wives golfed together as often as possible; at sea Henderson and Mitscher usually dined each night in the captain's cabin. Henderson had a lively sense of humor and a taste for "epic poems," some of a distinctly scatological nature, which he would occasionally compose when an incident amused him.[6]

The air officer, Comdr. Apollo Soucek, remembered by shipmates as a "great gentleman" and "a wonderful naval officer,"[7] had set a then-astounding world altitude record of 43,166 feet in 1930 and had flown off the decks of most of the navy's carriers. His father, a history professor in love with Greek mythology, had named his two sons Apollo and Zeus. Apollo, a genial-looking man with a broad forehead and thinning hair, had won a Distinguished Flying Cross for his aviation exploits. Artist-writer Tom Lea later wrote that "a quieter, more charming, pleasanter man would be hard to find."[8] Soucek believed that the key to leadership was getting his men to like him, not fear him, and he was instrumental in fashioning the character of "the happy *Hornet.*"

Comdr. Frank Akers, navigator and youngest member of Mitscher's senior staff, was a forty-year-old Tennessean who had become an electronics expert and the first pilot to make a blind instrument landing aboard a carrier. Akers was known as a "fuss-budget, a fuss-pot" and was possibly the least liked officer on board. Once at sea, other officers were annoyed to find that they could not enter his chart room even if they were on the way to flag plot to see the admiral or en route to the bridge to converse with Mitscher. As soon as someone poked his head around the chart room hatch, Akers would ask, "What are you doing in here?" He would not allow anyone to look at the plot to see where the ship was.[9] But Akers navigated the big carrier with unremitting precision, and he was respected for his abilities.

The engineering officer was Comdr. Pat Creehan, who later earned an enviable public reputation as a dedicated officer who for years had "blarneyed" navy medical officers into keeping him in service despite an unspecified serious ailment. Some of his men, however, considered

Creehan a bit fretful and perhaps afraid of his job. The gunnery officer, Comdr. James W. Smith, inevitably called "Smitty," loved Gordon Grant lithographs and Rockwell Kent woodcuts, which he brought aboard the *Hornet*, along with a sizable library of French classics.[10] Finally, there was young Lt. Stephen Jurika, who had spent several years in the American embassy in Tokyo and was both fluent in Japanese and knowledgeable about Japan's military ambitions. Jurika arrived just before commissioning to serve as flight deck officer. Mitscher had recruited him as much for his intelligence skills as for any other reason, and Jurika proved to be an invaluable addition to the ship.

Mitscher had reported to the *Hornet* in July, just as persistent Japanese aggression in the Far East had convinced the president to impose an oil embargo that threatened to cripple Japan's war machine. In retrospect, Roosevelt's action seems almost an act of war. But in the confused summer of 1941, with the Axis triumphant everywhere (Hitler had just invaded the Soviet Union, and his advance units were already deep inside the Russian steppes), world affairs seemed so fluid and Western military and moral weaknesses so obvious that it was difficult to make objective judgments about national interest. Nonetheless, most people, in and out of uniform, knew that the United States was drifting into deepening peril. Mitscher was determined that his new command would fulfill its mission, and a key to ensuring success was to weld the crew into a single community. After taking a month's leave—the longest in his naval career—to bask in the summer sun of Virginia Beach, Mitscher returned to his command to whip it into shape.

Every Saturday afternoon from early August until everyone began moving aboard ship in mid-October the captain and his wife held a cocktail party for the new officers. Lt. Henry Martin, fresh out of communications school, had already been exposed to the *Hornet* ambience when Henderson asked him what he wanted to do. Martin replied that he wanted something more than a simple communications job, so the exec assigned him a position in gunnery during general quarters. Martin found during the cocktail partying that the captain and his wife, who had no children, had more or less adopted him and three or four other young, unattached officers. He was flattered and grateful. Later, at sea, Martin discovered that Mitscher seldom slept. When Martin would bring a late-night message to the captain's cabin, he would find Mitscher in his bunk reading. "You busy?" Mitscher would ask. "No, sir." "Well, sit down. What's happening on the ship?"[11]

The fall of 1941, writer William Manchester recalled years later, "had been a fine, golden autumn, a lovely farewell to those who would lose their youth, and some of them their lives, before the leaves turned again in a peacetime fall. The girls, who would be women before the troopships came home, would never again be so willowy."[12] But although the weather remained gorgeous, the national mood was increasingly grim. Japan, undeterred by the American embargo, was continuing its assault against China; Japanese successes could threaten Malaya, the Dutch East Indies (Indonesia), and the Philippines.

Danger also lurked much closer to home. After returning in mid-August from his first meeting with Prime Minister Winston Churchill off Newfoundland, Roosevelt was determined to help tottering Britain any way he could. He promptly ordered the navy to extend its patrols far into the North Atlantic and to convoy merchant vessels west of Iceland in order to counter the Nazi submarine menace, which had reached crisis proportions. The warships were to darken their lights at sea, and, although the convoys were presumed to be composed exclusively of U.S. ships, the navy's operations plan stipulated that vessels "of any nationality" could join. The result was an undeclared naval war against Germany that could have only one outcome. On 4 September the destroyer *Greer* had narrowly avoided being torpedoed by *U-652* after helping a British aircraft find and track the sub. Six weeks later, on Friday, 17 October, a U-boat pack attacked a British convoy four hundred miles south of Iceland. Five U.S. warships steamed to the rescue. The new destroyer U.S.S. *Kearny* was torpedoed just as she reached the besieged vessels. The destroyer did not sink, but eleven men were killed. Roosevelt charged that the attack on the *Kearny* was part of grand scheme by Hitler to drive neutral U.S. shipping from the high seas. He added that history had recorded who fired the first shot and concluded: "We Americans have cleared our decks and taken our battle stations. We stand ready in the defense of our nation."[13]

Three days after the *Kearny* was attacked, the *Hornet* was commissioned on a sunny day at the carrier pier in Norfolk. Four thousand people, half of them crewmen, assembled on the big flight deck of the new carrier to hear Navy Secretary Knox praise the men of the *Kearny* as volunteers who had made the ultimate sacrifice so that people everywhere could "keep the hope of human freedom." The *Hornet* would be "a part of our guarantee that wherever we go on the seven seas our nation's power will always be exercised in the behalf of human liberty and free men."[14] Then Marc Mitscher stepped forward to read his orders and set the first watch.

The *Hornet* sails across Hampton Roads in the autumn of 1941. Note that 5-inch guns have not yet been mounted.

The new carrier was finally in the fleet, but she was far from a guarantor of power. That morning the last of the crew—seven hundred men—had reported aboard. Arriving from the Great Lakes Naval Training Station just north of Chicago, they were all raw recruits or barely trained ratings from the Middle West—schoolboys, soda jerks, and farm kids from Minnesota, Iowa, Michigan, and Mitscher's own state of Wisconsin. Some of the last products of the pre-Pearl Harbor navy, they would have to bear the brunt of the Japanese onslaught in the Pacific until more than a million of their countrymen and hundreds of new ships arrived. This was the navy of dress whites with blue collars over white sailcloth, of $21-a-month recruits and $36-a-month sailors (chiefs made $96 to $98). Two Michigan youngsters arrived in the *Hornet*'s final draft. Machinist's Mate Glen Dock, just eighteen, had grown up on a farm not far from Kalamazoo; before settling down, his father had been a young cowboy on the late nineteenth-century cattle frontier. Seaman Jim Walker from Detroit was not much older. Grinding his way through high school, Dock had seen two or three kids a year from the junior or senior classes run off to join the navy. As world war raged abroad in the spring of 1941 and selective service began cranking up, Dock decided to do the same. The United States would almost certainly be in battle soon, and he did not want to be a soldier. Jimmy Walker felt the same way.

The two boys endured their ninety days of boot camp at Great Lakes. Like all recruits, they slept in hammocks, not bunks, and each hammock had better be properly lashed to the steel rod hitching post with seven precise turns of the marlin spike or the boot was sure to get some kind of extra duty. The recruit company chiefs were ruthless but generally fair. Glen Dock's chief had been a gun turret captain out in the fleet, and Dock thought he was "a real bastard." With selective service in force, the navy was suddenly getting a markedly higher level of enlistee, and the chiefs at Great Lakes and San Diego began selecting one or two outstanding individuals in each recruit company to be informal training assistants. Invariably these young men were described by their disgusted recruit mates as "head suck-asses."

The recruits at Great Lakes spent long summer hours on the notorious "grinder," a two-block-long field of sizzling concrete, where angry chiefs, determined to teach discipline and obedience, would jerk the neckerchief of many a frightened, sloppy boy tightly against the Adam's apple and hold it there for agonizing moments. The chiefs obsessed about cleanliness, which was essential for good order and discipline on any warship. Those recruits who could not keep themselves clean received "KiYi scrubdowns" with heavy fiber brushes from their fellow recruits until their skin glowed pink and the blood ran. Nearly all learned quickly. The handful who did not were discharged and sent home. Any noise after lights out, any whispers, any laughter or stifled giggles, brought the always sleepless chief running to send the youngsters out for an hour or two of extra drill and push-ups on the pitch-black grinder.

After basic training Dock went to machinist school. He spent an additional month at Great Lakes, cramming algebra, geometry, and trigonometry into his tired brain. Next he went to the Ford Motor Company at Detroit, which had a government contract to provide advanced schooling for sailors. Dock spent ninety days there, learning the care and use of advanced machines. Then he found himself in the same group with Jim Walker, abruptly shipped eastward to "new construction."[15]

The eager, willing, but bewildered youngsters were completely baffled by the *Hornet*. Many had never seen, much less been on, any structure of her size. They spent their first hours aboard wandering in confusion, mouths agape, below decks or along the cavernous hangar bay. Akers,

"A barn door laid on top of a bathtub." Portside view of the *Hornet* in Hampton Roads, autumn 1941.

angry and impatient as the commissioning ceremonies neared, snarled: "Tie 'em together as best you can. If we don't watch out, they'll get lost."[16]

For the next six weeks the new carrier alternated sea trials with yard periods as she prepared for her shakedown cruise. Young crew members scrambled up and down ladders, through hatches, across the cavernous hangar deck, and along narrow steel corridors below decks, trying to find their way around the ship, one of the U.S. Navy's half-dozen largest then in commission. Peacetime practice dictated that new capital ships sail to the Maine coast for six or seven days of speed trials. But with an Atlantic war possibly only hours away, the navy could not afford the luxury of such a risk to its newest prize. Before her commissioning the *Hornet* had conducted speed runs in Chesapeake Bay without her heavy armament of 5-inch guns. In late October and throughout November, her heavy guns finally in place, she underwent a series of tests along the hundred-fathom curve just off the Virginia capes. The ship ran full ahead at flank speed for four hours, then slammed into reverse and steamed backward at high speed for an hour. She was twisted and pulled in every possible direction to test hull integrity, propulsion machinery, and turning radius.

As the tests went on, hundreds of eyes on board peered apprehensively at the gray waters of the Atlantic, looking for the telltale feather of a U-boat periscope, for by this time the United States had suffered its first total casualty of World War II: the torpedoing and sinking of the old "four-pipe" destroyer *Reuben James*. The U.S. press railed against Nazi insolence, isolationists were temporarily shamed into silence, and Woody Guthrie wrote a popular ballad about dead friends on "the good *Reuben James*." In mid-November the *Hornet* was back in dry dock at Newport News for minor adjustments and corrections to hull and machinery. Then she steamed back across Hampton Roads to the naval base to await her post-Christmas shakedown cruise. And there war found her.

2

Shakedown

THE *Hornet* was not the only carrier at Norfolk that first week in December 1941. The *Yorktown* was also there. She had been ordered from the Pacific Fleet late the previous spring to reinforce naval surveillance of German submarine activities in the North Atlantic. Thus four of the navy's seven precious carriers were on the East Coast: *Ranger, Wasp, Yorktown,* and *Hornet.* That was where the action was, or seemed to be. No one could imagine a sneak attack by Japan on America's back.

By this time the *Hornet* was beginning to jell, to take on a distinct form and personality. The experienced department heads and the older chiefs and petty officers were beginning to know their men and where and how to train them. In frequent wardroom conferences Mitscher did not criticize departments that reported slow progress. "Instead, he looked long and quizzically at the officers in charge."[1] It was worse than a reprimand, Akers recalled.

On Sunday, 7 December, the *Hornet* was moored starboard side to Pier Number 4 at the Norfolk Naval Base. Young Henry Martin had the early afternoon communications watch. Everything was quiet until a radioman brought a strange report. Uncoded messages were being received, saying that Pearl Harbor in distant Hawaii was under attack and that this was no drill. Then more messages, still in plain language: "Execute Battle

Plan X." Martin promptly informed Apollo Soucek, the senior duty officer, and Soucek immediately sent a young ensign over to the officers' club to tell Mitscher and Henderson, who had just come off the golf links and were having lunch with their wives. Mitscher opened Soucek's envelope and read his note. He turned to Henderson and said: "Pearl Harbor has been bombed; we're at war with Japan." He motioned for the check.[2]

Back aboard the *Hornet*, Lt. Gerald McAteer, a young doctor recently graduated from Georgetown University Medical School with a specialty in chest surgery, suddenly heard a lot of bugles blowing. McAteer had not been aboard long and was bewildered. But the veterans instantly knew what it was: general quarters. All noncrewmen were immediately ordered off the ship, and all officers were told to report to the armory to draw guns. When McAteer was handed one he protested. The Geneva Convention prohibited medical personnel from carrying or using firearms. Don't worry, he was told; the Japanese had never signed the Geneva Convention.[3]

Several miles away a group of *Hornet* sailors had taken up an entire row of a Norfolk movie theater to watch a long Sunday double feature. One of the boys who had gone to use the men's room quickly came back down the aisle. "We're at war," he whispered to his buddies. No one believed him until they left the theater and heard newspaper hawkers screaming out the headline. The shore patrol had not come after them with orders to report to the ship because the *Hornet* was still unfinished. But the boys returned anyway.[4]

It would be a somber, even frightening holiday season. A young torpedo plane pilot destined for the *Hornet* summed up the mood in a letter home to Indianapolis on Pearl Harbor night. Ens. Bill Evans had entered the navy from Harvard Law School, which had instilled in him a sober, coolly objective frame of mind. "People will not realize, I fear, for some time how serious this matter is," he wrote. "The indifference of labor and capital to our danger is an infectious virus and the public has come to think contemptuously of Japan. And that I fear is a fatal mistake—today has given evidence of that. This war will be more dangerous than any war the country has ever fought," he continued. "Once more the world is afire. In the period approaching Christmas it seems bitterly ironical to mouth again the time-worn phrases concerning peace on earth, good will to men. . . . I find it hard to see the inherent difference between men and the rest of the animal kingdom." But "faith lost—all is lost." Would Americans again summon the faith to fight for what they believed? "Let us defend these principles to the last ounce of blood. But then, above all, retain reason enough to have charity for all and malice toward none." For if the world ever embarked on another global conflict, "mankind is doomed. This time it has to be a better world."[5]

Three days after Pearl Harbor the *Yorktown* abruptly cast off her lines and sailed out from Norfolk, heading back to the Pacific. The men of the *Hornet* were allowed Christmas at home. Then the ship prepared to set forth into the seas of war. The mood aboard was mixed. Many people found it hard to give up the good food and drink and attractive women of the holiday season. But almost everyone who had been in service three or four years had friends stationed at Pearl Harbor and was "all hepped up" to get to sea, recalled one of the *Hornet*'s petty officers. "We didn't realize what was going on."[6]

In fact, the United States was in greater peril from abroad than it had been since the War of 1812, and if the carrier's enlisted men were not aware of the dangers, Mitscher's superiors in Washington and his friends in the Pacific Fleet were. Somehow the nation and its pathetic British ally had to wrest the global initiative from the Axis powers. To many the task seemed almost insurmountable.

Four days after Pearl Harbor Hitler declared war on the United States, thus opening up the entire East Coast and Caribbean as new fields of opportunity for his deadly U-boats. Japan was running wild, and Anglo-American disasters accumulated inexorably. Only hours after the shattering assault on Hawaii, Japanese aircraft caught most of the U.S. Far Eastern Air Force on the ground at Clark Field in the Philippines and delivered a devastating blow. By the night of 8 December two-thirds of all U.S. air power in the Pacific had been wiped out. Two days later Japanese planes caught and sank the *Prince of Wales* and the *Repulse*, Britain's only two modern capital ships in Asian waters. By 12 December the Japanese had landed large forces in Malaya and the Philippines and had seized Guam. After an initial repulse, Japanese forces struggled ashore on Wake Island despite a desperate defense by a handful of marines and their few Grumman fighters. Vice Adm. William Pye, temporary commander of the Pacific Fleet, bungled a relief expedition, and the island's gallant defenders surrendered on Christmas Eve. The next day Japanese forces completed their seizure of Hong Kong after a bitter struggle.

At home, optimists cried out that America had never lost a war. Pessimists countered that neither had Japan. Hysteria gripped the West Coast. It was fueled by confusing reports from Hawaii. Understandably,

Roosevelt did not reveal the extent of the Pearl Harbor disaster for another year, but every uncensored account was somber. There seemed to be no way to stop a Japanese invasion of California or Washington State. The United States was a besieged and uncertain giant, menaced on all sides by bitterly determined enemies.

Mitscher had "Remember Pearl Harbor" painted in huge block letters on the *Hornet*'s fat stack, and two days before Christmas hundreds of mechanics, yeomen, parachute riggers, ordnancemen, and plane pushers from Air Group 8 (the air group's number conformed to the ship's hull number) reported aboard. On Christmas Eve the carrier pulled away from her pier and moved to an anchorage in the Roads. Shortly after 0400 on the twenty-seventh the engineers started spinning the main engines for warmup, and thirty minutes later Mitscher ordered the special sea and anchor detail set. At dawn the big carrier got under way for sea. That afternoon in the cold, windswept seas off the Virginia capes the carrier received her planes. The clean, wooden flight deck was at last scarred with tire tracks and sullied with oil and gas trails. The *Hornet* was finally an aircraft carrier.[7]

But not a fully armed one. At full strength her air group would comprise eighty-three planes with room for another twenty in bays that cut across the gallery deck above the hangar. But only sixty-six aircraft had flown out of the pale winter sunlight to land aboard. They were the only planes that the United States could spare, and many were plainly inferior to the best that the Axis deployed.

An obsolete battle line had been destroyed at Pearl Harbor. Of the remaining fleet, half the destroyers and many light cruisers were of World War I–vintage, four-stackers with ancient, fragile engines and light gunnery. Although the heavy cruiser flotilla was comparable to almost all of the best Japanese models, the dozen or so active battleships, including those attacked at Pearl Harbor, were fossils at least twenty years old and built for the departing age of slow, big-gun combat. Naval aircraft were no better. The Grumman F4F-3 Wildcats flown aboard the *Hornet* by Fighting Squadron 8 were rugged but rather old and sluggish aircraft with batteries of .50-caliber guns in their tiny wings. One pilot called the Wildcat "a little beer bottle of a plane."[8] It was well protected with armor plating and a self-sealing gas tank, but it was too heavy to match the fragile but nimble and powerfully armed Japanese Zero in either speed or maneuverability. In a power dive on an enemy's tail the Wildcat was a terrifyingly effective warplane. But it took well over ten minutes for it to struggle up to the sixteen- or twenty-thousand-foot altitude where most combat took place. Although top speed for the F4F-3 was more than three hundred miles an hour, the Zero could outfly the American plane in a climb and in straight, level flight.

The men of the *Hornet*'s scouting and dive-bombing squadrons flew Curtiss SBC-4 Helldiver biplanes of 1930 vintage throughout the shake-down cruise. With a maximum speed of well under two hundred miles an hour even in a full power dive, these ancient bombers would be easy prey for most Japanese fighter and even bomber aircraft.[9]

The Douglas Devastators of Torpedo Squadron 8 were devastating only to their pilots and rear-seat gunners. Introduced into the fleet in 1937, the Devastators had been the navy's first all-metal, low-wing carrier aircraft. Although they could theoretically attain a speed of slightly more than two hundred miles an hour, they cruised at only about half that. Fighter, scout, and bomber pilots found it almost impossible to efficiently escort these slow-moving mastodons, and their vulnerability to both Japanese fighter aircraft and shipboard antiaircraft defense was obvious. The Devastator carried one half-ton torpedo. Submarine and aircraft experiences in the early months after Pearl Harbor demonstrated that America's torpedo technology was not only crude and unwieldy but wildly inaccurate.

Pearl Harbor was potentially a blessing in disguise, sweeping away an old navy in one dramatic if catastrophic stroke. The United States was building a huge surface fleet: carriers, battlewagons, cruisers, and destroyers of advanced design and incredible power and speed. America was poised to build thousands of warplanes that could rid the skies of Japanese aircraft and pilots. But months, even years, would pass before most of these vessels and planes appeared. Perhaps it would be too late. The fate of the nation rested on the handful of modern ships that had survived the Japanese attack, especially the aircraft carriers. For only these vessels now possessed the necessary speed and power to challenge the Japanese juggernaut. But there were only seven of them, and only five of these—the two of the *Lexington* class and the three of the *Yorktown* class—could be classified as full-fledged fleet carriers. Japan had used six such vessels at Pearl Harbor alone.

As the *Hornet* gathered in the last of her aircraft and headed south that second afternoon after Christmas, she followed in the curling wakes of the navy's first new battleships in more than twenty years. The *North Carolina* and *Washington* were handsome, powerful vessels but possessed neither the maximum speed nor the offensive capabilities that carrier war demanded.[10] The entire force was under the control of Commander Battleships, Atlantic Fleet, Rear Adm. John Wilcox. The three big ships and their accompanying destroyers built up speed and swiftly left the cold winds and waters of the North Atlantic. The Caribbean, the traditional training area for the Atlantic Fleet, was rightly deemed too dangerous because of the presence of Nazi submarines. The Gulf of Mexico, however, was beyond normal U-boat range. So when the force sighted Dry Tortugas Lighthouse in the Florida Channel several days after leaving Norfolk, Wilcox ordered a grateful Mitscher to proceed independently into the gulf, accompanied by the old four-stack destroyer *Noa*, to conduct his shakedown cruise. The battleships went off in another direction for their own training exercises.[11]

For the next month, as the carrier and her escorting destroyer steamed in a roughly triangular area defined by points several hundred miles off Tampa Bay, the Mississippi Delta, and an indeterminate point to the south, the men got to know each other and their ship. One of Mitscher's initial orders called for no ties, no ceremonies, no formalities, no dress courtesies of any kind. But, as the *Hornet*'s first historian, Alexander Griffin, recalled several years later, "discipline . . . clamped down upon the ship with a rigidity that never relaxed."[12] Every moment of every day was filled with activity. In the bright sunshine of the gulf winter, boys who had never before seen naval guns were soon learning all about them: ranging, loading, firing; ranging, loading, firing; stripping the guns down, changing barrels and ammunition; and ranging, loading, firing again, day after day. They blasted at sleeves towed behind Wildcats or Devastators until at last the sleeves were brought aboard, heavily perforated with holes from 5-inch, 1.1-inch, 20-millimeter, and .50-caliber guns. The chief petty officers in charge of the individual 5-inch guns or the cluster of lighter batteries never seemed to be satisfied. Do it again and again, they ordered, until their men were ready to drop from the exertion. Speed and accuracy were essential. Finally the gunners were consistently shredding target sleeves. Yet the order came down once more: Do it again.

By the end of the cruise Mitscher was delighted. He had seldom seen such accuracy on the more leisurely and relaxed peacetime shakedowns. Only the multibarreled 1.1-inch "Chicago pianos" proved disappointing. The *Hornet* had only two of the necessary four gun directors. Moreover, the guns themselves had always tended to jam. "Smitty," the gun boss, now found that they had difficulty tracking as well. All shot behind the targets. Smith and Mitscher consoled themselves with the thought that soon the Oerlikons would be replaced by newer and more efficient and accurate Bofors 40-millimeter guns.

The eight 5-inch guns were fired at both surface and aerial targets. Because no target sleds were available, the *Hornet's* carpenters built a "pyramid" and set it afloat off the ship for the gunners to shoot at. The results were as gratifying as the shooting at aerial targets, but there was one disturbing flaw in the 5-inch armament. As Mitscher wrote Admiral Stark, "someone" had "apparently" neglected to fix the problem of parallax in the mechanical computing instruments that directed the batteries, so it was "impossible to get the guns together in train." The problem was not serious on the starboard side, because that was where the gun director was, on top of the island, but with the port-side batteries it was "considerable." Smith was worried about the flaw; Mitscher was ambivalent. Lack of coordination might lead to a greater spread of gunfire coverage, the captain told Stark. But it might also lead to too much scattering. Despite this defect, the guns shot well. There were leaky joints in the elevating and tracking mechanisms, but that could be corrected during the forthcoming yard period.

Far below decks Pat Creehan and his handful of senior petty officers in the engine room never saw the sun as they taught the new boiler tenders, firemen, and enginemen their jobs under the pressure of constant orders from the bridge for changes in speed and power. The engineering plant proved to be excellent but not flawless. The youngsters learned to find and fix leaky fuel lines and gaskets in the turbines, while Creehan quizzed them unceasingly about the various components of the complex power plant, how they operated, and how they interacted.

One problem, however, disturbed Mitscher and Creehan, and it reflected a deeper, ultimately fatal flaw in the *Hornet's* design. Fuel lines were so connected that if only one was damaged, at least three of the nine boilers would be lost until it was repaired. The result would be a drastic loss of power. Neither Mitscher nor his engineering officer commented on the deeper, related defect that would eventually kill the ship. Although stoutly built, all three *Yorktown*-class ships incorporated fire and engine rooms together, rather than alternatively, and all possessed only four-inch armor plate over the engineering spaces. A torpedo penetrating this poor protection could immobilize the ships. Compartmentation offered some protection, but more than one torpedo hit could bring any of these big carriers to a dead stop.

Mitscher was obviously concerned about the structural integrity of the *Hornet*, for he conducted a series of damage control exercises during the cruise until he was satisfied that the ship was ready for war "from that angle." But he remained worried about stability. The *Hornet* was slightly heavier than her two sisters and required almost twice as much fuel oil in port-side tanks to balance the weight of the island. As the ship depleted her supply of fuel during steaming, the tanks had to be pumped full of water, which naturally became scummed with oil. If the oily water was pumped out and replaced with fresher water to clean the tanks, it would leave a trail that a Nazi U-boat could follow. If the oily water was left in the tanks until the ship returned home and then dumped, it would contaminate the waters of Hampton Roads. Mitscher decided to wait until the *Hornet* returned to Norfolk; he hoped that a sludge barge could remove most of the oily water.

Mitscher was also concerned about the aircraft radar, which simply did not work well. He took the extraordinary step of flying the radar officer off the ship to Washington to confer with experts. They concluded that the antenna was faulty. A new one was brought aboard, and the technicians worked almost daily to improve the radar's capability "within its limits." Fighter patrols were sent aloft to protect the carrier from mock enemy attacks that were conducted by the ship's torpedo and bombing planes. By the end of the cruise the *Hornet*'s air controller had succeeded in directing the fighters onto the approaching "enemy" aircraft within a twelve- to fifteen-mile radius of the ship. Mitscher feared, however, that this was not far enough out to employ the F4Fs effectively before they came within range of the carrier's guns. The fighters would thus run the risk of being inadvertently shot down. The real problem was the inherent limitation of the radar system itself, which could "only be solved by better equipment." Radar was a new technology. Surface as well as aircraft sets often displayed information susceptible to a variety of interpretations. Even personnel who had been well trained needed considerable practical experience to become expert operators. The uncertainties of war added their own stress. For the first several months of the *Hornet*'s life the radarmen were properly cautious, reporting nearly all contacts. One murky night in the Caribbean the entire crew was sent to general quarters, and Smitty's gunners on the 5-inch mounts blasted away at a supposed contact out in the darkness. After closer inspection, the foe proved to be a floating stump of a cypress tree.[13]

A good captain has no greater concern than the well-being and morale of those under his command. Mitscher was pleased that his young crew remained healthy and willing under the stress of the wartime shakedown. After a day of firing the guns, worrying over the radar, pushing planes on the flight deck, or crawling into and out of shaft alleys, the youngsters were allowed a brief respite during and just after supper; then they were brought back to mess halls, gun rooms, and radio shacks for more drilling. What would you do if a 1.1-inch round stuck in the barrel? What would you do if power were suddenly lost in main control? What would you do if you lost water pressure in the hoses during a fire? What would you do if a main fuel line broke? How would you handle a bomb hit on the hangar deck? Is this silhouette a Wildcat or a Zero? Think, sailor, *think!* It's your life and that of your shipmates! The quizzes went on and on. Just before the weary boys were ready to break from exhaustion, they were allowed to hit their bunks for a few precious hours until the next day brought the same unending round of drill, drill, drill.

Through it all they began to find their way around the big carrier and get to know it if not to love it. Mitscher and his officers understood that the ship and ultimately the country depended on these young sailors. The *Hornet*'s squadrons and their glamorous pilots who made up the carrier's main battery would be useless without the routine skills of boiler tenders, signalmen, telephone talkers, plane handlers, damage controlmen, bakers, supply clerks, hospital corpsmen, aerographers, fire control technicians, and quartermasters: hundreds of faceless youngsters toiling above and below decks, largely unknown to the captain, the fliers, or even the exec. These were the men who kept the ship afloat and fighting.

Decades later, slipping into old age, these once-youthful sailors remembered how things were then. Walking around the supercarrier *Dwight D. Eisenhower* at Norfolk, they recalled that the much smaller *Hornet* seemed to be a more comfortable ship: The passageways were wider, and the vessel was not so minutely compartmented. In the long years of cold peace and cold war after 1945, carrier air groups, when not deployed on their mother vessels, remained miles away at air stations. Thus when carriers were at sea there was always tension between the ship's company and the "airdales," who acted like visitors from an alien land. But during World War II air groups had to be aboard their carriers the entire time. They mixed easily with the seamen. Bob Taylor and Jack Medley joined the *Hornet*'s air group only after the ship had become a seasoned war veteran. Both were enlisted men; one was a mechanic, the other in ordnance. They recalled that they never felt crowded on board despite the presence of almost three thousand men in an 800-foot hull. Taylor also remembered that he never experienced fear aboard the *Hor-*

net until the last terrible day. When he later served on the 550-foot escort carriers *Altamaha* and *Nassau,* he was always nervous. These "jeep" carriers seemed to be sinking even when they were not, and he hated to be below decks.

The old men remembered how easily the *Hornet* moved in tropical seas and how smoothly she could take aboard her Wildcats and Dauntlesses. They remembered too the smell of fresh salt air and the play of buffeting winds across the unbroken flight deck, the loudspeakers on the island continually blasting forth orders or exhortations, the bugle calls and the scream of the bos'n's whistle. Life on the deck of a big fleet carrier in World War II might be dangerous, but it was also invigorating out there in the bright tropical or subtropical sunshine. "There was always noise on the carrier deck," pilot Frederick Mears wrote in 1943 of his brief time aboard the *Hornet* just before she went into battle: the ripping of the wind in the tall rigging above the island, the wash of water along the hull, the pounding of the ship in the sea, and at flight quarters the almost unbearable roar of heavy engines warming up and the shouts and balletic movement of men as the planes were pushed carefully into takeoff positions.[14]

Unlike the *Essex* and later supercarriers, the *Hornet* and her sister ships berthed the crew exclusively in the hull, not on the gallery deck. The men lived, sixty or more, in large compartments, sleeping on canvas-covered racks that were stacked four high and so close to each other that a man had to turn over carefully during the night to avoid bumping the sagging canvas above that held a shipmate. Each sailor had a locker just large enough for uniforms, dungarees, flat hats, white hats, shoes, and toiletries. One bulkhead contained a large locker for peacoats, and adjacent to each berthing compartment were the heads with showers, toilets, and shaving sinks. Three times daily at specified hours the men stood in long lines that snaked up ladders and along passageways and out onto the hangar deck, waiting for cafeteria-style meals in the large mess hall amidships on B Deck, two decks below the hangar. The crew's mess hall, which was adjacent to the ship's post office and laundry, was equipped with long benches and equally long tables. There were no round-the-clock feedings or snack bars, no exercise areas, no recreation compartments with games and magazines (although there was a small ship's library amidships available to all), no comfortable bunks with individual reading lights and personal drawers just below for storing candy bars.

Most of the officers were housed forward behind the forecastle and just ahead of the gun gallery in spartan two-man cabins or four-man bunk rooms, depending on rank. McAteer, the young surgeon, shared a cabin with the landing signal officer. The more senior officers and pilots lived in small staterooms scattered throughout the hull. There or at their work stations they had desk drawers or closet shelves large enough to hold a few cherished possessions. Lt. Comdr. Oscar Dodson, the communications officer, escaped "the appalling monotony" of waiting for enemy attacks by enjoying a small, cherished collection of old coins, none rare, none really valuable, but each possessed of a distinct individuality.[15] Lt. Comdr. William J. "Gus" Widhelm, a flamboyant scout pilot, lugged aboard a phonograph and fifty-two Bing Crosby records and a collection of Strauss waltzes and Wagner operas. The chaplain, Lt. Comdr. Eddie Harp, played sentimental old melodies and hymns on the ship's organ. Whether spartan or pleasant, each officer's room was cleaned by black mess attendants, who also made the beds, changed linen and towels, and shined shoes left outside doors.

The wardroom, which ran the breadth of the ship, was amidships on Deck A just below the hangar, right above the crew's mess hall. During feeding hours there was always congestion in that part of the ship as officers and men jostled to get to their respective compartments. Large and well lighted, the wardroom initially contained an old, dried-up hornet's nest hung from the ceiling, the only indication of the ship's name found anywhere aboard—except on official correspondence letterhead—for security was as rigidly imposed as discipline. The officers ate with monogrammed silver at long tables covered with crisp linens. Senior officers above lieutenant junior grade had a special table of their own. Everyone was served by "colored mess attendants who seemed ready to jump to your elbow at every moment."[16] Mitscher was ahead of his contemporaries in race relations. When a delegation of messmen approached him and asked to be allowed to do more than simply serve food, clean the officers' dishes, and make their beds, Mitscher immediately assigned them to one of the 1.1-inch batteries. He gave it special attention during gunnery drills, and the messmen quickly became some of the best gunners aboard.

There was little leisure at sea. Wartime watches and work meant that most men toiled fourteen to sixteen hours a day. On such a big ship friendships were rare beyond one's immediate work area on the flight deck or in gun galleries, signal bridge, or engine room. Everyone was just too busy carrying out an endless series of assignments. One constantly met strangers in the chow line, at the mess tables, sometimes even while waiting for the predawn shave. Recreation was sleep and, for those who

Enlisted aircrew quarters on a World War II carrier. Note the crowding and lack of privacy, which were typical of enlisted quarters on all ships of that period.

had spare time and energy once the shakedown cruise ended, numerous poker games or craps shoots at the single table in the middle of each berthing compartment or in the cabins in "officers' country." Chief water-tender Cardon Ruchti, who labored in the engine room, boasted that he never drew pay from the time the ship left the East Coast until it was sunk; he lived well, whether on ship or ashore, off his steady poker winnings. Movies were rare. They were occasionally shown on the hangar deck for everyone; more often, officers got to enjoy them in the privacy of the wardroom. Soon after the ship went to sea, some officers set up their own little convenience mess in a corner of the wardroom. It cost five dollars a share to join, and each officer could purchase a maximum of two shares to buy soft drinks, cigars, and other luxuries. Little touches such as these helped make life bearable amid the stress of war.

The only people who were not overworked were the five doctors and handful of hospital corpsmen who made up the medical department. McAteer remembered that he was often extremely bored and spent hours reading during the days and weeks when the ship was at sea but not in action and the crew's health remained sound.

Mitscher worried constantly, as would his successor, about supplies. Active young men constantly busy in a stressful environment required good food and plenty of it, but they often did not get it. Mitscher told Stark near the end of the cruise that the supply department rated only a "satisfactory." Not only had it not received essential spare parts and equipment, but "we ran out of fresh provisions some time ago and our diet since then has been out of a can. It has been sufficient but not varied." Some *Hornet* crewmen concluded that the spartan rations were part of a deliberate policy to see how long active young men could live on a diet of potatoes.[17]

But as much as Mitscher, Henderson, Akers, Creehan, and the others worried about the crew, the power plant, the guns, and a hundred other problems, their main concern was always the air group. For it was the air group that could not only project potentially devastating power but also defend the ship. Like any carrier, the *Hornet* was so packed with bombs, gasoline, and bullets that she could burst into flaming wreckage at the first detonation of an enemy missile. Naval guns alone could not protect the ship against swift Japanese Zeros, Zekes, and Vals. Taranto, where British carrier planes crippled the Italian fleet, the *Bismarck*, and the *Prince of Wales* and *Repulse* had demonstrated that no lone vessel could defend herself against a concerted air attack. The Wildcats of Fighting 8 remained the *Hornet*'s surest guarantors of life. And if the carrier was going to be the new queen of the seas, her bombers, scouts, and torpedo planes had to be honed to the finest fighting edge. The planes might not be the best; the pilots had to be.

As the *Hornet*'s air officer, Soucek was responsible for providing the pilots with all pertinent information and getting the air group off and back on board the ship. The commander of the air group itself—the "CHAG," or "Sea Hag"—was Lt. Comdr. Stanhope C. Ring. Four lieutenant commanders led the individual squadrons: Samuel G. "Pat" Mitchell, the F4F Wildcats (Fighting 8); Robert R. Johnson, the dive-bomber Dauntlesses (Bombing 8); Walter F. Rodee, the VSB-8 scout-bombers; and John C. Waldron, Torpedo 8. Each man was an Annapolis graduate with an apparently total dedication to his profession. The *Hornet* air group was the last to form before Pearl Harbor, and Ring and his squadron commanders were keenly aware of the need to bring their pilots up to a high professional level as soon as possible. But they had only fifteen fighters, twelve bombers, twelve scouts,* and nine torpedo planes that were consistently flyable.

Shakedown began badly for Air Group 8. On the fourth day at sea—the first involving full flight operations—the only operational spare aircraft was lost. It had taken off on a routine qualification flight, and the pilot, Lt. (jg) W. H. Highlands, was making his turn into the final approach pattern ("groove") when the engine abruptly failed. The plane pancaked into the sea and promptly sank; the destroyer *Noa,* acting as plane guard, quickly plucked Highlands from the water. The young pilot suffered head lacerations and possibly a skull fracture.

For the next month Soucek, Ring, Rodee, and the others worked their young aviators mercilessly. The youngsters flew every day for hours at a time in clear weather and clouds, high ceiling and low. There were group flights and operations; gunnery practice on towed sleeves and on the *Hornet*'s own pyramid, which bobbed up and down in the soft waters of the gulf; horizontal bombing practice; mock torpedo attacks against both the *Hornet* and *Noa;* and simulated dive-bombing runs. Takeoff and landing accidents were few. Several pilots missed the arresting wires and crashed into the nylon barrier amidships. One plane was severely damaged, but no pilot except Highlands lost flight time because of injuries. The flight deck crew was equally fortunate. The most serious accident occurred on 21 January, when Aviation Machinist's Mate R. L. Etter was knocked to the flight deck. A fellow mechanic had failed to shut off an ignition switch before turning the propeller on one of the planes, and a blade clipped Etter before he could get out of the way. He incurred a bruised thigh and several crushed fingers.[18]

Everyone aloft, as on board, watched constantly for U-boats. One could never tell when an especially bold member of Hitler's *Kriegsmarine*

---

*During the early years of World War II, the Douglas Dauntless was employed interchangeably as a scout and a bomber aircraft. During air strikes carrier "scout" squadrons were used as dive-bombers. Throughout the book the terms "scout" and "bomber" (or "dive-bomber") are used to indicate separate squadrons with the understanding that the scout squadrons possessed a dual function.

might try to stretch his fuel to the limit and search the gulf for a juicy target.

From the beginning the *Hornet* was on a wartime footing. For most men each day began at 0400, when bugles in officers' country and the bos'n's shrill pipe over loudspeakers in the crew's berthing areas roused all hands. The cooks, bakers, and messmen were already up and at work in both wardroom and crew's mess, for the pilots who were to fly the morning search mission and the enlisted mechanics and ordnancemen who were to service their aircraft had to be fed quickly. Often the wardroom was already full of officers who had awakened early, and the smell of early morning cigarettes and coffee was mixed with leftover odors from those who had just left after completing the midnight watch. Everyone else had fifteen minutes to wake, dress, shave, and be ready for general quarters, which sounded an hour before sunrise.

The call to quarters sent both officers and men racing up ladders and through hatches, cursing good naturedly or otherwise as they barked shins on hatches or bunched up behind a slow mate. For the one hour of morning GQ the ship was "buttoned up" tightly: All hands were at battle stations. Those above decks strained their eyes in the dawning light, searching for the watery feather of a periscope. Sunrise and sunset were the two best times of day for enemy submarines to strike, because the ship was backlit by the rising or setting sun. As the men watched and waited in the semidarkness, the search planes took off. Then up on the navigation or signal bridge, where men felt half-suffocated by stack gases, the first full light of the new day split the sea and sky, and soon the sun brilliantly lit the tropical waters. The bos'n's pipe sounded retreat from general quarters, and about two thousand men temporarily off duty trooped down to breakfast. After a day of incessant drills, GQ sounded again to carry the ship safely through dusk and sunset.

Only the mechanics, ordnancemen, and plane pushers of the air group were exempt from GQ. Their job was to keep every aircraft in top condition, which meant constant servicing, repair, and shifting about of individual planes. The men worked sixteen- to eighteen-hour days until their tasks were completed. During ship defense drills they would have been a hindrance on the bridges or in gun galleries, so they simply stayed out of the way.

Mitscher was especially concerned with meshing deck crew and pilots into a smoothly functioning team for flight operations. Landings and takeoffs were practiced every hour, and eventually the skipper expressed satisfaction with his pilots—apparently more so than did the CHAG or his colleagues. "Where the squadron commanders feel that their pilots should have a great deal more" training of all kinds, Mitscher wrote Stark, "I believe that in time of peace our standards have been entirely too high, and have tried to impress the squadron commanders with the fact that they must accept much lower standards in the future and try to strike a general average as the proper standard." Mitscher justified this remarkable defense of mediocrity by adding that most of the pilots had only recently graduated from flight school at Pensacola, Florida, "and at the present time have an average of only about 360 hours total flying time. They had never been aboard ship, probably had never seen a ship before." In a wartime emergency the best way to conduct forced-draft pilot training and indoctrination was to get the young men aboard and put them to work hour after hour. "And if this is done I think that very shortly they would snap into the routine and develop much faster than they do on the beach."

Mitscher's policy on the *Hornet* would become wartime doctrine, which would eventually reap enormous dividends for the United States after an initial period of heart-rending failures and near failures. Like the other great American commanders of World War II—Marshall, Nimitz, Eisenhower, and Patton, to name only a few—Mitscher intuitively understood that his country's genius lay in its superb mechanical and technical competence. A brilliant young Canadian historian, Chester Wilmot, also recognized this national trait, which he emphasized in the first important history of the Second World War in Europe. Hitler and his generals, Wilmot wrote in 1952, gravely underestimated American strength and skill. The high command of the Wehrmacht "was contemptuous" because the U.S. Army "had such a small professional core and so little military tradition or experience." Hitler listened with fascination to intelligence accounts of captured U.S. soldiers in France, who ostensibly told their captors that they were fighting in Europe for money or adventure. The Yanks, said one of the Führer's subordinates dismissively, had no political ideals; they were "rowdies" who turned and ran at the first sign of difficulty. Hitler himself added that the United States would never become a Rome of the future because Rome was a state of dedicated peasants. The Americans were not peasants and therefore could not be tough. Their armies lacked that deep inner fortitude that sustained dumb but staunch peasant armies. "To Hitler," Wilmot wrote, "it was as simple as that."[19]

But the Nazis failed to realize (although Adm. Isoroku Yamamoto and the Japanese naval high command certainly did) that "more than any other people, the Americans are mechanically-minded. In the United States the youth who cannot drive a car or has not operated a machine of some kind is a rarity." As late as World War II Americans often exhibited a lack of assurance among other peoples and betrayed a sense of inferiority about their behavior, "which Europeans [and Japanese] tend to regard as juvenile and even gauche." But in the realm of machines the Americans possessed "a self-confidence, indeed a sense of mastery, which European peoples do not know."[20]

The American genius for improvisation, for "jury rigging" solutions to mechanical problems, was exemplified by the *Hornet*'s air department, where machinists, mechanics, and electricians soon became expert repairmen under the pressures and exigencies of war. In 1942 American servicemen fought with what they had. There were no replacements. Air Group 8 compiled a remarkably safe flight record throughout its existence. Few planes were lost because of either enemy action or accidents on takeoff or landing. Those that suffered damage aboard were usually returned to flight status within a few days if not hours. Once the ship reached the Pacific there were usually spares aboard, and these were "cannibalized" as necessary to keep the group at or near its allotted complement.[21]

The instinctive American aptitude for technology blended naturally with another trait: love of adventure and movement. The European campaign, Wilmot contended, stimulated a revival of the frontier spirit, which had induced the great-grandparents of this wartime generation to break out across the Alleghenies and open up the Middle and later the Far West. "To the American troops driving across France" in 1944, "distance meant nothing. They had no qualms about thrusting deep into the military unknown. This was not the case with the majority of the British forces."[22]

Wilmot's observations about the U.S. character were especially applicable to the Pacific war, which from the beginning involved movement, distance, and the mastery and deployment of complex machines. If there was one overriding problem that defined the action in the Pacific, it was pilots. Japan had started the war with a large, superb cadre of trained aviators. As Jiro Horikoshi, the Zero's designer, wrote after the war, the "abrupt reversal of the Asiatic-Pacific balance of power" in the months immediately after Pearl Harbor "was accomplished with the total of only approximately one thousand planes of the Japanese Naval Air Force and . . . this same force suffered only the barest minimum of losses." But Horikoshi added that the Japanese, unlike the Americans, never mastered the problem of training equally competent second- and third-generation pilots to use when many of the frontline fliers went down, as they certainly would if the Americans could muster sufficient force against them.[23] Once Japan lost its best carriers and pilots in the Coral Sea, at Midway, and at Santa Cruz, it was doomed. The Americans kept their growing number of carriers at sea in 1943, training hundreds of pilots using the proven method of learning by doing, but the Japanese had to keep their handful of precious carriers and novice fliers out of combat and indeed out of the sea lanes. When they were finally forced to meet the Americans again in the first battle of the Philippine Sea, the predictable result was slaughter.

Thus Mitscher was right, at least in the long run, to insist that peacetime pilot-training standards on the "beach" were impossibly rigid and artificial. It was essential to teach America's apt young men the basics of flying and then get them to sea, where they could finish their education in the crucible of battle. But to an apprehensive if not demoralized service that was absorbing shattering defeats with often outmoded ships and faulty equipment, Mitscher's proposals were questionable at best, heretical at worst.

Nor did Mitscher apply them consistently. He, Soucek, and Ring never quite got a handle on Air Group 8, and its combat performance suffered accordingly. At least 70 percent of the air group consisted of green ensigns; even Pat Mitchell, boss of Fighting 8, had never flown an F4F onto a carrier deck. Mitscher and Soucek refused to admit that the few accidents were solely due to inexperience and grounded the hapless youngsters. The two men, wrote a later historian, "seemed to expect proficiency without practice, punishing mistakes by restricting flight time desperately needed to gain vital experience."[24] On one occasion Mitscher became enraged when a young pilot could not bring his plane in for a proper landing, and when the poor ensign finally made a shaky catch of number five hook, Mitscher vowed to ground him for the remainder of the cruise. Several days later Mitscher changed his mind, which angered Soucek. How could these kids learn to fly properly if they were not severely disciplined for mistakes? Mitscher said nothing, but the next week he ordered his air officer to put the ensign back on flight status. Mitscher may have been influenced by the experiences of squadron leader Mitchell, who was a very tentative flier and the last aboard the *Hornet* to complete his qualification trials.

There was also a problem with Torpedo 8. Whether it had been impossible to obtain sufficient weapons or whether the squadron leader decided to train his boys in a certain way, none of Waldron's men was allowed to fly with a torpedo under his aircraft. They took off, practiced, and landed with empty planes.

Mitscher, his air group, and the navy were feeling their way toward the best methods of combat training in the midst of war. No one had the right answers at first, and on one memorable occasion in the midst of battle Mitscher would clash with Stanhope Ring over the role and competence of the air group.

Mitscher realized that he was wielding a powerful but flawed cutlass of war, and as he prepared to turn the *Hornet* homeward at the end of January he was given further demonstrations of how tightly stretched and questionably capable the navy was. By this time Nazi U-boats were ravaging the East Coast, brazenly sinking unescorted ships within a few thousand yards of Miami, Jacksonville, Wilmington, North Carolina, and Atlantic City. The carrier had to remain in her training area for an additional week because there were not enough destroyers to convoy her safely back to Norfolk. Moreover, the *Noa*'s depth charges had persistently failed to work. Not only were the navy's older ships patently unsuited to modern war, so were many of the weapons aboard all ships, old and new. When the *Hornet* finally sailed north she went at full ahead: The carrier relied on speed, not old destroyers and faulty depth charges, for safety.

As the carrier prepared to come around the Florida peninsula on her way to Norfolk, she stopped for an afternoon at Key West, where Admiral Wilcox came aboard for approximately four hours. He sent a glowing cable to Vice Adm. Royal Ingersoll, commander in chief of the Atlantic Fleet, on the *Hornet*'s readiness for war, predicting "great things" for her. But Mitscher was ambivalent. The ship certainly was combat ready, but he continued to fret about the air group. At the end of his long letter to Stark he abruptly changed his optimistic tone. He reminded Stark that he had initially stated that the *Hornet* was ready for war under all conditions. "However, I will have to qualify that by stating that we must have our full complement of aircraft and spare aircraft before we will ever be ready for war."

Stark had just been relieved as chief of naval operations and was preparing to leave Washington for a London posting. Whether he was able to intervene on Mitscher's behalf or whether sufficient aircraft were already on the way to the *Hornet* is not clear. But when the ship reached California a month later, the fighter, scout, and bomber squadrons each received a full complement of factory-new F4F-4s and Douglas Dauntlesses, along with spare parts.

That was all in the future as Mitscher guided his ship past Thimble Shoal Light into Hampton Roads near dusk on 30 January 1942. The *Hornet* had been at sea for thirty-five grueling days, and everyone aboard looked forward to the brief post-shakedown yard period. They could not imagine—nor could most Americans—what would happen to the carrier after that.

3

Preparing

SCORES OF people would later claim credit for dreaming up the famous Doolittle raid against Tokyo; most had a more or less plausible argument. A bombing assault against the Japanese capital was an almost inevitable retaliation for Pearl Harbor and the countless disasters that followed. Something had to be done to stem the apparently inexorable tide of Japanese conquest, and the assault against Hawaii had demonstrated that aircraft carriers could indeed be employed as major strategic weapons. Moreover, the island empire of Nippon was as vulnerable to attack from air and sea as Pearl Harbor had been.

Roosevelt, Commander in Chief, U.S. Fleet, Ernest J. King and his staff, Lt. Gen. Henry "Hap" Arnold, head of the U.S. Army Air Corps, and a number of prominent aviators apparently all conceived the idea of bombing Tokyo in the weeks after Pearl Harbor. As one Pacific Fleet intelligence officer remembered decades later, "the Doolittle strike was expected to be a rather uncomplicated affair. There were no illusions of grandeur regarding the raid."[1] The problem was how to do it. One enthusiast for a Tokyo raid was Roscoe Turner, who, with the possible exception of James H. Doolittle, was the most famous flier in the United States. Turner and Doolittle had spent much of the previous decade developing and flying the world's most technologically advanced aircraft, and the two had competed amicably at air shows from Los Angeles to Cleveland.

Doolittle had returned to the air corps in 1940, and just after Pearl Harbor he ran into Turner in Cleveland. "Say, Jimmy," Turner said, "I've got an idea. You and I are probably two of the best aviators in the country. Why don't we get some of these kids organized on a bombing raid to bomb Tokyo?" Doolittle replied that that was a wonderful idea, but it would have to wait. "Hap [Arnold] brought me back in the Air Force and I haven't had time to do anything, except just work." Toward the end of January Doolittle ran into Turner again, and Turner reminded him of his idea. What idea? Doolittle asked. Why, the bombing raid on Tokyo. "Oh," Doolittle replied, "I'll talk to you again about that." Several months later Turner picked up a newspaper and read that "Doolittle Dooed it." Turner promptly walked into a Western Union Office, picked up a message sheet, and wired Doolittle through Arnold's office: "Dear Jimmy, you son of a bitch."[2]

Initially the White House and War Department thought about introducing air corps bombers into China or the Aleutians. But distance and the weather made the Aleutians infeasible, and a staging base in China would be vulnerable to a preemptive Japanese assault. Early in January 1942 Capt. Francis S. Low, an operations officer on King's staff, visited Norfolk to check on the readiness of the *Hornet*, which was then in the gulf. Flying into the naval base, Low noticed twin-engine bombers making simulated attacks on a carrier deck outlined on the runway below. He immediately conceived the idea of using air corps medium bombers launched from a carrier deck to raid Japan.

The navy needed all of its handful of Pacific carriers to harass the outer ring of Japanese island defenses in the Marshall and Bismarck Islands. Moreover, the *Saratoga* had been torpedoed and damaged in the early weeks of the conflict, leaving only the *Enterprise*, the *Lexington*, and the newly arrived *Yorktown* to hold the line against possible enemy assaults against Hawaii, western Australia, or Midway, the last remaining mid-ocean outpost. But the *Hornet* was still in the Atlantic working up. Once her shakedown was completed, she was a perfect choice to send to the Pacific to perform the Tokyo mission.

Low returned to Washington with his idea and immediately approached Admiral King. The two men often spent long evenings together, brainstorming various strategies and policies over drinks aboard the small flagship *Dauntless*, which King kept tied up at the Washington Navy

Yard. The chief of naval operations was intrigued with the idea and told Low to start planning a Tokyo raid with army B-25 medium bombers launched from a carrier off the Japanese coast. Low asked his air operations officer, Capt. Donald B. ("Wu") Duncan, to draft a proposal. Five days later Duncan handed a handwritten plan to King. No copy was ever made "so nobody except those who had to know about it would ever have a chance of seeing it." Duncan's proposal was in outline form, with annexes containing predictions of probable weather, a proposed route to the launch site, and thorough discussions of how to embark the medium bombers, what ships might be used—"everything I could think of," Duncan later said, "that was needed to present to the commander in chief of the Pacific [Chester W. Nimitz] and to General Arnold and to Doolittle."[3] King immediately approached Arnold, who was delighted with Duncan's work; the air corps had been searching for ways to launch a B-25 mission from "free China" and had modified several of its bombers with additional fuel tanks. But could B-25s actually take off from a carrier deck? No one knew, but by the beginning of February the *Hornet* was back at Norfolk and available to test the planes. Two B-25s en route from one East Coast air base to another were diverted to Norfolk Naval Air Station.

Already Mitscher and Jurika had learned that the carrier might be chosen for a highly secret mission. John Wilcox was not the only naval officer who had boarded the *Hornet* at Key West near the end of January. Jurika claimed in 1976 that both Duncan and Secretary of the Navy Knox had also visited the ship and that Mitscher "and I had been talking to them concerning the feasibility, the possibility, of launching a carrier strike or strikes against the Japanese mainland. Ultimately," Jurika continued, "we discussed the feasibility of Air Corps aircraft such as the B-25 or the B-26 twin-engine bombers being loaded aboard at some American port and launched on a one-way trip, bombing Japan en route, and landing either in China or in the Soviet maritime provinces."[4]

The *Hornet* was in good material condition after its shakedown; the mechanical problems that Mitscher and others had identified during the cruise could be quickly and easily fixed. But the crew was both weary and cocky. Even the rawest boot among the seven hundred novices who had reported aboard one hundred days before had gotten his sea legs and learned his job. Both officers and men believed they had earned some time off and were eager to show their dashing gulf and Caribbean tans to the pale-skinned natives of wintry Norfolk, where a light snow began falling soon after the ship docked. Instead, after one day in port with liberty for all except the duty section, Duncan suddenly came aboard to confer with Mitscher.

Once closeted in the captain's spacious in-port cabin below decks, Duncan asked: "Can you put a loaded B-25 in the air on a normal deck run?"

"How many B-25's on deck?" Mitscher responded.

"Fifteen."

Mitscher called for the *Hornet*'s flight deck spotting board, a scale replica of the flight deck, and made some rapid calculations. Yes, it could be done. Good, Duncan replied, he would put two of the air corps medium bombers on board the next morning for a test launch.[5]

At 0530 on 2 February Pat Creehan's gang lit the first fires under the carrier's boilers. Several hours later, in the foggy dawn of a new day, the crewmen on the decks above were astounded to see two B-25s taxiing carefully across the base from the nearby airfield toward the carrier pier. The *Hornet*'s big crane just aft of the island delicately lifted the bulky planes to the flight deck. The quartermaster was evidently told not to document the incident, for no record of army planes appears in the *Hornet*'s deck log. The sea and anchor detail was immediately set, and at 0900 tugs carefully pulled the ship away from the dock. The *Hornet* turned majestically and with gradually accelerating speed sailed through the gloom down Hampton Roads and out into the Atlantic. A light snow began to fall. Mitscher ordered the airdales on the flight deck to spot the two planes far apart: one well aft, the other forward opposite the island, the actual spot from which the first of the contemplated fifteen planes would have to take off. The wingspan on the forward plane extended to within six feet of the island; its left wing stretched far over the ship's port side. The two daredevil test pilots who would fly these aircraft— Lt. John E. Fitzgerald and Lt. James F. McCarthy—would have to hold their planes very close to the port side of the flight deck throughout the roll-off to avoid a fatal swerve into the catwalks and gun galleries just below. It would be a near thing.

The crew was mystified by the B-25s and the preparations. Scuttlebutt, "the wild and swift-spreading rumor of the Navy,"[6] was rampant. From fo'c'sle to fantail, from signal bridge to engine room, everyone was intrigued. The B-25's wingspan was much wider than that of a carrier plane; the takeoff alley down the flight deck might or might not be long enough, and even if the planes could be launched, they could never be

landed back aboard. Their thin bottoms were too fragile to accommodate the hook that protruded from each navy fighter, bomber, and torpedo plane to snag the carrier's arresting wires. Yet early that afternoon,
with the *Hornet* barely out of sight of land, twenty-five to thirty miles off
the Virginia coast, Mitscher, bundled up in foul weather gear on the port
bridge wing thirty feet above the deck, ordered flight quarters. An equally
chilly Duncan stood next to the skipper, worrying about wingtip clear-
ance, positioning of the airplanes on deck, and their ability to pick up
speed into the teeth of a strong, lifting wind. While the pilots manned the
B-25s, the carrier increased engine revolutions and turned into the raw,
wet gale.

At 1300 the first plane raced down the deck, its engines howling, and
lifted easily into the air with room to spare. Mitscher and Duncan exchanged triumphant smiles; their calculations had been correct.

Suddenly the ship received semaphore signals from the escorting destroyers, the *Jones* and *Ludlow*, which had sighted an enemy periscope.
The *Hornet* went to general quarters, and the remaining pilot killed his
engines and climbed down from his bomber. The two destroyers plunged
through the heavy seas toward the wavering feather and hurled depth
charge after depth charge. These weapons worked, and the sea churned
into broth. Huge explosions rocked the *Hornet*, which opened fire with the
5-inch guns in the port-side stern gallery. With the sea still heaving from
the depth-charging, an oil slick began to spread from the spot. Yet the
"periscope" remained where it was. Mitscher turned to Frank Akers, who
had the watch, and said, "This is the first blasted submarine that I've ever
seen like that." Within minutes the abashed destroyer commanders sent
more signals. The "periscope" was actually the mast of a sunken merchant ship. "Very realistic drill," Mitscher said, smiling. Turning to
Akers, he added: "Send them a 'well done.'"[7]

Just $2\frac{1}{2}$ hours after the first B-25 had arced skyward, the second raced
down the *Hornet*'s flight deck and into the sky ahead of the ship. The
carrier promptly swung around and headed back to port, where Duncan
debarked and rushed to Washington. Within hours Mitscher received
orders to get his ship ready to sail by 1 March.

For the next $3\frac{1}{2}$ weeks the *Hornet* alternated dockyard and pierside
availability, while the crew enjoyed the meager pleasures of Norfolk.
Perhaps the most startling transformation was the ship's new paint job.
The *Hornet* was given a "Measure 12 Camouflage": various brush streaks,
swirls, and combinations of navy blue, ocean gray, and haze gray that

were designed to lower a vessel's silhouette and reduce her visibility to enemy airmen and submariners. It is not clear whether this combination had the desired effect. It certainly made the *Hornet* and the similarly painted *Wasp* distinctive flattops in the Pacific carrier fleet and natural targets for the vengeful Japanese.

As the ship lay snugly tied to its Norfolk pier, Jurika began to subtly educate his shipmates about the forthcoming mission, which was completely unknown to everyone except him and Mitscher. Yes, the young intelligence officer said, "it can be done. . . . I know Tokio [*sic*] like a book. If our bombers could start fires in separate sections of the city, the Tokio fire department would never be able to put them out." His constant reiterations slowly convinced his wardroom mates to be "Tokio-minded."[8]

If U.S. planes were to raid the Japanese capital, only lightweight "medium" bombers could do the job. Thus army planes would fly from a navy carrier. But the carrier would have to bring the army planes very close to Japanese shores, and Jurika knew that Japanese aircraft routinely guarded the ocean approaches out to three hundred miles. Picket boats patrolled out to five hundred miles or perhaps farther. A carrier raid using army bombers would be a supreme risk for a navy that desperately needed all its flattops to stop an apparently relentless Japanese advance.

On 20 February Mitscher was informed that the *Hornet* would sail to the Pacific in company with the heavy cruiser *Vincennes*, the light cruiser *Nashville*, the fleet oiler *Cimarron*, and several destroyers. Air Group 8 reported to the ship on the twenty-eighth, and its planes were hoisted aboard during the next several days.

Life below decks on the big carrier had its own domestic dramas both large and small. Glen Dock, the apprentice machinist's mate from Kalamazoo, found himself "mess cooking" for the chief petty officers in their comfortable dining and lounge area situated on the fourth deck aft, next to the after elevator pit. He became an acceptable short-order cook, frying up eggs and ham every morning. But he had not joined the navy to work in the galley. He wanted to be in the machine shop, and so he shamelessly buttered up the "A" Division chief. But his efforts were unsuccessful. In the months just before Pearl Harbor, as the nation frantically rearmed for the war almost everyone believed was rapidly approaching, the navy had called back hundreds of reservists. Many were second- and third-class petty officers who had been tool- and die-makers in civilian life, and they were immediately put into the *Hornet*'s machine shop. After his tour of mess cooking was over, Dock was assigned to "B" Division and a job in the ship's fireroom.[9]

A third-class electrician's mate wrestled with a more agonizing problem. His brother had been terribly injured on the destroyer *Shaw* at Pearl Harbor. Invalided to San Francisco, the man had died, and the electrician's mate struggled for days with the Red Cross, trying unsuccessfully to obtain emergency compassionate leave. One day an astounding message came down from the quarterdeck: The captain himself wanted to see the electrician. When the uneasy youngster appeared in Mitscher's sumptuous in-port sea cabin, the captain sat him down and said: "I'm going to let you go because you will probably come home in a pine box just like your brother, and that will be too much for your mother and father. But I want you to promise me that if you come back and we're not at Pier 7, you won't mention this to anyone but you [will] go to the receiving ship and get yourself another set of orders." The boy immediately agreed, and off he went. When he returned to Norfolk, the *Hornet* was long gone, so he reported to the receiving ship, where a set of orders was waiting for him. He was to obtain immediate transportation to join Torpedo Squadron 8—aboard the *Hornet*. He got back to the ship weeks later.[10]

Fully provisioned, her crew rested and eager, the *Hornet* and her escorts left Norfolk on 4 March and headed for Panama and the Pacific. The small task force guarded a troop convoy whose ultimate destinations were Australia and Guadalcanal. Two days out of Norfolk the assistant secretary of the navy for air, Artemus L. Gates, came aboard and rode the carrier down to Panama, where he debarked. Long before the *Hornet* snaked its way through the Panama locks the air became tropical again. As the ship transited Culebra Cut on 11 March, Gerald McAteer, the young surgeon, felt the heat coming off the wooden flight deck through his shoes. Everyone wished desperately for air conditioning, which was confined to the squadron ready rooms just below the flight deck. The ship stopped overnight at Balboa long enough for officers and men to purchase precious personal commodities. Many of the crew had responded to wartime stress by taking up the smoking habit, but McAteer quickly tired of cigarettes. He preferred cigars and in Panama bought as many fragrant Havanas as possible. The shakedown had taught everyone that at least in the early, frantic days of a world war even a capital ship like the *Hornet* could rapidly run out of supplies.

Leaving the canal, the *Hornet* said farewell to the Australia-bound troop transports and swung north toward California with her cruisers, destroyers, and oiler. The crew was relieved; many had wondered if their beautiful new ship would be used for anything except test flights and convoy duty. Two or three days out of Panama one of the *Hornet*'s escorts suddenly made a surface contact with an apparent submarine. The carrier went to battle stations, while the destroyer raced to the scene with 5-inch guns blazing. The "contact" turned out to be a huge Galápagos turtle with a sea gull on its back, swimming hundreds of miles from land.

As the *Hornet* knifed her way through tropical seas, the hundreds of raw "boots" who had come aboard just before commissioning continued to experience the harsh realities of serving as nonrated seamen in the U.S. Navy. There was a rigid system of seniority. Glen Dock found himself in Number Eight Fireroom. His chief petty officer was a man named Vaughn, and the first-class petty officer was named Koch. The unrated men did not talk to these exalted figures unless spoken to or in the line of duty. "The chief," Dock remembered, "was just like Jesus Christ." All requests and problems in the nonrated ranks were handled by the "leading seaman" or "leading fireman" in each division. Half a century later Dock could not remember his department head's name; he was not sure that he had ever spoken to Pat Creehan and perhaps had never even seen him except at morning quarters. But he remembered Johnny Carroll, his leading fireman. Carroll ruled the nonrated men in Fireroom Eight. Only if he could not resolve a problem would a nonrated man be permitted to approach Koch. And only if Koch could not handle the situation would Chief Vaughn become involved.[11] The system would begin to crumble as days and weeks at sea gradually turned the hundreds of "boots" into more competent sailors, enginemen, and airmen and mutual trust replaced ironclad discipline. But it would be a slow process.

On Friday morning, 20 March, people on Point Loma saw the *Hornet*'s "lopsided structure" appear far out toward the horizon. Within the hour the ship entered the narrow ship channel and moved toward the carrier berth at North Island across from downtown San Diego. To novice aviator Fred Mears the carrier looked like a "monstrous perversion."[12] By noon the ship was moored. Her destination as she left Norfolk had been top secret, "but when we got to San Diego," one crewman remembered, "lots of wives were at the dock."[13]

The carrier was bare of planes. Air Group 8 had already flown into North Island Naval Air Station, where it would acquire and fly new aircraft during the *Hornet*'s brief stay in southern California waters. Fighting 8 received nineteen brand-new F4F-4s, but the pilots soon discovered that the new plane with its advanced design was a mixed blessing. The F4F-4's most celebrated features were the hand-activated, folding wings, which permitted storage of many more aircraft aboard ship, and the increase in firepower from a four- to a six-gun battery. But heavier armor plate, gunnery, and the folding wing mechanism raised the gross weight of the plane a full seven hundred pounds over its F4F-3 predecessor. In acceleration and general handling the F4F-4 proved "less perky," and its official range was considerably less.[14]

Bombing and Scouting 8 were delighted to replace the ancient Curtiss biplane with the brand-new Douglas SBD-3 Dauntless, "one of the great carrier planes of all time."[15] A tough, rather fast aircraft (250 miles an hour) that could carry a 1,200-pound bomb load, the Dauntless was one of the few carrier planes that would not be inferior to its Japanese counterparts in the early stages of the war.

The next morning Ensign Mears and his colleagues, comprising several training squadrons designated Red and Blue, were ordered aboard the *Hornet* for advanced carrier qualifications. Their minds on the difficult flying ahead, the pilots failed miserably to follow basic shipboard etiquette, forgetting everything they had been taught at Pensacola. As they climbed up the gangway many saluted forward instead of aft, where the national ensign flew. Instead of formally requesting the officer of the deck's permission to come aboard, most said nothing. One youngster did blunder: "May I please come aboard your boat, sir?"[16]

"Once on the quarter-deck," Mears wrote in 1943, "we wandered around bumping into busy seamen whom we envied for knowing what they were about and tripping over mooring lines until we were instructed to report to the captain's quarters with our orders." From there the novice fliers were sent to the first lieutenant's office to get room assignments. Mears was surprised to discover that the first lieutenant was not a lieutenant after all but a lieutenant commander. "It was very confusing."[17]

After a weekend in port, the "Horny Maru," as Mears and his colleagues called her, got under way at midmorning on 23 March and headed out into the Pacific. With the ship's air group ashore, the fledgling aviators were assigned Fighting 8's ready room under the flight deck, where they began to understand the pleasures and irritations of life on a carrier at sea.

The ready room was each pilot's clubhouse and office. Just before battle the enlisted aircrew who manned the torpedo planes and dive-bombers along with the pilots came in to attend briefings, but otherwise

Douglas SBD-3 Dauntless scout-bomber.

they were excluded. Most of the pilots spent their ready room time working on theoretical navigation problems, mastering radio codes, participating in enemy recognition drills, discussing tactics, playing cards, sleeping, reading, or just plain loafing. As the eyes and fists of the ship and the fleet they were understandably a pampered lot. Aboard the *Hornet* "there were refrigerators with cold cuts, the makings of sandwiches, and warm loaves of bread, which very quickly became cold . . . , and all kinds of fruit drinks and ades."[18] When not in or on the eve of battle the pilots were frequently as bored as the medical staff. The only fliers actually on duty were the handful assigned to combat air patrols. If another carrier was present, even these usually occurred only once every other day as the two ships alternated being "duty carrier." But no one could be sure when and where the Japanese might be spotted. The combination of boredom and anticipation bred a persistent tension that could be debilitating over the long run.

The *Hornet* set a course southwest from Point Loma, and early in the afternoon flight quarters were called.[19] The qualifying fighters and dive-bombers had been loaded aboard at North Island, and now eight bombers were lined up on the flight deck ready to go. "The sea was not rough, but the swell was mean and the wind high," Mears recalled. The *Hornet* was pitching "considerably," causing the stern of the flight deck—"the ramp"—to move up and down as much as thirty feet. Three of the dive-bombers were promptly sent below to the hangar deck when their engines failed, cutting out at high rpm. The reason, the instructor told the fliers in an acid tone, was that the engines had not been kept sufficiently revved up before takeoff and the spark plugs had failed. The other five planes "rumbled down the deck" and took off safely with room to spare. Now the problem was to get them back on board.

Those who were not flying, including Mears, climbed up the island structure and positioned themselves on catwalks and bridge wings above the flight deck to watch their colleagues try to bring fast, heavily loaded aircraft onto the long, narrow, pitching deck. The planes came back toward the carrier along its port side; when they were about one thousand yards behind the ship they turned and came "up the groove," following the wake toward the ship's rising and falling ramp. The first plane, flown by an Ensign Edmondson, landed perfectly in the middle of the deck, catching number three arresting wire, just as everyone had been taught to do. The next flier came smoothly up the groove, took the landing signal officer's cut, and set down just port side of center. The wire caught his hook and threw the plane's tail outboard, causing its left wheel to drag within a foot of the edge of the deck.

From then on flight operations went from bad to worse. Coming in for his second landing, Edmondson got a cut, but instead of dropping his plane on the deck, he let it float several feet above the flight deck until it smashed into both the island structure and the first of several large wire barriers, which were set up to catch errant aircraft before they could hit any planes that might be parked forward. The ship's alarm horn blasted as the aircraft landed heavily on the deck. Edmondson was not hurt, and there was no fire, "but the bent prop look[ed] like the petals on a flower, and his right wing [was] crumpled." Fortunately the plane's undercarriage was not damaged, and the deck handlers disentangled the aircraft from the barrier and pushed it forward with the shaken ensign still in the pilot's seat.

Several more planes came aboard without incident before "Ensign Goddard [had] the next crash." After taking the cut he landed too far to starboard, and when the wire caught the plane's hook the aircraft was tossed into the bank of 20-millimeter guns situated in the catwalk below and along the flight deck. The batteries were not manned because the ship was not at general quarters, but the plane's left shaft was broken and a wing was crumpled.

Several F4F fighters were next brought up from the hangar and took off without incident. Their pilots made good to excellent landings for a while, but then came "the most exciting crash of the afternoon." When Ens. Robert Dibb took the cut, his plane hit the deck heavily just forward of the ramp. The gas valve under the plane was knocked off, and the aircraft, bouncing high, burst into flames as it floated down the deck and crashed into the wire barrier. The *Hornet*'s alarm bell went off again. A blanket of fire shot from the nose under the belly of the plane, and Dibb literally dove out of his cockpit, hit the wing with his shoulder, and rolled off onto the deck and into the arms of the two asbestos-suited "Joes" who were racing to rescue him. As the unhurt but frightened pilot was rushed to sick bay, the fire crews squirted a soda preparation at the burning plane with CO_2 bottles and hoses. But within seconds the firefighters lost water pressure, the hoses slackened, and the plane began to burn fiercely, cracking and buckling from the heat. The wooden flight deck itself caught fire. One of the gas tanks burned a hole in the fuselage and shot a stream of fuel into the blaze; the cockpit windshield reached combustion and torched up. Fire call was sounded. Then water pressure was regained, and the fire crews quickly smothered the blaze with a flood of liquid white soda. "The two grotesque parts of the plane which remain[ed]" were hauled below on one of the ship's three flight deck elevators.

Mitscher was "dismayed" at both the ineptitude of the pilots and the damage to his new ship.[20] Nonetheless, flight quarters sounded again early the next morning. This time crack-ups occurred during both landings and takeoffs. One of the young ensigns roared off the deck, disappeared over the starboard bow, and splashed within 150 yards of the *Hornet*. He had forgotten to deploy his flaps. His plane sank, but he got free and floated past the carrier as it raced by. Within minutes the plane-guard destroyer picked him up. Another flier took the cut too far to starboard; his plane went over the side and hung briefly from the arresting wire. Then the wire snapped from the strain, dropping the plane into the sea. No one on deck was hurt when the heavy wire came whipping back, and the busy destroyer soon had another pilot on board. One of the fliers watching from the island looked toward the destroyer and cracked: "Only two more and they'll have enough for bridge over there."

Actually, one of the *Hornet*'s crewmen, apparently a veteran of an older carrier, informed them that they were not doing too badly for new pilots. Usually there were more accidents than this during carrier qualifications. The men qualifying that day had undergone rigorous training on the "beach," the kind that Mitscher had told Stark was well beyond anything really required. Yet their crack-up ratio was apparently as high if not higher than that of the *Hornet*'s air group during shakedown in the gulf. Perhaps Mitscher was right after all: Give the men minimal training ashore and send them to the fleet to learn by doing. Mears himself qualified with surprising ease, although on one of his approaches he missed a wave-off until the last minute and his plane hurtled over the port side stern of the *Hornet* at about five feet, causing the landing signal officer to sprain a thumb as he leapt into the safety net.

That Friday, 27 March, the *Hornet* returned to North Island, and Mears and his buddies went ashore. The crew received weekend liberty, and Mitscher awaited his next orders.

4

The Raid

BY THE time the *Hornet* had completed her pilot qualification exercises off San Diego, Allied prospects were at their nadir. In Europe and North Africa the Nazi juggernaut was again on the move. After spending the winter clinging to positions just one hundred miles west of Moscow, the Wehrmacht was now preparing for another summer offensive that would carry it deep into southeastern Russia. Erwin Rommel was threatening Cairo, and apprehensive armchair strategists, seeing arrows on a newspaper war map instead of men, equipment, and terrain, envisioned Nazi spearheads spreading across the entire Middle East toward India. In the Pacific, Japan was rapidly consolidating its gains behind a midocean defense line that included Truk, Rabaul, Wake Island, and Guam. American and Filipino forces were being pushed to their last defensive positions on Bataan. Singapore had already fallen: Thirty thousand well-armed British and Commonwealth troops had shamefully surrendered to a Japanese force half their size, which had besieged the city with bicycles and rifles. The last of the U.S. Asiatic Fleet had been destroyed in distant, hopeless battle off Java; the Dutch East Indies were on the verge of surrender; Japanese troops were invading Burma. Was it possible, the armchair strategists asked, that Japanese and German boys could somehow link up in the middle of India?

In the Pacific, the core of Axis power was the *Kido Butai,* Japan's magnificent Mobile or Striking Force of six frontline aircraft carriers under the command of Vice Adm. Chuichi Nagumo. From Pearl Harbor on, this force or components of it had seemed to be everywhere, supporting Japanese advances in the mid- and southwestern Pacific. Planes from the *Kido Butai* had backed the Japanese landings on Wake, had struck a sudden, shattering blow against U.S. naval and air forces at Darwin in northern Australia, and had supported the invasions of Java, Sumatra, and New Guinea. Now, under Nagumo, four of these carriers were steaming into the Indian Ocean to sweep away the handful of British heavy ships there. Meanwhile, the other two carriers of the *Kido Butai* were thousands of miles to the east, threatening Allied supply and communication lines from the United States through Samoa to New Zealand and eastern Australia.

As King and Nimitz struggled to contain the Japanese in the central and southwestern Pacific, plans proceeded rapidly for a carrier raid on Tokyo. In late January Hap Arnold had ordered his old friend, forty-five-year-old Lt. Col. James H. Doolittle, to gather a group of volunteers at Eglin Air Base in north Florida for a brief, hectic training period. Under the tutelage of navy Lt. Henry L. Miller, who had come over from nearby Pensacola Naval Air Station, the Army Air Corps pilots would learn to lift their B-25 medium bombers off a concrete runway that was about half the length of the *Hornet*'s deck.

Doolittle mustered his men on 1 March, just as the *Hornet* was pulling away from the carrier pier at Norfolk. Youngsters who were accustomed to using nearly a mile of runway to lift thirty-one thousand pounds of aircraft from the ground had to master the quick, high-powered runs necessary to take off with fewer than five hundred feet. After a frantic and difficult two-week training period directed by Miller at a remote satellite field, Doolittle informed Arnold that his boys were almost ready to go— although none of them, including Doolittle, was sure where he was going or why. Because of the short takeoff runs, along with Miller's coaching and lectures on shipboard protocol, it was obvious that the mission involved an aircraft carrier. Doolittle speculated that it might also involve a Tokyo raid, but he could not be sure. The *Hornet* was nearing San Diego by this time, so when Arnold summoned King to his office and told the chief of naval operations that Doolittle was ready, King asked that Doolittle come to Washington for a full briefing. Arnold spun on his heel and called out to a subordinate: "Get Doolittle up here right away, tonight!"[1]

After flying up from northern Florida through wretched weather, Doolittle met Captain Duncan the next morning at the Navy Department and was handed the single copy of Duncan's plan. "He read it once," Duncan remembered, "and . . . said, 'That's fine.'"[2] Doolittle may have been reassured that the mission would be based on the *Hornet*, for in the small aviation world of the 1930s he had gotten to know Mitscher, Henderson, and Soucek well. He would be sailing with friends as well as professionals.

Doolittle and Duncan agreed that the army contingent would leave Eglin as soon as possible for McClellan Field near Sacramento, where the fliers would await final instructions for joining the *Hornet*. Duncan, meanwhile, would fly to Pearl Harbor to brief Nimitz and Vice Adm. William F. "Bull" Halsey, commander of Task Force 16, which was built around the carrier *Enterprise*. As Duncan prepared to leave, King took him aside and told him to inform Nimitz that the Tokyo raid was "not a proposal made for [Nimitz] to consider but a plan to be carried out by him."[3] When Duncan met with Halsey and Nimitz on 19 March, he found both men enthusiastic, and he promptly cabled Washington to "tell Jimmy to get on his horse."[4]

Five days later, after some final training sessions in Florida to make up for time lost during fog and inclement weather, Doolittle awakened his men at 0300 and told them they would be on their way within eight hours to Sacramento via San Antonio and southern California. Meanwhile, the tireless Wu Duncan rushed back to San Francisco by Pan Am Clipper and then down to San Diego to brief Mitscher. The *Hornet* was tied up at North Island for weekend liberty, and once again the two naval captains huddled together in Mitscher's cabin. Duncan gave Mitscher the final plans, which included a mid-Pacific rendezvous with Halsey, the *Enterprise*, and Task Force 16, which would provide essential air cover. Mitscher promptly informed Henderson, Soucek, and Jurika, and on Monday morning, 30 March, the *Hornet* steamed down the San Diego ship channel, past Point Loma, and headed north toward Alameda. The carrier's entire complement of more than eighty mostly brand-new aircraft was packed tightly in the hangar deck, and the bare flight deck, gleaming in the Pacific sun, awaited strange, new tenants. Late the next afternoon Mitscher carefully took his carrier through the partially dredged channel into Alameda, sliding the big ship through mud to reach the pier, where the first contingent of Doolittle's planes waited.

Doolittle's men had flown west the previous week. Full of pent-up energy, they hedgehopped across the country, brushing trees and just missing power lines. "It was the craziest flying I had ever done," Capt. Ted Lawson recalled, "and I had done some kid-stuff tricks like banking a B-25 through a low, open drawbridge."[5] The young pilots were fatalistic. Whatever the mission, it obviously would be extremely hazardous. You might not be around much longer; it was time to do the things you had always wanted to do.

While the B-25s were being rechecked at McClellan, Doolittle warned his fliers that there would be no more hell-raising. Once the planes were certified as combat ready, Doolittle ordered them to a small airfield near Willows, north of Sacramento, where Hank Miller for the last time drilled everyone in short takeoffs. While his men were thus engaged, Doolittle flew to San Francisco for a quick, secret meeting with Halsey. As commander of the *Enterprise*, Halsey had already made a name for himself by directing quick, hit-and-run raids on enemy bases in the Marshall Islands and at Marcus, only 960 miles from Tokyo. Doolittle and Halsey hammered out final tactical plans, including the crucial question of how close to Japan Halsey might take the raiders. The navy initially argued for a launch position about eight hundred miles east of Tokyo, well outside the Japanese picket boat defenses, to ensure the safety of the two precious carriers. Doolittle just as forcefully argued for a launch point only four hundred miles away to ensure that his pilots and planes could make it to "free China." The two men compromised: The launch point would be six hundred miles east of Tokyo.[6]

On the first morning of April 1942 Doolittle's men made one more hop over the mountainous hump from Willows to Alameda. As they flew across San Francisco Bay toward the naval air station, they saw ahead of them the unmistakable shape of an aircraft carrier at the pier. "Three of our B-25's were already on its deck" when Lawson's plane arrived. Gazing down at the *Hornet*, one of his crewmen said apprehensively, "Damn! Ain't she small?"[7] Doolittle met each of the twenty-two B-25s that landed at Alameda and asked the pilot if everything was fine. If he received a positive answer, Doolittle ordered the plane to taxi to the pier, where the *Hornet*'s crane delicately lifted it onto the flight deck. Those pilots foolish or honest enough to admit aircraft troubles saw their planes pushed to nearby hangars, and they were informed that they had been scrubbed from the mission. That was how Doolittle got his best planes and possibly his best crews. Some of the dismissed fliers went along on the *Hornet* as backup crew, but none would be needed.

Lawson was stunned by the *Hornet*. "She was a great sight," he remembered. "I can't describe the feeling I got, standing there, looking up at her sides." Miller approached him. He warned Lawson not to tell the "Navy boys" anything; they had no idea where the B-25s were going. But then, neither did Lawson. Once again the carrier's deck log made no mention of army bombers aboard. It was as if Doolittle's men and planes did not exist.[8]

The men of the *Hornet* were less enthusiastic about their army visitors and the circumstances surrounding whatever mission was planned for the carrier. Young Dr. McAteer was appalled that the ship pulled into Alameda in broad daylight "in front of the whole city" of San Francisco and brazenly loaded army bombers aboard.[9] Jurika was unimpressed by the fliers themselves, especially since he knew where they were going. Obviously an all-volunteer bunch like this had to possess special flying ability and group dynamics. But the army boys seemed unkempt. Their shoes were scuffed and worn out; they wore open collars and short-sleeved shirts even though the early spring weather was cool. The hard linings of their caps—"grommets"—were either crushed or nonexistent. Yet these people had spent their time at Sacramento in bachelor officers' quarters, where they could at least have cleaned up sufficiently to board the *Hornet* with a vestige of neatness. Jurika was not amused.

Sixteen bombers were loaded by midafternoon on 1 April, and at 1500 Mitscher backed the *Hornet* out of Alameda as carefully as he had brought her in. He took the ship out to Berth Nine in the middle of San Francisco Bay for the night so the navigation team would not have to sail through the busy harbor at dusk or dark. Restricted liberty was granted to some, who privately worried then (and publicly complained later) that the secrecy of the mission was seriously compromised by the careless display of bombers cluttering the carrier's deck for an entire city to see. But nearly everyone aboard assumed that the ship was simply on another ferry mission, taking the B-25s to Hawaii or some other threatened spot in the Pacific. In fact, as apologists would patiently reiterate for many years, carriers were often used as ferries for the navy and army aircraft sent to defend Hawaii, Panama, or Australia. Few if any ashore could distinguish the exact type of planes on the *Hornet*'s flight deck, and even if they could, they would logically assume that the B-25s were being taken to any one of a dozen hot spots around the globe. Indeed, the carrier might have been heading back to Panama en route to England or Iceland. The *Hornet*'s crew thought the B-25s were meant for Hawaii.[10]

At midmorning on 2 April the carrier got under way through a light fog, destined never to return to the country she would so stoutly defend during the final six months of her life. Visibility was initially about one thousand yards, but, as is often the case, the morning fog bank extended only a few miles beyond the Golden Gate, and soon the *Hornet* was sailing under sunny skies. By noon Task Force 18 formed up only a few miles off the coast.

In addition to the *Hornet*, it comprised the cruisers *Nashville* and *Vincennes*, the fleet tanker *Cimarron*, and Destroyer Division 22. Because the carrier's planes were below deck, aircraft from the Western Sea Frontier provided cover until late afternoon. As they circled high overhead, navy blimp L-6 floated across the horizon to a point above the aft end of the *Hornet*'s flight deck. Two boxes of navigator's domes for the B-25s were carefully winched down, and then the blimp departed.

Soon Mitscher told everyone aboard where the ship was going and its precise mission. The sixteen B-25s would take off with sixty 500-pound bombs to strike Japan. When the word was signaled to the other vessels in the small fleet, exultant cheers and yells drifted across the water.

But there was unease as well as anticipation aboard the *Hornet*. Some, remembering the brazen way in which the carrier had both approached and departed San Francisco, believed that land was still too close to make such a critical announcement. Mitscher should have waited until the task force was far at sea. McAteer experienced a momentary surge of depression, and the next morning and thereafter more crewmen showed up for sick call than normal. This became a pattern in the days just before a battle. Everyone realized that for the first time in the war the *Hornet* was really venturing into the world's ocean. She had hugged the East and Gulf Coasts during her shakedown and voyage to Panama; then she had raced up to San Diego. Now she was finally steaming into the broad Pacific, where battle might come at any time. Fewer than sixty days before, a Japanese submarine had briefly surfaced off Santa Barbara and lobbed a few shells toward an oil refinery. The enemy had proved that he could literally be anywhere: The seas belonged to him.

Even the rawest sailor aboard now knew enough about aircraft carriers to understand that they were floating bombs packed with ordnance and gasoline. Under the right conditions the ship could be detonated by the spark of a ricocheting bullet. Moreover, the *Hornet* was a tinclad. Her strongest armor plating, which formed a girdle at and below the waterline, surrounding the engine spaces and firerooms, was only four inches thick. It was incapable of withstanding enemy torpedoes. The carrier was a fragile giant, terribly vulnerable to the assaults of a vicious and determined foe. And what did the U.S. Navy know about that foe? The only ships and men that had met the Japanese in the first months of the Pacific war had not returned to tell of their ordeal and defeat; few would. The carrier raids that were being made on Japanese island holdings in the central and southwestern Pacific were mere pinpricks, valuable for providing pilots and carriers with some combat experience but no substitute for sustained battle.

All those aboard ship knew or guessed the odds against them. No matter how well trained they were, the enemy was equally capable and far more battle-hardened. Chaplain Eddie Harp may have thought the crew was reacting predictably when attendance at Sunday services increased. Young McAteer discovered that other officers and men responded differently. Aboard a big warship a doctor got to know more people than did almost anyone else: enlisted men, chief petty officers, warrant officers, as well as the junior and senior authorities. Once under way in the Pacific, McAteer from time to time became the recipient of varied "offerings": knickknacks, food, or whatever a man could think to give. And with the present came the invariable request: "Doc, when we go into combat and there are ten to fifteen guys lying around hit, remember me." A few officers even brought McAteer some of the Cuban cigars he loved.[11]

Doolittle's men had other problems. Almost all except Doolittle himself and a handful of others had been assigned to bunk with the *Hornet*'s junior pilots, who were cordial and frankly curious but far from accommodating. At the outset the navy boys made it clear that their passengers would sleep on the small cots that had been placed in each already crowded cabin in officers' country. Once the nature of the mission became known, the ice broke. Some of the navy men insisted that their army colleagues take the comfortable bunks. The fighter and bomber pilots took Doolittle's men to the hangar deck and showed them the tightly packed F4Fs, Devastators, and Dauntlesses. Arrangements were quickly made to see who could empty whose pockets at poker. With their fighters and bombers immobile, the navy aviators had even more time to kill than did Doolittle's men.

Making arrangements for Doolittle's enlisted aircrew was more difficult. With every bunk full, it looked at first as if they might be sleeping in hammocks or on mattresses laid out on the decks of the enlisted berthing compartments. But airdales and ship's company were as hospitable as the air group once they discovered where the *Hornet* was going and what

Jimmy Doolittle's B-25s on the *Hornet*'s flight deck en route to Tokyo. The ship's log did not even mention the presence of the planes on board until takeoff.

Doolittle's men would be trying to do. Crewmen insisted that Doolittle's sergeants and corporals take their bunks, and the sailors went off to find other places to sleep. Some wound up sleeping in the big mesh nets that hung down at the after end of the hangar deck and held some of the ship's twelve-man life rafts.[12]

Once aboard the *Hornet* with their planes, the army pilots suddenly realized how cramped and narrow the launch area was. The *Hornet* might be a big ship, but in the history of her type she was relatively small. Some of Doolittle's fliers immediately paced the deck to determine just how many feet they had. Even Doolittle was not immune to the jitters. Soon after the carrier broke out into the sunshine beyond the Golden Gate, Hank Miller found him on the flight deck. "Well, Hank," Doolittle asked, "how does it look to you?" "Oh, gee, this is a breeze," Miller replied. The colonel was not convinced. He climbed into the cockpit of his plane with Miller next to him and said, "Gee, this looks like a short distance." To calm him Miller said, "You see where that tool kit is way up on the deck on that island structure?" Doolittle said yes. Well, Miller replied, "That's where I used to take off in fighters on the *Saratoga* and the *Lexington*." After gazing at Miller for a second, Doolittle retorted, "Henry, what name do they use in the navy for bullshit?"[13]

As the carrier and her escorts headed west for a midocean rendezvous with the *Enterprise* and Task Force 16, some aboard began to fear that Doolittle's men were not serious enough about the mission. At first the pilots were crisp and professional. They told Jurika, who acted as Mitscher's liaison officer, that they wanted to "cover Japan, not just Tokyo, but Osaka, Nagoya, and Kobe, as well."[14] The Doolittle raid would thus be broadly sensational rather than selectively destructive. Although a dispersed effort might create widespread panic, it would not guarantee the same strategic results as a concentrated effort. No great war installation, such as Fuji Steel, Japan Iron and Steel, or one of the major petrochemical plants, would suffer major damage.

Having chosen their targets, the fliers huddled with Jurika and representatives from the *Hornet*'s navigation department to plan routes both to Japan and on to the south and west to landing fields in China. Everyone agreed that the raid would be launched late in the afternoon of 18 April so that the bombers would be over Tokyo at night. Doolittle would go in first with a planeload of incendiaries to mark the target route through the city. Those bombing other cities would presumably be on their own. The raid would be completed in time for the fliers to use the dawn and early morning light to find their landing fields in China.

Those problems resolved, many of Doolittle's flight crews succumbed to a kind of lethargy—or perhaps a healthy dismissal of fears. It all depended on one's perspective. Certainly the army boys had plenty of activities. Jurika spoke to them incessantly about intelligence matters; Akers and his staff conducted daily classes to hone the celestial navigation skills necessary for successful completion of the long night flight to Japan and beyond; Lt. T. H. White, the Doolittle group's flight surgeon, who would make the trip, presented several courses on sanitation and first aid in case injured fliers would have to spend several days or weeks in rural China before rescue. Doolittle lectured on targets and gunnery, and the enlisted gunners on each B-25 practiced on target kites flown from the carrier.[15]

But Jurika fretted. Because he knew Japan and the violent temperament of its military, he felt responsible for imparting every scrap of information he could. But Doolittle's men seemed almost criminally negligent. "A briefing would be set up for 8:30 in the morning, after breakfast," in the wardroom, Jurika remembered, and "they would saunter in and the briefing scheduled for 8:30 wouldn't start before 9:00 or 9:15, sometimes as late as 9:30. And their attention span was very short, half an hour at the most. They would be interested up to a point, and yet, from my point of view, their lives were at stake. The success of a raid was at stake."[16]

Jurika talked about target identification and the location of all major buildings in the Tokyo area. "The Diet Building, for example, on one of the highest hills of Tokyo, was something that you could fly over, go a very short distance, and be in Kawasaki, perhaps three or four minutes, no more than that, on a bombing run, and the first major point under you would be the Tamagawa River, and just beyond that would be a major petro-chemical works." With these features to rely on, aircrews would not have to estimate or use a stopwatch to check their bombing runs. Jurika also identified the location of antiaircraft defenses and described their concentration on towers and high buildings throughout Japan's major cities. The batteries consisted of light pom-pom artillery, heavy machine guns, and even small arms that had first been used in China "and up at Nomonhan [on the Manchurian-Soviet border] against the Russians . . . something that we knew they had and the way they used it." But Doolittle's men quickly tired of the details. Jurika "felt they took it very, very casually, surprisingly so."[17]

Perhaps his briefings were too intense, too detailed, for restless, apprehensive young men. After all, if the raid was going to be conducted at night, would not Tokyo be blacked out, or at least "browned out," with only a few critical lights visible? It would be impossible to locate landmarks under such conditions. Nor would it be likely that Japanese flak batteries could shoot effectively at a handful of planes rushing by in the dark at low altitude. Jurika, of course, was hedging his bets. If the carrier met Japanese forces unexpectedly, the B-25s might have to be launched far offshore in morning daylight. Then the planes would be over Tokyo by noon or even earlier.

Although Doolittle huddled often with Mitscher, he attended Jurika's briefings only "on rare occasions, such as the day before they expected to be launched," when he gathered his men together "for sort of a pep and a brief session." As the *Hornet* sailed westward into increasingly stormy seas, Doolittle spent more and more time in the air office and in the adjacent "PriFly" (primary flight control), the small structure extending from the island out over the flight deck where the air officer and his assistants orchestrated air group launchings and flight deck activities. Doolittle asked aviators, air officers, landing signal officers, and anyone else about the problems of taking off from a twisting, steadily dropping and rising deck. He factored their observations into his own mathematical calculations, which he revised constantly. Finally he said, "The hell with it, I'll trust what I hear from the navy."[18]

The weather had turned bad almost as soon as the task force passed the Farallons. The northern Pacific exhibited its usual springtime conditions: heavy seas, high winds, and low, gray clouds accompanied by rain and squalls. It was almost identical to the pattern four months earlier, when Nagumo and the six carriers of his *Kido Butai* had been able to approach within 250 miles of Hawaii without being sighted. Even the *Hornet* and her escorting cruisers pitched and rolled uncomfortably; on several occasions the task force had to slow down to avoid structural damage to the low-riding *Cimarron*. Near the launch site a photographer aboard the *Salt Lake City*, part of the *Enterprise* escort group, captured the *Hornet* riding the crest of a huge wave that had thrown her entire bow out of the water.

From the time the force left the Golden Gate, Jurika sat for hours in flag plot, the small area reserved for admirals when aboard, listening patiently for any program discontinuities or abnormalities from station JOAK, Radio Tokyo, that would indicate discovery of the raid. Four days out "a strange type of numeral code was heard on 3095 kcs [kilocycles]," but no one could guess the meaning of this anomaly.[19] Tensions rose. Were the Japanese waiting in ambush?

Mitscher and a handful of his top people, including Jurika, believed otherwise. But no one could be sure. Cryptanalysts at Station Hypo in the basement of Pearl Harbor's Fourteenth Naval District had by now broken the top secret Japanese codes and were reading the enemy's most sensitive cable traffic. But because of frequent changes in Japanese codes and codebooks and the huge volume of messages, no one knew whether all of the pieces of any given jigsaw were together. The Pearl Harbor code breakers, led by Comdr. Joseph Rochefort and Comdr. Edwin Layton, had to endure constant distractions from Washington, where a rival group of cryptanalysts frequently reached sharply divergent conclusions on what the decoded Japanese messages portended. Fortunately, the Pearl group enjoyed Nimitz's complete confidence, and he was able to override the Washington group's influence with Admiral King. By the spring of 1942 both Pearl Harbor and Washington knew from radio intercepts and submarine sightings that the Japanese had flung a net of long-range aircraft patrols and a string of picket boats around the approaches to the home islands.

Rochefort and Layton were also reasonably certain by early April that continued Japanese aggression would be centered in the Rabaul–New Guinea area of the southwestern Pacific. The carriers of the *Kido Butai* would presumably concentrate there in support. This assumption was confirmed on 5 April, when the *Kido Butai* raided the British Far East naval base at Colombo, Ceylon (now Sri Lanka). Four days later its planes hit the British naval base at Trincomalee on the other side of the island, sinking cruisers and an old carrier. London promptly pulled its naval forces all the way back to the port of Mombasa on the East African coast; this retreat was exactly what the raids were designed to accomplish. As Japan succeeded in conquering all of the southwestern Pacific from Singapore to the Solomons, it no longer had to worry about British naval forces striking from the western flank.

By 17 April Rochefort and his staff had concluded that the *Kido Butai* would withdraw immediately from the Indian Ocean, that two new Japanese offensives were planned in eastern New Guinea and the Coral Sea just north of the heavily populated eastern coast of Australia, and that Tokyo was planning another Pacific operation whose objective and details were not yet clear. Where would the four carriers of the *Kido Butai*, now leaving the Indian Ocean, go next? To the Coral Sea? Or home to prepare for the new "Pacific operation"? If they were heading toward home waters, could they cut off the escape route of the *Hornet* and *Enterprise?* [20]

After a week at sea Mitscher was ordered to delay rendezvous with the *Enterprise* and the rest of Task Force 16 until 13 April. Halsey had not sailed from Pearl Harbor until the eighth. The *Hornet* "reversed course and slowed to comply." Mitscher then attempted to fuel the task force from the *Cimarron*, but it proved impossible. As the carrier approached the tanker, heaving gray waves swept across the tanker's low decks and washed overboard two sailors who had been breaking out the fueling lines. The *Cimarron*'s alert crew immediately threw several life rings attached to heavy lines into the sea, and one of the unfortunate men grabbed a ring and was hauled back aboard. The other sailor wallowed in the choppy water until the destroyer *Meredith*, with a fine burst of seamanship, rushed to him and brought him aboard. The *Meredith* had earlier rescued a sailor who had been swept off the *Vincennes* by the wild waves. [21]

Thereafter the seas moderated somewhat, and on the tenth the *Cimarron* was able to refuel both cruisers. Two days later, having set course 255° True for rendezvous with Task Force 16, Mitscher finally was able to bring the *Hornet* alongside for refueling. That same day the busy *Cimarron* also topped off the cruisers and filled the bunkers of Destroyer Division 22.

Aboard the carrier the army aviators were still proving to be somewhat of a trial to Jurika. It became customary during the late stages of World War II and later in Korea and Vietnam for naval aviators to combat the tedium and physical debilitation of shipboard life with vigorous exercise. But many of the Doolittle fliers seemed lazy. They began sleeping deep into the morning after late-night or all-night poker games in the junior officers' cabins. The enlisted aircrew from the torpedo and bomber squadrons had been allowed to use the ready rooms during the cruise and took their army buddies in for equally lengthy and hilarious poker games. The navy petty officers discovered that their army counterparts were cool and impressive men who "mixed real well with the crew."22 As the days passed, a few poker sessions in officers' country became virtually nonstop. While the cards were rhythmically dealt, bet on, and tossed in, "somebody would go to the wardroom during a meal and bring back enough to keep them from starving."23 Jurika also knew that some of the men, undoubtedly both army and navy aviators, kept liquor aboard.

He worried over the lack of organized sit-up exercises and at the failure to organize community jogs around the forward part of the flight deck, which was clear of planes. (The carrier's tireless photographers did record a few of the army aviators trotting around one day.) Capt. Paul Ryan, submariner and historian, later suggested that Doolittle himself had come out of the carefree, tomorrow-we-all-die "Dawn Patrol" environment of the First World War, in which physical conditioning was anathema and a good drink and good cards were all that a pilot needed to get through the nights before battle. Jurika agreed that this seemed to be the attitude of most of the Doolittle fliers.

There were a few exceptions—Ted Lawson was apparently one of them—men who were interested in the capabilities of Japanese aircraft, the Japanese character, and life and culture in Japan. Jurika spent some hours with these boys, warning them bluntly that "while I couldn't assure them of this . . . if they were captured dropping bombs on Japan, the chances of their survival would be awfully slim, very, very, slim." Jurika said the captured men would be paraded through the streets as Exhibit A, tried by some kind of kangaroo court, and publicly beheaded. "This seemed to settle them down quite a bit."[24]

While many of Doolittle's pilots slept, played, and occasionally talked to *Hornet* crewmen about the thrill of flying under the Oakland Bay Bridge on the way into Alameda, the enlisted gunners and mechanics took time out from cards to hone their marksmanship. One day the *Hornet*'s aerography department incautiously launched a weather balloon filled with delicate instruments while Doolittle's boys were in their bombers siting the guns. As soon as the balloon appeared over the ship, some trigger-happy sergeant or corporal shredded it with .50-caliber machine gun slugs.[25]

During the voyage the B-25s developed numerous minor difficulties. There were generator failures, spark plug changes that needed to be made, leaky gas tanks, brake problems, and engine trouble. The *Hornet*'s air department was equal to the challenge. Unlike their enlisted shipmates in the air group, who found the army boys to be cool and congenial characters in a poker game, the carrier's aviation mechanics shared Jurika's belief that Doolittle's men were lazy. Aviation Machinist's Mate 2nd Class Eugene Blackmer and his mates were disgusted that the sergeants and corporals seemed to know nothing about the mechanical structure of their planes and left all repairs to the navy; while the army slept and played, the navy worked. At one point Doolittle concluded that one of the precious bombers might have to be thrown overboard because of a persistent engine malfunction. The navy boys removed the engine from the plane and took it below to the shops on the side of the hangar deck. Opening it up, they discovered that the only problem was a broken washer. The machinist's mates quickly made another, and the mechanics placed it in the engine, which was promptly taken back to the flight deck by elevator and reinstalled on the B-25. Summoned from sleep, a poker game, or perhaps a briefing, the B-25 pilot turned the engine over. It worked flawlessly. Within hours Doolittle appeared on the hangar deck, introduced himself to the machinists and mechanics, and thanked them for a job well done.[26]

The army fliers constantly worried about takeoff length and aircraft weight, and every day they found more and more gear in their planes that was nonessential. Eventually it made a rather large pile, which was placed in the storage bays above the *Hornet*'s hangar. One turret on a B-25 stubbornly refused to function during the entire cruise, although the pilot swore it had been fine when the plane was lifted aboard at Alameda. For two weeks anxious navy mechanics fussed over the recalcitrant machinery, but it never did work, and when the pilot took off it was still unusable. As the weather steadily worsened, the carrier's air department reported that "constant surveillance and rigid inspections were required to make certain the planes were properly secured to the flight deck."[27]

Late in the afternoon of 12 April, far north of Midway Island, the *Hornet*'s radar system, probably the YE homing beacon atop the foremast, picked up transmissions bearing 230°, distance 130 miles. They were the *Enterprise* and Task Force 16 out of Pearl Harbor. The two forces joined at daylight on the thirteenth and headed west at a brisk speed. Everyone aboard the *Hornet* and her escorts could breathe easier. No enemy contacts had been made in the eleven days since leaving California, but now, as the carrier entered a more dangerous area, she would have essential air and antisubmarine protection.

Otherwise it was a somber week. Bataan had finally fallen just four days earlier. The last American garrison in the Philippines hung on despondently at Corregidor, knowing by this time that no help would arrive and that the hour of death or surrender depended only on the Japanese assault calendar. The *Kido Butai* had driven the British out of the Indian Ocean, and Rommel was running wild in the western desert of Egypt. Everywhere the Allies were not only on the defensive; they were being beaten.

As soon as the *Enterprise* and *Hornet* task groups rendezvoused, Doolittle dispatched a short message to Halsey, reopening the question of the launch site. According to Halsey's intelligence officer, "Doolittle pointed out that from a position six hundred miles off the coast he felt that he had very little chance of effectively conducting his strike" and getting his pilots "safely to the prearranged air bases in China during daylight. 'From five hundred miles my chances would be much improved,' he stated." But even five hundred miles was risky. If a strike was launched near dawn from four hundred miles off Japan, the raiders could bomb Tokyo in full daylight and still reach their designated bases before dark. Undoubtedly Doolittle anticipated the possibility that the primary airfields in China might be overrun by Japanese forces before the Americans could arrive. Intelligence from the Chinese coastal area was poor, and Japanese forces were constantly probing inland. A launch only four hundred miles off Japan not only would allow Doolittle's fliers to reconnoiter the airfields in daylight and make sure they were still in friendly hands but would also save enough fuel so that the B-25s could proceed farther to secure fields if the primary landing sites had fallen. Halsey reluctantly agreed to bring Doolittle's pilots and planes within four hundred miles of Japan. "But recognizing the existing military threats and particularly that of shore based air," Halsey insisted that "if the Force were sighted and reported at any time he would be obliged to direct an immediate launch of the Doolittle strikes."[28]

Three days after the *Enterprise-Hornet* rendezvous, the B-25s were completely fueled and spotted in their final launch positions. Mitscher noted that "the last plane hung far out over the stern ramp in a precarious position. The leading plane [Doolittle's] had 467 feet of clear deck for take-off."[29]

Japanese intelligence had become aware that something might be afoot. Earlier there had been jitters that the Americans might somehow try to mount an air raid on the home islands. But when the wolf failed to arrive, fears receded. Staff officers dismissed the news that many patrol aircraft had suddenly been spotted at Pearl Harbor. They also failed to respond after study of patrol plane traffic indicated that "a strong enemy surface force" might be operating south of the Aleutians; nor did they order increased alerts or traffic analyses after learning that the Americans had abruptly increased their submarine presence off the coast of Honshu. But around the fifteenth analysts suddenly awoke to the fact of "unusually brisk enemy radio activity" somewhere in the Pacific. Something obviously was going on among the confused, reeling Americans. Combined Fleet Headquarters ordered a precautionary concentration of naval air strength in the Kanto Prefecture around Tokyo.[30]

Meanwhile, the four most experienced carriers of the *Kido Butai*— *Akagi, Kaga, Soryu,* and *Hiryu*—and their escorts were on their way home from the Indian Ocean. The crews were exhausted but delighted after four months of steady victories. Aboard the huge flattops and the escorting cruisers and destroyers, now passing the Philippines, boiler tenders, signalmen, aircrews, and flight deck personnel shared a "happy excitement" at the prospect of several weeks' home leave.[31]

On the fifteenth, with radio silence still rigidly imposed on the U.S. task force, Doolittle read his men some "goodwill-Godspeed messages" composed earlier by King, Arnold, and Army Chief of Staff Gen. George C. Marshall. The sixteenth was camera day. Despite gusty winds and pitching decks, each of the sixteen aircrews posed for a photograph. Then everyone went back to work.[32] Task Force 16 passed the 180th meridian early on the seventeenth, and several hours later Halsey ordered his destroyers and oilers to remain behind while he took off with the carriers and cruisers on a dash west. The *Hornet, Enterprise,* and their escorts smashed through heavy seas at twenty-five knots, coming within twelve hundred miles of the Japanese mainland, then a thousand, then eight hundred. In the communication shack the radio programs from the United States—Jack Benny, Fred Allen, and the major league ballgames—faded. Now there were only Japanese programs, some of them in English. A female broadcaster was a particular favorite among the monitoring crew, who dubbed her "Lady Haw Haw," Japan's version of the famous Nazi turncoat.

That afternoon Mitscher and Doolittle arranged a brief ceremony on the *Hornet*'s flight deck. Despite windy conditions and heaving seas that occasionally sent the ship pitching a hundred or more feet, a few bombs were brought up on deck. In 1908 H. Vormstein, John Laurey, and Daniel Quigley had been among several thousand sailors who had received Japanese medals commemorating the visit of their ships to Tokyo Bay. Vormstein and Laurey were currently working in the Brooklyn Navy Yard; Quigley had retired in Pennsylvania. After Pearl Harbor the three men decided to send their medals back to the Navy Department, hoping they would be returned to Japan in proper fashion. Navy Secretary Frank Knox had immediately recognized the public relations value of such a move, and he promptly mailed the medals to Nimitz, who passed them on to Halsey for transmission to Mitscher. Now they were aboard the *Hornet,* along with medals that other army and navy officers had received from the Japanese government before the war. Ship's ordnancemen attached the pieces of metal to the missiles, while other sailors and members of the marine detachment gleefully chalked crude messages on the sides of the bombs. A typical scrawl read: "I don't want to set the world on fire [a reference to a currently popular tune back home]—just Tokyo."[33] Mitscher's personal orderly, Marine Cpl. Larry Bogart of Philadelphia, scrawled his girl's name on one bomb and his parents' names on another.[34] The *Hornet*'s photography department, which had been kept busy recording every aspect of the cruise since the ship had left the Golden Gate, scurried around the flight deck taking pictures of smiling airmen and sailors.

With the ceremony over, Doolittle called his boys together for a final briefing. Time was getting short. Everyone had assumed that takeoff would be on the nineteenth, but the navy was moving fast, and the launch would probably be late the next afternoon. Extra five-gallon fuel cans would be stowed aboard each plane, but once used they could not be thrown out because they might leave a trail right back to the *Hornet*. Each can had to be perforated; then all would be thrown out of the aircraft together.

As the *Hornet* pounded steadily westward, everyone from bridge to shaft alley knew that Japan's best planes, the Zeros, Zekes, and Vals, did not have the range to find the force. But what about submarines or a stray carrier or two that were not where Rochefort estimated? Mess halls, wardrooms, and bridges were tense. Launch hour crept closer.

Down on the flight deck the ship's increasingly efficient air department worked feverishly to arm and fuel Doolittle's aircraft. Soucek's "Air Department Plan for Friday, 17 April 1942" read:

(1) Complete fueling ships; tanker shoves off.

(2) Push [B-25s] #02268 and #02267 clear of number 3 elevator [aft].

(3) Bring incendiary bombs to flight deck via number 3 elevator; commence loading on accessible airplanes.

(4) Start bringing heavy bombs to flight decks via regular bomb elevators; commence loading on accessible airplanes.

(5) When all incendiary bombs are on flight deck, secure number 3 elevator and pull #02267 and #02268 forward far enough for loading purposes.

(6) One half hour before sunset, respot the deck for take-off.

All loading was done under the direct supervision of one of Doolittle's men. By sunset on 17 April the Doolittle bombers were spotted and ready for takeoff.[35]

At dusk the weather became abominable. Pounding rains and lashing gales whipped the small U.S. force. The plunging, pitching *Hornet* took waves over her flight deck, sixty feet above the waterline. Lifelines were set, both army and navy planes were double-lashed on flight and hangar decks, and all other movable gear was tightly secured.

As 18 April began, Ens. Robert R. Boettcher relieved Ens. J. A. Holmes as officer of the deck. The darkened ship and its companions were steaming on course 267° True, speed twenty knots. Shortly before 0300, as Boettcher stretched, yawned, and drained the last drops from a cup of coffee, radar operators aboard the *Hornet* and *Enterprise* began picking up unidentified objects on their screens. Boettcher's stomach knotted, and he promptly passed the word to Mitscher in his sea cabin a few feet away. At first the objects were dismissed as sea return, which the crude, first-generation radars unfortunately tended to record as ships.[36] But Mitscher was taking no chances. As the objects continued to appear, he came to the bridge and sent the *Hornet* to general quarters. Halsey swung Task Force 16 onto a new course to evade a possible Japanese picket line. The army fliers rushed from their bunks along with everyone else and manned their planes in the wet, windswept gloom, while Doolittle raced to the *Hornet*'s bridge. But the task force was not sighted.

At daybreak Mitscher secured from general quarters and sent the *Hornet*'s off-duty crew to breakfast. The weather seemed to be moderating somewhat; it might turn out to be a fine morning. High up in the island structure Yeoman 2nd Class Darrell Bost, on horizon lookout, peered out at the seas ahead but saw nothing. Down in officers' country just behind the fo'c'sle Ted Lawson began packing his small B-4 bag in anticipation of the flight later in the day. It was "bitterly cold," and Lawson felt the deck periodically heave and shift in response to the rough seas.[37] As he awaited the second call for breakfast, he tried to pile all his belongings in the bag: raincoat, shorts, shirts, shaving kit, shoes, handkerchiefs, and everything else. His roommate, Ens. K. B. White, watched indifferently. The army pilots had been told to report to the wardroom after breakfast and to remain there until takeoff. If Japanese ships or long-range patrol planes were sighted, the fliers would be in one place and ready to go.

Suddenly at 0745 everything happened at once. Just as the *Hornet* picked up radar signals very close aboard, Seaman Hubert H. Gibbons on the cruiser *Vincennes*, off the *Enterprise*'s starboard flank, spotted a Japanese trawler twelve miles away. He instantly notified the bridge. It was the *No. 23 Nitto Maru*. Almost simultaneously an aircraft just launched on dawn patrol from the *Enterprise* spied the picket ship heaving and tossing, and the *Hornet*'s radio direction finder obtained the vessel's range and distance. Up on horizon lookout, Bost through his binoculars barely discerned several distant, black specks against the backdrop of the gray dawn.[38]

Lawson, who was still trying to stuff everything in his bag, heard a "muffled, vibrating roar," followed immediately by general quarters. White leapt for the door and Lawson followed. As the two rushed up ladders to the flight deck, they encountered the rest of the army fliers heading in the same direction and *Hornet* crewmen racing to battle stations. Everyone flung out questions, but no one had any answers. Just as he reached the flight deck, Lawson felt the *Hornet* vibrate again from nearby gunfire. Looking out, he saw a cruiser, the *Nashville*, blazing away at the far horizon, where a low-slung fishing vessel soon began sending orange flame and black smoke into the early morning sky. Far below, in the *Hornet*'s always hot, noisy engineering spaces, water tender Cardon Ruchti, who was on watch at boiler control just above the middle boiler rooms (numbers four, five, and six), suddenly heard the announcement over the overhead loudspeaker that Japanese ships were present.[39]

Back up on the cold, wet flight deck someone yelled, "God damn! Let's go!" White turned and rushed back toward his cabin to get Lawson's gear. Lawson pounded along at his heels. McAteer was also on the flight deck at that "rainy, miserable" moment. When general quarters sounded, he went down to his battle dressing station in the small coffee mess just off the wardroom. First he supervised his hospital corpsmen as they broke out their equipment; then he sat down and read as the rest of the ship throbbed with purpose and excitement.[40]

As Lawson raced back down ladders and through passageways, he knew there would be no leisurely late afternoon takeoff after all, no time to follow carefully the directions of flight deck personnel and the launching officer. It was GO NOW! Everyone realized that the chances of getting to friendly airfields in China were now gone. Not only was the *Hornet* 642 miles from the Inubo Saki Light at the entrance to Tokyo Bay, but the carrier was recording surface head winds of 26 knots (29 miles per hour), far greater than anyone had anticipated.[41] But there was no doubt about the need to launch at once. Not one of the army crewmen shrank from his duty.

Certainly Halsey over on the *Enterprise* had no hesitancy. Radiomen aboard the carriers and cruisers heard the operator on the *Nitto Maru* tapping out a frantic message: three enemy carriers 650 miles east of Inubo Saki. Halsey's staff officer, Lt. Gilven Slonim, was in charge of monitoring enemy communications for any sign that the task force had been detected by air, submarine, or surface forces. The *Nitto Maru*'s message was received aboard the U.S. ships in garbled form. Had Tokyo heard it? Slonim wasted no time wondering; he advised Halsey to order a launch immediately. The task force had obviously run afoul of the outer ring of Japanese picket ships, which were farther out than anyone had guessed. The mission was in jeopardy. Halsey promptly signaled the *Hornet*: "LAUNCH PLANES X TO COL DOOLITTLE AND GALLANT COMMAND GOOD LUCK AND GOD BLESS YOU."[42]

Aboard the *Hornet* there was abrupt, organized bedlam as the *Nashville* and planes from the *Enterprise* continued to blaze away at the hapless *Nitto Maru* and then at another Japanese fishing vessel. Doolittle's men ran to

Colonel Doolittle struggles aloft: one of the most famous pictures of World War II. Note the angle and height of the aircraft, which seems to be just over the *Hornet*'s bow.

Doolittle's takeoff was a bizarre mixture of perfection and near disaster. Experienced carrier pilots had told him that lingering prop washes on a flight deck could pose a fatal hazard to air operations. He also knew that propeller planes naturally torqued to the left. So when an aircraft reached the edge of the flight deck, it was necessary to tap the controls to rotate slightly right for a moment in order to sweep away the prop wash before resuming the natural left torque. As he began to roll, Doolittle carefully brought his bomber five degrees to port, not quite enough to send the left wheel into the gun galleries lining the port side but enough to position the prop wash perfectly. As he rotated upward and off the deck, he swung his bomber slightly to the right and then resumed course. But the beautiful takeoff was marred by an incredibly steep rotation, which almost caused the plane to stall. Lawson, with a perfect view, saw his commander hang "his ship almost straight up on its props, until we could see the whole top of his B-25."[43] Jim Walker, from his position at a partially opened roller curtain on the *Hornet*'s hangar deck, saw Doolittle's plane appear forward of the ship and thought it would crash. But Doolittle brought the B-25's nose down, and, as hundreds aboard the *Hornet* cheered wildly, he swung his aircraft in one circle around the ship and headed west toward Japan.

As the *Nashville* continued to blaze away at a stubborn Japanese picket ship bobbing in the swells, Doolittle's men followed him off the *Hornet* in precarious fashion. "With only one exception," the carrier's War Diary recorded primly, "take-offs were dangerous and improperly executed."[44] The young pilots were excited and disoriented. Each had obviously counted on a full day to get psyched up for the dangerous, perhaps suicidal mission. Suddenly the Japanese and the navy had plunged them into the worst crisis of their young lives. Doolittle had gotten off—if he had not, perhaps no one else would have tried. But Doolittle was one of the greatest aviators in the world. Could a Lawson, a Manch, or a Gray do the same? There were forty knots of wind to fight over the bow, the huge *Hornet* was pitching and rolling like a chip in the steep, slamming seas, and the end of the flight deck, telescoped from the perspective of a B-25 cockpit, looked like it was ten feet away. What the hell were they doing here, anyway? Could they really trust the launch officer to get them off? The takeoffs from a stable concrete platform in far-off Florida seemed long ago.

But not one pilot flinched. According to the *Hornet* War Diary, the first few used the full back stabilizer to get off the deck. Films show that almost as soon as a B-25 began rolling, its pilot wrestled it up and off the *Hornet* in a frantic rotation as if the carrier were on fire. The planes stumbled into the sky in a near stall configuration. Each pilot struggled wildly to keep his plane's nose down, then fought the controls for several miles, trying to gain true flying speed and at least one hundred feet of altitude. In desperation Hank Miller held up a blackboard for the last few pilots that read "Stabilizer NEUTRAL," but few paid attention.[45]

Lt. Bill Farrow was the only one to take off as directed, but even he almost crashed. As Farrow's B-25 was being maneuvered into position on the pitching, sloping deck, Aviation Chief Machinist's Mate Tom Respess and a small detail struggled to hold its nose down with their hands in the high gale. Suddenly they were horrified to see one of their own, Aviation Machinist's Mate Robert W. Wall, lose his footing. Wall was instantly sucked like a blowing tumbleweed into the plane's left propeller.

One blade tore off an arm; another hit Wall in the rump, throwing him clear.

Farrow felt the jar and, looking back, saw the injured sailor on the deck. Just then he was given the signal to take off. Rattled, Farrow put his flap control lever in retract rather than neutral. With nearly seven hundred feet of flight deck to work with, he seemed on the brink of an almost picture-perfect takeoff. But as the plane raced along, the flaps slowly came up. As the B-25 sped over the bow, it dropped like a stone. Farrow instantly realized the problem and reset his flaps as the bomber rushed ahead of the *Hornet* at wave-top level. Slowly, ponderously, it rose and flew off to the west. Wall was taken below. His shipmates later raised more than $1,800 for him.[46]

Incredibly, all of the boys somehow horsed their small bombers into stable flight, circled the ship, and headed toward immortality. Meanwhile, the *Nashville* finally sank the first, second, and then a third enemy patrol boat. The cruiser expended more than nine hundred rounds in the process, an embarrassing display of gunnery. Contrary to expectations, the weather worsened as launch operations continued, and the last five planes flew into a raging storm.

As suddenly as it had begun, the *Hornet*'s part of the operation was over. By 0920, sixty-five minutes after Doolittle had flown off, the flight deck was quiet and empty. The two carriers and their cruiser escorts swung to a northeasterly course and raced away from Japan.

Tokyo received the *Nitto Maru*'s message in a garbled form, just as it had been intercepted by the U.S. ships. The patrol vessel had reported several minutes before 0800, but the message that Fleet Adm. Isoroku Yamamoto sent out from his flagship roughly an hour later stated that the enemy carriers had been sighted 730 miles east of Tokyo at 0630. Yamamoto's chief of staff, Vice Adm. Matome Ugaki, later wrote in his diary that "the fleet staff plunged into activities at once" and that Yamamoto ordered immediate operations against the U.S. fleet.[47] A submarine squadron en route to the great Japanese fleet base at Truk in the Caroline Islands was diverted to make a sweep around the Bonins, far south of Halsey's position. At the main fleet base at Yokosuka, twenty miles down the bay from Tokyo, Vice Adm. Nobutake Kondo ordered a cruiser force to get up steam and intercept the Americans. Two armed merchant cruisers operating close inshore off Honshu promptly sailed toward Halsey's reported position. Airfields in and around the capital were placed on alert to repel the anticipated air strike, while an extensive, armed air search was conducted to find and sink the enemy carriers. Even the distant *Kido Butai* off Formosa was alerted for a possible high-speed sweep northward.

But in the excitement and terror of sudden assault by a major enemy fleet, the little *Nitto Maru* had been unable to discern what kind of planes the American carriers had on board. Yamamoto and his colleagues assumed that the enemy was planning a conventional attack with naval aircraft; none of the Japanese dreamed that their enemy had already launched medium bombers from a small, narrow carrier deck. The Americans would have to steam to within at least two hundred miles of the Japanese coast for any kind of effective raid by Dauntless dive-bombers, which meant they could not reach their launch point until at least late afternoon and perhaps the next morning. There was plenty of time to prepare for them. Clearly the desperate Yanks were committing an act of folly; the Japanese fleet would be delighted to spring the trap that would destroy them.

Aboard Halsey's rapidly retiring carriers, the remainder of the morning was rather frantic. Slonim was relieved to hear the messages rippling out from Japanese naval and air headquarters. The abrupt launch had been justified after all. The course of the U.S. task force took it past another line of Japanese picket ships, which were difficult to spot and shoot in the persistently heavy seas. The *Nashville* and combat air patrols were kept busy destroying the small boats, none of which apparently radioed to Tokyo the true situation. On the *Hornet* wings were swiftly rebolted to the torpedo, scout, and bomber planes that packed the hangar bay, and the aircraft were sent one by one to the flight deck above by the three big centerline elevators. Then pilots pitched in with hangar deck and maintenance crews to quickly unlash the brand-new F4F-4s from the storage bays on the gallery deck, unfold their wings, and send them along as well. By 1100 the carrier's flight deck was full of armed and fueled aircraft. Fifteen minutes later, shortly after the *Nashville* returned from sinking Japanese picket ships, the *Hornet* began launching eight fighters for joint combat air patrol (CAP) with the *Enterprise* fliers. Then everyone aboard the carrier and on every other vessel in the task force waited to find out what had happened to Doolittle's men. At 1025 and again at 1215 the carrier's small radar room in the island picked up false aircraft contacts, which kept everyone tense. The crew was sent to the noon meal, while Jurika and his men continued to monitor Radio Tokyo. Far to the southeast Rochefort's super-secret communications intelligence unit at Pearl Harbor was doing the same thing.

At 1255 local time the quartermaster, who kept the log on the *Hornet*'s bridge, wrote: "Musical programs from Tokio [*sic*] still being received."[48] Thirty-two minutes later he made a similar notation. Doolittle and his men should be over the Japanese capital momentarily. Even with the worst luck they would surely reach Tokyo within fifteen minutes. Suddenly at 1400—noon in Tokyo—the men in the *Hornet*'s communication office heard low-frequency radios in the Japanese capital go off the air. Fifteen minutes later all Tokyo radio stations suddenly became silent just as Halsey's force encountered the last Japanese picket ship of the day. Within five minutes the Japanese vessel had raised a white flag, and the *Nashville* went alongside to take prisoners. Ten minutes after that, at 1430, Radio Tokyo abruptly came back on the air, announcing angrily that U.S. bombers had appeared over the city about thirty-five minutes earlier to bomb schools and hospitals. The word was promptly passed around the *Hornet* and then the rest of the task force that Doolittle's raiders had indeed "made it." Cheers and yells erupted on flight decks, in engine rooms, and in living compartments; broad smiles were exchanged on every bridge. Back in Pearl Harbor, Rochefort and his men monitoring Radio Tokyo had actually heard the wail of air raid sirens in the background as Doolittle's men came roaring over the city. Jurika and Slonim, his counterpart on the *Enterprise*, soon received further intelligence, and the *Hornet*'s quartermaster noted: "Army bombers got through o.k. Some reported shot down. Osaki [*sic*], Nogoya [*sic*], and Tokio bombed."

The boys in the scuffed brown shoes and scruffy caps who had seemed so foolishly nonchalant to Jurika had pulled off one of the most courageous raids in aviation history. Flying mostly alone over hundreds of miles of stormy seas in aircraft no larger than a modern jet fighter, they had found their targets in the center of the enemy's capital and in three other cities in broad daylight and had dropped their bombs before fleeing for distant, uncertain havens. Most survived, many of them rescued from behind enemy lines by Chinese partisans. An estimated 250,000 Chinese civilians would pay with their lives for the Doolittle raid and the courage of those partisans.

Just after the evening meal Mitscher addressed the crew from the bridge loudspeaker. The officers and men of the *Hornet* should be commended for their alertness, efficiency, and willingness in "their first taste of real action," which was "a complete success."[49] The next morning Chaplain Harp and the three yeomen who helped him prepare the daily *U.S.S. Hornet News Digest* in the print shop far below decks produced a collector's item. Beneath a huge headline, "Remember Pearl Harbor," was a cartoon of a tall Uncle Sam, striped pants and all, spitting a huge mouthful of bombs across a full-page map of the Pacific onto a small island labeled "Japan, or what's left of it."[50] Harp's story, in which relief was mingled with vengeful pride, was similar to those that appeared in U.S. newspapers during the next several days. America had a victory at last.

Air group commander Stanhope Ring even contributed a poem, which reflected the pent-up fury and frustration of a nation that had finally struck back after weeks and months of steady defeat.

> 'Twas the eighteenth of April in forty-two
> When we waited to hear what Jimmy would do,
> Little did Hiro think that night
> The skies above Tokio would be alight
> With the fires Jimmy started in Tokio's dives
> To guide to their targets the B-25s.
>
> One if by land and two if by sea
> But if from the air the signal was three
> When all of a sudden from out of the skies
> Came a basket of eggs for the little slanteyes
> So Hiro and Togo [*sic*] just buried their heads
> Under the carpets and under the beds.
>
> Their posteriors turned into rising suns
> As bombs they fell by tons and tons
> Then a stab of pain made Hiro shiver
> Was it his kidney or was it his liver?
> Or was it perhaps; alack, alas
> A returned Jap medal assaulting his
>   (Honorable self).
>
> For, long ago in nineteen eight
> The Japs made medals to commemorate
> Our Fleet's visit to their land
> But now returned by Jimmy's hand
> Strait [*sic*] as an arrow and without fail
> These medals impinged on Hiro's tail.[51]

Fright and vicious resolve were evident in those words. The country had been in economic collapse and social despair for a decade and then had been treacherously assaulted on a peaceful Sunday morning by a malicious, racist-minded foe. Years later, writer and veteran James Jones remembered "a sort of nervous inquietude and malaise of near-despair and insecurity" that beset the nation in the months just after Pearl Harbor. "The United States had been dumped and dumped hard. We were shaken by the catastrophe. The United States had been scared." Above all, "did we have the kind of men who could stand up eyeball to eyeball and whip the Jap?"[52] The Doolittle raiders and the men of the *Hornet* had proved that we did, and in their jubilation over a dangerous job well done they taunted the Japanese enemy with a crude racist outrage of their own. The Pacific war had become a holy crusade for both sides.

Yamamoto and the other leading military authorities in Japan, including Prime Minister Hideki Tojo, were deeply shamed. Not only had the audacious enemy bombed the capital, he had placed the sacred emperor in personal jeopardy. For hours after Doolittle's planes left, Yamamoto waited in vain for reports from his captains and pilots that the enemy fleet had been found and assaulted. But all his planes returned to base without a sighting; the frantically searching ships reported only empty ocean. The next morning Yamamoto ordered the entire Japanese fleet out of home waters, the Marshalls, and the Marianas to find and sink the Americans. The rapidly approaching *Kido Butai* was pressed into service despite the exhausted state of its crews. But Halsey and his nimble ships were never found, and Japanese naval and army general staffs, lashed by guilt and embarrassment, began another lengthy and vigorous argument over strategy in the Pacific war.

The Tokyo raid was one of the greatest exploits in aviation annals but also one of the most profoundly ironic. For Doolittle and his gallant fliers had inadvertently helped the navy prove beyond question that aircraft carriers could be successfully employed at the highest levels of warfare. The *Hornet* was the first U.S. carrier ever strategically employed, following in the footsteps of the *Illustrious* at Taranto and the six ships of the *Kido Butai* at Pearl Harbor. But the *Hornet* had done more than knock out a battle fleet; its planes had assaulted the heart of an enemy capital. America's sailors never forgot the implicit lesson of 18 April 1942; nor did their brethren in the Army Air Corps and later the U.S. Air Force.

As soon as Japan was crushed in 1945, sailors and airmen began quarreling over the future of American military aviation. To champions of the long-range bomber with its heavy payload, the comparatively small carrier with its air group of limited range and striking power was a distinctly inferior weapon. Navy spokesmen stressed the immobility of air bases and their consequent vulnerability to bombs, missiles, and foul weather. The Doolittle raid had proved the aircraft carrier's mobility and its capacity to find acceptable weather in which to launch devastating blows against an enemy heartland. If carriers were indeed superior strategic weapon systems, the air force countered, it was proper that they be operated by those charged with the "global mission" of projecting U.S. air power. Ernie King, Wu Duncan, Hap Arnold, Jimmy Doolittle, and Marc Mitscher not only salvaged America's pride in April 1942; they opened a Pandora's box of interservice conflict that has not been closed to this day.

Task Force 16 sailed back to Hawaii on a looping northern course. The *Cimarron* and *Sabine* with their patiently waiting destroyers were picked up on the day after the launch and reincorporated into the task force steaming circle, while the *Hornet* and *Enterprise* exchanged turns as duty and standby carriers. After weeks ashore or below decks, Air Group 8 finally began to come into focus as a fighting unit. In the next five weeks it would be sorely tested.

5

Sea Duty

AFTER A week of steaming, air operations, and listening to radio signals from vainly searching Japanese ships and aircraft, Task Force 16 sailed into Pearl Harbor on 25 April. The two carriers had already flown off their planes; Air Group 8 went to Ewa Air Station near Barber's Point west of Pearl Harbor.

As the *Hornet* carefully negotiated the narrow Pearl Harbor ship channel that morning with everyone at quarters for entering port, all hands were shocked at the unfolding panorama. For months the men had been exhorted to remember Pearl Harbor; now they finally saw firsthand what they had to remember. The small, cramped anchorage was still filmed with oil and filled with the wreckage of great machines of war, blasted and sunken at their berths: the *Arizona* smashed beyond recognition; the *Oklahoma* on her side in bottom mud; other units of the battle line—*West Virginia, California,* and the rest—in various stages of salvage and repair. Buildings ashore that were once spruce and military still showed the wounds and smoke stains from that awful Sunday morning. Much more than an outmoded battle fleet had been lost less than five months before; an entire naval culture, built on peace, practice, professionalism, and an unquestioned belief in the traditional supremacy of big guns aboard slow-moving ships, had been destroyed as well. Slowly, agonizingly, a small and hidebound but comfortable and dedicated old navy was giving way to a new service, huge in size, ultramodern in configuration and orientation, and always in flux, with professional demands and technical dimensions seeming to change almost daily. The *Hornet*, her men, and her fliers straddled these two worlds uneasily.

The carrier moored at berth Fox Nine off Ford Island shortly before 1000, and her men streamed ashore to find that prewar Hawaii, "old Honolulu," was no more. Yet much of what had been remained. On the one hand steel and construction workers, shipfitters, divers, electricians, and engineers were arriving from the mainland every day to help rebuild the shattered naval base and adjacent airfields. Concertina and double apron wire ringed Waikiki and the other beaches of Oahu; each major intersection in the city and between Honolulu and the outlying naval and military bases was blocked with barbed wire and guarded by armed soldiers. It would be several weeks before the wire on Waikiki would be modified with a few gates to allow people to swim in the daytime. Even then, few took advantage of the opportunity. Most striking of all, of course, was the total absence of tourists. Hawaii had been instantly transformed from a tropical playground to an enormous military staging area.[1]

But for boys who had never seen the fabled islands of the Pacific before, the perpetual sunshine, the palm trees, and the beaches, even if glimpsed from afar, were major treats after gray skies and heaving seas. Then, of course, came beers and perhaps a tattoo in the old, grimy bars and parlors on King or Hotel Streets. A few whorehouses even remained open. But all the sightseeing had to be done in the sunshine, for there was a rigid nighttime curfew. And this was still the old navy where RHIP—rank (and rate) has its privileges—remained the order of the day. Liberty for the hundreds of nonrated men expired at 1800, for the rated men at 2000. Chiefs could remain ashore until midnight. The ship's officers and pilots determined their own liberal off-duty schedules.[2]

There would be some hell-raising, but nothing out of the ordinary. Mitscher promised all hands at least two weeks in port. The *Hornet* had been under way virtually without rest for six weeks, all the way from the East Coast. It was time to relax and be amused by the know-it-alls, who filled every barroom in Honolulu with loud and confident assertions that, of course, Jimmy Doolittle's boys had taken off from this or that American island.

Unfortunately, the war would not wait, and the twenty-six hundred men aboard the carrier had only a few days to enjoy what wartime

Hawaii had to offer. Japanese and American strategists were busily plotting new missions for their precious, overworked carrier fleets. Nearly five months after Pearl Harbor neither Tokyo nor Washington was certain of enemy intentions or of its own. In Japan the army and navy remained deeply divided over the future course of the war. At its outset Yamamoto and his staff in the Combined Fleet had hoped that the conflict would be largely a naval contest in which the Imperial Japanese Navy would spearhead a blitzkrieg conquest or neutralization of Ceylon, the eastern and western Australian coasts, and Hawaii, killing off the remnants of the U.S. Navy in the process. If realized, this incredible project would ensure Japan a vast empire impregnable to enemy assault.

But within weeks after Pearl Harbor it became clear that Nippon did not possess anywhere near the resources needed to conquer all of Oceania and its adjacent landmasses. Thereafter the navy's central staff in Tokyo, opposing Yamamoto and the fleet, supported the army's more modest if still breathtaking timetable of conquest. The Japanese empire would be huge, but it would be manageable. The army would concentrate on expanding its control over the southwestern Pacific, specifically New Guinea and adjacent islands, in order to neutralize at least western and central Australia as Allied staging areas. Once eastern and southern New Guinea was conquered, especially the strategically critical town of Port Moresby on the western edge of the Coral Sea adjacent to northern Australia, all of Southeast Asia's oil, rubber, tin, hemp, and other tropical products could be exploited at leisure. For three months Nagumo's *Kido Butai* and its supporting warships had been invaluable spearheads of invasion in Malaya, the Philippines, and the Dutch East Indies while providing the essential shield against sporadic enemy counterattacks on Japanese staging areas in western and central New Guinea. Understandably intoxicated with victory, the army wanted the navy to remain firmly under its thumb and tied to its schedule of expansion.

Yamamoto and his staff rebelled. Time was not on Japan's side. Within two years the United States would have a big new fleet at sea. It was imperative first to smash what warships the Americans and their British allies could still muster in the Pacific and the eastern Indian Oceans and then to dishearten Washington with a series of audacious conquests that would force the Americans back to the West Coast long before their first new battleships and carriers were ready to sail. Pearl Harbor had been at best a half-success. The small but stubborn enemy carrier fleet remained at large and had to be brought to battle and destroyed before the admirals could feel comfortable tying the *Kido Butai* to army objectives. In the three months after 7 December American carriers had harried Japanese expansion from New Guinea to the Marshalls in daring hit-and-run raids. Yamamoto had urged that Japan focus its major effort on hunting down and killing these dangerous vessels. Once they were destroyed, the American ability to contest Japanese power would be destroyed. But the admiral had been repeatedly overruled by his superiors in Tokyo.

The Doolittle raid forced the government to reconsider Yamamoto's arguments. On the evening of 18 April his chief of staff, Admiral Ugaki, had written in his diary: "The enemy force seemingly withdrew to the east after launching the planes. We have missed him again and again. This is more than regrettable, because this shattered my firm determination never to let the enemy attack Tokyo or the mainland." For the next week Ugaki filled his diary with lamentations and speculations as the few captured Doolittle fliers began to talk under torture. Within days the Japanese high command obtained a reasonably comprehensive story of the attack. "More truth has been added to the statements of the POWs captured at Nanchow," Ugaki wrote on 22 April. "*Hornet* left the states with two cruisers and four destroyers and was joined on the way by another carrier, cruisers, and destroyers. At takeoff, the relative wind velocity was twenty meters per second. The length of her flight deck was seven hundred feet and takeoff run 550 feet." Ugaki was impressed with the Americans' skill and daring. He also obsessed that they might come again.[3]

In all the thousands of square miles of North Pacific Ocean stretching from Wake Island to Kamchatka, only Marcus Island and the thin line of converted fishing boats and trawlers guarded the home islands from further American assault. What good would it do, Yamamoto argued, to seize and exploit all of the southwestern Pacific and Southeast Asia if the home islands remained vulnerable to attacks by enemy carriers? Japan must at least complete a ribbon defensive line down the middle of the Pacific from the Aleutians through Midway and Wake to the Gilberts and southward. From such a line the ships and aircraft of the Japanese fleet could not only easily defend the enormous area that had been wrested from the Allies since Pearl Harbor but could also mount probing attacks against Alaska, Hawaii, and Australia that would force Nimitz's small collection of ships back to California, thus breaking American morale and destroying Washington's will to continue the war. This, at any rate, was Yamamoto's desperate hope.

The key to victory, if true victory was achievable, thus lay in two interlocking objectives: seizing Midway and destroying the handful of

American carriers long before the powerful new U.S. fleet was ready for battle. The *Kido Butai* had spent weeks bombing helpless towns, ships, and beaches. It was time to force a final showdown with the U.S. Navy.

Yamamoto would have his way. The Doolittle raid had been too great a humiliation to endure, and it pointed to future threats if America's still small Pacific Fleet was not obliterated. Four of the six carriers of the *Kido Butai*, comprising Divisions 1 and 2, had just returned to home waters from their long cruise to the South Pacific, which included an audacious raid against Ceylon, the closest Yamamoto would ever come to his dream of seizing that strategically rich prize. Division 5, consisting of the two newest fleet carriers, *Shokaku* and *Zuikaku*, remained in the South Pacific to support Japanese expansion from the New Guinea area eastward across the Coral Sea. The army argued that a seaplane base on Tulagi and an airfield on Guadalcanal would advance the southern flank of Yamamoto's desired ribbon defense system deep into the Solomons, thus menacing enemy supply lines to eastern Australia. Yamamoto would have liked all six carriers of the *Kido Butai* in Japan to prepare for Midway, but it was difficult to refute the army's logic. A quick naval strike eastward from New Guinea in support of a Tulagi invasion would not consume much time, and with luck the *Shokaku* and *Zuikaku* could be back in home waters in time for Midway. So Yamamoto reluctantly agreed to the army's plan.

King and Nimitz perceived strategy much differently. The United States was still on the defensive, still by far the numerically inferior naval power in the Pacific. Its only ace—a substantial one—was the ability of Rochefort and his desperately overworked handful of assistants to read the most secret Japanese naval and diplomatic messages. But that advantage could evaporate instantly if Tokyo decided to change its signal codes. Even if this did not happen, the incredible and diverse volume of cables, reports, and orders always threatened to overwhelm the Pearl Harbor code breakers. Thus, while Japanese generals and admirals agonized over the best way to probe and push to retain the initiative, their American counterparts agonized over the best use of scant resources to stop them. In one way the Tokyo raid *had* been an act of folly. If a stray Japanese submarine or two had sighted and sunk or damaged the carriers of Task Force 16, only the *Lexington* and *Yorktown* would have stood between Yamamoto and San Francisco Bay. Now, with the *Hornet* and *Enterprise* back at Pearl Harbor, the question was how to use them most effectively.

Lexington and *Yorktown*, designated Task Force 17, had been in the

South Pacific for weeks under the overall command of Rear Adm. Frank Jack Fletcher, who was ready to contest any Japanese advance eastward from New Guinea and New Britain into the Coral Sea. Should Task Force 16 be sent to support him? Or should it remain at Pearl Harbor to counter a possible Japanese assault somewhere in the central Pacific? At a Pacific Fleet staff meeting in Pearl Harbor held several days before Task Force 16 steamed in, Nimitz learned that the Japanese would probably begin operations in the broad New Guinea–Solomon Islands area sometime on or after 3 May. They were expected to employ a force of perhaps five carriers, two battleships, and supporting cruisers, destroyers, and auxiliaries. The admiral had to assume that all or most of the *Kido Butai* was in the Coral Sea, for Tokyo did not possess many light or auxiliary carriers. Nimitz was as eager as Yamamoto for a carrier clash, and his staff convinced him that if Fletcher's *Lexington* and *Yorktown* were reinforced by Halsey's Task Force 16, Yamamoto might be tempted to bring the rest of the Imperial Japanese Navy down from home waters for a climactic battle. If the U.S. show of force dissuaded the Japanese from attacking eastward, then the *Hornet* and *Enterprise* could remain in the South Pacific to relieve the *Yorktown,* which except for ten days had been at sea since early January. But time was crucial. Task Force 16 could not linger at Pearl; it had to be on its way as soon as possible so Fletcher could receive timely support to counter the impending Japanese offensive.

Only three days after returning from the North Pacific, Task Force 16 received orders to be under way in forty-eight hours. Scuttlebutt both aboard the *Hornet* and within Air Group 8 over at Ewa pointed to the South Pacific. But no one knew for certain.

As the *Hornet* prepared to depart, crewmen groused again that their elegant warship would be nothing but a ferryboat. Soon after the carrier had arrived in Pearl, cranes had lifted a dozen F4F-3s of Marine Fighter Squadron 212 onto the flight deck, where they were immediately pushed to the elevators and struck below in a corner of the hangar. The *Enterprise* took on a similar load. The planes would be flown off north of Efate, the southernmost island in the New Hebrides group on the western edge of the Coral Sea, a place that would assume major strategic importance if the Japanese seized Tulagi. Within hours the marine pilots, under the command of Maj. Harold W. Bauer, reported aboard. Like their army predecessors, they were assigned to room with the ensigns and lieutenants (jg) of Air Group 8. When he heard of the arrangement, John Waldron, skipper of Torpedo 8, was irritated. "Are we running a Navy or are we running a rooming house?" he growled.[4] He may have been irked because the navy boys, who had cleaned out Doolittle's men at poker on the way out to the launch site, had lost most of their winnings on the return voyage to the handful of backup army pilots who remained aboard after Doolittle's fliers departed.

On the morning of 30 April Pearl Harbor churned with action as the two carriers of Task Force 16 and three of their destroyer escorts slipped their moorings and again sailed out past the antisubmarine nets and the green waters at the harbor's mouth. The cruisers and the remaining destroyer escorts followed slowly throughout the day. The *Hornet*'s navigator, Frank Akers, and his counterpart aboard the *Enterprise* set course for a position north of Oahu to meet the 160-odd planes of Air Groups 8 and 6, which flew out that afternoon. Shortly after 1200 the two carriers turned into the wind and began taking their air groups aboard. The *Hornet* suffered only one mishap, but it was serious. On straight-deck carriers a barrier about twelve feet high was erected two-thirds of the way down the flight deck to prevent any planes parked forward from being struck by aircraft falling out of control when landing. Lt. Bruce Harwood, Fighting 8's engineering officer, brought his F4F aboard too hard, bounced it off the flight deck, and hit the barrier with his wheels and the *Hornet*'s island with a wing tip. The fighter flipped over on its back. The tall Harwood was protected from serious injury by the plane's strong headrest, but the F4F was a "write off," leaving Fighting 8 with only twenty-six frontline and backup aircraft.

As the small fleet headed south, a new feeling swept through the *Hornet* and Air Group 8. The ship was finally on her own to fight as she was designed to fight. Halsey swiftly reinstituted the duty carrier–backup carrier routine that had been employed on the return from the Doolittle raid, which meant that one carrier took the late morning, afternoon, and next dawn scout and patrol flights, freeing up the "off-duty" carrier to conduct training flights.

As always at sea, the day began before dawn, with flight quarters called just as the first small arc of sun split the tropical horizon and seascape with a shaft of light. The after two-thirds of the flight deck was filled with warplanes, which had been fully armed and fueled in the hangar the night before, brought up by elevator, and pulled and pushed into position by several hundred husky young men of the flight deck crew. The air officer in PriFly had the entire flight deck fore and aft spread out below him. Microphone in hand, he called out, "Prepare to start engines."

The dim shapes of scores of men could be seen below, swarming over and around the planes. The heavy naval aircraft of World War II did not start with the turn of an ignition key; their engines were too heavy. Nor could engines be started by spinning the propeller by hand as was done with the light, fragile aircraft of 1917. Instead flight deck crews opened a small door in each plane's engine cowling and inserted an explosive charge resembling a shotgun cartridge into a firing mechanism. Within moments came the next word: "Pilots man your planes." Fifty or more young men, carrying clipboards with flight information, dressed in light clothing, tennis shoes, and close-fitting helmets, and wearing goggles rakishly pushed back on foreheads, trotted up from their ready rooms below, jogged across the flight deck, and climbed up small, portable ladders to their planes. The enlisted "plane boss" assigned to each aircraft "snugged" them in, checking harnesses and parachute straps. As soon as the first pilots were aboard the order came: "Start engines." Each pilot pressed an electrical button in the cockpit, and starting cartridges began popping all along the flight deck. Propellers slowly rotated and small, blue flames flared from exhaust pipes. For a few seconds the noise of warming engines was tentative and exploratory (Will I go today or will I stay home?); then a thunderous noise engulfed the ship and surrounding sea as fifty or more engines firmly took hold. For five or ten minutes, as the *Hornet* turned into the wind to give each plane the greatest lift possible, the flight deck became a roaring, shaking theater of noise. Then the assistant air officer snapped on a green light attached to the outside of PriFly, and the first plane taxied forward to get the takeoff signal from the launch officer on the flight deck.

One by one the planes swiftly gathered speed and raced down the deck in the dawn light, rotating into the sky forty or fifty feet from the bow. The sequence was almost invariable: the Grumman F4F fighters first, the Dauntless scouts and bombers second, the Devastator torpedo planes last. "The fliers were like kids out of school," remembered one *Hornet* officer. "They had been standing around for weeks with their hands in their pockets, wet-nursing a lot of Army bombers." The frustration must have been almost unbearable, because the entire air group, except for Torpedo 8, had received brand-new airplanes. Now at last "they had their own wings back . . . and there was a general feeling of exultation." The men of the air group "ripped their planes off the flight deck"; the pilots "virtually threw them into the sky."[5]

From dawn to dusk fighter planes from the two carriers flew out on long, wedge-shaped patrols, searching for enemy aircraft and submarines, while the Dauntlesses, which could be used interchangeably as scout planes or dive-bombers, made practice diving runs on the task force or, together with Jack Waldron's Devastators, towed sleeves for the ship's gunners to riddle. To many aboard the *Hornet*, the new carrier seemed alive and vibrant as she swaggered easily through the tropical seas at twenty-five knots. "She's a good ship, Frank, a fine ship," Mitscher remarked to Akers, and everyone aboard agreed.[6]

But was Air Group 8 ready for war? Long days of patrol and practice were not equivalent to combat, especially since Torpedo 8 still flew its practice missions without torpedoes. The fliers on the *Enterprise* had been briefly tested in earlier hit-and-run raids against Japanese island outposts in the Marshalls. Airmen aboard the *Lexington* and *Yorktown* had also fought the enemy. Only the *Hornet*'s air group remained disturbingly inexperienced.

Group commander Stanhope Cotton Ring, who "lived, ate and slept aviation," according to the *Hornet*'s first historian,[7] remains a cloudy figure more than half a century later. A 1923 graduate of the Naval Academy and an experienced flier, Ring seemed to at least some of his men and to ship's officers an affected martinet who often spoke with a disdainful, phony British accent.[8] It is not clear whether his peremptory manners with subordinates and his angry defensiveness with superiors masked an inferiority complex or reflected a sincere belief that his air group—possibly including himself—was not yet ready for war. But he was not universally popular or respected at a time when the young, untested pilots in the air group desperately needed to believe in their leaders. Historian John Lundstrom's verdict was that battle "would reveal serious flaws" in Air Group 8's "combat effectiveness and cohesiveness."[9]

Fighting 8's leader, Pat Mitchell, although genial and evidently intelligent, was tentative both personally and as a flier. Essentially a passive individual, he seemed to harbor the same inner uncertainties as Ring, and at times he was obviously uncomfortable in the role of fighter squadron commander.[10] In fact, Mitchell had never served as a fighter pilot, and before joining the *Hornet* his only carrier duty had been quick tours aboard the *Langley* and *Saratoga* between 1935 and 1937. He had been working on theoretical problems for the Bureau of Aeronautics in Washington when Mitscher personally tapped him for aviation command on the *Hornet*. Mitchell had been the last member of Air Group 8 to qualify on carrier landings during shakedown. His executive officer, Lt. (jg)

Stanley Ruehlow, was a competent pilot, but some in the squadron thought he was too stiff and correct to lead a band of airmen whose intrinsically dangerous calling traditionally had been nourished by high spirits and irreverence.

Walter Rodee led the scout planes of VS-8. He was a round-faced man whose deep-set eyes were often crinkled in the professional pilot's squint. He wore a small, trimly barbered mustache above firm, narrow lips and a square jaw. By all accounts Rodee was a kindly, sensitive individual, quiet and affable when relaxed, a raconteur of sorts. Yet one member of the air department recalled that he was "no ball of fire," an "uninspired" leader at best. Another observer noted that "tension closed him up like a clam." Rodee was never able to accept pilot losses calmly or philosophically. "He carried the tragedy within himself when some of his kids did not come back."[11]

Rodee's executive officer, Gus Widhelm, was the most boisterous naval aviator of the early war years, "wilder than a March hare," in the words of one admiring *Hornet* officer.[12] Widhelm was a hot-eyed young man from Nebraska with a direct stare and slicked-back, dark hair. He loved gambling, booze, cars, and music. His penchant was poker, but he thought winning just before combat was bad luck. He never drove his Lincoln Zephyr at less than eighty miles an hour, and he carried a fifty dollar bill "just in case I meet a tough cop." That bill and another that Widhelm had obtained over the years had very low serial numbers. Gus was always looking for a sucker to play a game he called "Money Golf." "Low number takes the dough," he would tell friends, "and I've got five zeros on one of these babies."[13]

Bombing 8 was nominally led by Lt. Comdr. Robert R. Johnson, of whom little is now remembered. During the battle of Midway and perhaps before Ring designated himself commander of Bombing 8 as well as commander of the air group.

In the first months of the Pacific war the legendary hero of the *Hornet* air group was John Charles Waldron, squadron commander of Torpedo 8. A tall, lean, fierce-looking, hawk-faced man from Fort Pierre, South Dakota, Waldron was part Native American.[14] The oldest of Air Group 8's squadron commanders, he had been appointed to Annapolis in 1920, before some of his young charges had been born, and he treated the ensigns and "jgs" under him accordingly. Nearing forty, Waldron had devoted his professional career to advancing the science and technique of torpedo bombing, and with a command finally in his grasp he was determined to create the finest torpedo plane squadron in the world.

Waldron knew, and his men knew, that the Devastator was a "miserable" airplane, but it was all the navy had. To compensate for the plane's shortcomings, Torpedo 8 drilled and drilled both before and after going to sea. When the squadron had first gathered at Norfolk, Waldron had designated himself squadron morale officer, and he played the stern parent diligently. His boys flew six to eight hours a day, low and hard at any available target on land or sea. They had to be prepared to take their flawed planes and often inaccurate torpedoes right down the throat of any enemy that might be found, regardless of the consequences. Torpedo 8's motto was simple—"Attack!"—and the squadron insignia was a closed fist. After a full day of flying, Waldron ordered his pilots to take four hours of duty at night. He made them learn things about their planes that pilots had never had to learn before: how to make engine changes, how the hydraulic system worked, how to load a torpedo.

When the youngsters had begun to buckle under the unremitting pressure, Waldron had abruptly eased off, inviting them and their dates to his house, where he and his wife, Adelaide, hosted boisterous parties. Boys and girls, older men and women, would dance, drink, and get down on their knees to shoot craps, arguing and bellowing with each other in the sheer, liquored-up joy of stress release. The Waldron home was always open to the pilots of Torpedo 8; the Waldron car was theirs whenever the commander was not using it. But even in moments of relaxation Waldron gathered his men around and reminded them over and over again: "Attack!"

Now, as the *Hornet* sped toward the Coral Sea with the rest of Task Force 16, there were no parties, and Torpedo 8, along with the other squadrons, just flew endless patrols and studied. Unlike the other squadron commanders, Waldron let paperwork slide so he could spend as much time in the air as possible. His conception of command was personal leadership. He never asked his fliers to do what he would not. While he was aloft one day a fuel line suddenly burst, drenching him with oil. Waldron should have bailed out, because a single spark could have instantly ignited the cockpit. But he coolly brought his plane down onto the *Hornet*'s flight deck without mishap.

His men were typical of the naval aviators that a desperate nation threw against the Japanese in the year after Pearl Harbor. Most were in their early or mid-twenties, although there was a sprinkling of older, experienced men. They came from all parts of the country and from several social classes. Lt. Jimmie Owens, Torpedo 8's executive officer, a stocky, brown-haired man with chubby cheeks, was diligent and soft-

John Waldron insisted that his pilots know their airplanes. A prewar aviator prepares to personally crank up the engine of his biplane. Note the dangerous placement of the necktie.

spoken. He was the home-loving husband of the group, dividing his passion equally between wife and work. Lt. R. A. "Moose" Moore was the squadron's gunnery officer. Like many of Torpedo 8's pilots, he was an Annapolis graduate. A dark-haired, dark-complexioned man, he said little, "but when he did talk he did so in an engagingly shy manner, and there was usually a kind of wistful humor in . . . his words." Big, sandy-haired, rough-looking Ens. William W. "Abbie" Abercrombie had worked in meat-packing plants in Kansas City and was an avid booster of his hometown. When Waldron presented navigation problems, Abbie invariably asked how far a mythical Point A or B was from Kansas City. Everyone considered Abbie a good Joe; he was probably the most popular man in the squadron. Perhaps he was liked best because of his honesty. He called Torpedo 8 and its criminally obsolete airplanes the "Coffin Squadron" and always talked about leaving. But he never did.

Ens. Bill Evans from Indianapolis, Yale, and Harvard Law had written the eloquent, bitter letter home on Pearl Harbor night about war and the Christmas spirit. His amused mates considered him the Ivy League "smoothie" of the squadron and called him "Squire" because of his aristocratic attitude. When off duty he favored black and white saddle oxford shoes, and his closet aboard the *Hornet* was filled with tweed sport coats and gray slacks. But he was a genuine, unaffected young man, graceful and rosy-cheeked, who fitted in well. The rough-hewn Waldron loved having an Ivy Leaguer in the squadron and made Evans communications and intelligence officer. When Waldron posed a particularly difficult problem in torpedo tactics that no one wished to answer, he would chide the boys, saying they all had brains and were more educated than he; then he would invariably turn to Evans, who just as invariably gave a lucid response.

Ens. Whitey Moore from Bluefield, West Virginia, was the squadron clown and Waldron's favorite. A cherubic "half-pint" who spent an inordinate amount of time asleep, Moore had soft, fluffy brown hair and a Dagwood face that girls loved because they thought they could mother him. Young men liked him because he was witty and unassuming. He was also an ardent jitterbug dancer who had entertained at all of Waldron's parties back in Norfolk.

The biggest man in Torpedo 8 was Ens. Grant W. Teats, a former track star at Oregon State who had worked in lumber camps all over the Pacific Northwest. Teats was an individualist who was used to running his own life and did not like the navy telling him what to do, but he did his work, and his mates respected him for it.

Others in Torpedo 8's ready room aboard the *Hornet* included quiet, reserved Ens. Rusty Kenyon, who had married a nurse in Norfolk just before the carrier sailed for the Pacific; Lieutenants (jg) G. M. Campbell and J. D. Woodson, who had recently been promoted from the rank of enlisted chief; Ens. J. P. "Jack" Gray, tall and well-built, from Columbia, Missouri; Ens. Harold J. Ellison, a slight, nervous boy with slick, dark hair and a thin, feminine face who had been employed in a Buffalo insurance office, hated to work, and loved talking about girls; Ens. George "Tex" Gay, who had dropped out of Texas A & M to join the Army Air Corps but failed the physical, had worked on a construction gang for a time, and then joined the navy; and one enlisted pilot, R. W. Mills of San Diego. All these youngsters were eager to fly, and they did: day after day on antisubmarine patrols. But they still, for whatever reason, did not fly with torpedoes under their wings.

Things went badly for Fighting 8 from the first full day at sea. The *Hornet* was duty carrier, which meant that the F4Fs would be busy, but at the dawn launch two of the Grummans turned out to have bad engines and had to be replaced with standby aircraft. Ens. Stephen Groves, flying one of the replacement planes, could not coax flying speed out of his aircraft, which sailed off the bow, lost altitude, and pancaked into the water five hundred yards off the *Hornet*'s port bow. Groves was unhurt and quickly pushed himself out of the plane and away from the onrushing hull of the huge carrier, which nearly brushed the sinking aircraft. A destroyer rushed in and plucked Groves from the water. An investigating board on the *Hornet* subsequently concluded that the propeller governor had malfunctioned.

The next day Fighting 8 lost another Grumman because of low manifold pressure and the failure of the pilot, Ens. Charles Markland Kelly, to lower his flaps. As a result the plane raced down the deck, reached the bow, then dropped like a stone to the water below, only two hundred yards in front of the carrier. Kelly swam vigorously away from his sinking plane, then turned and watched the *Hornet* slice right through the fuselage, the bow wake tossing the plane aside with a gesture of contempt. Kelly joined Groves on board the destroyer *Monssen*, where they spent the next several days sampling life in the "tin can" fleet until they could return to their carrier during normal refueling operations. Thereafter fate left Fighting 8 alone, transferring its capricious whim to Air Group 6 aboard the *Enterprise*, which suffered a series of crashes, one of them fatal, during the next several weeks.

Task Force 16 crossed the equator on 4 May, the first time ever for the *Hornet*. Jurika later recalled that Halsey had forbidden the traditional high jinks. The ships were in a war zone, where a reduction in vigilance could be fatal. But no sailor can resist celebrating "crossing the line." Shortly after 1600 Mitscher himself took the *Hornet*'s conn while Davey Jones and his Royal Court presented subpoenas to thousands of "polliwogs." "Davey" formally departed after only ten minutes, so the resulting festivities were evidently brief, but they were also appropriately rough. The ship's log recorded several injuries because of excessive "skylarking," and Gerald McAteer remembered things "getting out of hand." He treated a broken arm, a broken leg, and a vicious scalp wound suffered by a young sailor who was running away from someone and forgot to duck going through a steel hatch. McAteer spent an hour patching up the man's head. Some of the more sober-minded aboard used the occasion to make a point about conservation. No one knew how long the *Hornet* would be at sea; adequate supplies to sustain a long cruise had always been a problem. The supply officer decided to vividly demonstrate to Cardon Ruchti and his fellow polliwogs how to wipe their anuses with only one small section of toilet paper and the middle finger if the need arose.[15]

While the planes flew, the ship's company settled back into the daily routine of life at sea. Dawn general quarters were followed by breakfast; then at 0800 the crew mustered on station. Occasionally at least some of the engineering department was formally mustered on the hangar deck to give the sallow, heat-enervated men an opportunity to escape their cramped working and living spaces below decks and get a bit of sun and wind. The rest of the day and evening was consumed with work, chow, sleep, and maybe, if possible, some poker or craps shooting. The endless sea stretched monotonously around the ship from horizon to horizon, broken only by the forms of dashing destroyers and stolid cruisers holding a steady course. Men woke, worked, ate, and slept with the sounds and rhythms of the ocean. It hissed along the side of the gliding hull; its salty smell mixed with the oil and gasoline fumes that filled the flight and hangar decks; its occasional swells lifted the steel plates on which men stood and walked. It provided a backdrop of uniformity and harmony for daily life.

Big and spacious as she was, the *Hornet* was crowded with men, planes, and dangerous machinery. Life aboard was always chancy, and people were constantly suffering minor injuries. Men cut their heels racing up the steps of the ship's countless ladders; they cut their fingers on bread slicers or had them crushed when heavy hatches were closed too quickly. They spilled hot coffee or soup on themselves as they were inadvertently jostled by shipmates on the crowded mess decks. Occasionally an unwary sailor walked into the wing of an airplane parked on a dark hangar deck, or an unsecured engine cowling fell on the head of an unwary mechanic. Heavy wrenches were dropped on toes. Men would back into hot steam lines while cleaning the bilges or would stumble over boxes in small working spaces, falling and cutting their hands or heads. One time a sailor stumbled across a heavy mat in the forward 5-inch gun platform and struck his head on the heavy gun barrel. In the most bizarre accident of all, a man let go of a heavy steel trash barrel, which fell through a hatch in the gallery deck down into the hangar bay, where a plane was being warmed up. The barrel struck the spinning propeller and was instantly chewed to pieces. Small, potentially deadly bits of steel shot through the air, injuring nearby crewmen.[16]

Several incidents disrupted the even tenor of the cruise and remained in many minds for years. One day the engineering department called the bridge with a routine request to blow tubes—that is, to clear boiler tubes and funnel intakes of accumulated fumes and gases by shooting a jet of pure air through them. The telephone talker on the bridge relayed the request to the junior officer of the deck, presumably a very young ensign, whose name has been mercifully forgotten. "Permission granted," the ensign said smartly; then, turning to the boatswain's mate of the watch, he added crisply, "Bos'n, order the bugler to blow tubes!"[17]

Frank Akers was the only senior officer aside from the captain who had a sea cabin in the island. It was essential for the ship's navigator to be close to his work and readily available at all hours of the day or night. But Akers did not always appreciate the privilege. He was especially irritated that water pressure up in the island was weak and undependable. Showers were often tepid little streams of water, and toilets seldom flushed fully after one or two tries. In the long weeks after leaving Norfolk, Akers's complaints became more frequent, bitter, and pointed. The culprit, he claimed, was the ship's first lieutenant, Lt. Comdr. Henry Moran, who was responsible for all deck work and repair activities. One day during the voyage to the New Hebrides, Akers left the bridge to go back to his cabin for a "rest." Suddenly he erupted back onto the bridge, sputtering and cursing; the bottom of his khaki uniform shirt was soaked and flecked with feces. Someone in the deck department had become fed up with Akers's bellyaching and had cut the main fire-fighting water line with its enormous pressure directly into the navigator's plumbing. Now Akers would have all the water power he needed for toilet or shower. Akers was furious. Mitscher and his exec, George Henderson, exchanged amused glances and promised to try to find the culprit. That evening an anonymous, highly scatological "poem" about the incident appeared on the wardroom bulletin board, no doubt the product of Henderson's fertile mind. Nothing more was heard from Akers about insufficient water pressure in his stateroom.[18]

Provision of adequate fresh water was both an obsession with and a daily headache for the engineering department. Somehow twenty-six hundred men had to have enough to drink and to keep clean in a tropical climate. Glen Dock's petty officers in "B" Division were wild on the subject of water conservation and had a fit about men taking showers.

Just the time needed to adjust the water temperature could waste precious gallons. Yet everyone in the division spent four of every eight hours at sea in firerooms and boiler rooms, where temperatures routinely reached 120 degrees. By the end of each watch clothing and bodies were foul with sweat.

Chiefs and petty officers quickly devised a remedy: Clothes and bodies would be cleaned together. Each sailor aboard the *Hornet* had his own standard, navy-issue bucket attached to a rack not far from his bunk. Each bucket had a stenciled number that was the same as the sailor's bunk number. Filthy "snipes" coming off duty from the engine, boiler, or firerooms went to their berthing areas, got their buckets, and went into the adjacent washroom. They filled the buckets with water from the showers and added strong "saltwater soap" that made tremendous suds in fresh water. The men dumped their sweat- and grease-stained clothes into the soapy water and let them soak for five or ten minutes. Then, still stripped, the men dumped the dirty, soapy water over themselves and cleaned their bodies with more saltwater soap. Still soapy, they refilled their buckets with fresh water from the shower, rinsed out their now fairly clean clothing, then used the water to wash the soap off their bodies, finishing up with just five or ten seconds under the shower spray (with no time allowed to adjust the water temperature) to wash off the last of the soap. Then and later men complained of poor food and minimal supplies, but the *Hornet* never suffered a catastrophic loss of fresh water.[19]

During the dawn launch on 21 May the *Hornet* suffered her first death. Standing in the catwalk just below the flight deck, Seaman 1st Class S. I. McGowan apparently mistook the natural exhaust flares on one plane for a fire. Grabbing a nearby extinguisher, he raced excitedly up the two or three steps to the still-dark flight deck and right into a roaring propeller. McGowan was cut to ribbons. The entire crew was stunned. That afternoon the task force briefly lowered colors as McGowan's body was committed to the deep in a brief but poignant service. Then the ship went back to work. But no one who witnessed the incident ever forgot it.[20]

Two hours after McGowan's burial, twenty-three-year-old Ens. Louise John Muery, from Houston and fresh out of Pensacola, went out on a routine scouting patrol with his gunner-radioman, Walter Richter of Nebraska. Out at the edge of its patrol run, two hundred miles from the carrier, Muery's plane suddenly developed engine trouble. The young pilot courageously refused to send a call for help, which might have given the task force's position away if answered, and went down. For twenty-four hours Mitscher ordered Waldron, Widhelm, and other members of the scout and torpedo squadrons to hunt for Muery and Richter; finally Halsey ordered them to give up. The task force had more important things to do.

Muery and Richter floated alone on their raft for twenty-three days under the merciless sun. Their food and water dwindled to nothing. Finally, they drifted toward an island ringed with surf. The two weakened men tried to get ashore, but Richter died in the attempt. Staggering onto the beach, Muery lay half-dead until several English-speaking natives decided that he was not a Japanese, came to his aid, and eventually returned him to American hands.[21]

The day after Task Force 16 crossed the equator Halsey and his carrier skippers learned from CinCPac intelligence bulletins that they were too late for battle. The *Lexington* and *Yorktown* were already engaging Japanese planes and ships in the Coral Sea, a thousand miles to the south. The next day, 7 May, word came that the American and Japanese carrier fleets had at last grappled, and the *Lexington* was rumored to be in extremis. Halsey also learned of a possible Japanese assault on the islands of Nauru and Ocean, which lay between the Japanese-held Gilbert and Solomon Islands. If these small bits of rock and coral were seized, Japan would substantially strengthen its ribbon defensive line in the South Pacific.

As Task Force 16 crossed the dateline, 9 May disappeared, and by the tenth Halsey knew that the *Lexington* had sunk, the *Yorktown* had been badly damaged but was still operational, and Japanese and U.S. forces had withdrawn from the Coral Sea. Port Moresby was, at least for the moment, safe from Japanese invasion.

Twenty-four hours later the marine F4F-3s were brought up from the hangar decks of the *Hornet* and *Enterprise* and sent on their way—not to Efate, whose airstrip was discovered to be unusable, but to Nouméa on the big island of New Caledonia, some two hundred miles south of Efate. For days the men of Air Group 8 had told the marine pilots the same thing they had told Doolittle's men: Don't panic; there is plenty of takeoff room; just launch normally. And, like the Doolittle fliers, the marines proceeded to race their engines and rotate their planes off the deck in near stalls even before they reached the end of the island. Someone heard Waldron mutter that God must look after drunks and marines.

With his mission accomplished, Halsey turned Task Force 16 north and west, hoping to catch the Japanese invasion force heading east to Nauru and Ocean from the naval base at Rabaul on New Britain. He knew from intelligence reports that fliers from the *Lexington* and *Yorktown* had heavily damaged the carrier *Shokaku*, one of the premier units in the *Kido Butai*. But *Shokaku*'s sister ship, *Zuikaku*, had not been hit, and he hoped that she might be accompanying the Nauru-Ocean invasion force. In fact, the *Zuikaku*'s air group had been so decimated by the Americans in the Coral Sea that she was heading for Truk, while the *Shokaku* headed home to the repair yards. Neither ship would be able to accompany the other four carriers on Japan's next offensive.

For a week Halsey maneuvered and patrolled in a restricted area around the New Hebrides while awaiting orders to intercept the Nauru-Ocean invasion force. To war correspondent Robert J. Casey aboard the cruiser *Salt Lake City* all this "churning up the edge of the Coral Sea" seemed futile. "So far as the scenery is concerned we might be on one of those two-week cruises to nowhere that used to run out of New York." On 12 May all of Task Force 16 suddenly changed course when one of the *Hornet*'s patrolling planes became lost because its homing device failed. The pilot made the whole fleet nervous "when he let off his plaintive cry for help."[22] Compounding the felony, he failed to switch off his long-range communication system when he began talking to his rear seat gunner-radioman over the aircraft's local circuit. Task Force 16 and unknown numbers of Japanese heard the youngster say: "Get that receiver working. What's this little switch for? Boy, this is serious. Can't you hear anything? I can't hear anything either. What the hell do you suppose is wrong with that thing? It worked all right yesterday. What the hell good is a radio beam when you can't pick it up?" Eventually the radioman got the homing system working, and the plane came along to meet the advancing fleet and was safely taken aboard the *Hornet*.[23]

Such incidents were the kind of mistakes that caused Ernie King, the chief of naval operations back in Washington, to fret over the safety of his few remaining carriers. The *Lexington* was gone, the *Yorktown* was damaged, and the *Saratoga* was completing repairs on the West Coast. King did not want his only two healthy flattops in the entire Pacific sucked into a trap laid by Japanese planes or submarines from the Gilberts. Nimitz was glad to exploit King's fears, for Rochefort had now begun to accumulate impressive evidence that Yamamoto was preparing a central Pacific offensive. So Nimitz ordered the limping *Yorktown* back to Pearl immediately and directed Halsey to make a show of force, but no more, against the approaching Nauru-Ocean invasion fleet, allowing long-range patrol planes from the Japanese base at Makin in the Gilberts to sight Task Force 16 repeatedly. The ruse was so successful that the Nauru-Ocean invasion force abruptly turned around and headed back west, bringing news that a powerful American carrier task force remained on duty in the South Pacific. With that mission accomplished, Nimitz on 15 May ordered Task Force 16 back to Hawaii.

The Japanese were clearly up to something new. On the way north, those in the wardroom and mess decks debated whether the enemy blow would fall on Alaska or Midway. But wherever Yamamoto did strike, this time the Yanks would be ready with a naval ambush of their own.

6

Mysteries at Midway

AT NOON on the last Tuesday in May, Task Force 16 again steamed slowly up the Pearl Harbor ship channel. By now the *Hornet*'s hull had sliced through so many thousands of miles of ocean that paint had peeled off down to bare metal at several places along the waterline. Twenty-four hours later Admiral Fletcher brought in the remnants of Task Force 17. As the harbor reverberated with cheers, the *Yorktown*, trailing an oil slick ten miles long, limped toward the open caisson gates of Dry Dock No. One. Within hours she was settled snugly on blocks, and under Nimitz's orders yard workers frantically began welding temporary plates below the waterline and bracing damaged compartments with timber. But only a few of the many sprung watertight doors could be fixed, and there was no time to repair the three boilers that Japanese bombs had knocked out in the Coral Sea. The *Yorktown* would make at most twenty-seven knots in the forthcoming operation: she remained a crippled lady.[1]

Early the next morning, 3,400 miles to the northwest, sixty-eight ships of the Imperial Japanese Navy—battleships, cruisers, and destroyers, headed by the *Akagi* and three other carriers of the *Kido Butai*—weighed anchor under cloud-flecked skies and steamed majestically through the calm waters of the Inland Sea and out into the Pacific. It was a lucky occasion, the thirty-seventh anniversary of Adm. Heihachiro Togo's smashing victory over the Russian Baltic Fleet at the Battle of Tsushima and Japan's traditional Navy Day. By 1 June the entire Imperial Fleet was at sea. Altogether nearly 150 warships and transports, including 8 carriers and 12 battleships, were ready to assault American positions from Dutch Harbor, Alaska, to Midway.[2]

More than half a century later Midway still bewitches both historians and laymen with its complexities, its might-have-beens, and its drama. Had the Japanese planned more intelligently, they could have won and perhaps ended the war; had the Americans employed their comparatively scant resources more efficiently and fought with greater imagination, their victory might have been conclusive. One commander lost an empire in the space of five minutes; the other gained an unbelievable but flawed victory. And in the process an American torpedo plane squadron immortalized itself with a doomed charge that instantly placed it on the same pedestal of heroism as the Light Brigade. Myths were made at Midway, but mysteries remain.

For the Japanese, "Operation MI" was the product of war by committee. Fleet Admiral Yamamoto had dreamed up the operation, but he was not a free agent. Not only did he and his fellow sailors have to recognize and often defer to the wishes of the Japanese army, but they were divided among themselves. The Combined Fleet Staff in Tokyo wanted to control strategy; so did Yamamoto, and so, in a way, did Vice Adm. Chuichi Nagumo, commander of the *Kido Butai*, and his brilliant young staff officer, Comdr. Minoru Genda. Opinions were divided, as always happens in councils of war.

Yamamoto originally conceived of Midway as a lure to tempt the tattered remnants of the U.S. Pacific Fleet into decisive battle. Even a threat to seize the island would force the Americans to fight, because loss of Midway would place unbearable pressure on Pearl Harbor, little more than a thousand miles to the southeast. But during innumerable conferences, conversations, and war games in the spring of 1942, Yamamoto and the Combined Fleet Staff both shifted the emphasis of the operation and expanded its scale. Midway should not be simply a lure but an objective in itself. And not only Midway; one or more Aleutian Islands should also be seized. A simultaneous conquest of Midway and the Aleutians would complete Japan's mid-Pacific ribbon defensive line, ensuring the safety of the home islands from assaults like the Doolittle raid. Midway could also provide an essential stepping stone to the conquest of Hawaii itself if that was needed to end the Pacific war on Japan's terms. If

Hawaii with its 400,000 American inhabitants could be captured, Tokyo could use it as a bargaining lever to force Washington to sue for peace.[3]

There seemed little immediate danger in scattering the Imperial Japanese Navy all over the central and northern Pacific. Only in retrospect did historians characterize Yamamoto's battle plan as one "that carried the Imperial Navy's predilection for the baroque to wretched excess."[4] This fateful stage of the war was the time to knock the Americans out permanently before their growing industrial might could decisively change the course of battle. Japanese intelligence estimated that in the first week of June 1942 the U.S. Pacific Fleet could muster two or at most three carriers, eight or nine escorting cruisers, and a score of destroyers. By attacking everywhere north and west of Hawaii, Japan would force its enemy to scatter thin resources to the breaking point and thus would maintain initiative and momentum.

But Yamamoto was uncomfortable with such a bold and far-reaching plan. So was Genda. On the eve of Midway Yamamoto wrote to a friend that Japan had so far had its way in the Pacific campaign. "The 'First Operational Stage' of Operations has been kind of a children's hour and will soon be over, now comes the adult's hour."[5] The combined Midway-Aleutians operation would place a terrible tactical-strategic burden on the *Kido Butai,* whose effective carrier strength had been reduced to four flattops after the Coral Sea. If the Americans contested the Midway invasion, the *Kido Butai* might be forced to operate tactically and strategically at the same time. Tactically Nagumo's four carriers would have to support another amphibious assault. Strategically they would have to confront and defeat enemy carriers, which would surely respond either to save Hawaii (the much more likely scenario) or Alaska. Like other weapon systems, carriers were most secure defensively and most effective offensively when massed. That was the prime lesson of Pearl Harbor. Yamamoto had thrown his entire heavy carrier force against Hawaii and had gained a brilliant victory. With two of its fleet carriers now out of action, the *Kido Butai* would have to be bolstered by some of the Japanese navy's better light carriers to ensure triumph at Midway. Yet the two best, the *Ryujo* and *Junyo,* which possessed fleet speed and a combined complement of nearly eighty planes, were earmarked for an air raid against Dutch Harbor to mask invasions of Attu and Kiska farther west in the Aleutians.

If the Japanese navy had agreed to cancel the Dutch Harbor–Aleutians enterprise, the two light carriers could have been brought into the Midway operation, probably providing Nagumo with a decisive margin of both power and flexibility. Operating ahead of the invasion force and on its northern and southern flanks, the *Ryujo* and *Junyo* could have detected any possible enemy ambush and attracted initial American air attacks while the undetected heavy carriers prepared a devastating counterblow. Alternatively, Nagumo could have divided his invasion fleet into tactical and strategic units, with the light carriers employed solely to soften up Midway while the heavy carriers awaited the American riposte. Nimitz and his admirals developed such a strategy during the great trans-Pacific offensive of 1943–45, when escort or "jeep" carriers provided the essential close-in tactical air support for island assaults, while the fleet carriers, heavy and light, roamed adjacent and distant waters with the strategic task of hunting down the dwindling enemy fleet and bringing it to battle. By failing to insist on a concentration at Midway, Yamamoto, Nagumo, and Genda sowed the seeds of disaster.

Yamamoto's deference to a foolish plan reflected his driving impatience to bring the Americans to decisive battle, which derived partly from his shame over the Doolittle assault. Captain Fuchida later recalled that Yamamoto had devoted considerable energy to ensuring that the home islands would not be assaulted from the east. "The defeat of all his precautions against an enemy carrier-borne attack on the homeland cut Admiral Yamamoto's pride to the quick, and he resolved that it must not be allowed to happen again at any cost."[6] But Yamamoto may have reluctantly deferred to a wider offensive because he realized that if Japan did not move quickly against the *existing* American carrier fleet, it would lose the balance of naval power in the Pacific not in a year or so but immediately. He could not afford to spend precious weeks quibbling and fighting over the scope and scale of Operation MI.

The size of the U.S. carrier fleet in early 1942 was common international knowledge disseminated through numerous prewar and even wartime publications. On Pearl Harbor day the United States possessed seven fleet carriers—*Lexington, Saratoga, Ranger, Yorktown, Enterprise, Wasp,* and *Hornet.* On the eve of Midway, Japanese intelligence assumed that the *Lexington* and perhaps the *Yorktown* had been sunk in the Coral Sea. That left five ships. The *Enterprise* and *Hornet* were known to be alive and well somewhere in the Pacific. The *Saratoga* had not been seen since she had been torpedoed off Hawaii, but she would surely return to battle before long. The *Ranger* and *Wasp* were not accounted for; both were known to have been in the Atlantic. German intelligence may have spotted the *Wasp* delivering critically needed Spitfires to Malta in late April and early May and may have informed Tokyo, but perhaps not. In any case Yamamoto had to assume that at least one of the Atlantic carriers had probably already sailed through the Panama Canal to beef up the Pacific Fleet. The *Nitto Maru*, after all, had reported three enemy carriers during the Doolittle raid, and no other Japanese unit had confirmed or denied that report.

Thus Yamamoto had to conclude that by late June or early July the *Kido Butai* might have to deal with four and possibly even five American carriers: the *Saratoga*, *Hornet*, and *Enterprise* for certain; perhaps the *Yorktown*; and the *Wasp* or *Ranger*. In fact, on the day the Battle of Midway began, five American carriers were in or very near the Pacific. Three were in the central Pacific; the *Saratoga*, fully repaired, was halfway from the West Coast to Hawaii; and the *Wasp* was preparing to transit the Panama Canal. If Midway had been fought a week later, the Americans would have confronted Yamamoto with four large carriers; if the Japanese had hesitated until July, the *Wasp* would also have joined the American carrier fleet. On the other hand, neither the *Shokaku* nor the *Zuikaku* would be ready to resume combat operations before September.

Moreover, the Japanese high command could not be absolutely sure that the enemy did not possess some auxiliary or converted carriers that had escaped the attention of the world's naval observers. The Japanese themselves had converted several merchantmen to reasonably fast auxiliary carriers. The United States was known to be building one or two such ships; indeed, the *Long Island*, the first of what would become a very numerous but very slow class of "escort" carriers, was already in commission. On the day after the Doolittle raid Admiral Ugaki, Yamamoto's chief of staff, speculated that "what the enemy intended in this attack . . . was to launch long-distance planes from converted carriers after closing in our homeland supported by [regular fleet] carriers, heavy cruisers, and destroyers."[7]

Midway thus had to be attacked before a widely scattered American carrier fleet of unknown size could be concentrated to face the depleted *Kido Butai*. But, of course, this was all the more reason for bringing together every available Japanese carrier at Midway to achieve maximum power and flexibility. Failure to do so was Yamamoto's major blunder, as Ugaki readily admitted. In a lengthy analysis of Midway written aboard the command superbattleship *Yamato* several days after the battle, Ugaki said that "after we learned that the Fifth CV Division

[*Shokaku* and *Zuikaku*] could not participate in this operation, the plan should have been revised so that one mission would be finished before dealing with another. I think we can't escape being blamed for negligence in not having taken the necessary steps."[8]

Yamamoto's fallacious strategy flowed naturally from a firm belief, shared with his colleagues, that the small American carrier-cruiser fleet was not physically able to immediately contest either the Midway or the Aleutians operation. The entire Japanese naval establishment accepted the assumption, based on faulty intelligence, that Halsey's Task Force 16 with two undamaged fleet carriers remained far off in the South Pacific and that Nimitz and the American high command in Hawaii had no inkling of the impending assaults against Midway and Dutch Harbor. Japanese planning was based absolutely on blind faith that there was no tactical-strategic dilemma because Midway would be assaulted and taken on 4–5 June and the Americans could not react before 7 June at the earliest.

Some Japanese and American historians, including Fuchida, Ronald Spector, and Gordon Prange, have suggested that the Japanese high command continued to believe that battleships remained the decisive weapons of war at sea and that this belief caused its improper employment of carrier forces in Operation MI. But the evidence does not support their claim. As in all previous assaults since Pearl Harbor, the *Kido Butai* was to be the spearhead of the Japanese attack, and the main objective of Operation MI, besides the capture of Midway, was the destruction of the U.S. carrier fleet. Yamamoto and his colleagues knew that if the American carriers could be destroyed or badly damaged, the Japanese battleships and supporting cruisers could easily sweep the handful of surviving American cruisers and destroyers from the seas. If that happened, opportunities for further Japanese victories, both naval and diplomatic, would be unlimited. With only two or at most three American carriers left to deal with for the next eighteen months (*Saratoga, Ranger,* and *Wasp*), Japan could turn its attention to isolating Australia and Hawaii. The *Kido Butai* could bomb the Panama Canal with virtual impunity, and with that vital waterway closed, the remainder of the American fleet, new and old, would be bottled up in the Atlantic. Hit-and-run raids of the Doolittle variety could be easily mounted against the American West Coast. Indeed, during the pre-Midway war games in April and May 1942, representatives of Japan's First Air Fleet Headquarters, speculating about a "second-stage operation" after the seizure of the island, suggested that with new construction and further conversions the *Kido Butai*'s operational strength could eventually be expanded to nine or even a dozen carriers operating together against Hawaii and other enemy targets.[9] It was an exhilarating prospect.

But when hasty war games were conducted in May aboard the *Yamato* in the Inland Sea, they clearly indicated that if an American carrier force were introduced into the Midway scenario at the beginning, Nagumo's carriers would suffer significant to catastrophic losses. Yet every time one or two units were declared lost, the umpires brusquely ordered them to be revived for the next round of battle. Neither Ugaki, who served as an umpire, nor anyone else objected. Yamamoto himself was not present. At Trafalgar, J. F. C. Fuller has written, "Nelson did not fight in order to carry out a plan, instead he planned in order to carry out a fight, and between the two there is a vast difference."[10] Indeed there is, and this crucial difference doomed Japan at Midway.

In hindsight it is easy to criticize the impatience, the faulty strategic grasp, and the tactical weakness of the Japanese naval command in planning for Midway. It is easy to forget that Yamamoto, Ugaki, and the others, like their American counterparts, were dealing with a brand-new weapon system, indeed a brand-new dimension of warfare. At Midway neither side had any precedents for guidance. The aircraft carrier had been developed during the final stages of the previous war; as late as 1939 it had been widely considered little more than a scouting arm of the fleet. Even after Taranto, Pearl Harbor, and the sinkings of the *Bismarck, Prince of Wales,* and *Repulse,* countless influential officials in many of the world's navies were highly skeptical of the carrier. Yamamoto and Nagumo themselves had not handled the *Kido Butai* with much imagination in the weeks and months after Pearl Harbor. Instead of vigorously seeking out the American carriers that had escaped the Hawaii ambush, Yamamoto had allowed his carriers to be used as they had been off China between 1937 and 1940: as aviation support units for the Japanese army. Only the quick rush of the *Akagi, Kaga, Soryu,* and *Hiryu* into the Indian Ocean in early April to strike at British installations and shipping in and around Ceylon conformed to later strategic uses of carrier air power. Even the Battle of the Coral Sea had not been planned as a carrier action but resulted from the American response to the Japanese lunge into the lower Solomons. Not until Midway did both the Japanese and American carrier fleets plan to confront one another.

Both sides had formulated carrier doctrines and tactics in the years of peace before Pearl Harbor, but only battle would test their soundness. Yamamoto would clearly need every bit of luck to escape disaster. But his enemies had serious tactical if not strategic flaws of their own.

The American carrier plane squadrons possessed widely disparate ability, experience, and capability. Air Group 6 on the *Enterprise* had never met Japanese fighter and bomber aircraft in large numbers; the *Lexington* air group was dispersed after the ship sank in the Coral Sea. Air Group 8 aboard the *Hornet* had not fired a shot in anger. "For Midway, the *Yorktown* aviators were the only ones in a position to profit from their hard-earned Coral Sea experiences," Lundstrom wrote.[11]

The Americans also lacked coherent, effective plans of attack. During the prewar years carrier advocates and aviators were preoccupied with the need to "sell" their new weapon system to the service and the country. Over the years they were able to demonstrate the aircraft carrier's potential as an offensive weapon against both shore- and sea-based enemy forces. But in the process the doctrine of blind attack took precedence over the defense of either the fleet or of attacking squadrons. "It is clear from the [1941] force structure," one aviation historian has written, "and from the [various fleet exercises and] problems that the aviators intended to defend the battleship by striking the enemy—his carriers and his battleships—rather than by intercepting him in the air. Air control, for the support of the battleship, was to be primarily achieved by destroying the enemy's floating air base, not by shooting his planes down."[12] In its 1938 manual of carrier and air doctrines, the U.S. Navy asserted: "It is highly improbable that control of the air can be gained by employing aircraft to shoot down enemy aircraft. The surest and quickest means of gaining control of the air is destruction of enemy carriers . . . by bombing attacks."[13] The 1941 manual contained an identical statement. With the battle line now in ruins at Pearl, American carrier admirals could throw their air groups at enemy island installations and carriers as they saw fit.

During the island raids of February and March and in the Coral Sea in May, Halsey and Fletcher had launched entire carrier air groups at the enemy with little coordination. The results had demonstrated the shocking disparity of the various aviation weapon systems available to the fleet. Although better than their predecessors, the F4F-4 fighter planes newly deployed aboard the *Hornet* and the other carriers had serious deficiencies. They were not particularly maneuverable and could not gain altitude quickly, throttle back easily, or fly slowly. Above all, their powerful engines gulped fuel at a prodigious rate, drastically limiting their air time and range. As a result they were almost impossible to employ effectively as escorts for either dive-bombers or torpedo planes. The new Dauntless dive-bomber–scout planes were the best and most efficient naval aircraft in the U.S. arsenal, but the torpedo squadrons were still saddled with the ancient Devastators, which were not only incredibly slow but were unable to attain the cruising altitude of either the dive-bombers or the fighters. Indeed, the Devastators would soon be replaced by much more capable and maneuverable planes appropriately nicknamed "Avengers." The first half-squadron of TBF Avengers, in fact, reached Pearl Harbor under the command of Torpedo 8's executive officer, "Swede" Larsen, just hours after the *Hornet* departed. Larsen took his planes out to Midway, where they participated in its defense, but Torpedo 8 was stuck flying its original complement of Devastators.

Some Pacific Fleet fliers learned quickly from combat. One of the lessons that emerged from the Coral Sea was that if skilled, well-trained pilots performed proper tactics, the tough but inefficient F4F-3s and -4s could match the faster, more nimble, but fragile Zeros.[14] Another critical lesson was that the Devastators could survive to do their jobs only if they were heavily escorted by fighter aircraft. The *Yorktown* and *Lexington* torpedo plane squadrons had fared well in the Coral Sea, but they had benefited from favorable circumstances. The distance to the enemy fleet had been short enough to allow the F4Fs to accompany the Devastators all the way to the target and back in close, S-patterned escort. Moreover, the first Japanese carrier they had attacked (and the only one sunk) was the light carrier *Shoho*, which could muster only six Zeros for its air defense. When the Devastators had assaulted the big fleet carriers *Shokaku* and *Zuikaku* the next day, they benefited from poor visibility and a dispersed Japanese combat air patrol. Even so, the Americans lost three escorting fighters and numerous torpedo planes. The *Yorktown*'s after-action report concluded unambiguously: "It is essential that they [the Devastators] be furnished with fighter protection."[15]

But if the bulk of the F4Fs were to stay with the torpedo planes, then the Dauntless dive-bombers and their equally slow scout plane escorts would have inadequate protection. Arriving first over the main Japanese fleet on 8 May, the bombers from the *Yorktown* and *Lexington* had been mauled as they began their final dives to the target. Altogether the Americans lost forty-three fighter, bomber, and torpedo aircraft in the Coral Sea.

It was obvious to both Coral Sea participants and analysts that each carrier needed many more fighter aircraft to provide adequate defensive air patrols and enough effective escorts for both the torpedo planes and the dive-bombers. Unfortunately, little could be done immediately. War production was just getting started. There were numerous calls for planes, tanks, ships, and guns, and not every order could be filled immediately. Throughout early 1942 the Pacific Fleet carriers would have to fight primarily with what they had.

Scarcity should have dictated tactical as well as strategic planning, but in two crucial, interrelated areas it did not. First, the all-out, helter-skelter assaults by entire carrier air groups should have been modified. The assaults against the Japanese fleet in the Coral Sea had revealed a deplorable lack of coordinated effort even within a single air group. At the very least each air group should have had a master coordinator, who, while proceeding toward the target, could intelligently muster and then divide his diverse fighter, bomber, scout, and torpedo forces for maximum effect. When two or three carriers were involved, a master coordinator in the sky was even more essential. But at Midway each commander of a carrier air group—the "Sea Hag"—would perform the coordinating mission.

Second, traditional takeoff sequences should have been modified to accommodate the disparate performances and capabilities of the bombers and torpedo planes. The slow torpedo planes should have been launched first, the bombers second, and the fast, fuel-guzzling fighters last; in fact, the sequence was exactly reversed. As a result fighters and bombers wasted precious fuel slowly forming up and climbing to altitude as they awaited takeoff by the Devastators. Moreover, launching the fighters first guaranteed that ships' captains and fighter squadron commanders, such as Mitscher and Mitchell, would instinctively choose an attack configuration in which the fighters escorted the faster, higher-flying bombers, leaving the slower, low-flying torpedo planes to fly alone.

No effort was apparently made within the U.S. carrier fleet to rethink air group launch and attack patterns in the admittedly hectic days between Coral Sea and Midway. Once back at Pearl Harbor, the *Hornet*'s intelligence team attended a frantic round of conferences to acquaint everyone with information from Rochefort and his staff about Japanese intentions, but the aviators failed to plan a more efficient integration of air group operations by single carriers or to develop a coordinated plan of attack among the three carrier air groups. Instead, command changes, concentration on repairing the bomb-torn *Yorktown,* and drinking and carousing consumed everyone's attention.

As soon as Halsey reported to Nimitz, he was ordered into the hospital for treatment of a raging skin disease, the result of too much stress and exhaustion in the frantic months since Pearl Harbor. Rear Adm. Raymond Spruance, Halsey's subordinate cruiser commander, who had been in charge of the escorts during the Doolittle raid but had never had a carrier command, took over Task Force 16. Spruance naturally was concerned with coordinating the forthcoming operation with Fletcher, commander of Task Force 17. Operational and signal arrangements had to be worked out or confirmed; orders had to be written and interpreted to the mutual satisfaction of both men and their respective staffs. The *Yorktown*'s people were frantically working with the Pearl Harbor shipyard to get the carrier minimally seaworthy.

The *Hornet* had another distraction almost as soon as her special sea and anchor detail was dismissed. Mitscher learned that after thirty-eight years of service he had finally attained flag rank. His replacement, Capt. Charles Mason, promptly reported aboard. Just before a battle was no time to change command, so Mason agreed to ride along on the Midway operation as passenger and prospective commanding officer. But the change could not help but disrupt the *Hornet*'s orderly and comfortable routine. Meanwhile, hundreds of stevedores and oilers steadily worked under both sun and arc lights to reprovision and refuel the ship for a prolonged stay at sea. At the adjacent anchorage hundreds more were toiling just as diligently to prepare the *Enterprise.*

The three carrier air groups were scattered on airfields all over Oahu, from Ford Island to Kaneohe to Ewa. The *Yorktown*'s air wing had to be rebuilt, which consumed every veteran aviator's time aboard that ship. The *Enterprise* pilots, however, went ashore as soon as the ship moored and binged at the Waikiki hotels.

Stan Ring was determined that his boys would not succumb to shoreside temptations. In a burst of martinet pique he ordered the entire *Hornet* air group confined to base at Ewa. Everyone would alternate standing alerts from an hour before sunrise to an hour past sunset, just as at sea. The pilots were furious; they had expected the kind of liberty their buddies on the *Enterprise* were enjoying. Several bomber pilots practically mutinied, and Ring promptly grounded them for insubordination. Waldron, of all people, was outraged. His boys had flown and practiced long enough at sea during the past $3\frac{1}{2}$ weeks, and according to his schedule it was time to party. But Ring was obstinate. So Waldron somehow found a jeepful of booze for Torpedo 8 and got gloriously drunk on a new concoction he called a "Barbers Point Special." Returning in the early dawn to his quarters, the still furious torpedo plane commander defiantly fired off an entire .45 clip from the door. Ring was smart enough not to press the issue, but as the foremost historian of the 1942 Pacific air war noted, "the *Hornet* air group was not exactly a band of brothers" on the eve of Midway.[16]

The only airman to make any attempt to circulate new ideas about carrier aviation at this time was Lt. Comdr. John S. "Jimmy" Thach, leader of the *Yorktown*'s fighter squadron. He had had some success coordinating new fighter tactics with squadron commanders aboard the *Lexington* during the Coral Sea campaign, but he admitted years later that when the *Yorktown* returned to Pearl Harbor he had very little contact with the *Enterprise* pilots. "The *Hornet* was rather new in the Pacific, and I hadn't even seen them."[17]

Everyone on hot, sweaty Oahu that last week in May 1942 knew that something big was about to happen. Correspondent Bob Casey, just ashore from Task Force 16, discovered that Honolulu had been in a state of alert for ten days. Army pilots were standing watches in the cockpits of their planes, and rumors abounded that Japanese carriers had been sighted only a thousand miles from Hawaii. Other rumors "had it on good authority that an advance detachment of the Japanese navy, complete with carriers, battleships and transports, had been sighted off Midway."[18]

Meanwhile, Rochefort and his intelligence crew were feeding accurate information on Yamamoto's Operation MI to Fletcher and Spruance. Rochefort's operation had been routinely working around the clock during the previous month, using two to three million IBM cards to break down as many top-secret enemy messages as possible. In the last days before the Pacific Fleet left Hawaii to meet Yamamoto's forces, Rochefort recalled, "we were all chewing no-doze and junk like that, and this went on for about 48 hours at a stretch." The enemy fleet was clearly regrouping in its home anchorage for a major operation. "We were not getting daily reports from the Japanese fleet," Rochefort remembered, "but we had broken the Japanese operation order for Midway and we managed to read almost all of it."[19]

The junior officers and men of the fleet knew nothing of Ultra or decrypts or any of the other arcane jargon of intelligence and had no idea who Rochefort was or what he did. But no major secrets can be kept in a huge, sprawling organization like the American military, and everyone guessed that within hours the fleet would be back at sea to battle a largely untouched and so far victorious Japanese navy. It would be Yamamoto's veteran carriers with a dozen battleships against Nimitz's handful of cruisers and flattops: the American David versus the Japanese Goliath.

For the men of one ship the looming conflict was coming much too soon. Jim Jones, an army corporal who was enjoying his first furlough in these uncertain days while Washington and Hawaii decided what to do with the "Pineapple Army," wandered into a Waikiki bar early on the morning of 28 May to find a petty officer and two seamen from the *Yorktown* already drinking heavily. "With their sun-blackened faces and hollow haunted eyes, they were men who had already passed on into a realm I had never seen, and didn't particularly want to see." The sailors told Jones all about the Coral Sea; then the petty officer added that it wasn't the going into battle once that got to him "but the going back again and again."[20]

It was an experience the men of the *Hornet* so far had escaped. Mitscher's boys happily went back to Hotel and King Streets, where a precious bottle of American whiskey cost $25.00, but a quart of day-old imitation bourbon, made from native cane, could be bought for $3.07. For those senior enlisted men who could stay ashore past dark, the blackout was not too onerous if they were inside some dive. Blackout was a normal condition when the *Hornet* was at sea. A few respectable women—young or not so young—remained who were willing to dance once with a sailor at the USO building. But on the evening of 27 May, less than forty-eight hours after the *Hornet* had moored off Ford Island, telephones suddenly rang in officers' clubs all over Oahu, USO officials walked onto crowded dance floors, and shore patrols, policemen, even duty details off the carrier itself appeared throughout Honolulu. Their message was simple: "All liberty cancelled. Report at once to the ship."[21]

Petty officers, ensigns, and commanders piled onto already jammed trolley cars and filled the few available taxis. Some lucky men had friends with ten- or fifteen-year-old jalopies or flivvers to take them the five or ten miles out to Pearl Harbor. Soon the two gates to the big navy yard were jammed with hundreds of men in white, showing their liberty cards and rushing toward the docks where their cruisers or destroyers lay or to the landing piers, where boats from the two carriers waited to ferry crewmen back to their ships.

"The whole goddam fleet is moving!" sailors told each other.[22] That was not quite true. The *Yorktown* would remain for another day of dry-docking and liberty; then she and the rest of Task Force 17 would chase off after the *Enterprise* and *Hornet,* hoping to meet them north and east of Midway before the *Kido Butai* appeared. Most in the fleet were eager for combat; for some old-timers avenging Pearl Harbor and even the Coral Sea was an overriding factor, but the majority of the sailors and airmen simply wanted a decisive battle with the "Jap" so that the war that had disrupted everyone's life could somehow move closer to an end. If you didn't fight, you couldn't go home; it was as simple as that.

Out at Ewa on the morning of 28 May the airfield teemed with pilots and ground crewmen rolling hastily tuned-up planes out to the flight line. By midafternoon, in conformity with existing doctrine and practice, Sam Mitchell's Fighting 8 was aloft, soon followed by Bob Johnson's dive-bombers and Rodee's scouts, with impatient Jack Waldron bringing up the rear with Torpedo 8. As Johnson's Dauntlesses formed up, Gus Widhelm discovered that they were one plane short. He turned back to Ewa, where he learned that the missing aircraft belonged to Stan Ring. Widhelm landed and raced up to Ring to see what the trouble was. Ring was cursing about "a couple of fouled [fuel] plugs." Widhelm had a reputation for being able to fly aircraft that no one else could, so Ring took his plane and Widhelm tried to get the balky scout-bomber into the air. But it was impossible. Fortunately, young Ens. George Gay of Torpe-do 8 had not yet taken off. He was beginning his taxi from the flight line when Widhelm raced up, shouting, "Boy, you got a passenger." He leaped into the vacant middle seat of Gay's Devastator.[23]

Meanwhile, Task Force 16 had begun its departure from Pearl Harbor. The antisubmarine nets opened at midmorning to allow first the destroyers, then the cruisers, to slip out. Bob Casey rode the *Salt Lake City* down the harbor and out to sea. It was a cool morning, "and the calm, sleepy atmosphere was broken only by black bursts from Fort Weaver ack-ack ominously thumping off our port bow."[24] At 1130, while Jim Jones was still listening to the three sailors from the *Yorktown* tell sea stories in a Honolulu bar, the *Hornet* slipped her moorings at Ford Island "in accordance with CinCPac Operation Plan 29-42."[25] The carriers, with Spruance and Halsey's flag staff riding the *Enterprise,* were last out. Turning past Hospital Point with their prows pointing into the green seas just off Pearl, the two big flattops were off again to find war. Their hundreds of crewmen, in dungarees and white hats, stood at their stations for leaving port.

The *Hornet* under way for Midway shortly after noon, Thursday, 28 May 1942. The southern shore of Oahu is in the background. The distinctive Measure 12 Camouflage, designed to lower the ship's silhouette, thereby reducing her visibility, can be clearly seen on the *Hornet's* upper works.

By late afternoon the two ships had reached their usual recovery zones off Kauai, and the air groups began coming aboard. Gene Lindsey, commander of Torpedo Squadron 6 aboard the *Enterprise,* suffered a bruising crack-up, but there were no mishaps aboard the *Hornet.* Within minutes after the last plane touched down, Mitscher used the ship's speaker system to inform all hands that Task Force 16 was off to intercept the Japanese at Midway. Over on the *Salt Lake City* Casey wrote: "The best thought on the subject suggests that we're heading for a slugging match."[26] By supper time the two carriers were moving through Kauai Channel, course 296° True, heading toward Point "Luck," an arbitrary spot in the ocean roughly 325 miles northeast of Midway, where they would be in flank position to ambush the *Kido Butai.*

Yamamoto's plan had already begun to unravel. A man of prudence as well as calculated daring, he had dispatched submarines to the Hawaiian area to find out whether any carriers were either at or leaving Pearl Harbor. But the subs did not arrive until after the *Yorktown* had sailed. Another plan for reconnoitering Pearl from the air with flying boats, refueled from a submarine at French Frigate Shoals, had to be canceled. When the submarine arrived, it found a small American force already in control of the shoals. As the various Japanese strike and invasion forces moved under cloudy skies from the home islands and the Marianas toward Midway during the last few days of May, intelligence received aboard Yamamoto's flagship *Yamato* suggested increased naval presence and activity in the Hawaiian Islands. But Yamamoto convinced himself that the U.S. carriers remained days away in the South Pacific. He refused to compromise secrecy by sending the *Kido Butai*, which was several hundred miles ahead, a message saying essentially that he had no definitive information. Any signal strong enough to reach Nagumo's flagship, *Akagi*, might also be heard by American listening posts. He saw no reason to gratuitously alert the Americans any earlier than necessary.

Aboard the *Hornet* life took on its characteristic complexion as Task Force 16 sailed under gray skies and through stormy waters toward Point Luck. On the first morning one of Bombing 8's planes, piloted by Ens. R. D. Williman, crashed about fifteen miles from the ship while on intermediate air patrol, probably because of engine failure. "No personnel were recovered."[27] Despite the tragedy Mitscher and his senior officers were in high spirits and ready for some horseplay. In Hawaii one of the senior doctors, Comdr. Sam Osterloh, had managed to bring aboard a crate of fresh grapefruit, which he jealously kept locked in the sick bay refrigerator. Chaplain Eddie Harp and the irrepressible Waldron somehow managed to steal it during general quarters one day. Osterloh immediately suspected Harp and put him on report. Mitscher promptly convened a mock court-martial and delightedly lectured the discomfited chaplain on the ways of the wicked.

On 30 May Mitscher held captain's mast and sent two seamen to the brig for short stays on bread and water. One had accepted cash in exchange for special privileges in the ship's laundry; the other had unauthorized clothing. The latter offense was far more serious than the former, for on any vessel, big or small, especially in wartime, shipmates have to trust each other absolutely; thievery is intolerable. The offender was fortunate not to suffer more informal—and brutal—punishment inflicted by his fellow sailors.

Meanwhile, the men of the *Hornet* grimly prepared for combat. As always at sea, the crew was sent to battle stations an hour before both dawn and dusk. The ship was tightly "buttoned up" after the evening meal each day. Every hatch and watertight door was secured, and if one had to be opened, someone made sure it was tightly secured once used. The air below decks soon became stale as the exhalations of twenty-six hundred men mixed with the fumes from engine room, torpedo shop, and photographer's shack. The air department was busy checking landing gear and arresting wires, making sure that ammunition hoists worked properly, that torpedo hoists functioned, and that aircraft spotting positions were well known to everyone. Usually the *Hornet* sent up at least four Dauntlesses, each armed with 250-pound bombs, every two to three hours during daylight hours to patrol for submarines out ahead of the destroyers. With most of the ship's aircraft on the flight deck in case of emergency, even the launch and recovery of so few planes meant that the several hundred blue-shirted plane pushers, red-shirted ordnancemen, and yellow-shirted plane directors were busy almost constantly, arming, pushing, and hauling Wildcats, Dauntlesses, and Devastators fore and aft of the big amidships crash barrier.

Steaming in tight battle formation provided invaluable opportunities for the *Hornet*'s junior officers, both ship's company and air group, to stand deck watches and learn the craft of seamanship, an essential prerequisite to eventual command. The weather steadily deteriorated on the way north and west.[28] Spruance over on the *Enterprise* shifted course and formation several times en route to the battle area. Task Force 16 maintained course 296° True until 31 May, when course was changed to 290° True and maintained until Point Luck was reached the next day. "Yesterday we were in a standard cruising formation. The oilers tagged behind," one *Hornet* pilot noted. "Today we are broken up almost into two forces, with the [*Enterprise*] group up ahead."[29]

Hundreds of enlisted men below decks prepared for battle by donning undershirts, which had been discarded in tropical and subtropical weather. Then they layered themselves in other work uniform clothing, buttoning sleeves at the wrists despite the sacrifice in comfort. They had learned from Pearl Harbor survivors what flash burns could do to a man and that the best protection was heavy clothing. Once Point Luck was reached, benches and tables were stowed away in the overhead areas of the messing compartments to minimize flying splinters from bomb or shell explosions below decks. Mattresses were readied so that they could be quickly piled together to localize outbreaks of fire or used to help shore up heavy plates below the waterline that might be sprung by torpedo hits or near misses from bombs.

Commander Henry Moran, whose duties as first lieutenant included responsibility for damage control, walked through the ship with phones on his head, trailing a long telephone wire and plug-in cord. He checked and rechecked every damage control station, ensuring that everyone knew his job, that foamite and sprinkling systems were ready, and that valves and lock-off apparatus in each watertight compartment were working smoothly. Down in the *Hornet*'s big galley, cooks and mess attendants continued to prepare hot food as long as regular meal hours were observed; after the benches and tables were cleared and secured, they began fixing setups for sandwiches and cold snacks and making sure that the "Joe pots" were ready to brew hundreds of gallons of essential hot coffee. Most of the cooks had battle stations elsewhere in the ship. When the *Hornet* spent hours at general quarters, designated messengers from bridge, gun galleries, hangar deck, engineering spaces, and damage control stations would come to the mess decks to get the food setups for their mates.

Aft of the galley in the sick bay and in seven battle dressing stations throughout the ship, Sam Osterloh, Gerald McAteer, and more than twenty doctors, hospital corpsmen, and pharmacist's mates made ready, checking surgical instruments and operating equipment. Once again crewmen appeared with various knickknacks and presents and the reminder to "remember me" when the wounded began to appear.

Up on the gallery decks that ringed the flight deck, Jim Smith's gunnery crews checked ammunition, gave swivels and loading devices one more practice twist, let off a few more bursts from the 1.1 Oerlikons and the 20-millimeter heavy machine guns, and made sure that everything was ready to go. And in a small, cramped compartment in the island, Steve Jurika, communications officer Oscar Dodson, and Dodson's assistant, Henry Martin, carefully read and assessed top secret intelligence messages from Rochefort and Spruance.

On the night of 30 May the *Hornet* received a CinCPac intelligence report "giving an accurate estimation of the Japanese Midway force organization,"[30] which was undoubtedly transmitted by Spruance aboard the *Enterprise*. It was the last such report that Rochefort and his cryptanalysts in their cellar beneath the Fourteenth Naval District Headquarters at Pearl Harbor could provide, for on 1 June the Imperial Fleet made a routine change of its codebooks; it would be days if not weeks before the new Japanese code could be broken. But Nimitz, Spruance, Fletcher, and now Mitscher and his fliers had all the information they needed to plan a naval ambush even more devastating than Pearl Harbor. Gilven Slonim had climbed aboard the *Enterprise* just as it was about to sail from Pearl Harbor. The young lieutenant had been with Rochefort for many weeks; now he was the liaison officer between Rochefort and Spruance. Slonim carried aboard with him "two packets Rochefort had prepared for Spruance containing not just an analysis of Japanese radio traffic but every single message about Midway that he'd received." Decades later Slonim recalled: "We knew the forces coming, their commanders, their intentions and their intended arrival time." The prebattle intelligence available to U.S. commanders at Midway "was probably the best ever enjoyed in the history of naval warfare."[31]

Nimitz had written the ten-page Operation Plan 29-42 with this intelligence firmly in mind. The plan directed Spruance and Fletcher to be "governed by the principle of calculated risk" and to avoid exposing their force to an attack by superior enemy forces "without the prospect of inflicting, as a result of such exposure, greater damage to the enemy." Lying in ambush on the *Kido Butai*'s left flank, Task Forces 16 and 17 would ensure maximum Japanese losses "by employing strong attrition tactics."[32] In 1951 Spruance remembered his interpretation of the plan: "All that I can claim credit for, myself, is a very keen sense of the urgent need for surprise and a strong desire to hit the enemy carriers with our full strength as early as we could reach them."[33] In other words, Midway would be a replication of the Coral Sea. Once again U.S. air groups would attack the enemy with full force. How they would attack and with what degree of coherence and effectiveness remained up to the individual air group commanders and the ships' commanding officers.

On the evening of 1 June, with Task Force 16 still steaming through foggy, cool weather, an unnamed "senior officer" aboard the *Hornet*, possibly Jurika or perhaps even Mitscher, summoned all pilots and enlisted flight crew to a rare meeting in the wardroom "for an explanation of our strategical situation." According to a flier who was present, the officer assured everybody that Midway was well garrisoned with patrol planes, which were searching the adjacent seas and skies minute by minute, heavy and light bombers, and even some torpedo planes and fighters. This small but powerful air force, it was hoped, would give the approaching *Kido Butai* and the invasion fleet all they could handle. Spruance and Fletcher hoped to launch the air power from Task Forces 16 and 17 as the planes from the Japanese carriers were raiding Midway to ensure that few if any Zeros would be around the carriers for combat air patrol. "Without air protection, the Jap fleet will look like a lot of wet ducks for our fliers. If we knock the carriers out the Jap planes are through as soon as they run out of gas. Then we proceed to demolish the remainder of their fleet—first the striking force, and then the other groups."[34]

The next afternoon, 2 June, Stan Ring convened a conference of squadron commanders to review Air Group 8's tactics in the impending battle. What they said may never be known for certain, but two members of Torpedo 8, Fred Mears and Tex Gay, later recounted Waldron's version of the meeting. Mears would never fly a mission at Midway. He had been on the *Hornet* briefly for carrier qualifications off San Diego the previous March. Now the vagaries of war had brought this rather foot-loose aviator to Torpedo 8 as a backup pilot. Waldron was not especially happy to see the young man and his colleague, Ens. Robert Divine, who had reported aboard the *Hornet* the night before she sailed from Hawaii. Waldron was undoubtedly upset over the prospect of having to incorporate two rookie fliers into his tightly knit squadron. He at first told the youngsters brusquely that they would not fly at all during the forthcoming battle. Later he relented, half-promising them that they might get a plane for the expected third raid on the Japanese fleet.

According to Mears, Waldron told the Torpedo 8 pilots on 2 June that they would make their first attack in the early morning of the battle day and then would return to launch a second attack from the *Hornet* at about 1100. "As many attacks as possible will be made during the day, and then after dark Waldron hopes to make another surprise sally, if he can persuade the command it is feasible. His theory is that the enemy will be in one hell of a mess after the day attacks, with their morale low and confusion rampant. Several ships probably will be on fire to serve as a beacon for our planes. If we can hit them again at night before they can rally it will make them that much more punch drunk the next day."[35]

Young George Gay remembered Waldron saying much more. Waldron reminded his boys that their planes were old and "could not climb [to] the altitude with the dive bombers or fighters and we expected to be on our own." Gay remembered also that the squadron "didn't expect to run into the trouble that we found of course, but we knew that if we had any trouble we'd probably have to fight our way out of it ourselves. Before we left the ship," Gay continued, "Lt. Comdr. Waldron told us that he thought the Japanese Task Forces would swing together when they found out that our Navy was there and that they would either make a retirement . . . just far enough so that they could again retrieve their planes that went in on the [Midway softening-up] attack and he did not think [the *Kido Butai* would] go on into the Island of Midway as most of the Squadron commanders and air group commanders figured, and he told us when we left [on the attack] not to worry about our navigation but to follow him as he knew where he was going."[36]

Waldron thus gave the impression of a determined maverick who mistrusted the judgment of Stan Ring, Sam Mitchell, or, if Gay's report is correct, any other squadron or air group commander in either Task Force 16 or 17. But Henry Martin, who knew him well, insists that Waldron had great respect for authority and would not flaunt it.[37] Whether Waldron shared with his fellow squadron commanders his intuition about what Nagumo and the *Kido Butai* might do can never be known. If he did, Mitscher, Ring, Mitchell, and Rodee obviously discounted it. Moreover, Ring apparently never questioned traditional launch practices that would send the fighters aloft first, followed by the bombers, leaving the torpedo planes to bring up the rear, flying slowly and alone. If Waldron challenged launch orthodoxy and Ring insisted on it, then Waldron's subsequent behavior in taking his squadron off by itself on the morning of 4 June can be interpreted more as resignation than arrogance.

Certainly some squadron commanders in Task Force 16 were trying to find ways to cope with the extreme performance disparities between the Wildcats and the Devastators. Over on the *Enterprise,* Fighting 6's leader, Lt. Jim Gray, and representatives from Torpedo 6 agreed that Gray would keep his F4F-4s at a high altitude, which was essential to preserve the advantage he needed over the much more agile Zeros, while providing cover for the Dauntless bombers. The torpedo planes would noodle along at their customary 1,500-foot altitude and 100-knot speed. But fighters and bombers would at least try to avoid flying out of sight of the torpedo planes. If Torpedo 6 was assaulted by Zeros, Lt. Art Ely, the squadron's operations officer, would simply call out, "Come on down, Jim," and Gray's fighters would dive to his aid.[38]

There is no indication that Waldron, Ring, and Mitchell ever tried to formulate such a plan. Torpedo 8 would be stubbornly, proudly on its own, in conformity with existing doctrines for carrier air groups. Whether this would be a suicidal gesture or a great tactical coup depended solely on luck. If American aircraft could find the *Kido Butai* while its planes were still busy blasting Midway to prepare for the invasion and if

Nagumo had foolishly stripped his carriers of protecting Zeros to ensure a successful Midway assault, then the lack of fighter protection for the torpedo planes would be unimportant. But if timing went awry and the *Kido Butai* was able to mount a powerful combat air patrol, Torpedo 8 would be doomed.

As with the charge of the Light Brigade, Waldron's proposed approach to battle might be magnificent, but it would not be war. In fact, if Waldron's impulsive action failed, it would be a criminal waste of both valuable weapon systems and irreplaceable pilots. Even before Pearl Harbor torpedoes were known to be the most deadly enemies of surface ships. The war in the Pacific decisively proved this. The only American carrier lost exclusively to bombs was the light carrier *Princeton* in 1944. The Japanese carriers that would fall to bombs at Midway were at their most vulnerable, with fully armed and fueled aircraft lined up on flight and hangar decks. Every other U.S. carrier lost in the Pacific and most of the Japanese flattops lost after Midway suffered torpedo damage. As the experience of the *Saratoga* had already shown, even a single torpedo could put a carrier out of action for months. But unless Waldron was fantastically lucky in finding the *Kido Butai* at just the right moment, he and his men would be wasted for no good purpose.

Shortly after the air group conference aboard the *Hornet* at Point Luck, Fletcher's Task Force 17, including the battered but indefatigable *Yorktown*, appeared over the horizon, and Fletcher immediately assumed overall command of the combined task forces. For the first and only time in their collectively brief lives, all three ships of the *Yorktown* class would be in battle together. They carried a total of about 220 operational fighters, bombers, and torpedo planes. Aboard the *Hornet* alone there were 27 Wildcats, 35 Dauntlesses, and 15 Devastators. The two task forces remained about ten miles apart, usually within visual contact under generally gray skies. The *Hornet* and *Enterprise* had passed this way only weeks before on the way to and from Tokyo.

As Spruance, Fletcher, and their staffs continued to receive top secret messages, the *Hornet*'s intelligence officers became uneasy. Their carrier was the only one without a flag officer aboard. Consequently the ship had not been issued a class five cryptographic allowance, which would permit them to immediately read the radio traffic from Pearl Harbor to the *Enterprise* and *Yorktown*. Moreover, the *Hornet* could not transmit vital battle information to her sister carriers by code once the enemy was found. So far there was no problem because the ships were in visual range of each other. A report of Japanese reconnaissance aircraft northwest of Midway on 31 May was quickly transmitted from the *Enterprise* to the *Hornet*. But if the three carriers became separated before or during battle while maintaining radio silence, critical information could only be transmitted to the *Hornet*, if at all, by the laborious and time-consuming method of semaphore.

Tense, ready, apprehensive, but confident, the men of Task Forces 16 and 17 approached the greatest battle of their lives. Just before 0900 on Wednesday, 3 June, the *Yorktown*, steaming through choppy, gray seas, picked up an unknown air contact at 045° True, and the *Hornet* went to general quarters and prepared to launch a combat patrol. But the "bogey" proved to be false, and the combined task forces went back to peaceful steaming around Point Luck. In the early afternoon Spruance and Fletcher received reports of a small Japanese raid on Dutch Harbor. Shortly thereafter a long-range patrol plane out of Midway sent word of a Japanese force sighted seven hundred miles southwest of the island and apparently inbound. This was the invasion force of transports and escorting battleships, cruisers, and destroyers that had sailed from Guam and Saipan in the Marianas a few days before. Some of the more cocky soldiers aboard the transports had already asked their postal officers to forward all personal mail to "Fortress Midway."

Intelligence had done its work; the Japanese were obviously on their way, although the precise location of the *Kido Butai* and Yamamoto's support force of battleships coming down from the northwest had not been determined. Both sides continued to enjoy sanctuary under a mass of heavy clouds. But the transports did not dare approach Midway without a preliminary air strike from Nagumo's carriers. The next day would obviously bring battle. Restlessly pacing the flight deck of the *Enterprise*, Spruance told Slonim that since there had been no unusual Japanese radio traffic, he could assume that submarines had not spotted the American force. The ambush still held. Slonim remarked years later that Spruance "knew that with such a flimsy force it was essential that he have the element of surprise and that he hit first, and hit hardest, with everything he had."[39]

That night on the *Hornet* everyone was keyed up. The next day the ship and its air group would have its first combat. Poker games sprouted all over officers' country and in various enlisted berthing compartments throughout the ship. Some of the pilots, like George Gay, had trouble sleeping. Others seemed relaxed. Mears, looking in on his mates in

Ensign Teats's room, found that "they picked up their cards and threw their chips as they always did, some recklessly, some conservatively. They were easy in mind." Abbie Abercrombie listened with delight to Jimmie Owens, Whitey Moore, and "Squire" Bill Evans squeal as he relieved them of $45. But the game broke up early.[40]

Big Jack Gray got tired of the poker games and of watching his roommate carefully carve a beautiful koa-wood fruit bowl. He took some of his classical records down to Gus Widhelm's cabin. Widhelm, who had decided not to test his luck with poker (he later claimed that he had lost nearly a thousand dollars the previous three nights, which had sufficiently primed his luck), was writing a letter and let out a yelp of complaint when the first strains of Wagner invaded his tiny compartment. "Gus, I fear you have no appreciation of the classics," Gray protested. Not true, Widhelm replied. He liked the classics fine; it was Wagner he could not stand. Gray quickly switched to Glenn Miller, and Widhelm was appeased. Back in the four-man cabin that Gray shared, Moose Moore nodded, half-asleep, over a four-month-old Western pulp magazine. Rusty Kenyon was working on some 20-millimeter cartridge cases, which he was making into a set of dresser lamps for his new wife. Glancing at the shoot-'em-up cover in Moore's hand, he asked his mate why he read such drivel. "Excitement," Moore drawled.[41] Soon the lights were out in every cabin and bunk room in officers' country.

Minutes after Thursday, 4 June 1942, began north and east of Midway, men on the *Hornet* and the other vessels of the combined American task force awoke. Little more than two hundred miles away to the west, those of the *Kido Butai* did the same. Two hundred sixty-one fighters, dive-bombers, and torpedo planes were on the flight or hangar decks of the *Akagi*, *Kaga*, *Soryu*, and *Hiryu*. The Americans were outmanned by about forty aircraft and confronted with some of the finest, most experienced combat pilots in the world.

Fliers aboard the *Hornet* were in their ready rooms by 0330, drowsing and waiting for something to happen. On the flight and hangar decks the air department soon was busy arming planes with bombs, torpedoes, and machine-gun bullets. Over on the *Yorktown* Fletcher decided that he would use his damaged carrier for scout and secondary assault duties, relying on the *Enterprise* and *Hornet* to make the initial strikes. At 0430 the *Yorktown* dispatched ten planes to search for the *Kido Butai* in a broad arc northwest of Midway. At precisely the same time Nagumo began launching the first of a 108-plane assault force against Midway. It was timed to hit the island just at dawn, two hours later. Everyone aboard the four

A typical aircraft carrier ready room on the eve of battle during World War II.

Japanese carriers and their supporting vessels hoped and assumed that one shattering, unexpected blow against the sleeping Americans on the small atoll would be enough. But Midway was not sleeping at all. At 0400 the first marine combat air patrol had flown off its runway, while out in the lagoon eleven heavy PBY patrol planes were skimming off the water and into the skies on long-range search flights.

Between 0500 and 0600 Torpedo 8's pilots in their ready room began to stir from their lethargy. The teleprinter screen informed everyone that during the previous day and night army bombers and navy PBYs had spotted a Japanese invasion force southwest of Midway that apparently included a carrier as well as battleships. This news snapped everyone awake. Quiet, reserved Rusty Kenyon suddenly began to tell limericks, and after a while even Waldron leaned back to listen:

> There was a young girl from Madras
> Who had a beautiful ass,
> Not rounded and pink,
> As you probably think,
> But with long ears, a tail, and eats grass.[42]

Kenyon joked on while everyone nervously waited for more news.

Off to the west the *Kido Butai* was experiencing an interesting early morning as it steamed closer to Midway. While ordnancemen were placing torpedoes and armor-piercing bombs on the remaining strike aircraft in case an unexpected enemy naval force was sighted, word reached the flagship *Akagi* at 0630 that the Japanese strike force had arrived over the island. For the next half hour flight leader Lt. Joichi Tomonaga and his men roared over the two small atolls, bombing and strafing, subjecting Midway to a savage pounding.

But this was no replication of Pearl Harbor. The defenders were awake and hopping mad. Radar had picked up the incoming attack formations at 93 miles, altitude 11,000 feet. Twenty-six aircraft, most of them obsolete Brewster Buffalo fighter planes but also a handful of brand-new F4F-4 Wildcats, met the invaders miles from the island. The Zeros brushed aside the Americans, downing most of them, but as the Japanese planes swept across Midway antiaircraft guns began blazing away. Immediate post-battle reports from the island claimed at least fifty enemy aircraft destroyed; even some recent accounts of the Pacific war state that Tomonaga lost thirty-six aircraft and that another thirty were so badly damaged that, although they were able to limp back to their carriers, they could not fly again. In fact, by the time Tomonaga and his mates departed at 0700, only six Japanese aircraft had not formed up for the return flight. But the Midway garrison had done its work. The slow old fighters and the angry marine gunners had thrown off the enemy bombing runs. Tomonaga had to radio Nagumo that a second attack against Midway would be needed.

Nagumo and Genda suddenly faced the cruel tactical-strategic dilemma inherent in the dual mission of the *Kido Butai*. If Midway had conveniently shattered under Tomonaga's bombs and bullets, the Japanese strike force would have been ready for any riposte by the U.S. fleet. But a second air raid against the island required rearming the bombers and torpedo planes on the Japanese carrier decks with high explosives. Did Nagumo and Genda dare take that risk, which would strip their force of all antiship strike capability, when they did not know whether any American carriers were in the area? Genda, recovering from an appendectomy, was still frail physically and probably not sharp mentally as well. A charismatic figure with an incisive intellect, he was not at his best during this crucial moment in Japan's quest for dominance in the Pacific.[43]

At 0500 the cruiser *Tone* had launched a scout plane to search a broad arc from northeast to southeast for whatever elements of the U.S. fleet might be lurking about. Almost immediately the pilot had reported an enemy submarine eighty miles from the rapidly steaming Japanese strike force. That was no great problem and seemed of little importance. At 0555 the scout reported that fifteen unknown aircraft were heading toward the *Kido Butai*. Nagumo sent fighters aloft from all ships, but the phantom planes, probably some of the scouts Fletcher had launched from the *Yorktown*, never appeared. Soon real aircraft, however, did arrive over the *Kido Butai*—a ragtag collection of high- and low-level bombers, torpedo planes, and even fighters from Midway.

Incredibly, the *Kido Butai* had no radar. Japanese technology lagged so far behind in this crucial new aspect of war that only two battleships, *Ise* and *Hyuga*, possessed even crude sets, and these two ships had been sent north with the Aleutians assault force. "As a result," one electronics expert has written, "Japanese fighter direction at Midway depended upon visual detection of U.S. aircraft, and visual signals to direct Japanese combat air patrols. The Japanese deployed their ships in dispersed formations to extend their visual detection range, and screening ships were forced to alert defending fighters by firing their heavy-caliber guns in the direction of approaching enemy aircraft." Without radar, Nagumo's fighters and gunners had no way of knowing the exact location of an enemy attack formation. Slow-flying Devastators coming in over the wave tops with the sun shining on them could be picked up visually, and gunners in the *Kido Butai* screen and the combat air patrol could easily destroy them. But if the Americans came in high out of a partially cloudy or sunny sky, Nagumo's defenders would be blind.[44]

Midway's gallant torpedo planes and high-level bombers harassed and distracted Nagumo's carriers, battleships, and supporting vessels for the next several hours. The determined American torpedo assaults were shot to pieces one by one without any damage to the Japanese, while Nagumo and his people simply ignored the B-17s, reasoning correctly that it was impossible to bomb fast-moving and nimbly maneuvering warships from twenty thousand feet. But the attacks confirmed Tomonaga's assertion that Midway must be hit again. Because no enemy warships had been sighted, Nagumo and Genda took a gamble and ordered that the torpedo planes and bombers aboard the four carriers be removed to the hangar decks below so they could be rearmed for a second raid on Midway.

At 0728, as American planes continued to buzz around the *Kido Butai*, the *Tone* scout pilot sent a heart-stopping message: "Ten ships, apparently enemy, sighted. Bearing 010°, distance 240 miles from Midway. Course 150°, speed more than 20 knots."[45] Who were these intruders?

They could not be Japanese, because the *Kido Butai* represented the easternmost tip of the Japanese assault fleet. They had to be American. Did they include a carrier? The tactical-strategic vise began to close tightly around Nagumo. What should he do? The admiral immediately ordered the scout to maintain contact and ascertain the composition of the small American force. As the *Kido Butai* continued to beat off sporadic air assaults from Midway, the *Tone* scout was silent for many minutes. Then at around 0808 he sent another message. The enemy force seemed to consist of five cruisers and five destroyers. Nagumo and Genda were relieved but remained suspicious. Why would such a weak force, helpless against determined air attack, be steaming so close to a major battle area?

At 0820 Nagumo was handed a flimsy message from the *Akagi*'s radio shack that gave him his answer: "Enemy force accompanied by what appears to be aircraft carrier bringing up the rear."[46] The report could not have come at a worse time. As the last of the Americans were being driven off, the first of Tomonaga's planes from Midway began to appear over the *Kido Butai*. A few were badly damaged; many others were low on fuel. Some of the finest pilots in the Imperial Japanese Navy were flying them. It was critical to get the planes and their irreplaceable men aboard as quickly as possible.

Nagumo did not hesitate. He swiftly issued a series of brief orders. The *Soryu* would send off one of her fast, experimental search aircraft to confirm what the *Tone* scout had seen. Soon thereafter the cruiser *Chikuma* was ordered to send one of her scouts on the same mission. Meanwhile, the *Kido Butai* would retire back along its northwesterly track to recover the Midway strike force. This would give the ordnancemen down in the carrier hangar decks time to switch weapons again, reloading the torpedo planes with torpedoes and the bombers with armor-piercing projectiles. Once this had been done, the *Kido Butai* would again be a coherent attack force that could seek out and destroy the small American fleet. But the transition would take time. Nagumo estimated that the *Akagi* and *Kaga* would be ready to launch torpedo and bomber strikes against the Americans around 1030; the *Soryu* and *Hiryu* would follow half an hour later. Down in the hangar decks of the four carriers, "crews sweating in their short-sleeved tropical shirts and shorts were unloading the 800-kilogram bombs, piling them helter-skelter near the hangar instead of taking the time to return the missiles to the magazine."[47]

The inherent foolishness of the Midway assault plan, excellent American intelligence, and the gallantry of the island's soldiers and airmen had succeeded in placing Japan's premier striking force in a potentially fatal situation. Now it was up to Spruance, Fletcher, and the airmen aboard the *Enterprise, Yorktown,* and *Hornet* to transform opportunity into victory.

The day broke strangely over the U.S. fleet. On the *Salt Lake City,* Bob Casey "looked out at a clotted sky, a black sea and odd gray moonlight." If there was such a thing as a special battle-day atmosphere, Casey thought, this was it.[48] At 0534 the *Enterprise* received the first report of a Japanese carrier from one of the Midway-based PBYs. Fletcher hesitated. The *Yorktown* still had its search flight in the skies, and the Japanese strike force would surely comprise more than one flattop. At the Coral Sea Fletcher had precipitously thrown both his air groups against an enemy light carrier, surrendering concealment and tactical initiative in the process; he did not want to make the same mistake again. At 0603 the *Enterprise* finally received from Midway a reasonably accurate report of the Japanese position and strength, and Fletcher hesitated no longer. The *Yorktown* would have to wait and recover its search flight, which was now returning. But Task Force 16 should attack immediately. After brief consideration Spruance concurred. He had wanted to move within one hundred miles of Nagumo to ensure that his fighters would have enough fuel to escort the strike and return. The Japanese were estimated to be 150 to 175 miles to the west-southwest, a dangerously long distance. But the need to strike first and hard was paramount. He ordered the *Enterprise* and *Hornet* to launch at once.

The *Hornet* had maintained a combat air patrol since half an hour before sunrise. Mitscher and Mitchell concluded that since enemy carriers were within range, not even half of Fighting 8 should be designated as attack escorts; the rest would protect the carrier. Only ten Wildcats would accompany the strike force. Evidently Mitscher and his squadron commanders accepted the doctrine in the 1941 carrier manual, which maintained that it was "highly improbable" that carrier airplanes could shoot down a significant number of enemy airplanes. Better to strongly defend the fleet and hope for the best than to disperse the fighters so widely that they could not be expected to shoot down any enemy aircraft.[49]

As was customary, the fighters would launch first, followed by the Dauntless bombers, with Torpedo 8 bringing up the rear behind and far below the rest of the assault force. The wind would be "an unfortunate aerological feature of the day's action," blowing at barely four knots and directly away from Nagumo's reported position. In his after-action report Mitscher noted that launch and recovery operations "were being conducted almost continually on a generally easterly heading and at high speed" in order to produce sufficient wind across the flight deck. Every time the *Hornet*'s combat air patrol was relieved or a forced landing was recovered on that busy day, "our attack planes had a longer run back to the ship and increased the distance between this force and the enemy."[50] The chances of a pilot returning safely to the ship would diminish with every minute in the air.

Shortly before 0730 Bob Casey watched the fleet break out of the light fog banks that had enveloped it for much of the past several days "and into a region of brilliant sky and glowing blue sea."[51] Over on the *Hornet*, where most of the pilots and flight crews were in their planes, Mitscher convened a quick meeting on the bridge with his squadron commanders. Navigator Frank Akers was there and probably Executive Officer George Henderson and Air Officer Apollo Soucek. According to the *Hornet* after-action report, the latest enemy position reported by Spruance on the *Enterprise*, based on a recent Midway plane sighting, was southwest, 239° True, distance 155 miles from the base course of Task Force 16. Mitscher, Ring, Mitchell, and Rodee, however, apparently decided that the *Hornet*'s fighters and bombers should fly on a westerly course, 265° True, since Spruance had ordered a search-attack procedure, indicating that he and Fletcher were not sure that all the Japanese carriers had been sighted. Mitscher and his air group commanders may have decided that the *Enterprise* air group could handle the two sighted carriers, whereas the *Hornet* would look for other enemy carriers a bit farther away from Midway. Waldron, who apparently disagreed with this decision, was determined to fly course 240° True.[52]

Either in the presence of the others or alone with Mitscher, Waldron told his captain that Torpedo 8 was ready and as well trained as any squadron in the world, "and that he would strike his blow at the enemy regardless of consequences." Mitscher later added that Waldron clearly understood "that there was the possibility that his squadron was doomed to destruction with no chance whatever of returning safely to the carrier." The young pilots of Torpedo 8 "asked only that they be allowed to share in the dangers and disastrous fate sure to follow such an attack."[53] Frank Akers later told writer Alexander T. Griffin that Waldron's "lean face [was] in repose now that the moment was almost here." The torpedo commander said, "Goodbye, Frank. . . . I'll take them in. You can count on us."[54]

Although it can never be known exactly what was in Waldron's mind, he may have been preoccupied with the necessity of attacking the enemy fleet while most of its planes were still engaged in the Midway assault. Only in that way would there be any hope of saving even a remnant of Torpedo 8, since Mitscher, Ring, Mitchell, Rodee, and Johnson had no intention of changing launch sequences or escort procedures to offer the squadron even minimal protection.

Mitchell lifted his Wildcat off the *Hornet's* deck just after 0700, followed by Rodee's Scouting 8 and Johnson's Bombing 8. There were thirty-four Dauntlesses in all, carrying 1,000- and 500-pound bombs.[55] Air Group Commander Stan Ring flew with Bombing 8. The *Hornet's* increasingly efficient launch team had the planes off in less than half an hour, and the air department promptly brought Waldron's Devastators up from the hangar deck. As Ring, Mitchell, and the others circled overhead, slowly gaining altitude and gobbling fuel, the torpedo planes soared off the *Hornet's* deck. By 0742 the carrier's flight deck was empty. So were the stomachs and hearts of the flight deck crew, who experienced the first of several battle-day letdowns once the entire air group was launched and they had nothing to do until the CAP had to be relieved.[56] Four minutes later, with Waldron's boys in flight position at only three hundred feet, Air Group 8 set off toward the distant Japanese. On the nearby *Salt Lake City*, Bob Casey and five hundred others on the cruiser's decks and upper works stood motionless, "each man prayerful after his fashion as the planes go quickly out of sight off our starboard quarter. . . . It would seem that the carriers are sending up all they've got. . . . Over the top and God bless!"[57]

For the first thirty minutes or so Air Group 8 maintained contact on the agreed heading, 265° True. The fighters and bombers climbed high above Torpedo 8. Then some of the fighter and bomber pilots saw Johnnie Waldron far below slowly swing his torpedo squadron off to the southwest, and it was soon lost to sight beneath the scattered cloud cover. For the next hour and a half the fighters and bombers droned on through empty, cloud-flecked skies, vainly searching the blue sea for the wakes of enemy ships.

It was at roughly this time that communication breakdowns began to add to the normal "fog of war." Planes from Midway were still harassing the *Kido Butai*, and the submarine *Nautilus* was also stalking the Japanese vessels. But air operations and communications officers in the task force, including Lt. Comdr. J. G. Foster, Jr., of the *Hornet*, later complained bitterly that Nagumo's course change had not been reported to the

American fleet. Spruance and others agreed that they received no signals about the position of the Japanese fleet from the time it was first reported until the *Enterprise* air group reached it two hours later. But the *Hornet* battle report states that "about one hour after the planes had departed, the enemy reversed his course and started his retirement. We did not break radio silence to report this to the planes."[58]

Where did this course change message come from? The immediate assumption would be from one of the Midway aircraft assaulting the *Kido Butai*. But Henry Martin told this author in 1994 that Waldron sent a message back to the ship, stating that he had so far found empty seas and was heading north along a course he believed would take him to the retreating enemy fleet.[59] Was this the message that the *Hornet* received? Or did the ship's battle report refer to a second, later message from Waldron reporting the exact position of Nagumo's carriers? Regardless of the source, some kind of sighting information apparently reached the *Hornet*, but not Spruance and Fletcher. Why did Mitscher refuse to transmit what he knew to his superiors? If the message came from Waldron, Mitscher could not assume that it had been picked up by either the *Enterprise* or *Yorktown*.

Historian Gordon W. Prange has strongly criticized Mitscher's decision not to transmit the sighting message, thereby dooming several squadrons and probably saving a number of Japanese ships.[60] But the mixup may have a simple explanation. Mitscher may not have dared to transmit an uncoded enemy sighting message to either his own squadrons or to Spruance and Fletcher. No one knew that the *Tone*'s scout plane had spotted the U.S. fleet. With enemy carriers close enough to pick up any powerful radio signals within the American fleet and between the fleet and its airborne squadrons, only Spruance or Fletcher could make the momentous decision to break radio silence. The *Yorktown* and possibly the *Enterprise* were too far away to contact by using either the low-powered TBS (Talk between Ships) circuit or semaphore. The only secure way to transmit such a highly classified message was through the class five cryptographic code, which the *Hornet* did not possess. Unable to communicate with his superiors, Mitscher must have concluded with anguish that all he could do was hope that the American fliers possessed the initiative and resourcefulness to somehow locate the enemy fleet on its new course.

Ring formed his composite group of Wildcats and Dauntlesses into a scouting line with him in the center setting course and speed. Although this formation broadened the search pattern, it also consumed more fuel as each pilot constantly shifted and adjusted his throttle to maintain an even line. Shortly after 0900, about 160 miles out from the carrier, one of the junior pilots in Fighting 8 began to fret over a steadily descending fuel gauge. Breaking formation, he flew over to Mitchell's wing, used hand signals to indicate his concern, and finally convinced Mitchell that it was time to turn back. Fighting 8 had gone as far as it could or would. The Wildcats abruptly broke formation and turned east toward the *Hornet*. Soon they became separated into two formations and lost discipline, flying at increasingly wide intervals as each man tried to conserve fuel. Homing instruments failed to work properly, and the squadron had taken off from the ship so quickly that most of the pilots did not have detailed information about Task Force 16's proposed steaming schedule. As a result, Fighting 8 flew just south of the task force. The pilots spotted ships' wakes (but not the ships themselves), which they erroneously identified as the Japanese fleet. Shortly after 1000 all had ditched either in pairs or in threes in widely separated areas northeast of Midway. Eight of the ten men were eventually plucked from the water, but their rescue was complicated because search planes assumed that the squadron had been lost northwest of the island.

With the fighter escort gone, Stan Ring maintained Scouting 8 and Bombing 8 resolutely on course 265° True. The sea remained empty. The *Kido Butai* was not anywhere near its previously reported position. Ring flew on grimly. When the planes were 225 miles out, with fuel levels dangerously low, the pilots apparently panicked and broke into two formations. Ring and his group, comprising primarily elements from Scouting 8, including Walt Rodee, turned south on a dogleg. If Ring had maintained course, he would have soon been over the enemy. But with fuel gauges proclaiming disaster, Ring abruptly brought his men to an easterly course and headed back to the *Hornet*. He thus flew just north of the *Kido Butai*. The other group, primarily composed of bombers and led by Bob Johnson, flew much farther south than Ring and then made a beeline for Midway. This course brought them just south of the *Kido Butai*. They, too, failed to sight the Japanese.

If the *Hornet*'s scout and bomber pilots had concentrated as much on finding the Japanese as on finding sanctuary, they might have been successful. For shortly before Bob Johnson turned his bombers toward Midway, Leroy Quillen, an aviation radioman second class riding with Ens. K. B. White, picked up the faint voice of John Waldron describing the fate of Torpedo 8: "Johnny One to Johnny Two. . . . How'm I doing, Dobbs? . . . Attack immediately! . . . I'd give a million to know who done that. . . . There's two fighters in the water. . . . My two wingmen are going in the water." Then silence.[61] Incredibly, either Quillen did not inform his pilot, or White did not pass the message to Bob Johnson.

Nearly all the bombers made it to Midway, including the one piloted by White, who had hosted Ted Lawson when the Doolittle fliers were aboard the *Hornet*. One pilot crashed far out at sea and was rescued days later. Another pancaked into the water only ten miles from the island. Upon reaching Midway the survivors jettisoned their bombs in the lagoon as a friendly gesture, but the defenders thought they were under attack and opened fire. Johnson and his mates barely made it onto the runway. Ring, seventeen planes of Scouting 8, and three bombers droned on toward the *Hornet*.

When Torpedo 8 soared off shortly after 0730 on the morning of 4 June 1942, none of its squadron members had ever flown with a torpedo before. As young George Gay recalled sixteen months later, Midway "was the first time I had ever carried a torpedo on an aircraft and was the first time I had ever taken a torpedo off a ship, had never even seen it done. None of the other ensigns in the squadron had either." Waldron had drilled and drilled his people theoretically, but they had not experienced the reality of combat flying and battle. "Quite a few of us were a little bit skeptical and leery" of flying a torpedo-laden plane off a carrier deck, Gay remembered. But Doolittle and his men had launched even heavier planes without ever seeing a carrier before, so "we figured by golly if they could do it, well we could too." The Devastator "could pick up the weight" of its torpedo easily, and the launch was a breeze for all. Buoyed by this good fortune, Waldron's squadron flew off cheerfully. "We had our tactics down cold and we knew organization and what we should do. We could almost look at the back of Commander Waldron's head and know what he was thinking, because he had told us so many times over and over just what we should do under all conditions."[62]

So when Waldron turned southwest, Torpedo 8 obediently tucked in behind him. Soon he too had his fliers arranged in a broad scouting line, and everything seemed to turn out exactly as he had promised. "He went just as straight to the Jap Fleet as if he'd had a string tied to them." When they arrived, Gay first thought that the squadron was too late, and his heart sank. One carrier and another warship seemed to be on fire.[63] What Gay probably saw was the initial antiaircraft fire from the protective cruiser-destroyer screen around the four carriers. Possibly the last Midway assault planes were still in the neighborhood.

Torpedo 8's attack was doomed from the start, and Gay sensed it. A Japanese float plane had spotted the formation on the way in, and Gay was certain the pilot had warned Nagumo (he had, but Nagumo had forgotten in the excitement of beating off the last of the Midway attacks and reorganizing the *Kido Butai* for an assault against "the" American carrier). A single escorting Wildcat could have shot the enemy out of the sky before the warning was sent. But there were no escorts.

For an instant Nagumo and his carrier skippers were nonplussed when the escorting cruisers and destroyers began signaling frantically at 0918 that torpedo planes were only a few miles out and coming toward them. Within seconds the guns of the screening ships opened up, confirming the worst. Waldron gave the Japanese a precious few moments to react as he slowed formation slightly to send a contact message to the *Hornet.* (This was undoubtedly the definitive position report that Mitscher concluded could not be retransmitted to either his pilots or his superiors.) Enemy gunners and the pilots of the combat air patrol recovered quickly, and the swift Zeros gleefully pounced on the torpedo planes as they crawled slowly toward the distant Japanese carriers. One by one the Americans died, their bodies ripped apart by machine gun bullets or broken as planes flying at slightly more than one hundred miles an hour fell out of control and slammed into the sea. Abercrombie, the Kansas City booster, died, and so did "Squire" Evans, the sensitive, eloquent boy from Yale with his locker full of tweed sport jackets. Moore, the cherubic squadron clown whom girls loved to mother, perished; so did Teats, the Oregon track star, and Rusty Kenyon, the limerick teller who had married the nurse in Norfolk just before sailing; and so did all the others except one. Waldron was one of the last to go; his plane suddenly caught fire, and Gay saw the skipper heave out of his cockpit seat in a frantic effort to jump. But the aircraft smashed into the water before he could escape and sank with his broken body still aboard.

Other young men also died with Torpedo 8: the enlisted rear seat radiomen-gunners whom no one ever mentions because history is written—although not often made—by officers. Robert Miles died in the back of his Devastator, manning the twin .50-caliber machine guns to the end. Tom Petty perished aboard another Devastator. Bernard P. Phelps died, and so did Amelio Maffei, William F. Sawhill, Horace F. Dobbs (Waldron's gunner), Otway Creasy, Jr., Francis S. Polston, Max Calkins,

George A. Field, Darwin J. Clark, Ross Bibb, Hollis Martin, Robert Guntington, Ronald J. Fisher, and Aswell Picou. Two of the boys were only second class seamen, probably eighteen or nineteen at most.

Aboard the *Akagi* and the other carriers, Japanese observers, throats tight and mouths dry, saw the flash of distant wings, the flare of fire, and the billows of smoke over bright water as Torpedo 8 came on with grim determination. Waldron had told his boys just before they took off that if things went badly and only one man was left, he wanted that man to get a hit. George Gay was the man. His gunner was already dead, along with all the rest of Torpedo 8, but Gay headed toward the *Soryu*. He was the only one who got close enough to be fired on accurately by the carriers and their escorts. The Zeros had to break off or be shot down by their own people, and Gay was able to release his torpedo. Unlike many that were launched by U.S. planes and submarines in 1942, it traveled straight and true. At the last minute, the 16,000-ton ship swung away, and the torpedo shot past harmlessly. The *Soryu* had turned simply to comply with a routine course change.

As Gay went zipping over the carrier and an escorting destroyer, he was hit in the leg and his Devastator died under him. He carefully pancaked the plane into the water and got out with a flotation cushion, under which he hid for most of the day, watching one of the great dramas in naval history unfold.

The *Enterprise* had launched its planes in tandem with Air Group 8. Faithful to his agreement with Torpedo 6, Jim Gray stayed high above but in constant contact with both Lt. Comdr. Gene Lindsey's Devastators and Lt. Comdr. Wade McClusky's Bombing 6. But differences in speed and performance plus heavy, scattered clouds soon broke up the fragile *Enterprise* formation. Lieutenant Gray lost sight of his torpedo squadron; while looking for it, he became separated from Bombing 6. Finally Gray found torpedo planes far below and followed them. In fact, he had picked up Torpedo 8, which was ahead of Torpedo 6. As Gray watched, Waldron began his attack. Gray thought it was too late to dive down and help; Bombing 6 might arrive any minute, needing an escort, and Gray's fighters were gulping fuel at an alarming rate. He could not wait long. Soon Torpedo 6 appeared below, and Gray, in an agony of indecision, watched it too futilely dash itself to pieces against the Zeros and guns of the *Kido Butai*. Only four of Torpedo 6's fourteen Devastators escaped destruction. No torpedoes found their targets. With his fuel dangerously low, Gray and his mates reluctantly headed back to the *Enterprise*, leaving Bombing 6 to its fate.

Down below, on the surface of the Pacific, the tide of war was definitely favoring the *Kido Butai*. Nagumo's superb Zero pilots had nearly obliterated two of the enemy's three finest torpedo squadrons and most of their skilled pilots. Although the Japanese could not know it, Bombing 8 and Scouting 8 had ceased to be factors in the battle. It was now shortly after 1000.

On the hangar and flight decks of the four Japanese carriers, aviation ordnancemen, fuel pumpers, and pilots scrambled across and around gas lines, bombs, and torpedoes as the air departments frantically reshaped their groups for a strike against whatever U.S. ships were out to the east. If the *Kido Butai* could hang on for another half hour or so, it would be safe. Down in the warm Pacific waters, George Gay, hanging onto his flotation pillow, saw a powerful carrier fleet frantically at work all around him. But almost as soon as the last planes of Torpedo 6 hit the ocean or vanished over the horizon, the alarm horns and bugles sounded again aboard the *Akagi, Kaga, Soryu,* and *Hiryu,* signaling the deadliest danger yet.

Fletcher had not launched his strike from the *Yorktown* until more than an hour after Task Force 16 had sent its planes aloft. The ship's air officer, Comdr. M. E. Arnold, astutely concluded that Nagumo would not keep a steady course toward Midway once he was assaulted by American aircraft but would double back. Arnold ordered his squadron commanders to stay east of the last reported enemy position. There Lt. Comdr. Lance E. "Lem" Massey of Torpedo 3 and Jimmy Thach with an escort of six Wildcats of Fighting 3 found Nagumo's fleet. Jim Gray had maintained pace with Torpedo 6 by flying a lazy S-pattern above. He consumed enormous amounts of fuel, but the move was effective. Thach did the same while escorting Massey and his fliers, but he stayed right with the torpedo planes rather than above, saving precious fuel by not climbing to high altitude. As Massey and his men closed in on the *Kido Butai* shortly before 1000, Thach and his fighter pilots engaged in wild, sea-level dogfights with the Japanese combat air patrol, which desperately tried to get in among the slowly advancing Devastators.

Soon the *Yorktown*'s torpedo planes began spinning and slamming into the sea, but the survivors droned on, bolstered by the determined efforts of their escort to protect them. Ahead lay the *Kaga, Akagi,* and *Soryu,* whose captains were frantically thrusting their big carriers away from the oncoming Americans in long, looping turns. Destroyer and cruiser escorts, with antiaircraft batteries blazing, maneuvered in every direction to stay out of the way. Just as he realized that his angle of attack was impossible, Massey spotted the *Hiryu* with her escorts about eight miles away from her sister ships. Without hesitation he turned his dwindling squadron toward that carrier. Thach and his fighters obediently followed, steadily dueling the excited Japanese pilots, who raced up from behind or alongside, trying to get in for the final kill of Torpedo 3.

Only three of Massey's Devastators managed to drop their torpedoes. Massey himself was shot down, and none of the torpedoes hit. But the *Yorktown*'s fighters and torpedo planes had pulled the entire Japanese combat air patrol away from three of Nagumo's four carriers.

As Thach and the handful of survivors from Torpedo 3 and Fighting 3 completed their fruitless assault, twisting and turning to escape for the long run home, Wade McClusky and Bombing 6 from the *Enterprise* appeared far above. McClusky had flown the same initial course as Stan Ring, but when the enemy fleet did not appear in a reasonable time, he guessed correctly that Nagumo had doubled back to recover the Midway strike force. McClusky took his squadron northeast. As fuel gauges tumbled, he might have turned back toward the *Enterprise* if one of his sharp-eyed fliers had not picked up the enemy destroyer *Arashi*, which was racing back toward the *Kido Butai* after unsuccessfully depth-bombing the submarine *Nautilus*. The destroyer led Bombing 6 right to Nagumo. As McClusky organized his squadron for the bomb run, Lt. Comdr. Max Leslie appeared with a portion of the *Yorktown*'s Bombing 3. Leslie, like Massey and Thach, had followed Arnold's briefing instructions right to the *Kido Butai*.

No carrier pilots before and no carrier pilots after would experience the unbelievable moment that McClusky, Leslie, and their squadron mates now enjoyed. The partly cloudy skies masked the American squadrons from the enemy CAP as McClusky and Leslie carefully formed up. Directly below, defenseless except for the ships' guns, were three of the six enemy vessels that had spearheaded the creation of a dominion stretching from Malaya to the Aleutians, from China to the Solomons. If Jellicoe in an earlier generation had been the only man who could lose an empire in an afternoon, these airmen were in a position to destroy an empire in minutes. The gallant fliers from Midway and the *Yorktown* had set the table for McClusky and Leslie. Men and the fates had given them the opportunity for an immortal feast.

Pushing over, McClusky's dive-bombers came down like a slow, silver cataract of death. Below, on the decks and bridges of the *Kido Butai*, men were congratulating themselves on one more narrow escape. If enemy

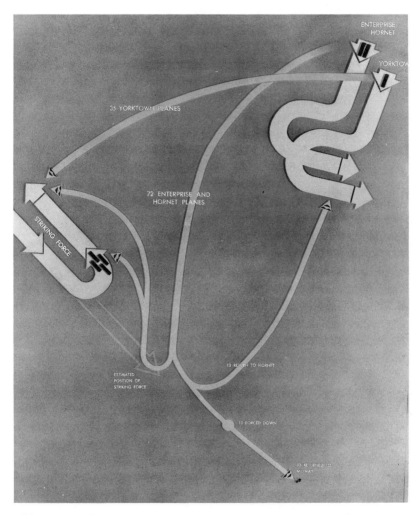

ENTERPRISE
HORNET

YORKTOW

35 YORKTOWN PLANES

72 ENTERPRISE AND
HORNET PLANES

STRIKING FORCE

ESTIMATED
POSITION OF
STRIKING FORCE

12 RETURN TO HORNET

10 FORCED DOWN

13 RETURNED TO
MIDWAY

Midway: a rough depiction of the American attacks on the morning of 4 June 1942.

assaults continued to be torn to pieces at this rate, Midway and whatever carriers lurked over the horizon would soon be out of planes and pilots. The balance of power in the Pacific was swinging decisively to Japan. Suddenly terror-stricken lookouts screamed the warning of a totally unanticipated attack from above. They were too late. It was 1020 local time, only minutes until launch for the *Akagi* and *Kaga*. Scores of planes were on the decks, armed and ready to go. Many more were below decks in the hangars being fueled. Bombs and torpedoes were still carelessly littered around them. Bombing 6's missiles detonated right in the middle of this mass of metal, explosives, and gasoline. Some bombs smashed through into the crowded hangars below before going off. Each carrier was instantly engulfed in huge, uncontrollable blasts of flame, and several thousand seasoned seamen and pilots were torn to bits, incinerated, or seared with fatal flash burns. Two great ships became vast funeral pyres.

George Gay, who was directly in front of the carriers, watched their death throes as escorting cruisers and destroyers desperately maneuvered around them, vainly hoping to provide assistance. Several times he feared he would be run down, and once he thought the enraged Japanese might pick him up. But the *Kido Butai* was busy attending to its horrible losses, and Gay was left undisturbed to watch as the two carriers blazed most of the day and then sank.

Over on the *Soryu*, rearming and refueling had not proceeded quite as far because the carrier was not scheduled to launch for another forty minutes. But her decks were also filled with planes; she too was potentially a gigantic bomb of open gas lines and unprotected explosives. Seeing that the *Akagi* and *Kaga* were already burning, Max Leslie sent Bombing 3 down after the *Soryu*. The result was devastating. As bombs detonated on the crowded flight deck, one more splendid Japanese carrier with her irreplaceable complement of sailors and airmen turned into a roaring, raging wreck. Six minutes after McClusky had launched his bomb, Nagumo was reduced to one operational carrier, the *Hiryu*.

Word swiftly reached the U.S. task force that the Japanese carriers had been found and attacked. But aboard the *Hornet* triumph was tinged with uncertainty. The fate of Air Group 8 was unknown. Where was everyone? Incoming messages did not identify attack squadrons, but "names used and voices indicated that no *Hornet* personnel were involved" in the attack on Nagumo's carriers.[64] This was a bitter blow. The prolonged silence that followed was worse. Finally, shortly after 1130, the remnants of Ring's flight appeared, with the air group commander in the lead.[65]

Ring and several of his colleagues landed with their bombs still slung under the fuselage. Word quickly spread that the other pilots had harmlessly jettisoned their bombs into the sea.

As soon as he landed, Ring went or was summoned to the bridge. Mitscher questioned him closely, then sent him below with orders to be ready to fly again. Dodson, Martin, and the rest of the communications department had monitored the various flights of the *Hornet*'s air group and had some idea of what had occurred. Only Torpedo 8 had not been heard from; it would soon be overdue. "We knew it was wiped out when they didn't return to Midway," Henry Martin recalled. "We knew they were in the ocean or gone." Men could only hope and pray that some pilots and aircrews had ditched and were awaiting rescue.[66]

Ring's apparent lack of aggressiveness in seeking out the enemy ranged from highly questionable at best to inexcusable at worst. Spruance commented in his after-action report that if the *Hornet*'s bombers had found the *Kido Butai* they could have destroyed the *Hiryu*, thereby avoiding the subsequent loss of the *Yorktown*. Some historians have agreed.[67] Certainly Mitscher was upset. The *Hornet* had apparently lost thirty-nine of its seventy-seven aircraft without accomplishing anything. Bitter staff people believed that as soon as Ring had found an excuse to stop looking for the Japanese fleet he had hightailed it out of the battle zone.[68] But the gloom lifted when word came that most of the *Hornet*'s missing Dauntlesses had managed to land at Midway. Once the island's overworked ground crews could get around to refueling them, they could be flown back to the *Hornet*. Meanwhile, the ship's company had other things to worry about.

Some crewmen would have a hard time remembering Midway. The ship was never attacked; everything was routine except the continual general quarters, which seemed to last for three straight days. The carrier was so tightly sealed that Cardon Ruchti never got back to his quarters; he caught catnaps when he could in a corner of the engine room with a rag for a pillow during the entire battle. Up in the ship's island, Henry Martin and everyone around him "slept on station." Officers and enlisted men were sustained by periodic infusions of coffee and doughnuts. The most grueling action, of course, occurred on the flight and hangar decks, where the air department was busy launching, landing, and spotting F4Fs of the combat air patrol.

The weather remained calm and beautiful; the sky was a delicate blue with a few soft clouds on the horizon, and the sea sparkled in the sun. At 1030 tickers in Fighting 8's ready room informed everyone that an enemy float plane was snooping around in the area and that the combat air patrol would investigate. All hands were warned to be ready for an air attack. But an hour later the bogey was identified as friendly.

Shortly after Ring landed, the *Hornet*'s loudspeaker cried out: "Stand by to repel attack." Task Force 16 immediately went into "a terrific lateral-pass maneuver"; Casey watched as destroyers, carriers, and cruisers began "running across each other's bows" to get into proper defense modes. On the *Hornet*'s flight deck Fred Mears nervously unloosened the flap on his .45 pistol holster, determined to fire away heroically at any Japanese plane that came within range.[69] But the bombers and torpedo planes that Nagumo had dispatched from the *Hiryu* found Task Force 17 first because it was closer to the Japanese fleet. The *Yorktown* was hull-down from the *Hornet*, but men topside on CV-8 had a "damned spectacular" view of the battle as the *Yorktown* and her escorts, along with the combat air patrol, which consisted of fighters from all three carriers, tried to break up the Japanese assault. Multicolored antiaircraft bursts filled the sky, and over the waters came the faint "crump, crump" sound of distant ack-ack explosions. Occasionally "the *Hornet*'s men would see a flash of flame and a mass of thick black smoke plunging downward to the sea. Another flash and another downward streamer. Finally the sky above the Yorktown was covered with smoke pencils, big and black as though written in the sky with a giant hand."[70] The *Hornet*'s crew not only saw but heard combat as Mitscher ordered the battle frequency cut into the ship's loudspeaker. Twenty-six hundred men from engine room to flight deck heard Lt. Warren Ford and three other pilots from Fighting 8 as they and the rest of the combat air patrol from the *Enterprise* and *Yorktown* tore into the enemy formation: "Watch out, watch out. Zero on your tail, zero [*sic*] on your tail." "Take the one on the right." "Now we'll go upstairs for that sucker." "You got one. Look at him burn."[71]

The Japanese assault was almost wiped out, but not before several bombs exploded on the *Yorktown*'s flight and hangar decks. A pall of black smoke arose over the horizon, and everyone aboard the *Hornet* realized that the "*York*" had been wounded again. Suddenly the ship's loudspeaker blared: "Torpedo planes approaching on the starboard bow." They were returning Japanese aircraft, their lethal loads expended. Apparently they were left alone.[72]

The combat air patrol came in to rearm and refuel. Several planes were almost out of gas; the engine of one F4F consumed its last drop just as the aircraft snagged the arresting wire. Jim Smith had to ditch close

"A terrific lateral-pass maneuver": The *Hornet* and her escorts assist one another during the Battle of Midway.

aboard after taking a wave-off. He was quickly rescued by a plane guard destroyer and was soon back on the *Hornet*.

With the *Yorktown*'s flight deck out of commission, her fighter director officer ordered to the *Hornet* all airborne planes, including the remnants of Massey's and Thach's decimated squadrons returning from their frustrating attacks on the *Kido Butai*. Half of the *Yorktown* pilots chose to land aboard the *Enterprise*, but Ens. Dan Sheedy of Thach's squadron "came aboard the first carrier he could see, which was the *Hornet*." Sheedy was painfully wounded in the shoulder and ankle; his plane was badly shot up, the cockpit "riddled with bullets." The F4F wobbled badly as it approached the carrier's ramp. Touching down, it skidded to the right, and the impact collapsed its already damaged right landing gear. Smashing onto the deck, the plane's tail hook caught an arresting wire, which swung wings and fuselage upward. Sheedy's hand was on the control stick, where the trigger of the wing machine guns was located. He had turned the master control switch to the "off" position, but he did not know that bullet damage had caused the circuit wires to remain welded in the open position. As the plane bounced on deck the six .50-caliber machine guns cut loose in a two-second burst.[73] Bullets ripped high across the flight deck and into a group of men watching the landing operations in the after part of the ship's island structure. Several slugs even tore through light armor plating and into "Battle II," the gunnery control room for the after 5-inch antiaircraft batteries.

Fred Mears instantly dropped on his back near four others. When the shooting stopped, a fellow pilot got up and calmly walked toward the nearest battle dressing station; he had been hit in the mouth and shoulder with bullets and "peppered with shrapnel." A nearby sailor had been shot in the knee but was not hurt badly. Covered with the seaman's blood, Mears stood up and looked around. Nearby was the body of a boy who had taken the machine gun burst full in the face. "The dead sailor lay in great peace, one leg flat on the deck with the toe outturned, the other with his knee drawn up. His arm was outstretched, the palm skyward in a relaxed gesture. 'My, he's quiet,' I thought. He had returned to simplicity." Mears walked toward a ladder. A marine sergeant was being carried below on a stretcher; his right arm was shredded, he had a bullet wound in his stomach, and he was crying out as if in disbelief.[74] He and four others, including brilliant young Lt. Royal Ingersoll II, son of the commander in chief of the U.S. Atlantic Fleet, died either instantly or soon after. Twenty of the ship's company were seriously wounded.

For two hours the skies and seas around the American task force were quiet, and officers and men could savor what was apparently an outstanding victory. By late afternoon it was clear that at least three Japanese carriers were so badly damaged that they would require months of repair. Perhaps they had already sunk. The *Yorktown*'s flight deck had been hastily patched so that flight operations could be resumed, and Fletcher sent out patrols looking for the *Hiryu*, now known to be the only undamaged Japanese carrier in the area. Then a second incoming Japanese assault wave was picked up, and the combat air patrols scrambled aloft once more and were vectored toward the attackers. This time the Japanese managed to evade many of the American fighters and struck the *Yorktown* again with both torpedoes and bombs. From the deck of the *Salt Lake City* Casey observed that the antiaircraft fire from the *Yorktown* and its escorts seemed ragged, "but the thunderheads of it blackened the horizon" briefly. Soon "the black puffs attenuate and lose color and mingle with the stratus clouds in the low distance." On the sea "the fires of the burning planes are quickly out."[75] Angry American fighter pilots "splashed" most of the Japanese attackers on their way out of the area. But once more the hapless "*York*" was put out of action, seriously damaged. Again half her combat air patrol and strike squadrons landed aboard the *Hornet*. Soon after the last enemy plane departed, Fletcher received word that the *Hiryu* had been rediscovered.

Once the *Hornet* recovered the combat air patrol, Mears went below to the "admiral's pantry," one deck below the ready rooms. Soucek had thoughtfully opened this most sacrosanct compartment for the pilots so they could have the best food and drink on board while the fighters were being rearmed and refueled for another launch. Everyone was hot, thirsty, and wildly excited.

The *Yorktown* pilots had been through this before, but the *Hornet* fighter pilots had finally tasted their first combat and had done well. Their hair matted with sweat held in by tight helmets, hands holding cups of lemonade or hot coffee that slopped over with every gesture, the pilots bellowed out their stories to each other around mouthfuls of sandwiches. Everyone was "having one hell of a good time," Mears recalled. "They had fought and won and were still alive, and they felt wonderful. All they wanted to do was go right out and fight again."[76] It was a tonic after the grim morning and the crippling of the *Yorktown*.

But misfortune continued to dog the "Horny Maru." Mitscher did not get word of the *Hiryu*'s sighting for more than half an hour after it was received aboard the *Enterprise*. Again the lack of adequate highly classified communication gear prevented effective coordination. Spruance did not signal Mitscher to dispatch Air Group 8, minus fighter escorts, until the *Enterprise* began launching a strike with planes from her squadrons and those of the *Yorktown*. Meanwhile, Lt. A. B. Tucker had led back the *Hornet* Dauntlesses that had landed at Midway after the fruitless morning flight. Once these planes were refueled, Scouting 8 and Bombing 8 were reconstituted as fighting units minus only a handful of planes that had been lost at sea. Shortly after 1600 Mitscher launched sixteen Dauntlesses from Bombing 8 and Scouting 8 toward a Japanese force estimated to be at course 278° True, distance 162 miles.

Ring apparently did not lead this strike, though he went along. Instead the honor went to Lt. Edgar E. Stebbins. "Steb," as he was invariably known, was slight and dark-haired "with a gap between his front teeth which gives his grin a quizzical, supercilious look." But far from being a snob, Stebbins was even-tempered, with a self-deprecatory sense of humor and a superb ability to fly warplanes. He was to command Air Group 5 aboard the new *Yorktown* in the later stages of the Pacific war.[77]

Once again the American fliers would be making a long, dangerous flight, and this time it would surely end in darkness. Stebbins reached the target area almost half an hour after the *Enterprise-Yorktown* strike group had slammed four bombs in close succession into the *Hiryu*'s flight deck, turning that carrier into as great an inferno as her now departed sisters. She would sink the next day. The heart of the *Kido Butai* had been cut out. Of the once-magnificent six-carrier unit, only the still damaged *Shokaku* and the *Zuikaku*, with half her veteran pilots at the bottom of the Coral Sea, remained. It was not the beginning of the end of the Pacific war, but it was the end of the beginning.

Coming over the Japanese fleet in the growing dusk, Stebbins saw that the *Hiryu* "was burning throughout its entire length and was assumed to be no further value as a target."[78] He led his dive-bombers over the escorting fleet, divided them into attack sections, and ordered them to attack a battleship and a heavy cruiser.[79] No Zeros were left to contest the Americans, "and even the antiaircraft fire seemed to reflect the despondency of Japanese crews who had been plastered all day with torpedoes and bombs."[80] Stebbins did not lose a man. The exultant pilots claimed that they had hit the battleship with two 1,000-pound bombs and a 500-pound bomb and had smacked the heavy cruiser with two of the smaller weapons. In fact, Air Group 8 had not hit the Japanese at all. Stebbins and his men returned to the *Hornet* uneventfully through dark skies, and all came aboard without incident, which, as Mitscher later observed, was a rather remarkable achievement since none of the pilots had ever qualified for night landings.[81]

Two of the sixteen bombers had returned to the *Hornet* with engine trouble shortly after takeoff. Perhaps one of the two was flown by Ring, or perhaps he had completed the mission. In any case Ring returned to the *Hornet* after this second strike of the day with his bomb still snugly secured aboard his aircraft. Once again he was summoned to the bridge, and this time Mitscher viciously lit into him for lack of aggression. Ring held his ground stubbornly. He was air group commander. His job was not to get killed but to see that his squadrons found the enemy and attacked aggressively. This he had tried to do, and he was not ashamed of it.[82]

Ring's behavior on 4 June generated great bitterness among the *Hornet*'s small family of aviators and bridge officers. But Mitscher evidently believed Ring had a point. After Midway, air group commanders generally assumed the role of strike coordinators. Later, as commander of naval air forces in the Solomons, Mitscher would make Ring his chief deputy.

The fourth of June had not been the *Hornet*'s best day. It seemed that everything that could go wrong with an untested and uncertain air group had gone wrong. Only that portion of Fighting 8 helping to defend the combined task forces had gotten results, although Stebbins's pilots had certainly tried hard enough. As Spruance pulled Task Force 16 back to the west that night, the mood aboard the carrier was mixed.

To most of the ship's company, even those who worked directly with the air group on the flight deck, the probable wipeout of Torpedo 8 was nothing more than the reality of any war in which good men died. To Jimmy Walker the death of a squadron was the "natural" outcome of battle. Keith Bancroft, a third-class aviation machinist's mate who reported aboard after Midway, was part of an eight-man plane-handling crew on the flight deck. He quickly became friendly with members of his crew and one or two others, along with a few of the "plane captains," the men responsible for the overall upkeep of their respective aircraft. But that was all. He saw the pilots from a distance. They did their job; he did his. Under the circumstances there was no personal sense of loss or tragedy.

Eugene Blackmer, who had become a plane captain in Fighting 8 by the time of Midway, took a surprisingly callous view of Torpedo 8's calamity, but his attitude reflected the realities of carrier warfare. Like the rest of his hard-working crewmen, Blackmer focused each day on a few critically important tasks. He knew his plane and he had formed an opinion of pilots that was not altogether flattering and certainly not worshipful. "They came aboard; here we are, there they are. It was hard to get to know the pilots." In those circumstances you expected to lose men, Blackmer remembered; it was part of learning how to fight a war. Many of the pilots were certainly good airmen; there were surprisingly few flight deck accidents on the *Hornet*. But most fliers were reservists who were perhaps slightly less professional than they should have been. Many drank too much when ashore; some flew too carelessly when at sea and got killed. Their deaths in battle were too bad, but the ship and its men carried on.[83]

The hundreds of cooks, firemen, telephone talkers, and damage control personnel who toiled below decks had no real idea of what had been accomplished and who had failed at Midway. Confined to small work spaces, living areas, and battle stations, they could no more mourn Torpedo 8 or condemn Stanhope Ring than anyone aboard an escorting destroyer or one of Task Force 17's cruisers. Even some of the ship's officers were comparatively free from anguish. Gerald McAteer later recalled that he spent 4 June in a small battle dressing station far below decks "drinking lots of coffee, getting caffeine poisoning." Occasionally, when things were very quiet, he undogged the hatch, went through the ship opening and shutting other hatches, and finally reached the fo'c'sle or flight deck, where he watched the *Yorktown* burning on the horizon. And that was all. With a sufficient number of doctors aboard he was not needed to tend to the men wounded in the afternoon's flight deck accident. When Mitscher came on the ship's loudspeaker system that night to report four Japanese carriers afire and escorting battleships and cruisers successfully bombed, the majority of the ship's company was proud and saw no reason to question Mitscher's "well done."[84]

But to the comparative handful of men who had worked with the lost pilots it was a somber night. The half-empty wardroom seemed like a cavern. Lt. Bill Rommens, the ship's electrical officer and generally considered an unemotional man, walked in, saw the rows of empty seats and napkin rings, and burst into tears. Gus Widhelm, the bomber pilot, felt sick, "sicker than hell." And he felt mean, too. "Mean and nasty. . . . It felt as though [the ship] had lost the fight, to use Gus' own words."[85] Even McAteer, when he learned about Ring's return with his bomb load intact, was angry. The air group commander "should have found something to drop it on."[86]

Ring was not the only villain to the disenchanted that night. The communications department had monitored Fighting 8's radio frequency that morning as Pat Mitchell accompanied Ring and the bombers toward the Japanese fleet. When Mitchell and his men turned back, ran out of fuel, and fell into the sea one by one, it was clear that the three senior pilots—Mitchell himself, Stanley Ruehlow, and Dick Gray—had ditched together, which was totally contrary to existing doctrine and standards of loyalty. A wing leader was supposed to ditch with his wingmen, because wingmen naturally consumed more fuel maintaining position than did their wing leader. It was their job to protect him in battle, and it was his job to protect them in an emergency by staying with them. Mitchell, Ruehlow, and Gray had apparently abandoned their men in order to stick together. The few aboard the *Hornet* who knew this were intensely bitter.[87]

Perhaps the most disoriented men aboard were Fred Mears and Bob Divine, the backup pilots for Torpedo 8. The whole squadron ready room belonged to them. There and in the pilots' small, cramped living cabins forward Mears and Divine joined others of Air Group 8 who were trying to figure out what had happened to an entire squadron. Torpedo 8 had certainly sighted and attacked the enemy; others had seen or heard that. But after? "How many had come through, and where were they?

On Midway? Afloat in rubber boats? Picked up by friendly destroyers or patrol boats" or perhaps by the Japanese? "We had no way of knowing." Late that night Divine, restlessly "ghosting about" the big, blacked-out carrier during the midwatch, happened across a small knot of men on the hangar deck forward. It was a funeral party, which was "sliding overboard the canvas-cased bodies of the five men killed that day, silently and in the darkness, after a two-minute prayer for each."[88]

Throughout much of the night of 4–5 June Task Force 16, with the wounded *Yorktown*'s air group split between the *Enterprise* and the *Hornet*, steamed east to remain out of range of any Japanese surface forces that might be trying to reverse the decision of the previous day. In fact, although the Japanese lurked around Midway for another twenty-four hours, they had no desire for an open fight with the American carrier planes. At 0200 on 5 June Spruance ordered his ships to turn due north; $1\frac{3}{4}$ hours later they turned west again. The task force, including the *Hornet*, received word from planes operating out of Midway that the enemy was bearing 320° to 340° True, 170 to 200 miles west-northwest of the island. One report claimed that there was probably one carrier capable of operating planes. If such a carrier had been sighted, it was either the *Hosho*, operating with Yamamoto's battleship support force, or the *Zuiho*, which was screening Vice Admiral Kondo's Midway invasion force. The *Hosho* carried only eight aircraft, the *Zuiho* twenty-four; neither was a match for one of Spruance's two undamaged carriers.

The Battle of Midway was nearly over, although it would flare intermittently for another forty-eight hours, bringing the Americans more but comparatively modest victories. The fifth of June began foggy and hazy. Aboard the *Hornet* some pilots and officers feared that the Japanese would either get away or would somehow manage to sneak an invasion force onto the island. Mears and Divine spent another eerie day in the quiet emptiness of Torpedo 8's ready room, while Spruance brought Task Force 16 up to twenty-five knots as it searched westward for remnants of the enemy fleet. Not until midafternoon did word arrive in the *Enterprise* that Japanese warships from the island had been sighted northwest of Midway. The source was either the submarine *Tambor* or a B-17. The report listed two battleships, four heavy cruisers, one carrier, and some destroyers. The *Hornet* launched twenty-six bombers, which were joined by a similar force from the *Enterprise*. Air Group 8 was again unfortunate. A determined 315-mile, three-hour search revealed only empty seas. At last, shortly before sundown, 278 miles from the ship, Bombing 8 sighted either an enemy light cruiser or destroyer. Japanese accounts indicate that it was the destroyer *Tanikaze*, which Yamamoto had dispatched to the area of the previous day's slaughter to determine the ultimate fate of the *Hiryu* and recover survivors.[89] Although short on fuel, most of the bombers dove down on the enemy. They achieved no hits, although the pilots claimed five near-misses with 500-pound bombs.

After the hasty attack, the planes headed back in the gathering darkness. Minute by minute the pilots nervously watched their fuel gauges sink toward empty as night approached. But they maintained formation and the homing devices worked perfectly. Suddenly Task Force 16 was below. The pilots turned on their running lights, and the ships responded by turning on all mast lights. The *Hornet* added its searchlight, waving it about for a minute; the beam picked up an escorting cruiser several miles away, turning the vessel into "a white model of itself." A nervous marine major aboard the *Salt Lake City* donned his life jacket. "We may complete this recovery right square in the middle of the Jap fleet," he muttered.[90] One *Hornet* pilot, out of fuel, was forced to ditch near the *Enterprise*. He was promptly picked up by the destroyer *Alwyn*. All the other planes landed safely aboard the *Hornet*, "Blue Base," as the carrier was known to communications officers and radiomen throughout the fleet. One Dauntless gulped its last thimbleful of gas just as it snagged the arresting wire.[91]

That night the *Hornet* received word that George Gay had been picked up. No one was yet certain, however, that he was the only survivor of Torpedo 8.[92] The fate of ten men of Fighting 8 was still unknown as Task Force 16 prepared for another day of battle. According to the ship's action report, course was set at 280° True, speed fifteen knots, "the enemy having been reported to be heading slightly south of west, probably to join the Southern forces."[93] Yamamoto was apparently trying to link up his battleship support group with Kondo's invasion force. He still hoped to lure the American carriers within range of his battleship guns, thus salvaging both the overall operation and the invasion.

Shortly before sunrise on 6 June the *Enterprise* launched a reconnaissance flight, which picked up what seemed to be a Japanese battleship, heavy cruiser, and several destroyers bearing 230° to 240° True from the task force, distance 150 miles. The contact message was garbled, and the battleship was misidentified as a carrier. Spruance held his forces back until the planes returned with an accurate verbal report. It was not until 0757 that the *Hornet* launched twenty-six bombers and eight fighters

The *Mogami* on 6 June 1942, after Gus Widhelm and fliers from the *Enterprise* had finished working her over.

against the enemy. "The latter were ordered along in case of previously undetected air opposition."[94]

What the *Enterprise* reconnaissance flight had actually seen was not a battleship and a cruiser but two large heavy cruisers, the *Mikuma* and *Mogami*, the last of Yamamoto's heavy units that had approached Midway. During their retirement after the loss of the *Kido Butai*, the *Mikuma* was damaged when it collided with her sister ship while evading the submarine *Tambor*. The two ships and their destroyer escorts were moving slowly because the commander of the *Mogami* was determined not to leave the *Mikuma* alone to face the American wolves. They were perfect targets for the *Hornet* aviators, who, led by Gus Widhelm, were lusting for blood. As the youngsters pushed their planes into the bombing dive, Widhelm yelled: "Throw everything at 'em but the kitchen stove, boys." His own thousand-pound bomb and those of several other pilots went through the armored upper decks of the cruisers, bursting deep inside with horrible effect. As the last plane dropped its bomb, the pilot cried out: "And here goes the kitchen stove."[95] For good measure, the dive-bombers strafed the cruisers as they finished their bombing runs. The fighters, with no enemy combat air patrol to worry about, enthusiastically joined in. The Japanese downed one plane from Bombing 8; Ens. Don Griswold and his gunner, Kenneth D. Bunch, died in a hail of antiaircraft fire.

As Air Group 8 finished its work and headed home under clear skies, Air Group 6 appeared overhead to continue the slaughter. The *Hornet* took aboard all its planes without incident, and most of the excited pilots rushed below for a quick meal.

As a Japanese submarine snuck past the *Yorktown*'s screen far to the southeast and pumped three torpedoes into that luckless ship, the *Hornet*'s efficient air department prepared another strike, and at midafternoon Widhelm and his mates again soared aloft. By this time the *Mikuma* was sinking and the *Mogami* was badly battered. Ens. Clayton Fisher, who had been unable to hit anything in the last two days, went down to funnel level and dropped his bomb squarely on the *Mikuma*, which went under the waves almost immediately. Widhelm turned his attention to the smoking but still floating wreck of the *Mogami* and laid another thousand-pound bomb right on target.

The Americans would not stop. Before taking off, they had ordered the .50-caliber wing guns loaded with armor-piercing bullets, deliberately excluding tracers and incendiaries. The boys knew that the .50-caliber slugs could tear the fragile upper works of a destroyer to pieces. As the frantic survivors of the *Mikuma* climbed aboard one of the escorting "tin cans," Widhelm and his colleagues brought their dive-bombers and fighters in low for vicious strafing runs. Their bullets chewed up the ship's slender, delicate upper works. "We were down so low that we could see the decks of the ships crowded with Japs," Widhelm told correspondent Stanley Johnston later. "They ran around trying to escape our machine-gun bullets, which ripped along their decks." Widhelm exulted as he blew away scores of Japanese sailors. Behind him, his rear gunner, Aviation Radioman 2nd Class George Stokely, blazed away at the destroyer with his own twin .50-caliber machine guns as Widhelm brought his plane out of its run. "Stokely, I think, got a lot of Japs in our sweeps. He's a wild man with a gun."

Widhelm decided on one more pass. But a handful of survivors on the destroyer's upper decks met him with a blast of gunfire that knocked out his engine. "Get ready to land," Widhelm yelled at Stokely. "O.K.," Stokely yelled back, still firing away. "For Cripe's sake, get ready to land!" Widhelm screamed. "Are you hurt?" Stokely shouted, continuing to fire. When Widhelm said he wasn't, Stokely said "O.K." again and kept firing. Just as Widhelm was ready to pancake into the sea, his engine miraculously started up again. He was able to nurse his hardy Dauntless the 120-odd miles back to the *Hornet*. On the way he sent a forced landing signal to the ship, warning that he had to get aboard on the first approach. Mitscher and Soucek "didn't seem overanxious for me to try the landing—my flaps and wheels wouldn't work," Widhelm recalled. But the determined flier came in anyway, slow and shot up but right in the groove, over the carrier's ramp, to snag a wire. "Inspecting the plane later, I discovered that all the intake stacks had been knocked loose by the blast of that shell. It sure was a close one."[96]

Everyone on the strike had seen Widhelm's incredible performance, and as soon as he landed, Mitscher summoned him to the bridge. The *Mogami* had not gone down. (In fact, the cruiser and its incredibly determined crew somehow struggled back to Japan.) Widhelm begged and pleaded to go out again. "Gus," Mitscher replied with his wry smile, "you're intoxicated with battle."[97]

And so Midway ended. It took a few days for everyone in the small U.S. fleet to absorb the facts: Nagumo's carriers were no more, Yamamoto's battleships had fled, and the Yanks had won a great triumph. The aircraft carrier had become the queen of the seas. The post-Midway patrol around the central Pacific became a victory parade.[98] Only with hindsight did it become clear that the victory could have been even greater.

Scattered across several hundred miles of ocean in rubber life rafts were pilots from all three American carriers. They would be rescued in the coming days; one, George Gay, would finally provide answers about the fate of Torpedo 8. Along the ocean floor close to where Gay was rescued lay the shattered hulks of the *Kido Butai* and the bleaching bones of several thousand of Nippon's finest sailors and aviators. Steel and flesh carried to the bottom Japan's dreams of empire.

In a seven-page after-action report, the *Hornet*'s assistant air officer, Lt. Comdr. J. G. Foster, Jr., admitted that since the strategic situation "was in our favor, it was only through errors on our part that we did not gain a more impressive victory."[99] He placed most of the blame on the navy and army pilots from Midway who had failed to report the *Kido Butai*'s presence in a timely manner on the morning of 4 June and then had failed to inform Fletcher and Spruance of Nagumo's major course change away from the island to recover his strike aircraft. Foster recommended more efficient and sophisticated communication links and enhanced cooperation between army and navy to rectify errors in searching, reporting, and responding. Such criticisms and recommendations were valid, but breakdowns in search patterns and communications, no matter how important, cannot completely explain the Americans' numerous failures at Midway, which could have cost them their triumph.

Half a dozen historians have accurately labeled Midway a "miracle," an "incredible" victory. But it was much more. It was the first battle in which two carrier fleets more or less intended to go looking for one another and made their plans accordingly. The primary Japanese blunder is easily identifiable: With insufficient resources Yamamoto placed a combined strategic-tactical burden on his carriers that was far beyond the ability of the *Kido Butai* to fulfill unless the American enemy conformed to every preconceived behavioral pattern assigned in the Japanese battle plan. Just by appearing unexpectedly, Spruance and Fletcher seized the strategic initiative.

But they and their carrier captains almost squandered this advantage. There is no evidence that Mitscher, George Murray of the *Enterprise,* or Elliott Buckmaster of the *Yorktown* ever developed a carefully conceived launch and strike strategy. They blindly adhered to peacetime practices that, no matter how apparently logical in concept, simply did not conform to reality. American carrier doctrine has always been based on the efficiency of sequentially launched individual squadrons to minimize fuel discrepancy. Dispatching each aircraft type "in a flock" ensured that each squadron could form up within minutes and head to the target, each with approximately the same amount of fuel. The alternative of taking off helter-skelter would mean that squadrons might have to orbit the carrier for many minutes, waiting for mates who were buried in flight deck traffic.[100] Since prowling American carriers during World War II were always vulnerable to sudden enemy air attack from either land or sea, it was necessary to launch at least some fighters first to provide a combat air patrol. This naturally led to the practice of launching all fighters first. But what was essential for air defense proved to be disastrous for efficient power projection as long as substantial discrepancies remained between the various aviation weapon systems.

Despite the obvious lessons of the Coral Sea, no effort was made at Midway to coordinate air group flights or assaults or to incorporate the much slower and more vulnerable torpedo squadrons into any coherent plan of attack. Walter Lord has emphasized that at Midway neither the *Enterprise* nor *Hornet* air groups "knew what the other was doing, much less what the *Yorktown*'s planes were up to." He claimed that Mitscher intended to send his torpedo planes ahead, while the faster fighters and bombers under Ring rendezvoused high above before setting off in pursuit of Torpedo 8, thus allowing a concentrated attack.[101] There is no evidence to support this contention; indeed, all evidence contradicts it. Mitscher insisted on continuing the practice of launching his torpedo planes last. So, apparently, did Murray and Buckmaster.

Why these commanders persisted in following this policy despite the evidence from recent combat and the varied capabilities of their aircraft is one of the great mysteries of Midway. There are others. For half a century John Waldron's final charge was glorified. "Torpedo 8 went to its doom in the finest American Navy tradition," wrote celebrated war correspondent Stanley Johnston in 1943. "It sighted the enemy. It attacked. It went to its death trying. No more could be expected of any fighting unit."[102]

The myth of Torpedo 8 begins to unravel under the most casual scrutiny. Much of the myth is based on the assumption that by attacking the Japanese carriers at low altitude, Waldron and his men deliberately drew down the combat air patrol, allowing McClusky's dive-bombers to strike unmolested. But subsequent scholarship, especially John Lundstrom's meticulous research, has destroyed that assumption. It was the assault by Massey on the *Hiryu*, with Thach as determined escort, that lured the defending Zeros away from the other three carriers, allowing McClusky's and Leslie's squadrons to mount the attack that destroyed the *Kido Butai*. Massey and Thach appeared minutes after the massacres of Torpedo 8 and Torpedo 6. Waldron's charge had no effect whatever on the outcome of the Battle of Midway. The courageous pilots and their gunners were uselessly thrown away.

Waldron could be fairly charged with criminal negligence in leading his command to such meaningless deaths if it were not for Mitscher's and Ring's insistence on maintaining traditional launch sequences and refusing to provide Waldron with fighter support. Buckmaster on the *Yorktown* did provide his torpedo planes with fighter escort, ensuring at least a minimal survival rate.

Employing traditional aircraft launch procedure in 1942 was inexcusable. Fred Mears later wrote that Waldron apparently did not believe that fighters would provide much protection for Torpedo 8. On the other hand, if Waldron had waited to begin his strike until the dive-bombers were attacking, the dual assault would at least have divided enemy antiaircraft fire and the combat air patrol "and thus give[n] the torpedo planes much more of a chance to get in, drop, and get out." Waldron knew this, Mears continued. He was an expert on torpedo plane warfare, "and it must have been obvious to him that an unsupported rush by his squadron against a large surface force, while it might net some hits, almost certainly would result in the destruction of most of the planes."[103]

What, then, were Waldron's motives for leading his squadron on a deliberately divergent course that would destroy any possibility of a roughly coordinated attack with the *Hornet*'s dive-bombers? And what were Mitscher's motives in letting him do so? If Mitscher believed that Waldron might find the Japanese fleet on a different course heading (the only justification for deferring to Waldron), why did he not order Ring and Mitchell to follow Torpedo 8? Did Waldron agree that Fighting 8's primary task was to defend the carriers and its secondary responsibility to escort the dive-bombers? Or did he try to alter launch sequences or at least obtain some fighter protection for his squadron? Why did he not seek some sort of coordination with Mitchell's fighter escort, as did Torpedo 6 aboard the *Enterprise?* Or did he make such a request and have it denied? Mears's only explanation of Waldron's behavior was that the man was willing to sacrifice Torpedo 8 to find the Japanese fleet and radio its position. If so, did Waldron tell Mitscher of his intention? Did Mitscher support it, even though it might mean the destruction of the *Hornet*'s entire torpedo squadron? Mitscher's after-action report on his final conversation with Waldron strongly supports that possibility.

But other factors may have been shaping the saga of Torpedo 8. Waldron's contempt for his air group commander and indeed for all senior aviators in Task Forces 16 and 17 was obviously profound. Did he believe that Spruance or Fletcher had doomed Torpedo 8 from the start with their demand for an all-out, uncoordinated attack? Or did he embrace such a strategy, believing that Torpedo 8 would somehow get through? Gay has told us that no one in the squadron expected the deadly Japanese response from the *Kido Butai*. The only explanation for Waldron's charge other than a suicidal determination to find the enemy fleet was that he—and perhaps Mitscher and Ring as well—gambled that Nagumo had sent nearly all his Zeros into Midway with the strike force and that if the *Kido Butai* could be found and attacked before this force returned, most of Torpedo 8 would survive.

In the end the historian can only speculate; the mysteries will always remain. Waldron was dead by midday on 4 June; Mitscher died in 1947 and Ring sixteen years later. None of the principals has left an account of his part or motives at Midway. But there are clues. Superb as Mitscher was, his leadership had limitations. He was always known as a doer, not a thinker, a man of action easily bored with detailed planning. His daring was always tinged with desperation, as he would clearly demonstrate in 1944 during the first Battle of the Philippine Sea, when he risked almost all the offensive power of his carrier force in a "mission beyond darkness" whose margin of success was as narrow as the American victory at Midway.[104]

Mitscher had told Harold Stark at the end of the *Hornet*'s shakedown cruise that the best way to train combat pilots was to get them to sea and put them to work flying and fighting. He was naturally attracted to the all-out assault, the grand gesture that was in itself almost as important as the result. If his after-action report is any indication, Mitscher was deeply moved by Waldron's undeniable sense of dedication and sacrifice. He seemed to believe that such traits by themselves would somehow guarantee triumph. In the case of Torpedo 8 he was tragically wrong, and the fate of that squadron mirrored the deeper flaws that beset the entire *Hornet* air group.

But Spruance and Fletcher encouraged the kind of reckless behavior that Waldron displayed and Mitscher applauded. Employing an uncoordinated "hit 'em with all you've got" approach certainly amplified the inherent tactical and doctrinal weaknesses of American carrier warfare. Midway was conducted amid the specter of Pearl Harbor and apparent Japanese naval superiority. Half a century later one senses both an apprehension and a keenness to meet a foe who had not lost a battle. Spruance, Fletcher, and the captains and pilots of Task Forces 16 and 17 seemed to approach Midway not so much as a tactical or strategic problem but solely as a battle of moral superiority between Japanese and American warriors. By indiscriminately throwing everything they had at the enemy, they would both demonstrate and fulfill America's will to win.

In the sense that Midway, like any battle, was a contest of moral fiber, the result was a draw. Japanese sailors and aviators were just as dedicated and courageous as their Occidental counterparts. They were betrayed by the faulty strategic and tactical planning of their superiors. Spruance, Fletcher, and their carrier and air group commanders nearly imposed the same fate on their men by employing inappropriate launch practices and undisciplined attack doctrines apparently derived from peacetime tradition.

The cost was high. Air Group 8 was not the only American squadron exposed to "bitter controversy" because of the events of 4 June 1942. Fighting 6's Jim Gray was torn by the same impossible dual responsibility to protect a bombing squadron above and a torpedo squadron below, and his ambiguous actions generated as much criticism as did those of Stan Ring. For the next twenty years Gray endured insinuations of cowardice from both armchair strategists and fellow aviators.[105]

Task Force 16 remained in the increasingly stormy central Pacific for several days after the battle, while aboard the *Hornet* Jurika and his small staff of intelligence experts grilled the pilots and debriefed the squadron commanders and section leaders, "attempting to find out how many direct hits and how many near misses that might have done damage were actually scored and by whom." The job was made easier because all aircraft of Bombing, Scouting, and Fighting 8 had wing cameras, which the pilots triggered just as they released their bombs or began their strafing runs. But Jurika remembered that the debriefing and report-writing "took an unconscionable time . . . many, many, many hours in the day and far into the night."[106]

On 9 June Nimitz released the remnants of Task Force 17, which headed for Pearl. Task Force 16 remained in the area and prepared to refuel. Shortly before 0900 the *Hornet*'s crew received a reminder of the inherent dangers aboard a large, complex piece of machinery like an aircraft carrier even when not in action. One of the fleet oilers had come alongside, and the hoses had been passed over to be locked into the carrier's fueling trunk on the starboard side of the hangar deck. A young sailor, James C. Hawkins, sat nearby glancing at a comic book. Suddenly a restraining strap on the heavy fueling block parted, and the loosened block swung around viciously, striking Hawkins and nearly tearing off his head. The youngster was killed instantly. Boatswain's mates immediately signaled the oiler to shut off flow to the hose until the block could be firmly restrapped in place. Meanwhile, the bloody corpse was taken below to be prepared for burial.[107]

Shortly thereafter the *Saratoga* appeared with a scratch air group consisting of squadrons that had been hastily brought together at San Diego just before the carrier had sailed. Mitscher announced to the *Hornet* that Task Force 16 was heading north to battle Japanese forces in the Aleutians. But Nimitz changed his mind. Everyone realized that the main Japanese fleet had been whipped and had left the central Pacific. It was time for everyone to go back to Hawaii.

On the *Hornet* the mood was a mixture of sorrow and elation. Good men and ships were gone. Mears and Divine had the depressing task of "inventorying" the personal effects of the fourteen fliers and fifteen gunner-radiomen of Torpedo 8. Hour after hour they listed and packed battered caps, girls' pictures, an earmarked prayer book, a wallet, a tweed sport jacket, and much else. They also had to scan the last few letters each man had received before shipping them back home and to censor for security reasons the final note each had asked to be sent to wives or families. This was the hardest part, for never had the power of love and affection been so evident, never had the waste and futility of war seemed so obvious. A year later Mears himself would die, and a friend would inventory his life.

But for thousands of victorious sailors Honolulu beckoned, and for the first time in six months the Japanese fleet seemed far away. A great battle had been decisively, if narrowly, won. It was time to rest, regroup, and reorganize for the many conflicts still to come.

7

Interregnum

TASK FORCE 16 got back to Hawaii just in time for Saturday night liberty. On the morning of 13 June the *Hornet, Enterprise,* and *Saratoga* launched all their planes for "a massive fly-in" to the airfields on Oahu, and at least one air group was greeted with beer and a band.[1] That afternoon the cruisers, carriers, and destroyers began steaming up the Pearl Harbor ship channel. They eased into their various piers and anchorages as the sun began to slip toward the western horizon. "We were welcomed as a victorious fleet," Stephen Jurika recalled, "with hula dancers and bands on the dock, just all manner of welcome."[2]

On ships and ashore the amazement over the recent battle had not abated. While the fleet was still in the combat zone, inflated intelligence estimates had placed the number of dead Japanese sailors and pilots at close to twenty thousand. "While we aren't wasting too much sympathy on our enemy at the moment, we are awed by the catastrophe that overtook him," Bob Casey noted in his diary. "There is chill in the thought that there, but for the Grace of God, go we. Had we been seen . . . had the Japs attacked us before making the try for Midway. . . ." Above all, there was the realization that "this incredible Navy has come of age and, not too greatly to the surprise of one who has lived with it in recent months, it is as good as it thought it was."[3]

Certainly the respectable ladies of Honolulu thought so. At the Royal

Hawaiian Hotel they placed a large sign announcing an "Appreciation Day" for the fleet. Such news was especially welcome for the men of the *Hornet*, who badly needed a rest. The carrier had been steaming virtually nonstop ever since it had left Norfolk. In only one hundred days the ship had left the Chesapeake, gone through the Panama Canal, picked up Doolittle's raiders at San Francisco, launched them off the coast of Japan, then sailed down to the Coral Sea and back up to Midway. It was time to sample some shoretime joys.

The *Hornet*'s junior doctor, Gerry McAteer, and a buddy saw the sign and promptly went into the hotel lobby. A middle-aged lady came up and said imperiously, "You come with me." The two young men happily climbed into a late model, wood-paneled station wagon to go to the "party."[4] The woman drove quickly through the fading sunlight, for the penalties if caught out after Honolulu's sunset curfew were draconian. She took the men to a lovely, large home with a golf course behind it, where they found themselves alone with the woman and her maid. For hours the woman talked about how difficult it was in wartime Honolulu. Food was at a premium; antiaircraft guns littered the golf course; the curfew had absolutely ruined social life. The two men became restless and thirsty, and it soon became clear that Honolulu society had decided that what the battle-weary fleet really needed was not merriment but peace and quiet.

After hours of inconsequential chat the woman finally asked the young men if they would like a drink. The reply was an emphatic affirmative. The maid disappeared into the cellar and soon returned with a small, near-empty bottle of whiskey. "We only use this for medicinal purposes," the woman said primly as she poured a thimbleful of amber liquid into two small glasses. McAteer's buddy, a tough kid from Brooklyn, was beside himself. The whole damned fleet was on Hotel Street or at the various "O" clubs around Oahu partying it up, and here they were stone-cold sober listening to a society lady's endless complaints.

The two men at last wangled a ride back to town. "I'll bet everyone's been partying," McAteer's buddy moaned pathetically as they approached the *Hornet*'s pier. To their astonishment everyone they met was sober as a judge. There was not a decent hangover to be found anywhere. Apparently the entire officer corps of the Pacific Fleet had been appropriated by one or more determined members of Oahu's upper crust. "Jeez," a shipmate told McAteer, "they gave us milk and put us to bed." Not us, McAteer and his buddy boasted, we had a helluva bash.

But there was a lingering bitterness in the determined search for fun.

Mitscher returned from Midway deeply depressed "for reasons beyond the loss of the pilots and crewmen." Although he had congratulated his crew on a job well done and recommended every member of the air group (including Ring and Mitchell) for a decoration, "he felt that the *Hornet*'s performance had not lived up to his expectations. He also felt that he had personally failed to deliver."[5]

Many ship's officers could not forgive the air group for its performance on the first day at Midway. Several days after the carrier docked at Ford Island, Stan Ring entered a Honolulu bar and grill full of the carrier's officers, including Henry Martin. Ring stood about purposefully for a moment, waiting to be recognized, as naval etiquette demanded. When no one stood up, Ring became incensed. It was customary, he told the tableful of officers in icy tones, for juniors to rise in the presence of their seniors. Martin and the others seethed. They thought that just before his takeoff on the morning of the fourth, Ring had preened and swaggered before the handful of civilian journalists standing on the side of the *Hornet*'s flight deck. Then he had twice gone out to find the enemy and twice returned with his bomb load. Now one of the junior officers looked up and replied to Ring's demand: "Not for you, you s.o.b." The furious air group commander spun on his heel and walked out. Martin never saw Ring again. Within hours of the incident he had been transferred.[6]

Perhaps this persistent sense of unease and uncertainty, along with inevitable post-combat exhaustion, explains why the fleet and its leaders let down after Midway. Some wardroom strategists realized correctly that the virtual destruction of the *Kido Butai* opened the central Pacific road to Tokyo. It is tempting to dwell on the might-have-been of another, hastily arranged B-25 raid on Tokyo or at least a strong carrier strike on Marcus in the weeks immediately after Midway. Such attacks might have induced the already shaken Japanese high command to transfer key naval and air forces back to the defense of the home islands and their approaches, thus ending Nipponese expansion in the South Pacific. But the *Enterprise, Hornet,* and *Saratoga* spent the rest of June and most of July "loafing in Pearl Harbor," while Nimitz and his staff explored ways to blunt the enemy advance in the Coral Sea–Solomon Islands area and air group commanders rebuilt their decimated squadrons.[7]

Across the Pacific the Japanese at first were equally indolent. Crushing defeat had induced lethargy. Returning home, Admiral Ugaki got his hair cut very short, partly to atone for the "failure" of the Midway operation. One afternoon in mid-June Vice Adm. Seiichi Ito, vice chief of the naval general staff, visited the *Yamato*, again anchored in the Inland Sea, to relay a message from the emperor. The Son of Heaven "was not too concerned about the recent defeat; such things were to be expected in war." The fleet should keep up its morale "and try again." Ugaki was not sure these were the emperor's true feelings. The admiral himself was "overwhelmed with trepidation" for the future. But Ugaki and his colleagues carried on as Hirohito wished. There were conferences about new carrier construction and aircraft production. The planning staff began drafting proposals for a naval offensive in the western Indian Ocean, presumably to support the army's advance through Burma toward the Indian frontier.[8] By the end of July the Imperial Japanese Navy was again ready to sail and to fight.

As the Pacific Fleet rested and restored itself in Hawaii, army and navy spokesmen argued passionately over who had really sunk the *Kido Butai*. Air corps bombers from Midway had struck at Nagumo's carriers first, and excited aircrew had insisted that they had delivered mortal blows. The navy knew better. How could bomber crews who had perched twenty thousand feet above the *Kido Butai*, safe from enemy Zeros, dare to assert that they could hit a ship twisting and turning at thirty miles an hour? But the army boys had gotten to Hawaii and the press briefings long before Spruance and Fletcher.

While army publicists insisted that the new queen of the seas was not the aircraft carrier but the B-17, the navy and Marine Corps veterans of Midway went to Waikiki and partied and rioted in every room and hallway of the Moana Hotel, which had been reserved for their exclusive use. "Some few were feeling tender enough to want to find a girl," Fred Mears remembered, "but for the most part their emotions were released in being just as mean as they could." Pilots who were the closest of friends on board the *Hornet* beat each other's faces with their fists, "not trying to duck or box, until they both had black eyes and were crimson with blood. Another pilot tried to throw his smaller friend out of a window."[9]

The unbearable post-Midway tension within Air Group 8 was part of a broader pattern. By the early summer of 1942 Hawaii was bursting with all kinds of warriors. Thousands of fliers "way-stationed" there before moving west or south to the war zones. Novices swiftly assumed the "hard, cruel, laughing bitterness" of the veterans, for the Coral Sea and Midway had revealed to everyone the enemy's deadly capability and implacable will. American airmen had "written themselves off," James Jones wrote. "None of them expected to come back, and they wanted everything they could get of living on the way out" to combat, "and that included fist fighting." Often the bloody protagonists staggered back into the Moana Bar or even the lobby of the Royal Hawaiian, which was supposed to be reserved for the submarine force, "arm in arm while their seconds and fans cheered."[10]

King and Nimitz recognized that the fleet and its "first team" of naval aviators were overly stressed after months of constant steaming and intermittent combat. They resolved the problem with characteristic vigor. Squadrons would be reorganized and carriers recharged with new leadership. Within days after Midway the *Hornet* had an almost entirely new command structure and air group.

Mitscher turned over his command as soon as the ship reached Pearl and left for the West Coast to await his new assignment. (In late October he would be named Halsey's deputy in charge of all naval air forces in the Solomons.) The *Hornet*'s new skipper, like the old, was a pioneer aviator. Capt. Charles P. Mason was a distinguished, gray-haired, gray-mustached, fifty-one-year-old sailor-flier whose slight paunch was restrained by a tightly cinched uniform belt. He had a passion for Robert Burns cigars, which he chain-smoked ashore and at sea. He had graduated from the Naval Academy in 1912. After four years in the surface fleet, he had gone to Pensacola, which was still a weedy naval coaling station with only a handful of fanatical fliers to keep it alive. When Mason won his wings in 1917 he was Naval Aviator No. 52. He served as a test pilot in France during the First World War and during the interwar years flew and commanded both planes and lighter-than-air craft. He had been the *Yorktown*'s first executive officer in 1938; then he had established the Jacksonville (Fla.) Naval Station until he was ordered to take over the *Hornet*.

Mason was a complex individual whose humor and impatience mingled to produce not confusion but fiery determination. The crew quickly realized that he was as much a prize C.O. as Mitscher had been. Artist-writer Tom Lea, who spent more than two months aboard the *Hornet* during her last days in the South Pacific, summed up Mason in a sentence: "With superbly delicate balance of judgment and conduct, he ran an efficient fighting ship." And, to the extent that any warship can be so characterized, it was also a happy one.[11]

George Henderson went off to a desk job in preparation for his first command, the light carrier *Princeton*, which was still a year from completion. Apollo Soucek moved up to executive officer. He and Mason quickly became close partners in the complex job of running a 2,600-man ship and airfield. "They were really a pair," one of the carrier's air officers later remembered. The *Hornet* "couldn't have asked for two finer gentlemen or steady hands at the helm than those two."[12] Frank Akers also left; he had been ordered back to the Navy Department in Washington for reassignment. His replacement was Comdr. Robert Lockhart, who kept the ship's navigation department running smoothly.

Soucek's replacement as air officer was Comdr. Marcel E. A. Gouin, a former test pilot. Gouin was a quiet man who got things done without a fuss. An officer who worked closely with him admired him because he was a "cool, calm perfectionist who invariably managed to know everything that was going on" and "keep accurate track of essential minutai [*sic*] in his little black book."[13] Gouin's chief responsibility would be to reintegrate the air group, to see that the planes and the men who flew and maintained them functioned perfectly. "A great and inflexible reserve set him apart from his fellow officers," Lea later wrote. "He spoke only when he judged it absolutely necessary. In the wardroom, even those who knew him best called him 'Commander.' There was no vanity whatsoever in this reserve, nor did it spring from his rank. It was simply the mark of a man who was eliminating everything from his life but his job." Of all the officers whom Lea wanted to memorialize with a portrait, Gouin was the most reluctant. But when he did finally agree, he was the least self-conscious subject. Beneath the quiet, steely exterior a "volcano burned," the artist thought.[14] Weeks later in the South Pacific a member of the ship's company questioned whether a planned air strike against Japanese positions would be strong enough to avoid being annihilated. Gouin glanced at the man briefly, said, "We're in this business to take risks," and walked away.[15]

As was customary, Mason had brought some of his own men from Jacksonville to fill his new command. One was Lt. Comdr. Francis Drake Foley, whose career in naval aviation eventually included postwar command of the *Shangri-La* and a rear admiral's stars. After graduating from Annapolis in 1932, Foley had routinely climbed the prewar tour and promotion ladder: battleships for a while, Pensacola, a tour in a patrol squadron, a carrier air group, then in 1939 back to patrol planes out of Jacksonville. He had been chafing at Jacksonville ever since Pearl Harbor, pestering the navy's Bureau of Personnel for a Pacific combat tour. When Mason asked if he wanted to go aboard the *Hornet* to get back into carrier aviation, Foley did not hesitate.

Foley and three others were briefly stranded in San Francisco. They finally got passage on a navy cargo ship, part of a convoy that reached Pearl Harbor early one evening in late June. In the gathering dusk the four men found their way to Ford Island and finally to the *Hornet*'s pier. By this time it was pitch dark. Hawaii was still rigidly enforcing blackout procedures because of the possibility that Pearl Harbor might again be the target of a sudden Japanese raid. The carrier "appeared as a huge black mass looming ominously alongside the dock." As Foley and his companions climbed the ladder to the quarterdeck, they saw parts of the vessel fitfully illuminated by a few battle lamps, which cast an eerie, blue glow. The officer of the deck briefly shined his screened flashlight in their faces as he checked their orders, then sent Foley along with an escort to his small stateroom forward and below decks. The next morning Foley met with Gouin and learned that he would be the ship's air operations officer. His principal function would be to help plan air strikes "and then to pass every conceivable bit of information connected with their successful accomplishment to the four squadron ready rooms below via teletype system." His work and battle station would be in the tiny "air plot" office in the island structure immediately adjacent to PriFly, from which Gouin or an assistant orchestrated the launching and landing of aircraft. Foley was delighted; his job was the next best thing to being a full-fledged member of the air group.[16]

When Task Force 16 had returned to Pearl, Nimitz had given his fliers four days off with forty-eight hours' notice. But liberty, no matter how raucous and tension breaking, could not solve the deeper ills that beset the carrier air groups. Each squadron aboard the *Enterprise* and *Hornet* was depleted both physically and emotionally. Each air group needed to be replenished and reorganized. The new *Saratoga* air group needed more training. It was not until 7 July, just two weeks before the *Enterprise* and *Saratoga* departed for the South Pacific, that new alignments jelled aboard each of the three carriers.[17] Battle-tested pilots were shuffled and exchanged among the air groups at a dizzying rate, and squadron ranks were then filled with newcomers. These changes took place in the midst of long, liquid liberties at Waikiki, in the better bars of Honolulu, and in officers' clubs at adjacent airfields and military installations.

The *Hornet* received an almost new air group. Within days after returning from Midway, Ring, Ruehlow, and other members of Air Group 8 had departed. Fighting 8 was gradually broken up and finally disbanded on 25 August; its veterans filled billets in other squadrons or left for the States. Mitchell became one of the *Hornet*'s assistant air officers.

With Ring's departure, Walt Rodee moved up to air group commander. Lt. "Abie" Tucker, who had brought the Dauntlesses back from Midway on 4 June, took command of Bombing 8, and Lt. Edwin Parker formed an entirely new torpedo squadron designated Torpedo 6. Parker had made a courageous attack on the *Shokaku* at the Coral Sea and thereafter had commanded a decimated five-plane torpedo squadron on the *Saratoga* until assuming his new position on the *Hornet*. On the surface he seemed a cold, distant man. Some, perhaps recalling Waldron's warmth, called him "The Flying Iceberg." But others accepted his coldness as part of an "iron discipline" that was essential if Torpedo 6 was to cope effectively with the ghosts of Waldron, Abercrombie, and the others.[18]

Gus Widhelm, the irrepressible grandstander and superb airman, became commander of Scouting 8. Tom Lea was soon one of his many admirers. Here was a man born to fly, born to fight, born to lead. Lea sketched Widhelm in the cockpit of his Dauntless, flight goggles down over his eyes, heavy cigar rakishly tilted between firm lips, left hand gesturing a thumbs up. "In all things he stuck his square chin out and dared the world to take a poke at it."[19]

Lt. Comdr. Mike Sanchez brought aboard a new fighter squadron, designated VF-72, which had previously seen duty on the *Wasp* in the Atlantic. Sanchez proved to be a leader in the Widhelm mold, audacious and scrappy.[20] Reminiscent of Jimmy Doolittle in both stature and manner, he delighted the hundreds of airdales on the *Hornet*'s flight deck by wearing cowboy boots for all battle flights. He even wore them for a formal squadron portrait. From a distance, plane handler Keith Bancroft got the impression that Sanchez was a man who knew what he was doing and was easy to get along with.[21]

Most of the fliers of VF-72 were scrappy. Lea described Lt. Al Emerson, Sanchez's executive officer, as "a consecrated fighter, with a burning hatred for the Japs." Still a young man, Emerson had "wide-open sharp green eyes" and prematurely gray hair; he moved "with a sleek, streamlined grace." Unlike Widhelm, Emerson was "utterly without pose or bravado."[22] He had a thousand hours of carrier flying, but like the rest of VF-72 he was just beginning his combat career. Killing and being killed were part of war, he told Lea. "The only way to fight," Emerson said, "is to get in there, and the hell with thinking about anything else."[23]

The transfers and shuffles frequently bewildered both enlisted men and officers. When Bancroft reported aboard in early July for assignment to Fighting 8, he was taken to his berthing compartment below, assigned a bunk and locker, and told to unpack. While he was emptying his seabag, the chief who had brought him down reappeared and told him to repack and get back to the hangar deck because Fighting 8 had been transferred off the ship. After he had stood around on the hangar with several dozen men for a while, word came over the loudspeaker that all enlisted men heading for Fighting 8 were to report back to their berthing spaces because they had been reassigned to VF-72.[24]

Not only were there new men; there were more and better aircraft as well. Heeding the lessons of both the Coral Sea and Midway, Nimitz had managed to scrape together thirty-six F4F-4s for Mike Sanchez and VF-72. The *Hornet* and her sister carriers would finally have enough fighters for both aerial defense and strike group escort. The introduction of the Grumman–General Motors Avenger was an even bigger bonus for the small American carrier fleet.[25] Designated TBF or TBM, depending on the manufacturer, the Avenger was a truly remarkable plane, a major leap forward in aviation technology from the Douglas Devastators that had carried Torpedo 8's pilots to their doom. With a maximum speed of 278 miles per hour, an operational ceiling of 22,000 feet, and a range of 900 miles at 215 miles per hour, the Avenger easily matched the performance capabilities of the Dauntless dive-bombers and scouts and the Wildcats of VF-72. The Avenger's 14,500-pound weight, 5,500 pounds heavier than the Devastator, allowed it to be used as either a torpedo or a bombing plane. In fact, although they were usually used as torpedo planes in the Pacific, Avengers were routinely used as bombers aboard escort carriers in the Atlantic, where their chief task was to seek out and destroy U-boats. The plane could carry one two-thousand-pound bomb or a comparably sized torpedo. Its bulk and versatility made it a rugged and effective combat aircraft. The component squadrons of U.S. carrier air groups had finally reached performance parity; the disparities that had caused such folly and tragedy at Midway were gone.

Despite weeks of hard steaming, the *Hornet* was in good shape and did not need any repairs in the Pearl Harbor shipyard. But the SC radar antenna had bedeviled Mitscher since the shakedown cruise. The carrier had been lucky at Midway. If it had been attacked, the faulty SC would have provided minimal intercept capability. Fortunately, Pearl Harbor had exactly what the *Hornet* needed. Two years earlier the battleship *California* had been one of the first vessels in the fleet to receive a new CXAM antenna, which proved to be quite effective. After the ship was badly damaged on 7 December, the set had been removed and installed as part of an army search unit on Oahu. With concerns about an enemy attack abated after Midway, the navy was able to get the set back, and in early July the CXAM was installed on the *Hornet*'s masthead.[26]

The carrier was not so fortunate in obtaining other upgrades and improvements. The 1.1 Oerlikon "machine cannons," which were subject to frequent jamming and even explosion, were to be replaced on all American carriers by heavier, much more efficient and effective Bofors 40-millimeter guns. But none reached Pearl in time for installation on the *Hornet* or the *Enterprise*. Both ships, however, did obtain more 20-millimeter guns, which were effective for close-in air defense. These supplemented the nearly useless .50-caliber machine guns placed on the port and starboard gallery decks just below the flight deck and on the bow.[27]

Foley quickly discovered that the *Hornet* "was feeling pretty damn good about herself, except for Torpedo Squadron Eight."[28] One incident exemplified the mood of the entire ship. Several of the carrier's veteran enlisted men were drinking beer in a Honolulu bar one night when they bumped into Metalsmith 2nd Class Lawrence Pettinati, who had served with them aboard the cruiser *Helena* before the war. An earnest young man, Pettinati was assigned to the Naval Air Station at Ford Island as a parachute rigger. He had survived 7 December when many friends did not and was eager to get into the fight. The war was passing him by, he lamented. His buddies agreed.

"You're wasting your life. We've got a real break. We're on the *Hornet*."

"That's a ship!" Pettinati said. Then he asked, "You use riggers, don't you?"

"Sure, we have a parachute loft on the *Hornet*," they replied.

"Boy, how I'd like to get on that one!" Pettinati said. "But it would take me years to get a transfer. How about it? . . . Do you think I could get one?"

"We'll bet you a beer in 1950 that you ain't on the *Hornet* yet."

"I'll take that bet," Pettinati said. They laughed and bought him a brew with the good-natured superiority that sailors feel toward landlubbers.[29]

Weeks later, shortly after the *Hornet* left Hawaii for the South Pacific, a grinning but frightened Pettinati was discovered aboard the carrier. He had snuck on as the last stores were being loaded at Ford Island. The prospect of fighting the war on the *Hornet* was too great a temptation to resist, even if it meant forfeiting an impending promotion to first-class petty officer. Desertion from one's post in wartime was one of the worst offenses a man could commit. Gus Widhelm was assigned to bring charges against Pettinati. But Gus was busy. Somehow Pettinati got out of the brig and began working in the *Hornet*'s parachute loft. And somehow Widhelm never found the time to file charges.[30]

In mid-July the *Saratoga*, with Admiral Fletcher aboard, the *Enterprise*, and most of the fleet again steamed out of Pearl Harbor and set sail toward the Solomons. The *Hornet* remained in Hawaiian waters to complete training of its air group. Just before Midway, Japan had seized the islands of Tulagi and Guadalcanal at the southern end of the Solomons chain. Japanese engineers had begun building a seaplane base at Tulagi and an airstrip on the north shore of Guadalcanal several miles away. The move upset the plans of Vice Adm. Robert Ghormley, Commander South Pacific Forces, to seize the Santa Cruz Islands slightly north and east of Guadalcanal in order to secure the supply line between the United States and Australia and to gain a jumping-off point for eventually undertaking a modest South Pacific counteroffensive. Now, U.S. forces would have to invade Tulagi and Guadalcanal as well as the Santa Cruz group. Whether they were ready or not, it was time for the Americans to initiate their first offensive of the Pacific war.

Ghormley mustered a marine division and seventy-five warships and transports, including three carriers and the new battleship *North Carolina*. It was the largest accumulation of Pacific Fleet vessels since Pearl Harbor, and at dawn on 7 August it suddenly appeared off the shores of Guadalcanal and Tulagi. Planes from the *Enterprise, Saratoga,* and *Wasp* (which had steamed to the area directly from San Diego) struck Tulagi and Guadalcanal, and minutes later the marines stormed ashore. Initially they met little opposition at Guadalcanal but a vicious reaction at Tulagi. After forty-eight hours of bloodshed, Tulagi was secured. Meanwhile, combat teams on Guadalcanal swiftly moved off the beachhead and through tall kuni grass and dense undergrowth to seize the half-completed airstrip and surrounding defense positions. The expected response materialized at midday on 7 August, when the Japanese conducted their first air raids over the anchorage in an unsuccessful attempt to destroy unloading transports and cargo ships.

As the *Hornet* prepped her new air group off Pearl Harbor, Guadalcanal grew from a modest operation into a major campaign that sucked in all available resources of both sides. The night after the initial landings, an audacious Japanese cruiser-destroyer force surprised and sank four Allied cruisers that were protecting the invasion beaches and the off-loading transports. Shocked by the Battle of Savo Island, Fletcher promptly withdrew his carriers, destroyers, and remaining cruisers from around Guadalcanal. Within hours the half-unloaded transports and cargo ships had rushed away too, leaving sixteen thousand increasingly embittered marines at the mercy of a determined foe. For days Ghormley refused to send in a resupply convoy, and Maj. Gen. Alexander Vandegrift and his men had to exist on large stockpiles of captured enemy food, mostly rice and canned fish, and what guns, vehicles, and ammunition had been hastily unloaded during the first thirty-six hours of the operation.

The Japanese did not immediately exploit their stunning naval victory. On 13 August Ugaki wrote confidently in his diary that

> some enemies still remained in the Tulagi and Guadalcanal area, but now they are supposed to have been left behind with small craft when the enemy withdrew. Both the [Japanese] Eighth Fleet and the Eleventh Air Fleet, therefore, turned out to be bullish.
>
> The most urgent thing at present is to send a troop there to mop up the enemy remnant, rescue the [small Japanese] garrison, and repair the airfield. The [Japanese fleet] support force should simultaneously carry out operations as scheduled while invasions of [Port] Moresby [on New Guinea], Ocean, and Nauru islands should be completed as well as attempting to reduce the enemy strength.[31]

But Ugaki was unable to convey any sense of urgency to army and air force commanders at Rabaul. For two precious weeks the marines were largely left alone to battle deadly mosquitoes, stifling tropical heat, the dense jungle, and the small enemy garrison that had melted into it. But Guadalcanal was a large island with difficult terrain. After a week ashore, the marines could claim at most 15 square miles of the roughly 1,500-square-mile piece of rock, jungle, underbrush, and grasslands. Moreover, their vanished cargo ships carried nearly all the heavy equipment needed to complete the airstrip.

The gallant marines confounded both Japanese strategists and Japanese naval and military power. Construction troops, using a single bulldozer, working in often torrential downpours, and coping with slowly intensifying enemy air raids from Rabaul, completed the strip on 17

August. Three days later the first dozen marine Dauntless dive-bombers flew into what was christened Henderson Field. Twenty-four hours after that Maj. John L. Smith brought in fifteen F4F-4 fighter planes.

The Japanese high command was astounded at "the speed with which the Americans completed the construction of an airstrip at Guadalcanal" and impressed with the capabilities of the bulldozers, a few of which had been captured at Wake Island the previous December but had never been used. The number of U.S. planes deployed at Guadalcanal seemed to increase daily.[32] Finally the Japanese army bestirred itself. Aerial resupply missions were sent to the besieged garrison on Guadalcanal, and accompanying leaflets begged the troops to hang on until reinforcements arrived. One air-dropped message that fell into the hands of the alternatively amused and alarmed marines read: "The enemy before your eyes are collapsing. . . . Friendly troops: a landing party (marine naval brigade) relief is near. . . . We are convinced of help from heaven and divine grace. Respect yourself. By no means run away from the encampment. We too will stick to it."[33]

As the marines slowly expanded their perimeter, Ghormley recovered his nerve. The navy began slipping in occasional resupply convoys during daylight, using air cover from Henderson Field and the three carriers. Slowly but inexorably the campaign became a test of both sides' will. To the Americans the task was simple: Hang on until their country, which was rapidly developing the potential to lavishly supply a two-front global war, could provide the men and equipment to knock the Japanese out and initiate an offensive that would ultimately sweep right up to the enemy's home islands. To the Japanese, American-held Guadalcanal became the "Port Arthur of the Pacific." Imperial Navy strategists recalled how difficult it had been during the 1904–5 war with Russia to conquer the well-defended forts that had protected the strategically critical city, but the task had eventually been accomplished and the war had been won. Japan would display the same will and tactics in breaking and overwhelming the enemy garrison at Guadalcanal. As at Port Arthur, the navy would blockade and isolate enemy positions, and the army would then seize them. This time, however, air power was an essential factor. Yamamoto's carriers and the air force at Rabaul would be jointly responsible for destroying enemy air power on Guadalcanal and in adjacent ocean areas.[34]

But the Japanese experienced serious difficulties from the beginning. Tulagi and Guadalcanal were more than 600 miles from Rabaul (560 nautical miles). Refusing to consider the possibility of an American coun-teroffensive, the Japanese had built no intermediate airstrips on the islands that stretched between. "Our air crews of the smaller bombers were forced to the limit of their endurance, and too frequently these bombers dispatched from Rabaul failed to return because they ran out of fuel."[35] The strain of intense aerial combat against a tenacious enemy at the end of a debilitating 600-mile flight further contributed to Japanese losses and a rapid decline in fighting ability. A Japanese staff officer later wrote eloquently of the airmen's ordeal:

> Bomber crews soon wearied of the strain of missions from which their return was mathematically doubtful and often, in the cases of their flying mates, impossible. We could not maintain the pressure indefinitely, even with experienced and excellent air crews. . . .
>
> Medium bombers and Zero fighters based at Rabaul had sufficient range to attack American forces in the lower Solomons, and still return. Our Type 99 dive bombers, however, were dispatched in missions on which their crews despaired of survival. Simply stated, the airplanes could not carry sufficient fuel to make the round-trip flight from Rabaul to Guadalcanal and return. Within two days of the American invasion, we lost eighteen Type 99 bombers, but only a few planes fell to the enemy's guns. Their fuel ran out as they struggled to reach Rabaul, and all bombers crashed.
>
> It was a terribly depressing situation. At the outset of the [U.S.] invasion, our Zero fighters were superior in almost every respect to the American planes which they opposed, yet their combat effectiveness was steadily being sapped by the strain which the pilots suffered from too many hours spent in the cramped confines of the planes' cockpits. This disintegration of our effectiveness in air attack was enough to drive the combat commanders to the verge of insanity; they had spent years in developing their air units to peak efficiency, only now to have them shackled by strategic blindness.
>
> Had Japan possessed even one fifth of the American capacity for constructing air bases, the Guadalcanal air campaign might have ended differently. Had we possessed such air bases, we could have brought several times as much power to bear upon the American forces. One of Japan's greatest blunders in the Pacific War certainly lay in its failure to devote proper study to such matters as logistical and engineering support of our combat air forces.[36]

The Japanese were now beginning to be fatally affected by the lack of a coherent offensive framework in which every element from construction needs to battle plans had been carefully considered and integrated. The American enemy with its enormous industrial potential could ultimately overcome mistakes by the sheer force of material superiority. Japan could not. With a growing horror that indeed bordered on "insanity," Japanese field commanders watched their precious, irreplaceable cadre of superlative "first-team" pilots and aircrews melt away in the skies around and above Guadalcanal.

But if Japan failed to rule the skies, it still seemed to dominate the seas. It was clear to both sides that if Yamamoto decided to send his entire fleet into battle, its half-dozen heavy and light carriers and dozen or more battleships would be decisive. Guadalcanal would then become at best an American Dunkirk, at worst another Bataan. The still depleted Pacific Fleet needed to muster all its slender resources in a desperate attempt to avert disaster.

Far to the north, the *Hornet* spent most of July and the first half of August at her pier, being fitted with new guns and antennae. But Charlie Mason was able to take his carrier to sea for a week, and in the protected channel between Molokai, Lanai, and Oahu, Marcel Gouin and Walt Rodee exercised the new air group while Soucek and the department heads got the ship back to fighting trim. "The air group operated and got back its sea legs," Jurika remembered, "did a few carrier landings, a few bombing and strafing exercises, both against towed targets representing ships and air-towed targets representing aircraft." Days and nights in Pearl were spent "empty[ing] the bottle a little bit," lying on the sands of Waikiki after being admitted through the barbed wire gates, and "watch[ing] the hula dancers at Kapiolani Park."[37]

As pilots and officers relaxed in the finest hotels and better bars of Honolulu or in plush officers' clubs, the enlisted men found a variety of entertainments. There were always the dives on Hotel, River, and King Streets, and the cathouses with their endless lines of soldiers, marines, sailors, and civilians waiting outside for a few moments of frantic pleasure. Enlisted men were also allowed to eat, drink, and dance at the Royal Hawaiian. But since their liberty ended at 1800 or 2000, there was little time to indulge in such luxuries. A small shot of whiskey or a beer at the Royal Hawaiian was seventy-five cents. A good drunk could thus cost half a month's pay; only a proficient poker player could afford much of that. There were also "very damned few" women around, and a sailor "had to be pretty sharp to get one."[38]

As the days and weeks passed, it became increasingly difficult to enjoy the joys of Hawaii when others were grappling with the enemy far to the south. So the men of the *Hornet* felt both relief and regret when they received orders to sail into battle again. Keith Bancroft was keeping a brief, sporadic diary, although it was strictly against regulations. "We are going out somewhere looking for trouble soon," he wrote on 5 August, "when or where I don't know but it won't be long."

The evening before the carrier "wrenched herself away from Pearl,"[39] Bancroft returned from liberty to find his chief petty officer waiting for him. Get below, he was told, and get into dungarees; there was work to be done. The ship had just taken aboard an additional twenty-one F4Fs, which were to be stowed until needed to replace losses. Bancroft and several hundred other members of the air department worked until 0400 the next morning to strip the planes of their engines, props, and guns, which were preserved in Cosmoline. The men also removed rudders and elevators from all the planes and stowed them far below in storerooms on the fourth and fifth decks. Then they hoisted the F4F carcasses, with wings folded, from the hangar deck into the many storage bays that interrupted the gallery deck overhead. One of the aircraft was a new, experimental model designated F4F-7, "a photographic reconnaissance plane with a fantastic range, 2,900 miles in still air."[40] To make room for the fighters, the crew had to remove from the overhead bays a "cache of unessential equipage" left over from the Doolittle raid. It made a pile on the hangar deck of roughly one thousand cubic feet that was guarded by members of the *Hornet's* small marine detachment. But within an hour scavengers managed to break through the cordon—helped by generous bribes, no doubt—and carried away every piece of gear to keep or sell as invaluable memorabilia.[41]

On 17 August 1942, while Keith Bancroft and his exhausted mates slumbered in their bunks after hours of work, the *Hornet* sailed out of Pearl Harbor with more than one hundred aircraft aboard. She was accompanied by two cruisers, six destroyers, and an oiler. These final remnants of the Pacific Fleet not yet committed to battle comprised a reconstituted Task Force 17. On the carrier's flag bridge stood Rear Adm. George Murray, task force commander. It was the first time the ship had had a flag officer aboard. That night Bancroft wrote in his diary, "We're out looking for Mr. Jap."[42]

8

Harm's Way

NOT EVERYONE aboard the *Hornet* was eager for battle. Little more than an hour after Task Force 17 had formed up off Pearl, with the Hawaiian Islands still visible to the north, east, and west, officers and crewmen in the island structure suddenly discovered that a sailor had climbed the ship's mast and crawled out along the starboard yardarm. He obviously intended to jump overboard. Signalmen on their small bridge at the foot of the mainmast had seen the man go up, but they had assumed he was a radar technician or someone else doing a routine job and had not attempted to stop him. Suddenly there he was, riveting everyone's attention, clinging tightly to the yardarm, and trying to muster the nerve to let go and drop the 120-odd feet into the sea.

The task force was making eighteen knots, the top cruising speed for the oiler. It could not slow down because Japanese submarines were thought to be constantly lurking in the area. Everyone began yelling at the sailor to come down. "The poor fellow became scared as hell but was apparently determined to go through with it," Francis Foley recalled. Mason appeared and told everyone to quiet down. The chief master at arms went aloft and climbed out on the yardarm. The wind whistled in the rigging, and the ship rolled gently in the calm seas far below. The chief pleaded quietly with the sailor, while flight deck personnel broke out a cargo net and rigged it between two tow bars on the starboard side to try to catch the boy if he slipped. Chaplain Eddie Harp and one of the ship's doctors went up the high mast to add their pleas. They finally convinced the sailor that suicide was not the solution to his fears. Slowly, carefully he crawled back from the yardarm to the mainmast. At the first opportunity he was sent ashore, then back to the States for psychiatric evaluation. Foley later heard that the sailor returned to the ship just before she was lost, "thus having to face up to the same situation he had tried to escape!"[1]

For the next week the task force was routed almost due south toward Tongatabu, then westward toward the New Hebrides and the war zone. The news from there was unrelievedly grim. Deep divisions were increasingly apparent between Nimitz and Ghormley and within Ghormley's own command. Eight months of incessant defensive war had frayed men's nerves.

The Guadalcanal invasion probably should never have been undertaken, at least not in the way it was. Indeed, American planning for the campaign was hauntingly reminiscent of Yamamoto's hastily cobbled together and poorly conceived assault on Midway. In the summer of 1942 Nimitz's carriers had a chance to gain the initiative with further hit-and-run raids against Marcus and possibly even B-25 raids against parts of the homeland. If this opportunity had been exploited, it is unlikely that Tokyo could have sustained any kind of South Pacific offensive, and the entire complexion of the war might have changed. Instead, the Americans ignored the opportunity and went charging 3,500 miles south, gratuitously returning the initiative to Yamamoto and the Japanese army and air force.

The Guadalcanal campaign resulted from Washington military politics, especially the fractious relations between the Joint Chiefs of Staff and Gen. Douglas MacArthur, the vainglorious southwestern Pacific field commander whose headquarters were in Melbourne, Australia. From the time he had escaped the Philippines in the spring of 1942, MacArthur had dreamed of leading a great crusade of reconquest. He would allow no one in Washington or elsewhere to stand in his way. But Joint Chiefs Chairman George C. Marshall and Chief of Naval Operations Ernest J. King were forced to look at priorities globally rather than regionally. Marshall, FDR, and the British desperately needed the U.S. Navy's concurrence in and resources for an eventual cross-channel invasion of Western Europe. The navy, however, was obsessed with avenging Pearl

Harbor, and Admiral King naturally considered the Pacific the major theater of war. After Midway he was determined to go on the offensive; unfortunately, he focused on stopping Japanese expansion at its farthest point, the eastern Solomons. He and Marshall were forced to strike a deal: The navy could have an immediate, limited offensive in the Pacific if it agreed to support an eventual cross-channel invasion in Europe. King grudgingly concurred and ordered Nimitz to plan a counterattack in which the United States would seize Japan's most advanced South Pacific base at Tulagi.

In their deal King and Marshall completely ignored MacArthur, who envisioned mounting America's first Pacific counterattack at Rabaul. But King convinced a skeptical Marshall that the army did not know how to manage either air or sea power; moreover, MacArthur simply did not possess sufficient resources to crack such a tough nut as Rabaul. America's first Pacific offensive would be primarily a Navy–Marine Corps show in the Solomons, and military theater responsibilities were redrawn so that the eastern Solomons would fall within Nimitz's field of operations while the western Solomons remained MacArthur's preserve.

According to historian Wilbur H. Morrison, "MacArthur was livid at King's insistence that Nimitz be responsible for the seizure of Tulagi. He sent angry messages to Washington that valuable time was being lost and that the Japanese were recovering quickly from their defeat at Midway. In a letter he reminded Marshall that the army had supreme command in Europe, and he expected no less in the Pacific." But his protests had no effect. Ignoring MacArthur's warning that the army might be reduced to little more than an "occupation force" in the Pacific, Marshall maintained his commitment to a naval offensive.[2] Relations between Nimitz's headquarters at Pearl Harbor and MacArthur's at Melbourne became frigid.

Fearful that King's agreement with Marshall might crumble under the weight of MacArthur's displeasure, Nimitz took only forty-five days to turn the chief of naval operations' 23 June order into reality. Rear Adm. Richmond Kelly Turner's orders not only called for the seizure of Guadalcanal and Tulagi; he was also to occupy the Santa Cruz archipelago several hundred miles to the east with his reserve troops as soon as Tulagi was captured and sufficient lodgments were made on Guadalcanal. Everyone realized that air power would again be dominant and that the *Enterprise, Wasp,* and *Saratoga* would have to bear most of the burden. In effect, Admiral Fletcher's carriers would perform the same functions at Guadalcanal that Yamamoto had asked his flattops to perform at Midway. The three ships would have to fulfill the tactical role of supporting an island invasion and subsequent buildup and simultaneously perform the strategic function of defeating both enemy land-based aircraft (from Rabaul and Buka) and Nagumo's still-powerful carrier fleet. Lundstrom emphasized the difficulties involved: "The Tulagi-Guadalcanal operation required close air support from the carriers. To accomplish this would pin the carriers to a narrow arc 80 to 100 miles south of Tulagi and render them vulnerable to air attack and also prey to submarines certain to flock to those waters."[3] Only a miracle could prevent the loss of one, two, or perhaps all three of Fletcher's precious carriers.

Ghormley, widely appreciated by his peers as a first-rate strategist, immediately understood the risks involved. He was also well aware of MacArthur's displeasure, which was expressed as disdain for the whole operation. After meeting with the general in Melbourne during the first week in July, Ghormley dutifully cabled King, urging that "Operation Watchtower" be postponed because of the overwhelming enemy land- and sea-based air strength that could be employed in the eastern Solomons region. Ghormley understood, if planners and strategists in distant Hawaii and Washington did not, that the Guadalcanal campaign was being undertaken too hastily with insufficient and uncertain resources and "shockingly inadequate" air power. "He estimated the invasion convoy required from 36 hours to four days to unload and thought it would be 'extremely doubtful' that the carriers could offer close air support during this whole time." But his plea merely raised the ire of army and navy planners in Washington and sowed "the seeds of doubt about Ghormley's own morale." King and Nimitz had worked too hard to let this opportunity slip. Fearing a Japanese buildup in the Solomons, neither man would countenance any delay. Ghormley compounded his growing isolation by refusing to attend the single preinvasion conference of the Expeditionary Force flag officers, held on 26 July off Koro Island in the Fijis. "This denied him both critical information and the opportunity to intervene to address the" crucial "question of air support for the invasion."[4]

If Ghormley had attended, he would undoubtedly have received support from a "visibly exhausted" Frank Jack Fletcher. The fifty-seven-year-old carrier chief, who had been in combat command at sea for more than six months without respite, was "flatly skeptical of the prospects for the campaign."[5] He believed that his carriers were being asked to do too much. Tempers flared between Fletcher, Turner, and Ghormley's representative, Rear Adm. Daniel Callaghan, over how long the carriers and their escort ships could or should stay in direct support of the landings. When the Japanese subsequently responded with unexpected vigor to the invasion of Tulagi, Turner was forced to commit his reserves, thus canceling the proposed invasion of the Santa Cruz Islands. The debacle off Savo Island the following night cracked American morale.

Ghormley "virtually locked himself into a small sweatbox of an office" in distant New Caledonia, where he worked for hours trying to analyze and react appropriately to the marines' increasingly desperate situation at Guadalcanal. He was not helped by consistently poor staff work. The admiral never visited the island for a firsthand look, which confirmed a rapidly crystallizing opinion among Vandegrift's ragged troops that they were about to be abandoned. Up in Pearl Harbor, Nimitz began to seethe quietly.[6]

Neither morale nor prospects had appreciably improved as George Murray brought the *Hornet* into the South Pacific little more than two weeks after the beginning of the campaign. A few convoys had gotten into Guadalcanal, but the marines were desperately short of manpower, supplies, and arms. Steaming south, the carrier conducted daily air operations to complete the training and integration of the new air group. From his perch in air plot, thirty feet above the flight deck, Francis Foley saw it all: blue-gray planes packed together in "stacks" with engines snarling; scores of young airdales in colored jerseys and matching, close-fitting cloth helmets dodging in and out of aircraft and around roaring propellers; signal flags whipping in the stiff, tropical breeze; ears vibrating as each plane slowly pulled out of the bunched pack near the stern and crept toward the start line; taxiing instructions relayed by hand signals from flight deck crew to pilots; and finally, thirty seconds apart, the checkered yellow and black flag swinging smartly downward from the flight deck officer's hand to launch the racing takeoffs. From dawn to dusk Foley passed every bit of information that flowed into his tiny office to the squadron ready rooms by teletype, while Wildcats, Dauntlesses, and Avengers took off and plunked down on the flight deck below. Air plot was just above the crude, cramped combat information center, and through an open scuttle Foley could look directly down at the radar screen that the fighter director officer, Lt. Allan Fleming, used to vector the combat air patrol onto incoming aircraft.

Gouin, who was continually busy keeping in touch with Mason on the bridge and his various squadron commanders in ready rooms below or in aircraft aloft, was determined not to lose any more pilots than necessary because of navigational errors. He told the pilots to relay their navigation solutions to Foley for recheck before they went on any specific mission, either to a search sector or any point with a particular objective assigned. "No flight could leave the ship until I checked their navigation calculations," Foley recalled. Fortunately, the air operations officer had "crackerjack" assistants, a junior officer and an enlisted teletype operator, both competent and experienced. This allowed Foley to devote sufficient time to the calculations so that "we didn't hold up a single operation. Nobody ever had to wait to man their planes while we checked their navigation, and no pilot ever left the ship without a confirmation."[7]

It was hard work: Foley seldom had time to visit the rest of the ship. Like the other men aboard, he shuffled daily between bunk, eating quarters, and work station. He was usually in air plot from 0800 until 2200 or even midnight each day, collecting intelligence, collating information, providing data to the squadrons, and helping keep Air Group 8 aloft or bringing it safely aboard. In such ways, small and large, the *Hornet* and her handful of sisters were developing the combat traditions of carrier warfare that would be applied in the great push across the central and north Pacific and later in Korea and Vietnam.

Artist-writer Tom Lea later sketched from memory some indelible scenes aboard the *Hornet* during this time. A drawing depicting PriFly shows Assistant Air Officer Pat Mitchell leaning out of one of the compartment's open windows to replace one solid-colored banner with another on the flag holder outside, which was above the flight deck and easily visible to both pilots and deck crew.[8] To Mitchell's immediate left inside PriFly is a small, waist-high table with a ledger; it provided basic information such as the number of aircraft aloft, on deck, and ready to launch. Below the table, welded into the bulkhead, is a small, round ashtray with a smoking butt. Steady nerves were required to orchestrate the launch, landing, and precise placement of eighty-odd high-performance aircraft day after day. Many if not most of the men in key positions on World War II aircraft carriers became chain smokers.

Like traffic lights, the flags that Mitchell placed and replaced in the holders outside PriFly controlled flight deck traffic during air operations: green for launch, red for emergency, yellow for alert. In Lea's drawing Gouin stands behind Mitchell, writing a notation in the little notebook that he invariably carried. To his left, a sailor with earphones clamped over his blue "white hat" (enlisted men attached to the air group or flight deck crew were allowed to dye their hats) is turning to watch a plane framed by the open window, probably a wave-off since aircraft in normal landing or takeoff configurations would be below PriFly. The sailor is wearing a heavy knife at his belt, a rather strange addition to the work uniform on a capital ship like the *Hornet*. Permission to carry such a weapon reflects the underlying anxiety of the ship's command structure that the carrier might not survive many more weeks. If this sailor and his nearly three thousand buddies had to go into the water, a knife might be needed to cut away the numerous life rafts carried along the ship's side and to provide at least some protection against sharks.

On the way down to Tongatabu the crew experienced both boisterous fun and senseless tragedy. Admirals and captains might worry about the distractions of ceremony in wartime, but the rowdiness that attended "crossing the line" was too time-honored a tradition to be suppressed. Mason grudgingly permitted a brief relaxation of wartime battle stations so that a huge tub could be brought up to the flight deck, and several hundred polliwogs, most from the recently reconstituted air group, received rough dunkings. Then they were given mohawks and other bizarre haircuts with heavy shears. An army captain on board as an observer was determined not to let the navy impose its ways on him. It took six husky sailors and a few nosebleeds and cut lips before he was subdued and dunked. A few polliwogs were lucky. "Had a big initiation when we crossed the equator," Keith Bancroft confided to his diary, "but they missed me, thank goodness."[9]

Bad weather struck the task force one morning while Abie Tucker had a flight from Bombing 8 out on a routine patrol-training flight. Toward noon some of the Dauntlesses came racing back. Instead of landing, the plane in the van swooped low over the *Hornet*'s deck and dropped a weighted note. The engine of Tucker's plane had died; he was down at sea about 180 miles from the ship. He and his gunner had bailed out at low altitude, and squadron mates saw their parachutes open. But by the time the fast-moving planes could bank and return, there was nothing on the surface of the sea. For twenty-four hours the task force tarried while Widhelm led a wave of flights over the area, trying to find some trace of the missing men. The pilots took their planes within fifteen feet of the ocean surface, and two of Task Force 17's six destroyers were detached to search the area. But the men were never found. Admiral Murray reluctantly ordered the task force on its way.

Air Group 8 was devastated: It was hard to believe that fun-loving, hard-fighting Abie, who had brought the Dauntlesses back from Midway, would perish in a routine flight. That night in the wardroom a brooding Widhelm sat down in his normal seat next to Tucker's place. A mess man, not knowing Tucker was still missing, had set the table routinely. Widhelm slowly picked up Tucker's monogrammed napkin ring and dropped it in the drawer under the table. Then he softly asked the mess man to please take Tucker's plate away.[10] The next day Lt. James "Moe" Vose was appointed head of Bombing 8.

Having reached a point just north of Tongatabu, Task Force 17 swung west toward the New Hebrides. On 24 August, as the ships were refueling, word was received of a vicious carrier battle in progress in the eastern Solomons, the result of Yamamoto's initial effort to implement the "Port Arthur" strategy.

On the night of 18 August six Japanese destroyers had landed a crack, one-thousand-man assault force on Guadalcanal. Col. Kiyonao Ichiki had promptly launched a foolish bayonet charge against marine outposts along the Tenaru River. Well-entrenched marines, using heavy machine guns, had massacred the attackers. For the next five days Japanese planes from Rabaul threw themselves at Henderson Field, which Ghormley frantically reinforced with army and marine aircraft from the escort carrier *Long Island*. The air battle was a standoff.

Both navies continued their attempts to reinforce the garrisons, but with little success. Rochefort and his people at Pearl Harbor, although ten days behind in reading Japanese military communiqués, had warned Ghormley that a substantial proportion of the enemy fleet had left home waters and was probably heading toward the Solomons. In fact, Admiral Kondo was lurking on the north side of the Solomons with a fifty-eight-ship task force, including the remnants of the *Kido Butai*, still commanded by Nagumo. Meanwhile, a large group of loaded troop transports, escorted by the heavy cruiser *Tone* and light carrier *Ryujo*, headed from Rabaul toward Guadalcanal down "the Slot" of islands that comprise the upper Solomons. Kondo and Nagumo stood ready to counter any American attack on the convoy.

Fletcher was determined not to be caught in his patrol area south of Guadalcanal. He swung his task force northeast to a point 150 miles east of the island of Malaita, north of Guadalcanal, and sent out air patrols to search for enemy ships. The admiral then committed two blunders. Although battle was imminent, he yielded to his chronic anxiety over depleted bunkers and left the *Wasp* behind to refuel. That left the *Enterprise* and *Saratoga*, with 153 planes, to face three Japanese carriers with 177 aircraft. On 22 August aggressively patrolling navy PBYs discovered the Japanese transport group and its screen off Bougainville, and Fletcher made his second mistake: he lashed out at the *Ryujo* with his entire force without waiting to determine whether there were other, larger enemy carriers in the area.

Airmen from the *Saratoga* sank the enemy light carrier while she was frantically refueling her combat air patrol, but the American flattops were almost defenseless when Nagumo unleashed the air groups from his two big carriers, *Shokaku* and *Zuikaku*. The Japanese assault left the *Enterprise* dead in the water. Fortunately for Fletcher, a second attack, which might have sunk the ship, missed the American position by fifty miles, and the engineering department of the "Big E" was able to get the carrier under way again. The *Enterprise* limped back to Hawaii.

Despite American mistakes and the damage to the *Enterprise,* the Battle of the Eastern Solomons and its immediate aftermath represented a major turning point in the struggle for Guadalcanal. Yamamoto's chief of staff, Admiral Ugaki, mourned lost opportunities for a major Japanese victory over the elusive U.S. fleet ("most deplorable. Again we lost a valuable carrier").[11] Determined U.S. air strikes from Henderson Field and by B-17s from Espiritu Santo forced the transport group in the Slot, now lacking local air cover because of the loss of the *Ryujo*, to turn back without delivering its precious cargo of men and supplies to the island. The Japanese lost a light cruiser and a cargo ship to U.S. bombs.

"It is apparent that landing on Guadalcanal by transports is hopeless unless the enemy planes are wiped out," Ugaki noted on 25 August. "So the plan was revised to transport reinforcements by minesweepers and destroyers, which would shuttle from our place [Rabaul] to that island at high speed every day."[12] Thus was born the famous "Tokyo Express," through which Yamamoto exploited the Japanese superiority in night navigation and combat to pursue three interrelated objectives: to land troops and supplies on Guadalcanal well after dark, neutralizing U.S. air power; to exhaust and disrupt the American garrison through nightly bombardments of the beachhead and Henderson Field; and to lure the small U.S. cruiser and destroyer fleet into decisive battle.

Despite Yamamoto's shrewd tactics, air power would remain decisive, as Ugaki acknowledged. There simply were not enough hours in the night for the Japanese to bring in and unload men and supplies safely and then escape beyond the range of daylight bombing by aircraft at Henderson Field. The battle for Guadalcanal thus hinged on the ability of the Americans to keep a powerful air presence on and around the embattled island. If they could do this, they would eventually whittle down Japanese power while steadily increasing their own. But if they lost too many planes to Japanese attack, either ashore or at sea, if Henderson Field was overrun, or if Fletcher's remaining carriers were badly damaged or sunk, Guadalcanal would eventually fall. This was the situation in the last week of August as Task Force 17, with the *Hornet* at its core, steamed up to strengthen Fletcher's depleted fleet, which was again maneuvering south and east of Guadalcanal.

Not surprisingly, the *Hornet*'s first task was to assist the aircraft shuttle missions that were constantly replenishing the "Cactus Air Force" at Henderson Field. Almost as soon as the carrier joined Fletcher's force, she retreated again several hundred miles to the east to prepare the twenty-one extra F4Fs, which were triced up in the storage bays above the hangar deck, to reinforce Guadalcanal. The process proved to be rather complex. Because the air department needed to concentrate on refurbishing the F4Fs, those planes flying combat air and antisubmarine patrols over the *Hornet* were based on the airfield at Espiritu Santo, the northernmost island in the New Hebrides. While Avengers from Torpedo 6 flew off to Guadalcanal without their radiomen and gunners to bring back marine fliers from Henderson, the F4Fs were lowered from the storage bays to the hangar deck, which soon resembled an airplane factory. Rudders and ailerons were brought back up from the storage rooms far below decks. As they and the wings were rebolted onto each plane, the steel curtains on each side of the hangar were rolled open, bringing in a flood of tropical air and sunshine. Clouds of smoke soon billowed out of the hangar as engines were remounted, started, and cleared of preservatives. Once each plane was mechanically certified, it was pushed over to an open roller curtain, where its machine guns were cleaned, sighted, and then test-fired over the ocean. For hours the ship reverberated to a steady rat-tat-tat of gunfire.

In early afternoon the Avengers returned from Guadalcanal with the eager marine pilots, who were sent below to a squadron ready room and given a crash course in carrier takeoffs. Their new aircraft, now in top condition, were brought up to the flight deck. To the clean, well-shaven crewmen and pilots of the *Hornet*, the marines looked like South Sea pirates. Conditions at Henderson Field, like the other precarious U.S. positions on Guadalcanal, were primitive at best. Pilots endured the same rain, mosquitoes, heat, hunger, diarrhea, and omnipresent mud as the riflemen. Nocturnal bombardments from the Imperial Japanese Navy had recently been added to the ordeal. The young marines had heavy, unkempt beards and dirty flight clothes. Their boots left trails of dirt clods on wooden and steel decks. The airdales and plane pushers who had been at sea for two weeks picked up these souvenirs of jungle warfare with wonder: "Look, Mac," they said to each other, "mud. Isn't it wonderful? Mud!"[13] Within hours the marines were on their way back to Henderson Field. They arrived just as a big enemy bomber formation with fighter escort came into view. In the wild battle that followed the marines shot down several Japanese aircraft and lost only one of their own.

With her shuttle mission completed, the *Hornet* steamed swiftly to rejoin the other two carriers. There was talk in wardrooms and berthing compartments that Fletcher, with three big flattops at his disposal, might raid Rabaul or even Yamamoto's headquarters at Truk, "Japan's Pearl Harbor," far to the northwest in the Caroline Islands. "We're expecting to go into action any time now," Bancroft wrote on the twenty-sixth.[14] But Yamamoto's submarine sailors had ambitions of their own.

Before the end of August 1942 fleet engagements in the Pacific war had been strictly two-dimensional. Despite strenuous attempts by both fleet commanders, submarines had played no important role at Pearl Harbor, the Coral Sea, or Midway. Nimitz and his staff believed for some time after Midway that the *Nautilus* might have sunk the *Soryu*. But it was later determined that the sub had fired on the already fatally stricken *Kaga* and that although three torpedoes hit, none had exploded.[15] Suddenly in the two weeks between 31 August and 15 September Japanese submarines for the first and only time became a major factor in the Pacific war.

At 0700 on the morning of the thirty-first, as crews aboard Fletcher's ships were at breakfast, the submerged submarine *I-26* fired six torpedoes at the *Saratoga* from a range of 3,500 meters. Less than three minutes after the firing, crewmen aboard the submarine heard several explosions. So did men aboard the *Hornet* and every other ship in the task force. As Griffin wrote, "No matter what the eye tells, the realization of a [torpedo] hit comes through a man's stomach, like the dull thud of a blow buried deep in flesh."[16] Fletcher's destroyers quickly pounced on the Japanese sub, while the rest of the task force took evasive action. For four hours *I-26* was pounded with depth charges, but she finally sneaked away.

The *Saratoga* was in bad shape. The torpedo hit caused a major electrical breakdown in main control, and the big vessel glided to a stop. Within an hour the *Minneapolis* took the *Saratoga* in tow, and soon the cruiser had built up sufficient speed to permit flight operations. The "Sara" flew off thirty of her aircraft to Espiritu Santo, where they were refueled and sent on to reinforce Henderson Field. Meanwhile, the carrier's innovative damage controlmen used part of the ship's degaussing cable to replace a main power line, and the *Saratoga* crept out of the battle area and headed north to join the *Enterprise* in the Pearl Harbor repair yards.

With her went Frank Jack Fletcher, perhaps the most controversial carrier commander of the war. He had been slightly injured in the torpedo attack, and Nimitz clearly believed the man had been at sea long enough. It was time for a rest. In fact, Fletcher never returned to command in a major theater of war.

Rear Adm. Leigh Noyes, who had been in charge of the air support force and thus of the three carriers, took Fletcher's place. Rear Adm. George Murray aboard the *Hornet* remained in the shadows for a time. Murray was one of those men whom fate and personality seemed to conspire to deny top combat command positions. He was a hard worker and was liked and respected. But he was never given the opportunity to demonstrate talent for innovative tactics or strategy. His personality undoubtedly held him back. Americans want warmth or at least a modicum of humor and humanity in their commanders. They want a Mitscher, who in 1944 as task force commander would begin a message about a forthcoming invasion by quipping, "I cannot tell a lie; D-Day is Washington's birthday."[17] Or a Nimitz, who once replied to the submarine *Darter*'s request for permission to continue tracking an important Japanese force: "Yes, my darling *Darter*, but don't go any further than you arter."

George Dominic Murray was a stiff but not frosty individual. He "was a very formal person. Everyone addressed him formally and everybody regarded him formally and prefaced every remark by 'Admiral.' That was the way it was," one staff officer aboard the *Hornet* recalled. "He was a very nice man to work for. As I say, he could not have been more courteous, but he was very impersonal as regards his entire staff, very, very impersonal." Like Charlie Mason, Murray was one of the navy's pioneer aviators. He had competently commanded the *Enterprise* at Midway and was given Task Force 17 as a reward. Tall and silver-haired with a slight paunch despite eating and sleeping little, Murray was somewhat eccentric. He had a habit of pursing his narrow lips, then holding them with his hands hour after hour as he sat deep in thought on his flag bridge or in his adjacent office, flag plot. Except under immediate battle conditions his working habits were Churchillian. He arose at dawn, shaved, dressed, and ate a light breakfast in his spartan cabin next to flag plot. He spent the rest of the morning on the bridge. In the afternoon he had a short lunch, then retired to his sea cabin, where he slept soundly for an hour and a half or two hours. Afterward he returned to flag plot or the flag bridge, where he remained until very late into the evening, digesting intelligence reports, talking with his staff, and occasionally summoning Mason for a quick conference.[18]

Murray was certainly a fighter. Tom Lea concluded after their brief acquaintance that the admiral "lived only for the times when he could use his force to slug the Japs." Keith Bancroft wrote on 26 August: "The Admiral says it's open season and no bag limit on Japs. I hope we make it OK."[19] But despite his feistiness, circumstances would force Murray into an essentially passive role when the last big carrier action of 1942 occurred.

Shortly after assuming command, Noyes wisely decided that his force needed a break. Some ships, such as the *Wasp* and *Salt Lake City*, had been steaming for weeks. Men on the cruiser claimed to have been at sea for 105 days; the carrier was down to block beef, flour, and water as basic provisions. Both were sent to Nouméa on the island of New Caledonia for a week's rest and replenishment. In the interim only the *Hornet* and Task Force 17 guarded the supply lines to Guadalcanal. It was the first time the *Hornet* was the only operational carrier in the South Pacific.

From the time she joined Fletcher's task force until going briefly to Nouméa six weeks later, the *Hornet* was a frantically busy ship whether working alone or with another carrier. Operating from a base position west and south of Espiritu Santo, the small U.S. carrier-cruiser-destroyer fleet made frequent high-speed runs toward the Solomons. Carrier air groups had two tasks: to search the Slot for evidence that the Tokyo Express or even larger formations of enemy warships and transports were heading toward Guadalcanal for nocturnal supply and bombardment runs, and to provide air support and cover for the daylight movement of U.S. supply ships into Guadalcanal. Planes from Henderson Field were protecting the island itself and its immediately adjacent anchorages from enemy bombers. Flying in pairs, the *Hornet*'s reconnaissance aircraft—Dauntlesses whose fuel tanks had been topped off after warmup—could range as far north and west as four hundred miles with 250-pound bombs under each wing.

The work was "hectic" as scout and support flights were launched and recovered from dawn to dark. "We were operating almost around the clock, day in and day out, day in and day out," Jurika recalled, "and we knew there was no place to anchor, no place to go in and rest." Underway replenishment, ammunition replenishment, and countless other exercises filled the hours. Periodically a "small boy" (destroyer) would be detached from the task force on a high-speed run to Nouméa, several hundred miles away, to obtain mail and supplies. Whenever a destroyer came alongside to send passengers over to the carrier, take them off by high line, or pass precious mail, the *Hornet* always sent back several hundred gallons of ice cream from its "mechanical cow." As Jurika remembered, "We had lots of it and all kinds of facilities, and we knew that they certainly didn't have it."[20]

Even before the *Saratoga* was hit, everyone feared submarines, and with good reason. American carriers were operating in a dangerously narrow zone because of the ongoing, often petty bickering between MacArthur and CinCPac at Pearl Harbor over their respective boundaries and turf. Noyes, sensitive to the conflict, had interpreted his orders to mean that his task force was to remain strictly south and slightly east of Guadalcanal and not stray into waters farther to the west and north, which were technically under MacArthur's command. Nimitz, however, intended no such restrictions on Noyes's movements. Yamamoto, seeing his enemy's folly, sent in his submarines. Noyes should have recognized the danger after the *Saratoga* was torpedoed and asked for a clarification of his assignment. He did not. Nimitz should have sent a message of his own. He did not.

The South Pacific seas at this time of year were often as unruffled as a table top. The still air made flight operations very difficult. The *Hornet* had to put all boilers on line and race across the water at thirty knots to create enough wind across the flight deck for takeoffs. As days passed, the stress on the engineering plant grew, and the carrier often did not reach sufficient speed to allow takeoffs with full combat loads.[21] The advantage of these conditions was that they would make a submarine periscope or a torpedo wake easier to spot.

Bancroft wrote on the twenty-eighth that although no Japanese forces had been sighted for days, "our sound detectors picked up 4 subs last night." On 7 September, the ship had a close call. Ens. John Cresto, piloting an Avenger from Torpedo 6, was returning from the first leg of a routine antisubmarine patrol. According to custom, he flew down the starboard side of the *Hornet* so that men on the bridge could check the plane's identification number before it flew off on its second and last leg. Just as Cresto came abreast of the island he saw what he believed was a submarine below the surface. On the flight deck Bancroft and his buddies watched the Avenger suddenly cross the carrier's wake, "roll over" in a sharp right-hand turn, open its bomb bays, and drop the depth charge. Almost immediately a big explosion and water geyser erupted off the port beam. Up in the *Hornet*'s island Mason was resting in his sea cabin. On the bridge Ens. Earl Zook, the ship's junior assistant navigator, had the conn. Zook had gone through accelerated graduation at Annapolis the previous December and was brand-new at his job. But he did not hesitate. When Cresto's depth charge detonated, Zook immediately ordered hard left rudder. As the big carrier steadied on its new course, hundreds of men, including Zook and Bancroft, saw torpedo wakes pass down either side. When Cresto landed, he was immediately ordered to the flag bridge, where Murray congratulated him on his initiative. "This morning," Bancroft added in his 7 September diary entry, "more torpedoes fired at us but none hit." Although Bancroft did not see the torpedoes himself, he remembered that lookouts did. "I hope we are not working on the law of averages," the uneasy young petty officer wrote that evening, "because if we are it's going to be bad one of these days."[22]

With the *Wasp* and her fighter aircraft temporarily gone from the seas, the men of the *Hornet* were delighted to see an old friend appear above the horizon one morning. The battleship *North Carolina* had come to the Pacific with the *Wasp*. Her top speed was insufficient for the most rapid carrier operations, but her multitude of antiaircraft guns were always welcome. The first battleship completed in nearly twenty years (she beat out the *Washington* by only a few weeks), the *North Carolina* was known affectionately or derisively as the "Showboat." According to legend, the name was introduced by jealous members of the *Washington*'s band, who serenaded their sister ship with songs from the popular musical as she steamed into harbor one day.

Then the *Wasp* and her escorts came back refreshed, reprovisioned, and rearmed. As the second week in September began, the two carriers, the battleship, and their cruisers and destroyers again accompanied a major supply convoy toward Guadalcanal. The warships broke off a short distance from the island and withdrew to their support area several hundred miles to the southwest. The timely arrival of the convoy was a significant factor in the hurling back of another major Japanese offensive to capture Henderson Field on the thirteenth.

Two days later, on 15 September, disaster struck again. The *Wasp*, duty carrier that day, was responsible for providing combat air patrol over the task force, which had just assumed a loose protective cover for five transports and cargo ships. Embarked on the transports, commanded by Admiral Turner, were crucial reinforcements for Guadalcanal, including the Seventh Marine Division. Noyes and his Japanese counterpart, Admiral Kondo, were looking for one another, and the *Hornet* had dispatched a search mission to the northwest that morning, hoping to find an enemy concentration that reportedly included at least one carrier. But the seas were empty. Widhelm and Iceberg Parker came back frustrated at midday and went below for lunch.

It turned out to be an uncharacteristically windy, sunny Tuesday afternoon. The seas were choppy and full of whitecaps, perfect cover for submarine periscopes and torpedo wakes. Shortly before 1500 the *Wasp* was preparing to launch a new combat air patrol. All fuel lines were out and full; ammunition elevators were loaded with bombs and bullets for rearming planes on both flight and hangar decks. Ens. John Jenks Mitchell, a twenty-two-year-old Annapolis graduate from Washington, D.C., stood in the carrier's forward 5-inch gun gallery on the starboard side some sixty feet in front and slightly outboard of the base of the island. He had just been relieved of the watch and had started to go below "when a seaman in the crew of my gun station said in a somewhat unseamanlike way, 'Mr. Mitchell, what's 'at funny-looking thing out there?'" Mitchell saw a torpedo wake heading right for the *Wasp*, toward a position directly under him. "I sounded an alarm in a voice that may be described as similar to a thrilled tenor," Mitchell recalled from his hospital bed several weeks later. But it was too late.

On the admiral's bridge another ensign, C. G. Durr, saw three rapidly incoming torpedo wakes. He turned to Noyes and said, "Those have got us." One "fish" detonated in gasoline storage tanks; another exploded abreast of the forward bomb magazine. The entire area went up with a blinding explosion and a convulsive shock wave. The blast jolted spare aircraft from the *Wasp*'s storage bays above the hangar and sent them crashing down onto parked and armed planes below and onto the heads of stunned crewmen. Scores of sailors perished immediately. Mitchell was blown thirty feet into the air; he landed sixty feet away at the captain's feet on the bridge wing. Shipmates and journalists later claimed it was the world's distance record for an explosion survivor. Mitchell, who suffered a broken leg, said, "The record for a survivor in the last war was believed to have been thirty feet high and a few feet away." After the two torpedoes struck "the third one did not matter. It was just a kick in the head of the dying body."[23]

Over in the *Hornet's* wardroom, thirty officers, the maximum number allowed to congregate in any section of the ship at one time while in enemy waters, were watching a movie, "Tough As They Come," starring a group of supposedly streetwise New York teenagers known as the Dead End Kids. Lt. Bill Rommens, who had worked for a telephone company before joining the navy, had rigged up a small projector and put together a crude sound system out of odds and ends. No one liked the film much. "It seemed a little tame after Midway."[24]

Six hundred feet astern, Cardon Ruchti stood on the fantail getting a rare breath of fresh air. For days he had been cooped up below decks on watch at his steaming station in boiler control, in the mess hall, or in his bunk. Now he was enjoying the wind and tropical sunshine. Bancroft was lounging up on the flight deck with his plane-handling crew. Since the *Hornet* was not duty carrier, he and his mates had little to do. Suddenly at 1451 the boatswain's pipe shrilled and the bugle sounded general quarters throughout officer's country. At the same moment Ruchti felt the thud of a torpedo exploding against a distant hull and saw the *Wasp* several miles away erupt in sheets of flame. Officers in the wardroom snapped to shocked attention, then leapt from their seats and raced for ladders. Somebody heard a seaman say: "The *Wasp* got three fish in her."[25] "Disheartened," Ruchti raced back below thinking, "So much for fresh air!"[26]

Up on the island and throughout the flight deck gun galleries it looked as if the entire Japanese submarine force had shown up. Every ship seemed to be ducking torpedoes. From the *Hornet's* port quarter came the thud of another torpedo hit, and a great spurt of water appeared above the *North Carolina's* port side forward. Looking out from air plot, Francis Foley saw a column of smoke appear and spread out horizontally from the bow of the big battleship, which seemed to shudder momentarily "but then came on majestically." McAteer, on the flight deck, saw that after being hit the battleship "just got up speed and took off."[27] The *North Carolina* had absorbed a deadly 24-inch "long lance" torpedo, which opened a gash measuring thirty-two by eighteen feet below the waterline next to the forward main battery turret barbette. The blast sent a flash into the number one handling room and spewed acrid smoke into forward compartments. Even as it increased speed, the big ship took on a five-degree list.

Within seconds an "appalled" Foley and his men saw the destroyer *O'Brien*, two thousand yards off the port beam, suddenly engulfed in a huge pillar of smoke that momentarily obscured the ship from view. The tin can had apparently taken a torpedo meant for the carrier. "Scratch one Small Boy," Foley's enlisted telephone talker sang out. The seaman turned and crossed the destroyer's name off a nearby blackboard that listed the names and positions of all screening vessels.[28] Abruptly the *O'Brien* appeared amid the pall of smoke with most of her bow gone but still plowing gamely through the bright waters.

On the *Hornet*'s bridge, Mason conned the big carrier in rapid evasive maneuvers. "Hard right rudder"; "Now hard left rudder."[29] Soon the messages came across the water. From the *O'Brien:* "Torpedo hit forward. CPO quarters destroyed . . . casualties. Can make 15 knots. Request permission to remain in company." From the *North Carolina:* "Large hole well below waterline. Five known dead. Damage under control. Can make 25 kts."[30]

Forty years later historians concluded that a single Japanese submarine, *I-19*, was responsible for the incredible carnage. The Japanese skipper, Takaichi Kinashi, had launched six torpedoes, three of which found the *Wasp*, one the *North Carolina* in the midst of a routine course change, and one more the *O'Brien* after the destroyer had avoided one "fish." Kinashi's remarkable daring had been matched by incredible luck.

After the attack all eyes turned toward the *Wasp*. The 720-foot, 14,700-ton carrier was small for her type, but she was still a large, tough ship that theoretically could have survived twice or perhaps even three times as many torpedo hits. Now she lay rolling in the swells, exploding and burning, McAteer said, "like a fourth of July bonfire: fuel, ordnance, planes, everything."[31] It was Midway all over again, with the *Wasp* reprising the roles of the *Akagi, Kaga,* and *Soryu.* Men on the *Hornet* peered at the stricken carrier "in dry mouthed horror."[32] Almost immediately Mason, Soucek, and Gouin got the crew back to work. The *Wasp*'s combat air patrol had to be landed, and the *Hornet* had to deploy replacement air and antisubmarine patrols of its own to avoid further disaster. No one could be sure that the attack was not part of a broader, coordinated two- or even three-dimensional assault by surface, air, and submarine forces.

The *Hornet* and her escorts moved farther away from the doomed vessel while the *Wasp*'s escorts hovered solicitously around her. The *North Carolina* dropped back to assess damage but then raced ahead; Bancroft watched her pass the *Hornet* with a magnificent burst of speed even though both ships were zigzagging wildly in case there were any more enemy torpedoes.[33]

For a while Capt. Forrest P. Sherman, the *Wasp*'s skipper, had hopes of saving his ship, although he knew that she would be an almost total wreck if she ever reached port. The after engine rooms were intact, and if power could be restored the carrier might be salvaged. He turned his stricken ship into the prevailing breeze blowing from the starboard bow, then went astern with his undamaged engines to keep the flames away from the after part of the vessel, while the determined crew started working with fire hoses amid a lethal rain of exploding ammunition. But the first violent explosions had destroyed all water power forward, including the hangar deck sprinkler system. In the bedlam no one had thought to isolate the intact rear loops of the ship's main water system from the ruptured forward sections, and only trickles of water came from the fire hoses. Soon the flames were uncontrollable.

Bancroft watched as the *Wasp* was gradually obscured by smoke and flame. As men on the *Hornet* and other ships of the task force looked across the water from six miles away, the *Wasp* was racked by the worst explosion of the day. A sheet of flame erupted from the hangar deck and engulfed three sides of the ship's island structure. Watching from his bridge on the *Hornet*, George Murray felt sure his superior, Admiral Noyes, had perished. In fact, Noyes was burned on his face and head but survived and retained command. Shortly after 1600 Sherman wisely ordered all hands off, and destroyers came alongside to aid in the rescue work. Noyes ordered the carrier torpedoed by destroyers from her screen, and she sank shortly after dark.[34]

Mason temporarily dispatched all ready aircraft aboard the *Hornet* to Espiritu Santo to make room for twenty-six of the *Wasp*'s search and patrol planes. Scouting 71 landed aboard virtually intact. It was nearly all that remained of Air Group 7; all other aircraft were destroyed and some pilots had perished.[35]

The loss of this carrier scared the men of the *Hornet*. It was the first major casualty any of them had seen. When the *Yorktown* had "gotten it" at Midway weeks before, she had been hull down on the horizon. The *Saratoga* had stopped briefly after her torpedoing sixteen days before but then had recovered sufficiently to limp off. But the *Wasp* was an uncontrollable inferno from the beginning. Everyone above decks could see as the ship kept exploding and exploding horrendously for several hours. The destruction was especially unnerving aboard the *Hornet* because one of her squadrons and a large portion of her airdales had come from the *Wasp* just a few months before. Good shipmates were dying hideously only a short distance away, and no one could do anything about it.

How soon might it be the *Hornet*'s turn? Down in the engine room, Ruchti brooded about the growing loss of ships. The *Saratoga* had been hit one week, then the *North Carolina* and the *Wasp*. "We were losing a capital ship a week. It was scary." Suddenly his mates realized that the *Hornet* had been "so goddamned lucky it wasn't funny." After all, half the crew were nothing but "raw-assed recruits." How long would good fortune last? Bancroft also wondered. Was the U.S. Navy good enough to whip the Japanese? Not only were the carrier task forces losing ships, but cruisers and destroyers seemed to be going down every week in "Ironbottom Sound" off Guadalcanal. Up in air plot Foley also brooded. The *Hornet* was suddenly America's last operational fleet carrier in the Pacific. It was "kind of grim," he remembered years later. "We felt we'd get it eventually."[36]

Ghormley demonstrated uncharacteristic boldness by allowing Turner to push his small but vital convoy through to Guadalcanal three days after the *Wasp* sank, while the Japanese were still savoring their victory. But this success meant little to the men of the small American battle fleet. Not only was the *Wasp* gone but the *North Carolina* was steaming carefully back to Hawaii for repairs. (The *O'Brien* sank on the way.) The *Washington*, another friend from shakedown days, was the last modern battleship left south of Pearl.

The Japanese were delighted with the sinking of an enemy carrier, which submarine *I-15* confirmed. It was time to sweep the last U.S. flattop from the seas. And Tokyo and Truk knew which ship she was; the Japanese also knew her role in the enemy's desecration of the homeland, since captured Doolittle raiders had been beaten until they divulged the *Hornet*'s identity. Now, the Japanese exulted, it was payback time.

Rochefort's people at Pearl Harbor decoded and sent to Ghormley a message from Yamamoto to all Japanese commands. Destruction of "Blue Base" and "Blue Planes" had become "the primary objective of the entire Imperial Fleet!" Ghormley's staff passed the message on to Charlie Mason, who had it read over the *Hornet*'s public address system. Hundreds of men cheered defiantly, and Foley was heartened. The Japanese ploy, if such it was, had backfired. Others, however, worried about the deadly threat. Too many good ships had gone down or been put out of action recently to dismiss enemy bluster.[37]

But the minute-by-minute demands of war at sea helped ease apprehension. So did a series of drills and exercises designed to prevent the fate of the *Wasp*. First Lieutenant Moran ordered a major program of paint removal throughout the ship to lessen the danger of spreading fires. By the end of September 50 percent of the carrier's "smoke and fire hazard paints" were gone. Much aluminum paint remained, but "the dangerous oil paints, such as hangar deck paint, bulkhead and overhead paint, were cut down substantially."[38]

Meanwhile, the damage control department fabricated special fire shovels designed to throw overboard "incendiary bombs, especially small bombs and phosphorous pellets." The air officer kept the gasoline tank compartments filled with nonflammable carbon dioxide at all times, "and, with the aid of the First Lieutenant, devised a method of keeping gasoline hose and piping filled with CO_2 gas whenever the gasoline system was not in operation." All departments cooperated in maintaining saltwater hoses, foamite, and CO_2 firefighting equipment in constant readiness.[39]

The deck department checked all knotted heavy lines and cargo nets "at all accessible places about the ship" to ensure what was euphemistically called a "safe approach to the water in case abandonment became necessary." In addition, life jackets were checked and upgraded and battle problems were held frequently for repair parties and interior communications personnel. Damage control drills were conducted daily, and Soucek ordered that placards containing directions for operating damage and fire control gear and for guiding personnel to escape hatches and first aid kits be posted throughout the ship. The medical department snapped out of its at-sea lethargy and equipped six emergency battle dressing stations for treatment and care of wounded. The supply officer devised better ways of providing food for men at battle stations.[40]

While the ship's company toiled below decks to prepare the *Hornet* for any battle ordeal, frequent trips toward Guadalcanal and the Slot could not slacken. On 24 September Bancroft wrote in his diary that "we sighted land for the first time since August 28 day before yesterday, and then again today. They are just small islands. We have a large task force now, but we are the only carrier."[41]

Gus Widhelm, Moe Vose, and Iceberg Parker sent their Dauntlesses and Wildcats up every morning, noon, and afternoon toward the Slot or north of the Solomons, looking for Kondo and Nagumo. With continuous flights it was inevitable that planes and men would be lost. The various combat and antisubmarine patrols involved flying over the Solomons or shuttling between the *Hornet* and airfields in the New Hebrides. Bancroft noted on 24 September that seven or eight scout-bombers had gone down in the past month, "but only three men" had failed to return. One Dauntless caught fire and the pilot had to bail out. Lt. (jg) William Woodman of Maplewood, New Jersey, missed the airfield at Efate and spent two days on a nearby island that was inhabited by French-Indochinese planters. Another lieutenant (jg), Donald Kirkpatrick, just months out of Northwestern University and Pensacola, misjudged either fuel or distance and had to make a dead-stick landing of his Dauntless on a coral reef somewhere in the Solomons. He and his gunner-radioman spent several days on a tropical island that was nothing like those depicted in Hollywood films; finally, a PBY pilot saw the two men and plucked them from their prison. Woodman and Kirkpatrick were soon back aboard the *Hornet* and flying again.[42]

It was a busy time not only for pilots and airdales but also for communications and intelligence personnel. Since Murray was the only admiral with a flattop, information flooded into his flagship: intelligence on Japanese nighttime landings on Guadalcanal, on the location of enemy transports and warships, on the possibility that major enemy fleet units might be lurking nearby. The *Hornet* was the source of all operational plans, and the carrier's intelligence officers helped Murray's small staff develop daily schedules, which then had to be passed down to Mason, Soucek, the air group squadrons, and the ship's busy air department. The airdales—plane pushers, mechanics, ordnancemen—worked sixteen- to eighteen-hour days. They stood no watches; their jobs were done when the last Wildcat or Dauntless engine was repaired, the last fighter or scout-bomber armed and fueled, and the last torpedo plane struck below to the hangar or pushed to its proper position on the flight deck for the next day's dawn launch. Jurika and Henry Martin in their small offices in the island worked as much as was needed. Three hours' sleep a night was fine, Martin recalled. An hour was acceptable.

To those who would man the fifteen to twenty great fleet carriers of 1944 and 1945, when the U.S. Navy was the mightiest on earth, such schedules would be routine.[43] But the 1942 navy was still groping its way from the peacetime culture to that of total war. Men like Jurika, Martin, and Mason in the island and boys like Bancroft, Blackmer, Aviation Mechanic 2nd Class Jack Medley and Aviation Ordnanceman 1st Class Bob Taylor on the flight and hangar decks, along with hundreds of shipmates on the *Hornet* and throughout the small cruiser-destroyer escorting fleet, were shaping a new culture of steady, unremarkable combat efficiency that was essential for ultimate victory over a determined foe. Some historians have asserted that America's only advantage in World War II was its unprecedented ability to produce, that otherwise its soldiers and sailors were rather inferior to the youngsters whom Hitler and the Japanese warlords put into the field and onto the seas.[44] In actuality, Axis efficiency at sea, on land, and in the air peaked during 1942 and then began to decline. Once the "first teams"—ships' crews, pilots, and soldiers—were destroyed or overwhelmed, their replacements proved to be decidedly inferior. America and its allies, on the other hand, held the line with their first teams, sacrificing many in the process and learning from the inevitable mistakes of combat, until their successors, well-trained, competent, confident, and determined, stepped forward to achieve final victory.

But no harsh regimen can be sustained forever. By the end of September daily life was becoming grim aboard the *Hornet*. Supply problems, always present, were becoming acute; the food was "horrendous." Beans were being ground up and called potatoes, and there were beetles in the flour.[45] The situation was even worse on the destroyers. One of the skippers, Lt. Comdr. Joe Worthington, recalled that some of those on the tin cans "had almost gone hungry, the supply system was so poor." Worthington had prudently provisioned his ship as fully as possible before leaving Pearl, but the food was marginal. "We were still eating on Spam and canned goods and this kind of artificial potato you have."[46]

Despite the critical situation in the lower Solomons, it was time to break off patrolling and head to port. Task Force 17 sailed for Nouméa on 27 September. Most of Air Group 8 flew to Tontouta Air Field near the port. For some reason, however, a dozen of the *Hornet*'s Dauntless scout-bombers were sent to an airfield several hundred miles north on Efate.

Task Force 17 spent only five days at Nouméa, but it was long enough for Moran to institute realistic abandon ship drills, in which 60 percent of the crew actually left the ship down lines and by raft or small boat. The great fuel bunkers far below decks were filled to the brim. Supplies came aboard, too, but the food was simply more of the same—"block" beef (Spam), flour, and dehydrated potatoes. The supply department would retain on board the few remaining delicacies for battle rations; officers and crew would dine on the same coarse food as before. After the hasty reprovisioning was complete, there was time only for a few quick beers in the tropical heat of dusty French colonial bars, and then it was back to sea.

9

Alone

TASK FORCE 17 cleared Nouméa harbor at noon on 2 October 1942 at the beginning of the greatest moral and strategic crisis the United States would face in the Pacific war. Several hundred miles to the northwest General Alexander Vandegrift and his marines grimly hung onto their narrow beachhead and airfield perimeter on Guadalcanal, waiting for reinforcements and supplies and cursing Admiral Ghormley in distant Nouméa for his growing pessimism. Nimitz, too, was upset. He had appeared in New Caledonia at the end of September, just before the *Hornet* arrived for her brief rest. Eight transports sat in the big, palm tree–fringed harbor, and three thousand tough soldiers of the army's Americal Division languished ashore. Why were they not heading for Guadalcanal, Nimitz wanted to know. He ordered Ghormley to send them up to reinforce Vandegrift as soon as possible.

Task Force 17, spearheaded by the *Hornet,* would screen the rapid-fire, two-part operation. The small fleet would first rush to the top of the Solomons to hit Japanese air and naval concentrations before Yamamoto could deploy them in one more climactic effort to throw the Americans out of the southwestern Pacific. Then Murray's ships would rush back south to escort Admiral Turner's reinforcement convoy almost to the beaches of Guadalcanal.

Nimitz was determined that the island be held at all costs. The United States could not afford another Bataan. On 29 September he flew into Henderson Field and spent a typically hot, muggy night with Vandegrift and his men. Nimitz's message was simple: Hang on until reinforcements arrive. Down in Nouméa, Ghormley, caught between the demands of his superior and the obvious determination of the enemy to destroy his forces, had no choice but to order a high-risk operation, which, the *Hornet*'s biographer said, would be "planned in desperation and carried out in bravado."[1]

Japan occupied all the Solomons above Guadalcanal. Just to the northwest was the big island of Santa Isabel with a major seaplane base at Rekata Bay. Further west was New Georgia, where Yamamoto had ordered the building of a big, new airfield at Munda. Then there were Vella Lavella, the Treasury and Shortland Islands, and, at the top, Bougainville, home of the Japanese Eleventh Air Fleet, which was based mainly at Buin and at large, freshly built airfields at Kahili and Kieta. Bougainville also provided deep-water anchorages for the cruisers, destroyers, transports, and cargo ships that made nightly runs down the three-hundred-mile-long, fifty-mile-wide Slot to Guadalcanal.

To sting the Japanese, to throw them temporarily off balance, bombers from the Cactus Air Force on Guadalcanal would hit enemy airfields and shipping at Rekata Bay; B-17s from Espiritu Santo would strike Japanese bases on the island of Buka off the northern tip of Bougainville. Air Group 8 from the *Hornet* would assault the airfields on Bougainville itself as well as enemy anchorages at Faisi and other small islands in the Shortlands group just southeast of Bougainville. Throughout the mission America's last operational fleet carrier in the South Pacific would be easily in range of the Japanese Eleventh Air Fleet. As Task Force 17 formed up off Nouméa that Friday noon, George Murray sent Operation Order 18-42 to all ships.

The mission threatened to unravel at the outset. By 1600 the *Hornet* had recovered thirty-two fighters and ten scout-bombers that had been sent to Tontouta Field just before the carrier entered Nouméa. But the dozen Dauntlesses that had flown to the airfield on Efate had not responded to Murray's orders to rejoin the task force; a combination of poor communications and abominable weather had grounded them. When no more planes appeared above the *Hornet* by evening, Mason impatiently dispatched two Dauntlesses back to Nouméa to find out what was happening. The South Pacific Force communications center confirmed that the twelve scout-bombers at Efate were tied down by a local weather front and would not be available for at least forty-eight hours. After the two planes returned with the news, Murray and Mason decided to press on. The six spare planes remaining in the storage bays above the *Hornet*'s hangar deck, all scout-bombers, were brought down by Gouin's efficient airdales, rebuilt, armed, and fueled. The air department had sufficient ordnance on board to bring the strike bomb load within one ton of the weight originally contemplated.

As Task Force 17 started north, Lt. Comdr. Art Cumberledge, the *Hornet*'s aerologist, sweated over charts and weather maps, striving to find the faintest clue to meteorological conditions for the operation. Weather in the tropical Pacific was always unpredictable. To make matters worse, every observing station in the northern Solomons was in enemy hands. The only information available came from occasional reports from patrolling PBYs or a submarine that had mentioned the weather while surfacing for battery recharge.

Murray set Task Force 17 on a northwesterly course at moderate speed. As the ships passed Guadalcanal on the evening of 3 October, they picked up a welcome weather front. The night was heavy, hot, and black; the next morning broke gray and muggy. At 1000 the task force reached the jump-off point. Murray ordered the destroyers to remain in position; the strike force would go on, make the attack, and return the next day. The *Hornet*, heavy cruisers *Northampton* and *Pensacola*, and light antiaircraft cruisers *Juneau* and *San Diego* revved up to twenty-eight knots, steering base course 325°. Murray chose not to mount a combat air patrol because its inadvertent or emergency communications with the carrier might give away her position. No enemy planes ventured out under the low cloud cover. Eventually one bogey did appear on the radar screen in the *Hornet*'s small combat information center. Although the CXAM system did not pick up identification signals from B-17s and PBYs, there was every reason to believe the aircraft was friendly. For the Bougainville-Shortlands area was not only occupied by the Japanese; it was within MacArthur's southwestern Pacific theater of operations. Task Force 17, under Nimitz's overall control, was intruding on both Japanese territory and MacArthur's domain. The bogey, friendly or not, came no closer to the task force than eighty miles.

Throughout the day the small fleet pounded north with all hands at modified general quarters. By this time the *Hornet* was beginning to show the strains of six weeks at sea and nearly a year out of her shipyard.

Because of progressive fouling of her bottom and early indications of "service deterioration" in the boilers, which caused high injection temperatures, engine revolutions had to be set at thirty knots in order to maintain the force's base speed of twenty-eight knots. This was fifteen revolutions faster than a normal full-speed run, "an increase of about 8% over the clean bottom curve."[2]

Murray placed the antiaircraft cruisers on the *Hornet*'s port and starboard bows, the heavy cruisers on the carrier's port and starboard quarter. At sunset the task group rearranged itself in open order: antiaircraft cruisers ahead of the carrier and heavy cruisers astern. Everyone was tense. Did the Japanese know their enemies were coming? Had they laid a trap? Preparing for a brief sleep in his berthing compartment, Keith Bancroft hastily scrawled a diary notation: "It's going to be a tight one."[3] When launch position—33.5° south latitude, 154.46° east longitude—was reached one hour forty minutes before daybreak on 5 October, the Japanese had no indication that a U.S. force was anywhere within three hundred miles.

Once again the *Hornet* went to full general quarters and a familiar regimen. All galley fires except one had been doused the evening before after food for the next day—doughnuts, sandwiches, oranges, mincemeat pies, candy, and gallons upon gallons of coffee—had been set out. "Fires were permitted in the Officer's galley long enough to prepare a satisfactory breakfast for the pilots who were scheduled to make the early flights." Toilets ("heads") were kept open in the island structure for use of all hands; so were one engineers' washroom far below and one near the officers' wardroom. Otherwise all water was cut into the main firefighting system.[4]

Murray and Mason took no chances of prematurely revealing the task force's presence. The five ships had broken out into a clear but dark sky illuminated only by a quarter moon, which provided just a faint glimpse of the horizon. Murray would launch under these conditions. He ordered the carrier and escorting cruisers to dim their mast lights. The launch area was slightly lit by flap-type landing lights "plus three dim colored flashlights on the edge of the flight deck forward."[5]

Standing in the early morning gloom, waiting for the brown-shirted plane captains to warm up their aircraft and the red-shirted ordnancemen to fill them with bombs, Air Group 8 cursed the fates that so far had been kind. A heavy weather front stood between the *Hornet* and the Bougainville-Shortlands area several hundred miles to the north. Flying in low or no ceilings toward and over mountain peaks was no one's idea of a healthy or productive mission. But turning back was unthinkable. If Guadalcanal was to survive, it was essential to do everything humanly possible to knock the Japanese juggernaut off stride.

Working briskly and efficiently, Gouin and his air department, including Lt. Comdr. Wayne Smith, the hangar deck officer, and Lt. Ed Osborn, the flight deck officer, launched the first attack wave of twenty-five aircraft at 0500. Twenty-five minutes later another thirty-two aircraft had been brought up from the hangar, spotted for takeoff, and were on their way. The *Hornet* launched a total of fifty-seven fighters, scout-bombers, and torpedo planes in fifty-five minutes. Without the Efate squadron, the carrier's onboard plane capacity was reduced to sixty-eight: thirty-two Wildcats, twenty-four Dauntlesses, and twelve Avengers. Because of the increased number of Wildcats, Murray was able to maintain a strong combat air patrol of eight to twenty fighters throughout the day while still providing the attack force with a modest escort. Murray, Vice Adm. John Towers, Commander Air Forces, Pacific Fleet, and Nimitz applauded the growth of fighter strength on the *Hornet* and urged that in the future all American carriers maintain fighter squadrons of at least thirty-six planes to ensure maximum effectiveness in both defending the fleet and projecting its air power.

Air Group 8 experienced serious problems in getting off the mission. One Avenger had engine trouble during takeoff, and as the pilot, Lt. (jg) Ivan Swope, struggled to gain speed and altitude, he "was transfixed by the unexpected sight of a rapidly oncoming red light dead ahead."[6] It was the truck light of the *Northampton*, and Swope almost crashed into the cruiser's upper works. He swerved at the last minute as the ship turned its mast light onto full power.

Once aloft, the pilots had difficulty forming up properly in the dark skies, "and in some cases, rendezvous was not effected." As each aircraft had reached its launch spot on the flight deck, the pilot had turned on his running light, but once in the sky these lights were no help in identifying specific squadrons. Moreover, Dauntless pilots were half-blinded by the bright glow of exhaust gas from their planes. Gouin, Sanchez, and the other squadron leaders consequently urged that the planes of each squadron be equipped with colored identification lights—white, red, green— "to aid in joining up at night."[7] And they asked that something be done to reduce the glare from the scout-bombers' exhaust.

The air group had no better luck once it started on its way. Because of the "doggone ball of weather," as Air Group Commander Walt Rodee called it,[8] sections and individual planes became scattered in the dense clouds. The post-battle report stated that "the group became separated into several groups of varied size and composition."[9] One group of seven Dauntlesses and another of three failed to find their target area or any enemy installations; they returned to the carrier in frustration. Of the seven fighters that accompanied the first wave, only two spotted suitable targets.

For those Dauntlesses and Wildcats that did break out of the clouds in the right places, pickings were slim. VF-72 Commander Mike Sanchez and his wingman were the only two fighter pilots to find Faisi and "were challenged by a very large CA [heavy cruiser] with her foretruck light."[10] Instead of heading back into the clouds, Sanchez daringly rocked his wings, which seemed to satisfy the cruiser's gunners that he was a "friendly," and they let him go. Sanchez picked out a line of six four-engine Kawanishi flying boats nearby, flipped over, dove down to 250 feet, and raced in to strafe them with his .50-caliber wing guns. His wingman, Lt. (jg) William V. Roberts, did the same to a second line of four Kawanishis. Both pilots, however, were overexcited and hasty. Although both airmen observed bullet splashes close aboard, they scored no hits. Sanchez then went after a small destroyer, which opened up with 20-millimeter antiaircraft guns but missed. Sanchez strafed the destroyer's upper works; then he and Roberts headed for home.

Gus Widhelm, flying with his wingmen Lt. (jg) Benny Moore and Lt. (jg) Jimmy Forbes, discovered that flying a combat mission in clouds over a mountainous island was a frightening experience. Back on the *Hornet* Widhelm's frustration was audible over the air group communication system: "Watch out on your right. . . . What's your bearing? How far are you wrong?"[11] Widhelm and his two wingmen were dodging rocks in the clouds; one plane nearly hit a peak that suddenly appeared dead ahead. Twisting and turning to avoid the mountain, the three fliers suddenly broke into clear skies over southern Bougainville and quickly found the Japanese base at Kieta. There were no planes on the ground, so they bombed a landing strip and adjacent buildings, but with little effect.

The ceiling at Tonolei Harbor in the Shortlands was only three to eight hundred feet. Five Dauntlesses, led by Lt. (jg) Frank Christofferson, glided out of the clouds over the estimated position of an enemy ship, which had been provided by Jurika based on coast watchers' reports. Christofferson had been told that if no ship was in his sights when he broke into the clear, he was to climb back into the clouds and try again. But he and his men spotted a few cargo vessels and one heavy cruiser.

The Americans claimed a 1,000-pound bomb hit on the cruiser and one 1,000-pound and one 500-pound bomb hit on a cargo ship. But in the rush of battle they understandably exaggerated.

The second attack wave consisted of all the *Hornet*'s Avengers and eight fighters. The Avengers were loaded with bombs, not torpedoes. Rodee flew without a bomb load, apparently acting as overall strike coordinator. One Avenger was forced to return to the carrier with engine trouble. With the skies now clearing, the rest of the planes formed up easily. But this strike also became separated in the heavy weather front that shielded Bougainville and the Shortlands. Rodee ordered a descent to eight hundred feet "and at this time seven VTB [Avengers] and 5 VF [Wildcats] remained together" to strike Faisi and the nearby anchorage at Buin.[12] Two other Avengers ultimately reached Tonolei; the rest returned to the *Hornet* with bombs in their racks.

Once again the Japanese were caught napping. There were no Zeros aloft, and at Faisi the U.S. pilots strafed two light cruisers, four destroyers, and a cargo ship. A Zero configured as a float plane and evidently attached to one of the cruisers tried to take off, but Lt. E. W. "Red" Hessel shot it down. One pilot claimed he hit the cargo ship amidships with his 500-pound bomb, and "numerous near misses" were claimed. At Buin Lieutenant Parker claimed "1 certain and two possible hits" on an aircraft tender at neighboring Shortland harbor. But no enemy ships were sunk. Within minutes the American raiders were back in the clouds and on their way home.[13]

By midmorning Air Group 8 was back aboard the *Hornet*. Those who thought they had laid their bombs on target were euphoric. They had knocked Tojo's pants off. Others were disgusted. Unable to claim anything but near misses, they "snapped that the whole mission was the bunk."[14]

As the pilots trooped below to clean up and eat, Jurika and his intelligence staff tagged after them. "What did you get . . . what did you get?" "Well, we got a cargo vessel."

Someone else grinned that he had really laid one on a cruiser.

"Start a fire?"

"I don't know. Low ceiling. Weather was lousy. Why can't we get some decent weather reports?"[15]

On the flight deck one of Mike Sanchez's pilots approached plane captain Eugene Blackmer and several other airdales. In the days before the raid the flier had become convinced that the key to success and survival in battle was a highly polished airplane, which would surely fly at least five knots an hour faster. He had offered a carton of cigarettes to the flight deck crewman who would burnish his F4F-4 to the highest sheen. The boys had responded enthusiastically, and the pilot had flown off to Bougainville with his plane shining like a mirror. Now, after his first brush with combat, the airman told Blackmer, "Hey, screw the polishing. Just make sure the guns work."[16]

In terms of ordnance expended for results achieved, the 5 October raid was a distinct disappointment. Eight 1,000-pound and thirty-two 500-pound bombs had been dropped with little effect. Poor weather confounded what seemed a promising operation. But in other ways the mission was a success. With the Japanese off balance Turner could start the Americal Division on its way to Guadalcanal, providing the exhausted marines with their first reinforcements since they had stormed ashore exactly two months before. The raid also sent a message to Yamamoto and his colleagues that the Americans still possessed the ability to take the offensive in the Solomons, to appear anywhere in the Japanese backyard. As long as one enemy carrier was afloat, the Japanese conquest of the Solomons remained in doubt.

On the *Hornet* the early morning hours had passed uneventfully. As soon as the strike force finished launching at 0524, the carrier and her cruiser escorts retired to the southwest at twenty-five knots. They rejoined the destroyers shortly after 0800. The wind was from the southeast, just as Commander Cumberledge and his "weather guessers" had anticipated. Once the air group was recovered (with only one wound, a .50-caliber bullet hole in one of the Avengers), the fleet immediately began a hasty withdrawal from "Indian country." But the now aroused Japanese were determined to find it.

Shortly after 1100 the CXAM long-range radar atop the *Hornet*'s island picked up an unidentified aircraft. Part of the combat air patrol was immediately sent to the scene. It discovered one of MacArthur's B-17s on a long-range reconnaissance. No sooner had the friendly been confirmed than the CXAM picked up another bogey bearing 140° True, speed 140 knots, distance forty-two miles, altitude 1,500 feet. Lt. Robert W. Rynd and three of his mates handling the "low" combat air patrol at 5,000 feet were directed to intercept. Thirty-two miles out they pounced on a twin-engine Mitsubishi 97. The crew of the heavy bomber were apparently so intent on finding the enemy that they were not looking up during the minute between Rynd's visual contact and the completion of his attack.

Diving down on the plane's port quarter, Rynd opened fire first, setting the Mitsubishi's left engine ablaze and slowing the big bomber sufficiently to allow his wingmen an easy target. The stunned Japanese never attempted to return fire as each of the other three Wildcats raced in to score hits all over the stricken aircraft. The bomber simply glided into the water; its port engine and tail assembly tore loose before it hit the waves. There were no survivors.

Forty minutes later the *Hornet*'s radar picked up another bogey forty-two miles out bearing 330°, speed 190 knots, altitude roughly 1,500 feet. This time Lt. John F. Sutherland and his section, flying the 15,000-foot "high" patrol, were sent to knock down the snooper. Sutherland headed north, and when he came to the storm front he divided his four planes into two sections, one above and one below the 2,500-foot cloud layer. Ten minutes after radar contact, the lower section sighted the bogey, another Mitsubishi 97 with a silver belly and many 7.7-millimeter guns. As the American pilots shouted "Tallyho," the enemy nosed down and initiated evasive tactics consisting of gentle and then jerky turns. At full throttle, the Mitsubishi was just a little too slow against the Wildcats. Lt. (jg) Henry A. Carey got into position first. Attacking astern, he knocked out the Mitsubishi's port engine. His mates delivered the coup de grace. The bomber was tough. Its determined crew fought back with several machine guns. But after several ripping and slashing attacks the big plane caught fire inside its fuselage, and, with most of the crew undoubtedly either dead or overcome, it slanted down sharply. It exploded as it hit the sea. "One occupant was seen to leap from the plane just before it struck the water."[17] His smashed body sank from sight along with his plane and his mates.

Task Force 17 steamed on south unscathed. The men of the *Hornet* had been at general quarters, condition "affirm," since sunset the previous evening. As daylight waned on the fifth, the last planes of the combat air patrol came aboard, and shortly thereafter the men went to the mess decks for their first full meal in more than twenty-four hours. Despite the ordeal of a full day at the guns or the engines without respite, morale was high. "All hands were anxious to meet the enemy," Charlie Mason wrote in his report, "after spending a considerable time in this area without contact with other than submarines."[18] By the next morning Task Force 17 was back in its usual patrol area south and west of Guadalcanal, waiting to escort Turner's convoy coming up from Nouméa.

By now both the Japanese and American high commands were prepared to throw all their resources into the battle for Guadalcanal, which had become a test of wills between Yamamoto and Nimitz. A defeat for either side was simply unthinkable. More than an island was at stake; national destinies had become involved. "Whatever happens, we must succeed in the coming operation of recapturing Guadalcanal at any cost," Ugaki wrote on 9 October. "If even this fails, what other plans can we make? It would mean the Combined Fleet would become incapable of doing anything."[19] The Japanese admiral knew, moreover, that time was steadily eroding his nation's position. Every hour, every day, in which the Americans fought Japan to a standstill brought defeat closer. Within months the great new U.S. fleet would begin to appear in Pacific waters. American manpower, far greater than Japan could muster, would be employed relentlessly. Yamamoto would have to win a major victory quickly or face certain defeat. At present only an aircraft carrier, a battleship, and a handful of cruisers and destroyers stood in the way.

But the crews aboard this handful of ships were quickly becoming more proficient. One day in early October, soon after the Bougainville–Shortland Islands attack, the *Hornet*'s airdales were called to attention for a brief ceremony. In the six weeks since leaving Pearl Harbor, only one life had been lost during air operations; no pilots had been killed and few planes had been lost. The *Hornet*'s safety record was remarkable. Many minor accidents had occurred. The heavy Dauntlesses and Avengers had occasionally landed at too a high a speed, causing tail hooks to rip out. The planes had then either nosed down hard onto the flight deck or more frequently had sped down the deck and crashed into the heavy nylon barrier amidships, resulting in twisted propellers or wrenched fuselages.[20] But such damages were mostly reparable. The few planes that could not be salvaged were cannibalized by the adept electricians and machinist's mates in the hangar deck shops. At a time when every plane counted, the *Hornet*'s air department kept a remarkable number flying.

As Task Force 17 again assumed position 170 miles southwest of Guadalcanal, the four battleships, five carriers, eight heavy cruisers, three light cruisers, and thirty-seven destroyers of the Japanese Combined Fleet left Truk under the immediate command of Admiral Kondo. The five flattops were in two divisions. Division 1, commanded by Admiral Nagumo, included the fleet carriers *Shokaku* and *Zuikaku* and the powerful light carrier *Zuiho*. It constituted the strike force of the Japanese fleet. Division 2 consisted of the light sister carriers *Junyo* and *Hiyo* under the command of Vice Adm. Hiroaki Abe. It remained with Kondo's battleships as a reserve and support force. Altogether the five carriers could put 267 warplanes into the sky. At Rabaul the Eleventh Air Fleet had been brought up to 220 aircraft.

Kondo's objective was to seal off the southern Solomons again. Lurking just north of the Stewart Islands, small bits of rock one hundred miles north of Santa Isabel, the Combined Fleet would use its carrier air power to deny Vandegrift and his troops reinforcements and to cover and if necessary strengthen a series of nighttime, high-speed resupply missions by fast destroyers from Rabaul. The Japanese garrison on Guadalcanal would be built up sufficiently to drive the Americans into the sea.

The small U.S. fleet covering the island had been divided into three forces: the *Hornet* with her few cruisers and destroyers, still designated Task Force 17; a surface action group consisting of the battleship *Washington* and a handful of destroyers; and a cruiser-destroyer group, under Rear Adm. Norman Scott, which screened Turner's convoy right up to the beaches of Guadalcanal and was ready to defend the island directly with nighttime sweeps through adjacent waters.

Turner's convoy triumphantly entered Ironbottom Sound off Guadalcanal on the afternoon of 9 October and swiftly unloaded the Americal Division and its equipment. Then it scuttled back south, while Scott prepared to battle any forces the Japanese might bring against him. On the nights of 11–12 October Scott's Task Force 64 collided with Rear Adm. Gunichi Mikawa's cruisers off the northwestern coast of Guadalcanal in what became known as the Battle of Cape Esperance. The Americans won the first round, the Japanese the second. When the confusing actions were over, two of Mikawa's valuable cruisers had been lost and a third damaged. Scott's cruisers were banged up but still battleworthy; only the destroyer *Duncan* had been sunk. Under cover of combat a Japanese convoy reached the garrison at Lunga Point, but on the morning of the twelfth Cactus Air Force bombs sank two more destroyers as they tried to leave the battle area at high speed.

As Scott and Mikawa lunged and parried, Task Force 17 was keeping busy 150 to 200 miles south of Guadalcanal. Modified general quarters were routinely set aboard the *Hornet* from one hour before sunrise to one hour after sunset each day because Japanese "snoopers" constantly lurked near or just over the horizon, teasing the carrier's combat air patrols. The task force steamed on a broad racecourse pattern, sailing away from Guadalcanal during daylight hours, then approaching the island swiftly at night so it could be in position at dawn to launch aircraft

in support of the Cactus Air Force at Henderson Field and Scott's embattled ships.

As the carrier and her escorts maneuvered ceaselessly, tension aboard
the *Hornet* built steadily. After ten months at sea, several thousand men
had become accustomed to a radical new life-style. But the stresses of
daily life aboard a large carrier and of dangerous, unceasing work were
compounded by the strains of war. Every American sailor in the Pacific
in 1942 had learned to live with the odds against him, but the *Hornet* had
become Japan's primary target. It was anyone's guess when an enemy
bomber, torpedo plane, or submarine might turn the big carrier into a
blazing torch like the *Wasp,* when a pilot might suddenly be killed or go
down with engine failure hundreds of miles from base, when a flight deck
crewman might be sawed in half by a propeller, run over, or thrown into
the sea by a taxiing airplane. Such thoughts were stifled even as they
formed, but they rattled even the strongest nerves. The poker games in
officers' country had become wild affairs, with the stakes on a single hand
occasionally reaching $1,500 (roughly equivalent to $15,000 a half-
century later). Down in the chiefs' quarters and enlisted spaces, bingo
fever suddenly broke out. No one quite knew how it started. For days a
clear-voiced yeoman on the mess deck sang out scores and awarded
prizes from the ship's store as hundreds of men played, thirty at a time,
during every change of the watch. Perhaps the games somehow echoed
other games that had been played in church basements and Grange halls
all across peacetime America. A coding officer on Murray's staff, determined to read the entire Bible from Genesis on, came to Deuteronomy
7:20—"Moreover the Lord, thy God, will send the *hornet* among them
until they that are left, and hide themselves from thee, be destroyed."[21]
The young lieutenant showed it to the ship's communications officer,
Oscar Dodson, who promptly quoted the phrase to every colleague he
met on watch in the island or in the wardroom. Chaplain Harp printed
the verse on the masthead of the ship's newspaper. Even George Murray,
isolated in flag plot and on the flag bridge, claimed he was moved.

As the days passed, many of the sailors and airdales, pilots, ship's
officers, and the enlisted aircrew lived more within themselves. Welded
into one of the finest carrier teams ever created, these men worked as part
of a unit during the long predawn to postdusk hours, but nighttime
moments were cherished for quiet privacy. In navigation and personnel
offices, under the bright lights in the wardroom or the illumination of
battle lamps shining dimly down long, steel corridors after taps, men

throughout the ship snatched time to read quietly, to ponder that day or the next, or to write to those they held most dear, all the while wondering when the probing enemy would finally find "Blue Base."

On the morning of 12 October the *Hornet* was "steam[ing] on Southerly courses, maneuvering to launch and recover aircraft or avoid suspected dangers."[22] At 1000 the carrier's plotting team in the combat information center made radar contact with an unidentified aircraft bearing 000° True, distance thirty-five miles. By now Lieutenant Fleming had fused his small fighter director team into a highly efficient unit. While Radarman 2nd Class J. S. Poffenberger maintained contact with the bogey, Ens. V. M. Burkman vectored Lt. (jg) George Formanek and his wingman, Ens. Richard Z. Hughes, onto the target. It was a typical tropical morning, partly cloudy, ceiling unlimited, ten miles visibility. The two men, flying at 10,000 feet, almost immediately sighted a four-engine Kawanishi ahead and slightly above them. They forced their Wildcats up to 13,000 feet, then dove on the hapless enemy, who fired a few futile rounds from his 7.7-millimeter upper and side guns but took no evasive action. Coming down on the Kawanishi's right side, Formanek shot over the fuselage, setting the port inboard engine afire with his first pass. Hughes, racing in behind, destroyed the outboard port engine. The big plane began to burn and spiraled down into the ocean. There were no survivors.

Two hours later the *Northampton*'s CXAM radar picked up an unidentified contact bearing 150° True, distance sixty miles. By this time Formanek and Hughes had been relieved by Lt. (jg) Robert E. Sorensen and Ens. R. B. Dalton. Fifteen minutes after radar contact the two Americans saw what seemed to be a Mitsubishi 97 at 7,000 feet. The enemy promptly "turned and ran" as Sorensen and Dalton pursued him at close to their maximum speed of 250 to 260 miles an hour. There were no nearby clouds in which the desperate Japanese pilot could hide, and after a long chase Dalton got into attack position, coming toward the Mitsubishi's left side from slightly above. Sorensen attacked almost immediately from below. The Mitsubishi responded with a few 20-millimeter rounds from a "turtle back" gun turret but failed to hit either U.S. plane. As .50-caliber incendiary and tracer slugs chewed up the Mitsubishi's wing between the port engines and the fuselage, a fire erupted, probably in the wing fuel tanks. The enemy bomber "glided to [the] water," where it exploded spectacularly. Again there were no survivors.[23]

The rest of the day was quiet, and at 2045 Task Force 17 changed course to a generally northwestern direction. At dawn launch (0615) on the thirteenth base course was again set to the southeast at twenty-three knots. Later in the day Murray ordered more course changes to prepare for a rendezvous with a tanker the next morning.

At 1145, under light clouds, with ceiling and visibility unlimited, the *Hornet*'s radar and plotting team picked up an unidentified aircraft bearing 025° True, distance twenty-nine miles. Once again Poffenberger kept the plane pinned on his radar screen, while Burkman directed a combat air patrol section onto the bogey. This time three Wildcats, led by Al Emerson, were patrolling at 10,000 feet. Emerson and his two wingmen soon spotted the snooper from 12,000 feet, but they quickly lost him against the water because he was flying only 500 feet above the waves. Racing down to 1,500 feet, one of Emerson's wingmen, Lt. W. J. Moran, picked up what seemed to be a Mitsubishi 97 several miles away, still at 500 feet. The Japanese pilot spotted the Americans at the same time, and the big reconnaissance bomber "turned tail and ran—diving for speed. Made two gentle turns."[24] Pinned against the water by the oncoming American planes, the enemy fought back desperately with 20-millimeter rounds from the upper and tail guns. Moran came in first from astern, killing or wounding the enemy gunners as he shot up the Mitsubishi. The starboard engine began to smoke as the plane glided toward the water. Emerson and his other wingman, Ens. J. O. Weimer, dove on the dying plane from either side as it hit the ocean. For a moment the Mitsubishi floated serenely on the sea; then it burst into flames that spread across the water.

Shortly before dawn on the fourteenth some of the economizer tubes in the *Hornet*'s boiler number eight began to leak, and Creehan had to order the entire superheated boiler unit to be cut out. It was not a serious casualty, but it demonstrated again that the carrier was beginning to show wear after months of steaming relieved by only a few weeks in port. Soucek noted that "probably new economizer tubes will have to be installed throughout number eight boiler in the future." Such repairs would require a trip to Pearl Harbor, if not the West Coast. "High engine speeds during the campaign have placed rather a severe strain on the Engineering plant," Soucek added, "and no doubt brought on the above mentioned casualty sooner than normally would be expected." The high speeds were needed to make up for the lack of true wind force over the deck during flight operations in tropical climes "and drag due to foul bottom."[25]

The fourteenth was spent refueling Task Force 17, and the correspondents who had been aboard the *Hornet* since Hawaii departed by breeches buoy. Tom Lea and John Hersey would never forget the two plus months they had spent aboard the big flattop. Lea, in particular, had caught the raw excitement of hundreds of men engaged in running a new ship with cutting-edge technology in the midst of war. Although busy crewmen seldom commented or even thought about it, aircraft carriers had suddenly become essential; a revolution in naval warfare and maritime glamour was taking place, and the *Hornet* was at the center of it.

Meanwhile, at Guadalcanal, the situation had become desperate. Scott had been forced to withdraw after the battle of Cape Esperance just as Kondo's Combined Fleet took up position off the Stewart Islands. Once more the nights on Ironbottom Sound would belong to the Japanese. Yamamoto poured more men and matériel onto the island and welcomed the Americal Division with incessant bombardments of Henderson Field. Japanese warships pounded American positions for hours on the nights of 13 and 14 October. Very early on the morning of the fifteenth a large contingent of warships, including the 14-inch-gun battleships *Kongo* and *Haruna*, which had been detached from Kondo's Combined Fleet for one day, came in to pulverize the dazed, exhausted garrison. The shelling was merciless, hellish, and effective. At dawn the marines counted only six operational planes on the airfield. The runways were so cratered that construction crews would need hours to return them to some semblance of operational efficiency. The Japanese on the island, fit, reinforced, and aggressive, finally seemed ready for a showdown.

"It now appears we are unable to control the sea in the Guadalcanal area," Nimitz concluded gloomily at Pearl Harbor. "The situation," he concluded, "is not hopeless but it is certainly critical."[26] Ghormley was even more pessimistic. "My forces totally inadequate to meet situation," he cabled from Nouméa.[27]

Vandegrift had only one option if he was to maintain control of the air and counter the ongoing Japanese buildup. He would have to call in the *Hornet* to act as the Cactus Air Force at least for a day while Henderson Field was repaired. But Kondo was using his carriers aggressively to complement the night assaults on Guadalcanal. On the fifteenth Zeros from the *Zuikaku* found a small American supply convoy heading for the island, sank the destroyer *Meredith* and a seagoing tug, and forced the rest of the ships to turn back. The next morning a lone seaplane tender arrived off Henderson Field and discharged her cargo of aviation fuel before being bombed and forced onto the beach at Tulagi. To send

America's last carrier into such an environment was more than risky. But the fate of Guadalcanal depended on her.

Murray initially had other ideas. At daylight on the fifteenth, with refueling completed, he set his task force on a looping course that would take it north of Guadalcanal; he apparently contemplated surprising Kondo's five carriers off the Stewarts with a sudden flanking attack. Murray soon changed his mind, however, and prudently decided to keep his force south of San Cristobal Island immediately to the east of Guadalcanal, where he could easily support Vandegrift's hard-pressed forces. Perhaps contact with a Kawanishi shortly after noon had an effect; with five enemy carriers somewhere in the vicinity, risking the *Hornet* north of Guadalcanal would have been an act of incredible folly.

Al Fleming's efficient plotting and vectoring team sighted the enemy snooper at 1235, bearing 180° True, distance thirty miles. Formanek and Hughes were cruising on combat air patrol at 5,000 feet in cloud-flecked skies with ceiling unlimited and visibility ten miles. As he headed to the enemy's last known position, Formanek dropped down a thousand feet. At 1300 he saw the bogey below and slightly to the right. With Hughes behind, Formanek dove and made a high side attack on the Kawanishi's left side with "no apparent result."[28] Hughes blazed away too, but the big bomber flew on, and one 20-millimeter cannon fired back from the top turret in the fuselage. Formanek and Hughes shot past and recovered to the right. Formanek came in again, blasting several hundred rounds of tracer and incendiary bullets. Hughes had just started his second run when the Kawanishi abruptly blew up in his face. Jurika and his people had speculated that Japanese patrol planes carried auxiliary fuel tanks in their fuselages. The spectacular demise of the Kawanishi seemed to confirm it.

At 1915 that evening Charlie Mason sent his men to general quarters, where they would remain for the next twenty-five hours. Food was served on station, and "wherever and whenever practicable, men were permitted to lie down on stations and get some slight degree of rest." In the soft tropical night above decks, sleeping was not difficult. The caress of trade winds under starry skies, amplified by the carrier's own speed over the water, actually made sleep easier there than down in the muggy berthing compartments, where no air stirred to dissipate the body odors of hundreds of sailors. But in the fire and engine rooms, with their constant vibrations, high temperatures (often approaching 130 degrees Fahrenheit), and lack of space, the loss of restful sleep soon resulted in reduced efficiency. "No one was tired out to the point of exhaustion at the end of daylight on October 16," Soucek recalled of that brutal twenty-five-hour period, "but it is believed that a continuation of Condition One would have exhausted many within another twenty-four hours."[29]

At 0650 on the morning of the sixteenth the *Hornet*, in position only ninety-five miles from Cape West Point on Guadalcanal, began launching her first strike of the day. There would be two attack groups, both with orders to search the Guadalcanal–Santa Isabel–Russell Islands area for enemy ships that were either withdrawing from the previous night's supply run into Guadalcanal or preparing to slip into the island the next night. The first attack group consisted of sixteen Dauntlesses of Scouting 8 and Bombing 8. They were escorted by eight Wildcats from VF-72, led by Al Emerson. Murray and Mason had wisely waited until dawn so that forming up would not be as complicated as it had been on the Bougainville-Shortlands raid eleven days before. Rodee again went aloft with a two-plane fighter escort, apparently to act as attack coordinator.

For 4½ hours the twenty-four planes roamed over a broad sector, but the sea was empty. The Wildcats were equipped with new belly tanks for increased range. They were mounted on the center line of the fuselage to minimize drag and thus loss of fuel and maneuverability. Emerson and his men were delighted with them. The F4F-4s could finally match the Dauntlesses and Avengers in range and yet maintain fighting efficiency.

With time running out and nothing to show for the strike, Rodee or Widhelm—it is not clear who—led the formation to the Japanese seaplane base at Rekata Bay. There the Americans found eight to twelve aircraft: seaplanes riding in the water close to shore and biplanes and monoplanes on the ground. Nearby was a large gasoline dump with tents and huts. While the Dauntlesses swept in low to drop their 1,000-pound bombs, the fighters strafed. All the enemy aircraft either sank or burned "except one biplane and it was riddled with bullets." The gasoline dump blew up, and several huts were set afire with .50-caliber incendiary bullets. One enemy plane had just taken off when the Americans arrived. It raced to the north, hotly pursued for a while by several Wildcats, but they finally had to let it go.[30]

The second attack group began taking off at 0705. It consisted of fourteen Avengers from Torpedo 6, eight carrying 500-pound bombs and six carrying torpedoes. This force first searched the area around Cape Esperance. Finding nothing worth attacking, the Avengers flew toward Lunga Point, where they spotted two enemy transports. Both were in extremis—one beached and virtually sunk, the other burning on a coral reef. Nonetheless, the frustrated Americans bombed them. What happened next is unclear from the after-action reports. Torpedo 6 claimed that all aircraft returned to the *Hornet,* whereas Mike Sanchez of VF-72 reported that the attack force flew south across the sea to the Russell Islands, then to the Savo Island area, and finally north to New Georgia but sighted no enemy ships or planes.

Over New Georgia, Lt. Warren W. Ford, leading the fighter escort, suddenly discovered that the right magneto on his Wildcat had cut out and the plane was throwing oil. He promptly broke away with his escort and headed back to the *Hornet* via Guadalcanal. Arriving over the north shore of the island west of the Kukum River, he spotted many small and a few large landing barges drawn up on the beach. As he and his section swooped down to investigate, they were challenged by light antiaircraft fire from several points along the beach. Ford led his men in a low strafing run, which he claimed destroyed two of the large and two of the small barges "and put one AA gun out."[31] Nearby the Americans found a small nest of Japanese barges, antiaircraft guns, and installations. Ford and his men rushed back to the *Hornet* with the news.

Throughout the day Mason maintained a combat air patrol ranging from eight to sixteen Wildcats. No one knew exactly what the Eleventh Air Fleet was up to or where Kondo's carriers might be. During the early morning the hot, clear sky, broken by only a few scattered clouds, remained empty of Japanese aircraft. But conditions suddenly changed just before the two attack groups were scheduled to return. At 0942 a bogey was spotted only eighteen miles from the task force, bearing 220° True. Closest to it were Lt. (jg) Minuard F. Jennings and his wingman, Ens. Philip E. Souza. Souza was the first to find the enemy. Flying at 8,000 feet, he saw the plane 5,000 feet below trying to hop from one small cloud to another while keeping the task force in sight. Souza promptly nosed over and went down after the Kawanishi. His high rear attack was met by determined fire from the upper and side turrets of the Japanese seaplane. Jennings, following Souza in, had to break off his own attack because the excited ensign, refusing to let go of an almost sure kill, remained between Jennings and the enemy. Souza then pulled up and away to make two more passes from the starboard side and above. In the midst of Souza's last attack the Kawanishi suddenly caught fire and exploded; it fell into the sea in two pieces.

Three hours later another Kawanishi drew within twenty-five miles of the task force. Murray had augmented the combat air patrol that day with half a dozen Dauntlesses flying antisubmarine watch. Frank

Christofferson, at the controls of one of the scout-bombers, picked up the enemy plane visually. The Japanese pilot saw him at the same time and flew into a nearby cloud. Christofferson gave chase and called for reinforcements. The Dauntless was scarcely faster than the Kawanishi, which meant his attack would be slow and vulnerable, but the lieutenant did not hesitate. As the Kawanishi flew out of the cloud, he made five passes at the stubborn enemy, which responded with one freely swinging 20-millimeter cannon. On Christofferson's fifth pass, approaching from behind and below with one .50-caliber wing gun already out of ammunition, his plane was hit several times and began to shudder. He broke off and made for the *Hornet*. Fuel oil pressure began to fall, and as the Dauntless approached the task force its engine suddenly froze up and quit. Christofferson made a clean water landing near the destroyer *Morris*, but his gunner-radioman suffered a broken arm in the jarring impact with the sea. Both men were pulled from the water by the destroyer's crew and were soon back aboard their carrier.

Christofferson's call for reinforcements had brought Formanek and Hughes to the scene. Coming in at four thousand feet, they spotted the enemy three thousand feet below. As their Wildcats raced down, the Japanese pilot pushed his plane over in a shallow dive to get as close to the water as possible and try to break up the American attack. Formanek made a high side pass from the left side, blazing away at the enemy plane with no apparent effect. Hughes followed; the result was the same. Recovering, Formanek came in from the right side and began to rip up the Kawanishi with sheets of .50-caliber machine gun fire. When Formanek was only three hundred yards away, the Kawanishi suddenly burst into flames, leaving only an oily smoke ring and a rain of small bits of metal and other materials. One other snooper approached the task force that day and was sighted by the *Hornet*'s air patrol, but it managed to escape.

During the morning patrols over the carrier one pilot stopped everyone's heart when he reported seeing an enemy cruiser "and 3 merchant type vessels in the bay" just north of Cape de Entrecasteaux on nearby San Cristobal Island.[32] After the first strike returned at midmorning Mason ordered another raid to hit the enemy ships. A dozen Dauntlesses and four Avengers, armed with bombs and torpedoes and escorted by eight fighters, went aloft at 1230. Racing over to San Cristobal, the pilots found nothing but a few rocks where the "enemy ships" were supposed to be. Once more an overzealous and inexperienced pilot had initiated a wild goose chase. But he would learn.

Ford's report of the enemy barges near the Kukum River was as enticing to Mason and Murray as a swinging skirt to a sailor on a dance floor. At 1350 they sent five Dauntlesses, nine Avengers, and eight Wildcats back to the area to shoot up the barges and gun emplacements. It proved to be a frustrating mission, for the Japanese had learned from Ford's morning attack. While the Americans swooped lower and lower over the beach, the Japanese in their hidden gun emplacements bit their lips and remained quiet. They would risk death from strafing for an opportunity to shoot down a U.S. plane. But the planes never got close enough for the perfect shot. Finally the bombers and fighters expended their ordnance on the handful of barges that the enemy had not been able to get off the beach and headed back to Blue Base, landing at 1630.

It had been a frenzied day on the *Hornet*'s flight deck. Three major attacks had been launched, one just after dawn, one just after noon, the last an hour later. Combat air patrols had been sent aloft and recovered steadily throughout the morning, afternoon, and early evening. Francis Foley looked down on the constantly changing flight deck, watching hundreds of young men in brown, red, green, blue, and white T-shirts hauling and pulling planes, refueling them, rearming them, and guiding them to spotting and takeoff positions. "Plane pusher teams were on the run during push backs with plane captains in the cockpits manning the brakes and chock men riding the wings, chocks in hand." There had scarcely been a moment's peace on the long, narrow strip of wood above the hissing sea as the air department had "improvised short-haul raids" to nearby Guadalcanal "throughout the afternoon, sending off mixed flights irregardless of their size as soon as we had a reasonable ratio of fighters to bombers on hand." Every pilot had been used to fly either combat missions or air patrols.[33]

Perhaps it was on this day, perhaps on another, that the flight deck crew experienced one of its most freakish accidents. A plane making a routine landing snapped the arresting wire, which went snaking across the flight deck. As the wire began to lose velocity, it struck a sailor and wrapped itself around his neck. Incredibly, it did not kill him. Badly winded, the young man fell to the deck and waited patiently while his mates carefully unwrapped the wire from his throat.[34] He was saved only because the comparatively light war planes of 1942 did not require strong arresting wires and the wire was rapidly losing force when it struck. In later years, with heavier planes, especially jets, the arresting wires had to be so strong that if one snapped and struck a man it could cut him in half.[35]

Far below, in the *Hornet*'s bowels, Pat Creehan's men were also kept busy in the enervating heat and pulsating noise of the engineering spaces, for continual flight operations on a hot, breezeless day necessitated maintaining the carrier at nearly flank speed. And as the big carrier twisted and turned through the sparkling seas to launch and recover her aircraft, the rest of Task Force 17 remained at a respectful distance, allowing the ship all the space she needed.

Never had the *Hornet* been more efficient as a fighting machine, and for those who understood her deadly competence these were exhilarating moments. Henry Ford, the profane flight deck chief, was in his element. "O.K.," he screamed at the boys who were riding the wings to keep the planes firmly on deck in the thirty-knot winds whipped up by the carrier's momentum. "I don't mind you bastards ridin', but quit draggin' your Goddam feet!"[36] When the last Wildcat came aboard in fading light at 1842 and flight quarters were secured, some pilots, such as Warren Ford, Red Hessel, and Emerson, had flown four missions—some as strike escorts, some as combat air patrol.

In terms of damage inflicted, the *Hornet*'s air strikes of 16 October accomplished little. Few enemy were around, and much ordnance was expended for little effect. Certainly the fliers of Air Group 8 were not in a boasting mood. They told correspondent Stanley Johnston several months later that the Bougainville-Faisi raids had been spoiled by bad weather; as for the 16 October raids, they admitted, "our punch wasn't very heavy."[37] But in the narrower scope of the October struggle, which could be considered the pivotal point of the entire Guadalcanal campaign, the *Hornet*'s raids on both the fifth and sixteenth were crucial. They demonstrated to the brave, stubborn Japanese that the Americans would never give up, not for a day, not for an hour, that somehow Nimitz would find ways to maintain pressure on Guadalcanal no matter how bleak the situation or how desperate the odds.

But Nimitz could not do it all. South Pacific Command Headquarters at Nouméa had to be revitalized. Ghormley was clearly exhausted from bearing too much responsibility for too long with too few resources. Defeatism among his subordinates was rampant. As the *Hornet* pulled away from the Guadalcanal–San Cristobal area on the night of the sixteenth, Nimitz had already decided to replace Ghormley with a man whose aggressiveness was legendary: Bull Halsey. After finally shaking off the debilitating skin disease that had kept him from command at Midway, Halsey had gone to the South Pacific, ostensibly for an inspection. When ordered by telegram to proceed immediately to Nouméa and relieve Ghormley, Halsey's response was typically explosive: "Jesus Christ and General Jackson! This is the hottest potato they ever handed me."[38] On Guadalcanal, throughout Task Force 17, and all across the South Pacific, American fighting men exulted. "One minute we were too limp with malaria to crawl from our foxholes," Vandegrift recalled; "the next we were whooping it up like kids."[39] Now the "Japs" would be put on the run by a fighting admiral! But one of Halsey's first orders would doom the *Hornet*.

One good day was left to her during her final week of life. October 20 was the ship's first anniversary. At Norfolk a year before—a lifetime ago to all aboard who remembered it—the ship had been put into commission in an America now far away in both space and time. Whenever they would return to it, and whatever the circumstances, the twenty-six hundred men aboard the *Hornet* would find a new country, one that had thrown off economic and mental depression and was feverishly caught up not only in the miracle of war production but also, inadvertently, in the creation of a prosperity that would last for decades. Cruising far down in the South Pacific, thousands of miles from a home that seemed more elusive and magical every day, sailors and airdales, officers and pilots, could not conceive of the depth and breadth of their sacrifice or the incredible riches and security that it was buying.

The ship had been at sea for eighteen days, and supplies were again dwindling. There were still enough cigarettes, but the mess rooms were down to block beef and dumplings. The dumplings were still made of beetle-infested flour. The block beef, no matter how it was cut or prepared, was obviously Spam. The cooks also served "potatoes," but everyone knew they were the usual ground-up beans.[40]

But the supply department managed to produce a birthday surprise on the evening of 20 October. Comdr. R. H. Sullivan—"Pay Sully," as he was known to the crew—had struggled for a year to provide the ship with the best food and equipment he could. It had not been an easy job at a time when the country was just shifting to a war footing after starving its armed forces for years. Sullivan, who had asked for sea duty again although he was near retirement age, had not always been appreciated. But he was about to provide the men of the *Hornet* with one of their happier memories.

Pieces of chicken à la king and mounds of potatoes suddenly appeared in the great aluminum mess pans and were doled onto hundreds of trays or were elegantly served by mess attendants onto officers' plates set on snowy linen. There was lots of butter and big hardtack crackers to spread it on. To a famished crew used to Spam it made little difference that the chicken was canned and the potatoes were dehydrated.[41] As mess trays were emptied and plates whisked away, another treat appeared to complete the memorable meal: ice cream from the ship's mechanical cow. It was the usual grainy kind made from dehydrated milk, but it was still ice cream. And for the officers there was something more: A large, three-tiered cake with "Happy Birthday Hornet" inscribed in confection on the top was brought into the wardroom. Then Apollo Soucek rose to make a few heartfelt remarks before a hushed, attentive audience. All hands, he said, had worked hard to make the *Hornet* represent American resolve and competence. "The going hasn't always been easy and undoubtedly there will be more rough times ahead. But this ship is a great ship and I know you all well enough to say that you will make it one of the greatest of all in the tradition of our Navy."[42]

Twenty minutes later evening general quarters sounded and several thousand men raced to battle stations. As Oscar Dodson stood on the bridge, he saw great thunderheads out beyond the ship; the rays of the rapidly setting sun slanting through them seemed to turn the sea red, as if the *Hornet* were sailing through an ocean of blood. As he turned away, Dodson experienced a sudden queasiness in his stomach, a dread for the morrow.[43]

10

Death

FOUR DAYS after her birthday party, the *Hornet* was steaming north of Espiritu Santo with Task Force 17. At the end of the afternoon watch men on the carrier's bridge saw the foretops of Task Force 16 appear over the horizon. The *Enterprise* was back in the South Pacific, and she had brought with her not only the usual handful of cruisers and destroyers but also the brand-new battleship *South Dakota*, which, in addition to nine big 16-inch naval cannons, also bristled with 5-inch surface and antiaircraft guns, 20-millimeter AA batteries, and, most important, new 40-millimeter guns. The two task forces were welded into one, designated Task Force 61, commanded by Rear Adm. Thomas Kinkaid aboard the "Big E." The two carrier groups, however, would retain their individual designations and a degree of independence. They would operate roughly five to ten miles apart. Murray thus remained in command of Task Force 17 aboard the *Hornet* but was subordinate to Kinkaid. Together, the *Enterprise* and *Hornet* could muster 170 aircraft against the nearly 500 planes available to the Japanese aboard Kondo's carriers and at Rabaul.

Halsey wasted no time in testing his new fleet. He would do with two carriers what Murray had wisely decided not to do with one: go after the Japanese Combined Fleet, which was still maneuvering somewhere above the Stewarts. Apparently hoping to catch Kondo's ships in a flank attack, as had been done at Midway, he ordered Kinkaid to sweep north of the Santa Cruz Islands as soon as rendezvous was completed.

Both sides were in a state of nervous anticipation bordering on exhaustion. Up at Truk, Admiral Ugaki reflected the worry of his nation, his emperor, and his commander as a string of frustrating messages arrived from Guadalcanal during the third week in October. The garrison there had been greatly augmented by the heroic efforts of the naval convoys; the army commander, Lt. Gen. Harukichi Hyakutake, had promised Hirohito that he would deal the enemy a fatal blow. On the twentieth Hyakutake predicted a glorious victory as his troops began working their way from base camps at Lunga Point through the tortuous, fetid jungles toward the American lines around Henderson Field. Kondo's carriers, now reduced to four because a fire in the *Hiyo*'s engine room had forced the light carrier back to Truk, maintained constant daylight air patrols near the island, evading the still feeble Cactus Air Force but also failing to find the major units of the small U.S. fleet. The great offensive against Henderson Field was planned for the twenty-second, postponed to the twenty-third, then postponed again as tropical rains slowed the advancing Japanese columns, whose formations were breaking up and fragmenting in the nearly impenetrable jungle.

Ugaki was obsessed by supposed sightings of U.S. battleships off Guadalcanal. There were at least three ships of the *Colorado* or *Texas* class, he guessed. In actuality, there were none. Japanese pilots were turning enemy heavy cruisers into prewar battlewagons in their reports. But where were the American carriers? Ugaki evidently believed that at least two, perhaps more, were around Guadalcanal, but his fliers and submariners could not find them.

Finally, on the twenty-fourth, Hyakutake began his offensive, tentative and piecemeal at first. The initial effort was hurled back along the right bank of the Matanicau River with horrendous losses. "The Oka regiment doubled its disgrace," Ugaki wrote scornfully.[1] Compounding Japanese problems, Kondo had moved the Combined Fleet too far north of the Stewarts to support Hyakutake's troops. Because communications between Hyakutake's headquarters and Kondo's flagship were nonexistent, there was no significant cooperation or coordination.

Just before midnight on the twenty-fourth electrifying news came from the island: Despite all obstacles, Henderson Field had finally been captured. "This settled everything," Ugaki wrote triumphantly just before going to bed. "March, all forces, to enlarge the result gained! Hesitation or indecision at this moment would leave a regret forever."[2] But within hours Ugaki was awakened with heartbreaking news: Henderson had not fallen after all; the Americans had been pushed back to the perimeter of the airfield but were hanging on grimly.

Ugaki was not discouraged. The Combined Fleet had been ordered back south at high speed to support the offensive, and the army had promised to resume its attack that evening. The troops would "charge in at 1900. If so, it will be all right. Now our last hope is that they will succeed tonight." October 25, 1942, would be a turning point in the Pacific war. But the naval high command was uneasy. Search planes from Kondo's carriers and cruisers had not found the enemy fleet. Where was it?[3]

A thousand miles south of Truk, sailing at high speed near the Santa Cruz Islands, Kinkaid and Murray had the same worry. Rochefort's men up at Pearl Harbor had done their usual superb job of interpreting Yamamoto's operational orders, which united Kondo and Hyakutake in a combined ground and naval air offensive designed to rid Guadalcanal of the pesky Americans. But, as always, the cryptanalysts were ten days behind in reading the enemy's flood of daily messages. Kondo and Nagumo were known to be lurking two to three hundred miles north of Guadalcanal with their powerful battleship–carrier–cruiser fleet. But exactly where? And what did Yamamoto know of American intentions? Were the Japanese preparing to swoop down on Task Force 61 as it rounded the Santa Cruz Islands?

Kinkaid had a problem that Kondo did not: untrained pilots. Air Group 8 aboard the *Hornet* was now a veteran outfit, but the *Enterprise* had a new air group; her fliers and radiomen-gunners were only ten days from the classrooms and training fields of Kaneohe. Except for a handful of veterans—Lt. Comdr. Jim Flatley, Lt. John A. Leppla, Lt. Stanley Vejtasa, and a few others—these "Grim Reapers," as the *Enterprise's* fighter pilots called themselves, had never been in battle, had never experienced the ordeal of navigating with partial information over miles of ocean to find and strike an elusive, determined enemy.

But Kinkaid got the first break. Around 1430 on the afternoon of the twenty-fifth word reached the *Enterprise* that a PBY patrol plane out of Efate had sighted Nagumo's carriers three hundred miles north of Guadalcanal. Within minutes another message came in, this time from Halsey at Nouméa. The three words signaled a drastic change in the mood at South Pacific headquarters: "ATTACK REPEAT ATTACK."[4]

Kinkaid immediately called a staff conference aboard the *Enterprise*, and thirty minutes later Comdr. Richard Gaines, Walt Rodee's counterpart on the Big E, dispatched sixteen Dauntlesses with fighter escort to search a broad area from the southwest to the north, two hundred miles from the task force. Meanwhile, Kinkaid ordered Murray to bring Air Group 8 up to the *Hornet*'s flight deck, armed and ready for a major attack. Once more the ammo hoists and elevators aboard the *Hornet* were filled with torpedoes, 500- and 1,000-pound bombs, and belts of .50-caliber ammunition, while the carrier's three swift elevators brought the Wildcats, Dauntlesses, and Avengers up from below. Once again several hundred blue-shirted "plane pushers" spotted them for launch.

As the air department readied the strike, Charlie Mason ordered his ship squared away for battle. "Gun boss" Jim Smith tested his fire control equipment; status boards down in damage control central, far below decks near amidships, were checked and rechecked; First Lieutenant Henry Moran had all hoses, foamite, and fire-fighting canisters accounted for and saw to it that fire buckets were filled with water or sand; each officer and crewman made sure he had his steel helmet, flash-proof clothing, a life jacket, and a shark knife. The medical department inspected first aid boxes throughout the ship and took inventory of medical supplies and surgical equipment. Officers were issued morphine to ease the pain of the wounded, and the ship's cooks prepared the usual battle rations—doughnuts, sandwiches, canned fruit, mincemeat pies, and coffee.

The *Enterprise* search group fanned out in pairs and droned south, west, and north. Pilots flew for hours over an empty ocean as their fuel gauges sank toward the halfway mark and below. Nagumo had turned sharply north, out of reach of the carrier planes. Finally, with no enemy in sight, the *Enterprise*'s bitterly disappointed fliers broke off their search and headed homeward over a darkening sea.

Now the vulnerability of the new air group became clear: These young men had never made night landings before; nor had they ever had to fly with rapidly diminishing fuel in a real flight situation. With throttles set back, constantly babying fuel mixtures and prop controls, each pilot sweated his way toward "Red Base." Forty miles from the *Enterprise*, Lt. Frank Miller's Wildcat fell out of formation and smashed into the sea. A destroyer was sent back to look for the veteran flier, but he was never found. The rest of the squadron made it back to the task force, but half a dozen planes had insufficient fuel to maneuver into landing position; they went into the "drink." Although most of the men were saved, Kinkaid had lost precious aircraft on the eve of a crucial battle.

Undeterred, the admiral ordered the *Hornet* to prepare for a night strike under moonlit skies if Japanese carriers could be found. Within hours another PBY out of Efate spotted Nagumo's force heading south toward Guadalcanal to support Hyakutake. The Japanese were now three hundred miles away on Kinkaid's flank. The patrol plane pilot audaciously attacked Nagumo's force and nearly torpedoed the carrier *Zuikaku*. Nagumo, who had been apathetic and despondent ever since Midway (Ugaki had always thought him a bit of a coward), could not have been cheered by being spotted by enemy patrol planes.

Charlie Mason received word of the new sighting on his bridge thirty feet above the *Hornet*'s flight deck. "Well, here it comes," he thought. He handed the message to a young communications officer with a brief "thank you" and in the fading light gazed seaward at the cruisers and destroyers around him and the *Enterprise* and *South Dakota* about seven miles away. The *Hornet* had missed the Coral Sea and Eastern Solomons; she had never been attacked at Midway. She could not be so lucky again. "Like the night before the Big Game," Mason thought. As word spread throughout the ship of the most recent sighting, many officers and men thought the same thing.[5]

Irrepressible Gus Widhelm ran to the bridge to suggest a plan. Let's go now, he urged Mason. The Japanese were at extreme range. Surely they knew that U.S. carriers were around. Nagumo would not be foolish enough to be caught with his pants down; his carrier decks, too, would be filled with armed, fueled aircraft awaiting an early morning launch as soon as the Americans were spotted. If Kinkaid struck first at night with fighter aircraft, Japanese planes and flight decks could be torched with .50-caliber incendiaries, destroying Nagumo's air power. Dive-bombers could finish off the damaged carriers in the morning.

When he heard about it, Doc McAteer thought the plan was splendid; half a century later he had not changed his mind. But Mason, Murray, and Kinkaid knew better. The *Enterprise*'s air group was not ready for such a daring undertaking at this stage in its young life. And what would happen if Widhelm missed the enemy? The Americans would have to fly back from a fruitless mission in the middle of the night and land in the dark; how many planes and pilots might be lost at sea or during landing crack-ups after such an exhausting, demoralizing flight? How fresh would they be to go after the Japanese again the next day or to face rested enemy fliers diving in on Task Force 61? Widhelm's plan was never seriously considered.

As Widhelm was coming down from the bridge, precombat gambling fever broke out in officers' country and the enlisted berthing areas. Bob Hope was right, Francis Foley later decided; a carrier was simply a crap game with a flight deck over it. Widhelm joined the festivities, and to his disgust he won big. Would it affect his fabled good luck? As he put the money in his safe that night he wondered if the safe would still be there when he got back from attacking the Japanese the next day. Oscar Dodson, the communications officer, filled a briefcase with his most treasured possessions: a miniature portrait of his wife, Polly, in her wedding dress; a snapshot of his son; an autographed photo of Johnnie Waldron; and his treasured collection of coins. He took the briefcase up to the flag bridge and left it at his battle station.[6]

By now the idea was widespread that in every battle you lost a carrier. It had happened at the Coral Sea and Midway; it had almost happened at the Eastern Solomons when the *Enterprise* had barely survived. Whose number would be up this time?

To those in the know, apprehension was undoubtedly amplified by Kinkaid's decision to center fighter direction control for the entire task force on the *Enterprise*. The *Hornet*'s fine group would be subordinate throughout the coming battle. The fighter director officer (FDO) aboard the *Enterprise*, Lt. Comdr. Jack Griffin, was new at his job, having been temporarily assigned to Kinkaid's staff from his permanent position as director of the Naval Radar School, which had just been moved from San Diego to Pearl. Griffin had studied under Royal Air Force radar officers during the later stages of the Battle of Britain, but he had never directed a combat air patrol at sea, whereas Al Fleming and his team aboard the *Hornet* had become experienced and proficient. In the aftermath of Santa Cruz at least one *Hornet* officer charged that Griffin had "naturally" favored his own ship and task group.[7]

But there was nothing to be done about the morrow till it came. The frantic gambling ended early, and the men of the *Hornet*, in ready status throughout the night, enjoyed a fitful prebattle sleep.

Task Force 61 was awake well before first light. At 0600, twenty-three minutes before dawn, while all hands in the fleet were at routine general quarters, Kinkaid launched another search from the *Enterprise*. As Lt. Comdr. "Bucky" Lee and his men headed out, they encountered an enemy float plane from one of Nagumo's cruisers only eighty-five miles from the task force. Disdaining to waste time and fuel to shoot it down, they proceeded on their way. Soon the snooper was close enough to spot Kinkaid's force and notify Nagumo that a U.S. fleet including two carriers was roughly two hundred miles east-southeast of his position. Aboard the *Shokaku, Zuikaku,* and *Zuiho,* Japan's best carriers, several score Vals (dive-bombers) and Kates (torpedo planes), already armed, fueled, and on the flight decks, were immediately warmed up and rushed off with their escorts of Zeros. The remaining Japanese fighters and gunners throughout the Combined Fleet awaited possible enemy attack. Nagumo ordered the *Zuikaku* to move under cover of a small weather front several miles from the other two carriers. He had learned something from Midway.

Back on the *Hornet* the nerves of twenty-six hundred men were stretched to the breaking point. When thirty-seven-year-old war correspondent Charles McMurtry left his cabin in officers' country for breakfast, a lieutenant commander called out: "You'd better hurry and eat. It looks like action soon." McMurtry found "a quickening atmosphere in the wardroom" as everyone awaited the announcement to return to general quarters. After a hasty breakfast he dropped into Air Group 8's ready rooms and heard the same complaint from keyed-up pilots: "When do we go?" Finally Mason sent the ship back to action stations, while Gouin completed preparations to send every plane aloft for either attack or patrol.[8]

At 0730 Kinkaid received information from two of his scouts that they had found an enemy battleship-cruiser fleet. The admiral paced and fretted on his narrow flag bridge; he declined even to plot precisely where this particular enemy concentration was in relation to his task force. Nagumo's carriers were the prize. Where in hell were they?

Twenty minutes later he got the answer. At 0750 Bucky Lee and his wingman, Lt. (jg) W. E. Johnson, spotted the *Shokaku* and *Zuiho* with their cruiser-destroyer escorts two hundred miles northwest of Task Force 61. Kinkaid plotted the information, but according to the *Hornet*'s after-action report, he did not inform Murray of even the battleship-cruiser sighting until 0822. By this time Mason had sent up eight Wildcats to join a similar contingent from the *Enterprise* on combat air patrol.

At 0832 the *Hornet*'s first assault wave soared aloft under Gus Widhelm's command, responding to Kinkaid's message ten minutes earlier concerning the enemy battleship-cruiser formation.[9] Apparently Widhelm and his colleagues had also been informed of the carrier sighting.

The core of the raid was fifteen Dauntlesses from Scouting 8 and Bombing 8. Widhelm led the group, and Moe Vose commanded the rear section. Each Dauntless carried a 1,000-pound bomb. Eight Wildcats, led by Mike Sanchez, escorted the formation, which flew at 12,000 feet, while six torpedo planes, led by Torpedo 6's Iceberg Parker, traveled along at 800 feet. Gouin promptly brought a second wave to launch configuration and by 0909 had sent it off after Widhelm. This "cleanup" formation included seven fighters of VF-72, led by Warren Ford; nine Dauntlesses with 1,000-pound bombs, led by Lt. John Lynch; and nine Avengers with four 500-pound bombs apiece, led by Lt. (jg) Ward Powell. Walt Rodee accompanied this flight in a bombless "command" Dauntless, acting as strike coordinator, as he had over Faisi and Guadalcanal.

Over on the *Enterprise*, Capt. Osborne B. Hardison had launched "every flyable plane aboard except for 20 fighters" of the combat air patrol. Comdr. Richard Gaines acted as air group attack controller.[10] The new *Enterprise* air group took an inexcusably long time to form up, and then, like Rodee and his mates, it tagged raggedly after Gus Widhelm's flight, Wildcats and Dauntlesses throttling back to keep pace with the slower Avengers.

It was Midway all over again: Throw everything available at the enemy, whose exact position could only be ascertained by visual sighting. But this time, historian Eric Hammel observed, the American strike groups "went off as a stream of separate mixed units, each one composed of whatever aircraft happened to be available at the time of launch. Indeed, each of the three strike groups lacked internal cohesion; each was itself strung out over distances of several miles."[11] The only improvement since Midway—and it was substantial—was that each formation had fighter protection. Sanchez and his counterpart from the *Enterprise* were determined that there would be no futile suicide charges by unprotected American aircraft. And the F4Fs with their new center-line fuel tanks could provide protection all the way to the target and back. But Parker's unwillingness to fly high in formation with the rest of the attack group (the Avenger was capable of high flight), at least until nearing the enemy, made the fighter escort's job a nightmare.

Moreover, Nagumo had beaten Kinkaid to the punch. His carrier decks had already been cleared when Lee and Johnson had appeared overhead shortly before 0800. The two fliers had done enough; they could have gone home. But their planes carried 1,000-pound bombs, and their sighting report had brought two of their squadron mates racing over from a nearby search pattern. There were no Zeros about; inexplicably, Nagumo's combat air patrol lolled unaware several thousand feet below. Replicating Wade McClusky at Midway, Lee and his wingman pushed over and made long dives toward the *Zuiho,* the smaller carrier beneath them. In the rear seat of each Dauntless gunner-radiomen lay pressed flat on their backs, searching for enemy aircraft as the sky rushed dizzyingly past and the ocean rotated slowly beneath them. In each cockpit the pilots, their eyes glued to tubular target scopes, sent their planes screaming down closer and closer to the unsuspecting enemy carrier. At a thousand feet or less, with the *Zuiho's* yellow, wooden flight deck filling their sights, they dropped their bombs, corkscrewed down another several hundred feet, then flattened out of their dives just above the white-caps as Japanese pilots finally came alive and raced after them while gunners on the ships below opened fire. Only one bomb struck the *Zuiho,* but it was perfect. Bursting on the stern of the ship, it tore a thirty-foot hole in the after end of the flight deck, making further landings impossible, and started a major fire in the hangar below. As Lee and his mate raced away at wave-top level, weaving desperately to throw the Zeros off their tails, the *Zuiho* fell out of formation with badly damaged steering gear.

Declining to wait for Rodee or the *Enterprise* squadrons, Widhelm and his mates pushed on to the west-northwest in search of Nagumo's carriers. Before they were halfway to the sighting point the Americans saw in the distance an enemy air formation coming toward them. It was Nagumo's attack group, which had apparently taken its time forming up. As the two formations passed each other, each pilot, Japanese and American, determinedly looked ahead, while squadron leaders radioed their respective carriers that the enemy was on the way and closing fast. But a few minutes later, when the Japanese came upon the *Enterprise* formation, they could not resist. Zeros peeled off to tangle with Wildcats in a melee of dogfights that left the Americans badly battered. The shaken remnants of the *Enterprise* formation staggered on after Widhelm.

Widhelm found the Japanese battleship force where the *Enterprise* scouts reported it, but he refused to attack. When one of his pilots asked why he was letting the battlewagons go, Widhelm replied: "They're only chicken feed. We're looking for carriers."[12] But the Americans were in trouble. For some reason Sanchez's escorting F4F-4s had fallen far behind and, instead of flying above the Dauntlesses, were at the same altitude. Fifteen miles beyond the battleships, Widhelm's formation was jumped by a host of Zeros from the carriers' air patrol. They quickly focused on Gus as formation commander; if he could be shot down, the whole formation might break apart in confusion. American pilots followed the same practice when attacking Japanese assault squadrons.

Spotting the enemy, Widhelm patted the side of his plane in the classic "close up" gesture. As the Dauntlesses swung in close aboard, the leading Zero came right at Gus head to head. Widhelm coolly blasted him with his wing guns and then dove when the mortally stricken Japanese tried to ram. The Zero flashed by overhead, then started a long spiral toward the sea. A second Zero came up from below, and Widhelm dropped his nose and again fired away with his wing guns. The Japanese pilot flew straight into a hail of .50-caliber machine gun slugs as he completed his attack climb, and the Zero exploded. George Stokely, Widhelm's long-time partner and one of the outstanding rear seat gunner-radiomen of the Pacific war, began to act as local fighter director controller, informing Widhelm of the direction each Japanese attack was coming from. Widhelm passed the word to the other Dauntless pilots.

Seeing the enemy attacking Widhelm's formation, Sanchez made a desperate but futile effort to catch up. Then the Wildcats saw that Iceberg Parker's six Avengers, flying far below and between Sanchez and Widhelm, had been attacked by another cluster of Zeros, and Sanchez and his fliers promptly dove down into that melee, which broke up into a series of wild, individual dogfights. Roaring down from 12,000 to 800 feet, the American fighters began blasting Zeros from the sky, while the slower Avengers ducked away. In the confusion Parker and his fliers never did sight Nagumo's carriers.

Sanchez's initial luck in ambushing the Japanese combat air patrol could not hold; there were too many Zeros. In the midst of the swirling combat Ens. Phil Souza became so mesmerized by the quickness of the Zeros that he was nearly shot down. Lt. (jg) Thomas Johnson, his wing leader, was killed. The other escort section of VF-72, led by Lt. Jack Bower, was also having a rough time. Bower's wingmen, Lt. (jg) Robert Jennings and Lt. (jg) Robert Sorensen, each blew Zeros apart, but Bower went down in flames.

Up ahead Widhelm and his boys continued to fight off the determined enemy. The pilots flying in close formation behind Gus kept a constant watch on their "weaving, bucking, bobbing" leader. Whenever a Zero or two approached the formation, the group turned toward it head on and blazed away as the enemy flew through the formation. Widhelm had trained his men superbly: "No amount of gunfire, no amount of diving and twisting and weaving by the Japanese fighter pilots could break the integrity of the American formation."[13] But the fighting was wild. A pilot far back in the formation glanced across at his wingman and saw a fresh belt of .30-caliber ammunition ripped from the rear gunner's hand by the slipstream.

The Japanese pilots' bulldog courage began to exact a toll. Lt. (jg) Phil Grant was the first to fall. He managed to pancake his plane into the water. A moment later Lt. (jg) Clay Fisher's Dauntless rolled out of formation and glided toward the sea. He and his rear gunner were never seen again. Lt. (jg) Ken White was shot in the left hand and shoulder and dropped out of formation. He managed to get away and made a shaky landing on the *Enterprise.*

Meanwhile, an expert Zero pilot had fastened on Widhelm. "The guy sat up above me," Widhelm later related. "He'd start down and I'd feint him. He was an old-timer and stayed right up there. He made three passes. On the fourth pass, when another Jap was coming in from the right, he came down and deliberately took a full deflection shot. He hit the oil lines, somewhere in the cooler (the oil radiator). I knew I was hit when I heard the bullets drill into the metal. Then the oil sprayed into the cockpit. It gushed all over me."[14]

Widhelm flew on, determined to do as much as he could to complete the mission. The wild air battle had taken both sides right over the *Shokaku* and *Zuiho,* and Widhelm broadcast a sighting report to Task Force 61—and to Rodee and the *Enterprise* attack force coming up from the rear—three times in a clear voice. He hung on as long as he could, not wanting a subordinate to take the punishment he was receiving as formation leader. His Dauntless was incredibly rugged. It flew on with its tail assembly half shot away and huge bullet holes all over both wings. Finally, however, the engine froze up; Widhelm dropped his thousand-pound bomb harmlessly into the sea and brought his aircraft down in the choppy water. Miraculously, neither he nor Stokely was hurt.

Moe Vose assumed command. There were eleven Dauntlesses left. Vose deployed his formation into a single dive-bombing line as the rear-seat gunners struggled to keep the Zeros at bay. Then one by one the eleven aircraft pushed over and headed down toward the undamaged *Shokaku.* Once again a Japanese carrier crew experienced the gut-wrenching sensation of watching a disciplined flight of enemy dive-bombers plunge toward them as they blasted away futilely with their ship's guns. Vose and his men were as successful as McClusky had been at Midway. They claimed three to six bomb hits right in the middle of *Shokaku*'s flight deck. Half a century later Ugaki's published diary confirmed four. The carrier was ripped open from bow to stern. If any of the *Shokaku*'s air group had been aboard, with fuel lines and magazines open, the carrier would surely have gone the way of her sisters at Midway. As it was, the *Shokaku*, which had been in commission one month less than the *Hornet*, suffered hideous blast and fire damage. She immediately swerved out of line, burning badly. Nagumo on the bridge must have felt an almost overpowering sense of déjà vu as explosions again racked his command. Once more he was forced to transfer to an escorting cruiser, where he carried on grimly. Widhelm and Stokely watched in glee from their raft nearby. Superb damage control kept the fires and explosions in the *Shokaku*'s upper works from damaging her main hull and engineering spaces, and she still had power to fight fires. The carrier managed to stagger back toward Truk, but she would be out of action for nearly a year.

Vose and his men pulled out just above the wave tops and headed home, darting and weaving to escape the stubborn Zeros. No more planes were lost, although several gunners were badly wounded. As pilots hungrily munched on candy bars for quick energy and set a course for the *Hornet*, the Japanese ships burned behind them. But a day that had begun so disastrously for Japanese fortunes was about to turn with dramatic suddenness.

Nagumo and his battered carriers never saw another enemy plane that day. The *Hornet*'s second wave and the *Enterprise* attack group should have found the Japanese without any trouble, but they never did. If they had, they surely could have sunk the *Shokaku* and perhaps the *Zuiho* with just one or two torpedoes. Apparently the jarring, twisting dogfights and the beating that Widhelm's plane absorbed knocked Gus's sensitive voice transmitter off its precise broadcasting frequency. His call did reach the *Hornet* and perhaps a third of the radios in Rodee's formation. But no squadron leader heard it, and no retransmission was made by those who did, presumably because Rodee and his counterpart leading the *Enterprise* attack group were determined to maintain radio silence and because those who did hear it assumed that their commanders had as well. The two groups sped directly west, just south of Nagumo's fleet, and never saw a thing. They disconsolately turned toward home.

Nor did Parker and his six Avenger torpedo planes find Nagumo's formation. Having successfully slipped away from the dogfights between

Sanchez and the Japanese combat air patrol, Parker led his men out to the specified 210-mile extremity, then stubbornly flew another fifty miles farther above an empty sea. Remembering the cruiser-battleship formation that Widhelm had seen en route to the enemy flattops, Parker led his men back and found the vanguard group protecting Nagumo's carriers. He might have found the *Shokaku* and the *Zuiho,* but both flattops had joined the *Zuikaku* under concealing rain squalls. Parker picked out a heavy cruiser, divided his six planes into two divisions for a classic "hammer-and-anvil" attack on both sides of the bow, and went in through heavy flak. The Americans thought at least two torpedoes hit, but actually the *Suzuya* managed to "comb" every one. Parker did not lose a man, but neither did the Japanese.

When Widhelm subsequently learned that leaders of the second attack formation had not received his radio reports and the reasons for the foul-up, he was understandably livid. He shot off a furious memo to appropriate authorities, emphasizing the need to "harden" communication systems so that they were guaranteed to work efficiently. Two, possibly three, precious Japanese carriers could have been sunk if Rodee and his men had been vectored to the right position. But even if they had, Task Force 61 would not have been spared a vicious and beautifully coordinated enemy attack.

Murray received reports of incoming Japanese aircraft shortly after 0930. For many minutes enemy and friendly planes remained mixed on radar scopes on both the *Hornet* and *Enterprise.* "It is understood," the *Hornet* after-action report stated, "that the two groups passed within 5 miles of each other, about 60 miles from our force."[15] Marcel Gouin had just recovered the dawn combat air patrol, comprising fifteen fighters under the command of Lt. Ed Hessel. The flight deck crew quickly refueled the planes, and the entire patrol was in the air again in sixteen minutes. As the last plane took off, Eugene Blackmer and his hundreds of mates on the flight deck experienced a familiar sense of emptiness. With all planes gone, their jobs were done. They were nonessential personnel until the air group returned.[16] Gouin ordered the entire aviation refueling system blanketed with CO_2 and directed all flight and hangar deck personnel to take cover immediately in unoccupied island spaces, along those portions of the catwalks lining the gallery deck that did not contain antiaircraft guns, or in the small shops and offices along the sides of the hangar deck. Many airdales lingered near the few planes that were still parked on the hangar deck. Men were told to stay out of the way of gun crews, ammunition passers, and damage control parties unless asked to help.

Meanwhile, Jack Griffin, the *Enterprise*'s fighter director officer, was understandably confused about which formation on his radar scope was friendly and which was not. Only when the Japanese formation unmistakably emerged from the welter of planes on the scope and headed toward Kinkaid's fleet could he begin to direct elements of his thirty-eight-plane patrol toward it. But Griffin had already committed two serious mistakes. First, he had stationed one formation too far south of the *Enterprise*. Second, the Wildcats in the patrol carried their new auxiliary gas tanks not on the center line but on the edges of their wings. Consequently they could not climb quickly. Griffin had positioned the planes too low to meet the enemy head on or take them from above in rapid dives. Once the Japanese, led by Lt. Comdr. Mamoru Seki, were identified, Griffin made a third error. He excitedly vectored his planes out, using the *Enterprise* as the point of reference. For those pilots who could not see the Big E through the clouds, such orders as "Hey, Rube [the traditional circus cry for attention and help], look for hawks on port quarter" had no meaning. Captain Mason included in his after-action report four pages from the cruiser *Pensacola*'s radio log, which recorded talk between the fighter director officer and the combat air patrol. The interchanges revealed persistent confusion among Griffin, section leaders, and individual pilots regarding where the air patrol was in relation to the fleet and to the Japanese.[17]

Ed Hessel was as confused as everyone else. His formation was split into two divisions, one under himself, the other under Lt. Robert Rynd. Ens. George Wrenn was flying with Rynd when the enemy came barreling in. "We climbed out in the direction of the reported enemy force under control of the Fighter Director (FDO) in ENTERPRISE," Wrenn remembered. "When things became a little confused, the eight of us [in Rynd's division] were turned over to the FDO of HORNET," Al Fleming, who immediately gave Rynd a perfect vector. Within minutes the eight Americans plowed into a formation of about forty enemy planes just as the bombers and torpedo planes were ready to split up for their separate but coordinated attacks. All coherent formation was lost on both sides as planes maneuvered to kill or escape. Lt. Claude Phillips raked two Val bombers from nose to tail; Rynd downed two Vals back to back; Rynd's wingman, Lt. (jg) Ken Kiekhoefer, got a "probable." George Wrenn followed Rynd in violent twists as the leader blasted away at several Japanese planes. Wrenn then fell out of a climbing turn and found himself just above a group of Kate torpedo planes about to race in on the *Hornet*.[18]

As Lieutenant Hessel was claiming one or two enemy aircraft "splashed" and the *Enterprise* pilots in the combat air patrol were declaring two other kills, it became clear that the *Hornet* was going to be hit. Task Force 17 lay closest to Nagumo's carriers, and as the Zeros, Vals, and Kates came on, Kinkaid's two groups, maneuvering at twenty-eight knots, steamed farther apart. Shortly before 1000 the *Enterprise* and *South Dakota* entered a small rain squall, which hid them for more than twenty minutes. The *Hornet* and her escorts remained in bright sunshine.

The morning was typical for the area north of the Santa Cruz Islands: partly overcast with the cloud level at around 1,500 feet, perfect conditions for both Kates and Vals to emerge into the clear at the last minute to make their runs. Gunners would literally have little more than the blink of an eye to track them and fire.

Everyone waited tensely, silently. Below decks, with all hatches closed and battened, the temperature in the long hull, warmed by engineering machinery running at top speed, reached at least one hundred degrees. Ventilation systems merely recirculated dead air. More than a thousand men stood in tightly enclosed compartments, waiting for whatever lay ahead. Down in the engine room was a sailor who had been on the *Lexington* when she had been hit and sunk at the Coral Sea. He had survived, transferred to the *Yorktown,* and experienced her agony at Midway. Again he had come through. Now he was on the third carrier that might be hit and sunk beneath him in less than six months. He had never seen the enemy.

In his battle dressing station in the small coffee mess next to the wardroom one deck below the hangar, Gerald McAteer sweltered as the temperature steadily rose during the early morning. His face and hands were smeared with anti-flash burn ointments, causing him increasing discomfort. Finally he took off the heaviest of his protective clothing, which was already sodden with sweat. No doctor could work efficiently with such a burden around him. But under his surgical gown he kept his regulation uniform collar and sleeves tightly buttoned to prevent flash burns.

At 0959 word reached Charlie Mason that enemy aircraft were in the vicinity. On the island several quartermasters came running along the catwalks to the navigation bridge, where Mason stood ready to conn his ship. They began to secure the heavy, steel coverings above the bridge portholes. "Leave them open," Mason said pleasantly. "I want to see the show, too."[19] Then he stepped out on the starboard bridge wing, accompanied by his assistant, Lt. Comdr. H. F. Holmshaw, a tall, calm chap from Los Angeles. Oscar Dodson rushed up from the flag bridge to the signal bridge just below and forward of the *Hornet's* big funnel to make sure that his eighteen signalmen were properly prepared for battle. He found that many had not put on their helmets or their flash-proof jackets. After ordering them to do so, he turned to watch the Japanese far out on the horizon form up and start to come in. Behind him the signalmen gave war correspondent McMurtry an aviator's yellow rubber life vest and some rubber bands and twine so he could tie down his pant legs to prevent flash burns.

By 1006 observers on the *Hornet* could see Hessel and his men taking on the enemy formation roughly twenty miles away. Just as at Midway, long pencils of smoke and flame began to fill the sky. All hands were at battle stations, Condition Affirm, and the flight deck was clear of planes. Aviation Machinist's Mate 3rd Class Chuck Beck, one of VF-72's plane captains, left his damage control station forward to get his blue denim flash jacket a few feet away in the island. As he ducked inside he heard the marine gunners in the nearby catwalks talking about incoming bombers. Emerging a few seconds later, pulling sleeves and hood tightly around him, he saw that the fifteen-man fire hose team he had left forward was gone and all the guns were pointing skyward. Suddenly the destroyers forming the outer protective ring of the task force opened up with their 5-inch antiaircraft batteries. Almost immediately the cruisers on the inner ring joined in, and the enemy was there at last: small, gray planes, Vals and Kates, diving out of the nearby clouds in a nearly flawless, coordinated attack. At 1010 the ship's loudspeaker brayed: "Stand by to repel attack." Beck began running down the middle of the empty flight deck, suddenly wishing he had wings.[20] As he ducked into a makeshift bomb shelter on the catwalk rimming the flight deck, hundreds of men throughout the carrier fell to the decks or dove under tables with hands cradling heads.

It was Midway in reverse. The Japanese brought their dive-bombers in first, then the torpedo planes. George Wrenn was right on the tail of two Kates. He got the first one quickly, then dropped to wave-top level and sent the other smashing into the sea. As he pulled up he found himself in a curtain of antiaircraft fire from the *Hornet's* escorts. Turning sharply away from the task force, he flew on for a few minutes and spotted two Kates, which had already completed their torpedo runs, joining up for the flight home. Wrenn blasted head on at one of them and sent it into the water in flames. The second Kate raced away as Wrenn and "someone from VF-10" aboard the *Enterprise* gave chase. Almost immediately the Kate was in Wrenn's gun sights, and he sent it spiraling into the ocean. Then the entire combat air patrol was instructed to protect the *Enterprise* and headed off to the south. Over Kinkaid's group Wrenn shot down another enemy plane, giving him five in one morning.[21]

But the Japanese had their sights on the *Hornet*, not the Big E. They did not come in from bow or stern or from the quarters but simultaneously from all four directions. No matter how he twisted and turned his big ship, Charlie Mason could not avoid all of the deadly bombs and torpedoes loosed against her.

Navy Gunner's Mate Alvin Graham of Roseau, Minnesota, realized that most of the men in his department had never fired live ammunition at an enemy. Now all the hours of practice so long ago in the Caribbean and later in the Pacific would be put on trial. "The boys were making bets on the chance of getting a crack at dive bombers and torpedo planes." Gun directors yelled, "'Here they come! Commence firing.'"[22] The *Hornet*'s gallery deck erupted in a sheet of flames as 5-inch, 1.1-inch pom-pom, 20-millimeter, and .30-caliber antiaircraft guns blasted away. In the sudden din, blue skies and white clouds were filled with mushrooms of orange and black, and small, gray aircraft disappeared in flaming balls or cartwheeled into the ocean. Cliff Butterfield, a twenty-two-year-old gunner's mate from Idaho Falls, Idaho, saw the enemy come in all around the ship, with machine guns blazing from the wings of Vals and later Kates. "We let them have it and they let us have it, but so many things happened I couldn't say how many we got in the first few minutes. It was like shooting wild geese."[23] Martin J. Melvin, Jr., a marine gunner from Oak Park, Illinois, remembered the assault as "pitiless . . . amalgamated hell. . . . It seemed to me those Japs would never stop coming in."[24]

From the corners of their eyes, gunners and gun trainers saw smoke trails fall through the sky as Wrenn and his mates got in among the attacking and departing enemy planes. No one ever got an exact count of the number of Nagumo's remaining few veteran pilots who were brought down that morning by Air Group 8 and the *Hornet*'s gunners, but later reports suggested more than twenty. Up on the signal bridge McMurtry

Santa Cruz: the *Hornet* under attack.

saw a Japanese dive-bomber miss a cruiser's bow by ten feet as it spun into the sea. The cruiser heeled far over to escape the flaming shower of gasoline from the exploding plane. Then the *Hornet* received the first blow of her life.

At 1013 a flaming Val, with bomb racks loaded and machine guns on full, came through the hail of shellfire, screamed over Charlie Mason on the starboard bridge wing, and headed right for McMurtry. It was probably piloted by attack commander Seki.[25] "For a thousand feet I never took my eye off him, and he never wavered an inch from a straight line to the signal bridge," McMurtry said. Next to McMurtry a young signalman fell to the deck as the plane came on. Another threw himself against McMurtry's legs, knocking the correspondent to the deck. The boy lay "sprawled, knees and elbows across my feet." The Val crashed into the forward top of the funnel. Spewing gasoline from ruptured tanks, the wrecked fuselage fell right onto the signal bridge, crushing three men to death and spreading a lake of flame over about twenty others. Oscar

Dodson, standing nearby, was shielded by one of the heavy, steel legs of the ship's big tripod mast. All around McMurtry men were turned into instant torches, saved from immediate death only by the steel helmets on their heads and the flash-proof clothing on their bodies. Although he had watched the bomber race by only a few feet from him, McMurtry was surprised to find that his hands and face suddenly felt hot. He was annoyed at the abrupt sting and throb but did not feel wounded. Within the flames four men died quickly.[26]

Dodson leapt into the lake of fire, trying to save people but hampered by his heavy antiflame gloves. He jumped back in horror as an uninjured signalman rushed into the arms of his twin brother in the middle of the pool of burning gasoline. The young men died together, locked in a final embrace. Six others were horribly burned before their mates could rip burning clothing from their backs.

In nearby air plot, Foley heard a tremendous roar and saw a sheet of flame cascade downward as the wrecked Val fell off the signal bridge, past PriFly, and onto the flight deck, where its first bomb detonated, dropping the last of the wreck, including a second bomb, into the cluster of compartments in the gallery deck below.

Lt. (jg) Ben Tappan, a twenty-five-year-old scout plane pilot from Baltimore, was one of Air Group 8's excess fliers that day. His roommate, Lt. (jg) Bill Woodman, had gone off with Gus Widhelm, but Tappan remained aboard; perhaps he might fly a second mission once the first strike came back. Tappan and a handful of buddies sat in their big, comfortable chairs in Scouting 8's ready room just below the flight deck as a few reports trickled in regarding what was happening outside. Apparently no one thought to take cover. Suddenly, as the pilots sat quietly talking, "one of our planes from the flight deck fell into the room." It was, of course, the remains of the Val. Lt. (jg) Ivan Swope was knocked completely out of his chair as a searing flash of fire swept the compartment. Swope passed out for a moment, then awoke to find burning fuel within inches of his face. Several feet away, Tappan covered his face with his hands, an instantaneous reflex that may have saved his life. He and his mates had had the foresight to tuck their pants into their sock tops to prevent flash burns from racing up their legs.[27]

Yeoman 2nd Class Ralph L. Cotton was with the squadron duty officer at his battle station in the back of the ready room. As hot oil spewed about, he "beat a hasty retreat." He saw the Val's bomb roll out from beneath the wreck and come to rest under a table. Someone

The shattered signal bridge at Santa Cruz. Note the heavy tripod that supports the mainmast; one of the legs shielded Oscar Dodson from blast and flame.

reached through the hatch from Bombing 8's adjacent ready room and pulled Swope to safety; the rest of the fliers got out of the burning compartment however they could. Tappan burst into the nearby air plotting room, "a great puff of smoke behind me." He found "two full commanders, lying flat on the floor. . . . They looked up. 'You can't come in here,' one of them shouted." Indeed, air plot was off limits to all except designated personnel. "Where the hell else can I go?" Tappan screamed back. They all lay on the deck together as the battle raged around and over the ship and fire filled nearby compartments.[28]

Within minutes one of Henry Moran's damage control parties fought its way into the area and began battling the blaze. Wayne D. McFetrich, a twenty-three-year-old enlisted man from Warren, Ohio, discovered the unexploded 500-pound bomb under the ready room table. With great care he and his mates eased the deadly weapon out into an adjacent passageway reasonably far from the flames. But the *Hornet* had now come to a stop and was rolling gently in the soft swells of the South Pacific. If the live bomb were allowed to carom from one side of the passageway to the other, it would surely detonate. George Marsh, another member of the repair party, crawled down through the bomb hole in the flight deck with a tool kit and several two-by-fours. Using the lumber, he braced the bomb securely. For the rest of the day, while the *Hornet* fought on and hundreds of men struggled to save her, McFetrich stood by the bomb to make sure it remained tightly secured. He won a Silver Star for his vigil.[29]

Seconds after the signal bridge was destroyed, a strange procession staggered out of the wreckage and onto the catwalk leading to the bridge. Four men, their clothing almost burned away, their skin seared and bloated, carried two others. As they came to the hatch leading to the navigation bridge, Mason saw them. Even though he was conning a ship under attack, he called out to ask where the pathetic little group was going. To the nearest dressing station, one of the burn victims replied. Impossible, Mason responded; the ship was so tightly buttoned up that only a vertical ladder led to the flight deck below. The injured men would never make it. "Bring them in here," Mason ordered.[30] The bridge gang laid the men out of the way in the narrow compartment and went back to work. Whenever possible Dodson and others checked on the wounded. One of the worst off was a boy named Russell, who had been the butt of much teasing because he was too young to shave regularly. As Mason bent over him, the boy looked up and asked, "Sir, am I being brave enough?" Yes, the captain assured him, he was. Russell died that night.[31]

As the fires flared and died down on the ruined signal bridge, Lt. Bob Noone stood braced against a dangling stanchion, watching the air attack still in progress. Despite a shattered knee and a badly burned face, Noone had remained to see all of the wounded evacuated. Now he wondered aloud to McMurtry and others if his injuries would keep him out of flight school at Pensacola.

Within two minutes after the Val delivered the first devastating blow, the *Hornet* received five others. Two 500-pound bombs struck aft of the island. The first dropped through the flight, gallery, and hangar decks and exploded on the fourth deck, deep within the ship, killing several men, bulging slightly a large part of the after hangar deck, and starting large fires in the supply department storerooms and adjacent chief petty officers' quarters. The second bomb struck just a few feet farther aft, near the starboard gun galleries behind the island. Detonating on impact with the flight deck, it caused little structural damage to the ship, but shrapnel killed thirty gunners and wounded many others. The blast also killed a number of men in the hangar deck below and jarred loose a Dauntless hanging in one of the storage bays. The plane fell onto the hangar deck with a crash, but no one was hurt. The reverberating uproar within the cavernous hangar bay and flying shrapnel terrified Jimmy Walker, Jack Medley, Bob Taylor, and the several hundred other airdales who had thrown themselves to the deck beneath planes or against bulkheads and roller curtains. Walker quivered and prayed. But the young men got up when ordered and went to work fighting the fires.

The last bomb was something of a fluke. Whether by accident or design, the enemy pilot had released it in such a way that it just missed the *Hornet*'s narrow island structure and hit the starboard side of the flight deck at an angle from right to left. The bomb passed through the flight deck only a few feet from the spot where the wrecked Val had crashed into the gallery deck. Leaving a small hole, it passed through the gallery and hangar decks without exploding. It detonated on the port side of the crew's forward mess hall just below where Gerald McAteer was manning his emergency battle dressing station in the officers' coffee mess.

Storekeeper 3rd Class R. L. Lewis was stationed with Repair Party IV in the forward mess compartment. All were quiet as they awaited the enemy attack. They were divided into two groups. Lt. Comdr. Nowell, leading the repair party, stood with phones on his head, keeping in touch with Moran in damage control central just a few compartments away and one deck down. With Nowell were a number of enlisted men, Lt. (jg)

Gillette, Lt. Litt of the air group, and Chief Petty Officer E. G. King. These men stood ten to fifteen feet from the compartment's port bulkhead. Lewis and the rest of the repair party, all enlisted men, were on the starboard side of the compartment. When Nowell heard from damage control central that twenty-four enemy planes had been sighted thirty-one miles away, heading for the ship, the entire repair party dropped to the deck and took cover between two steam tables.

Crashing into the compartment without warning, the bomb detonated near the port bulkhead with a horrible roar. The concussion raised everyone several feet off the deck. The blast transformed steam tables, servers, lockers, and ladders leading to the deck above into blazing hot shrapnel that swept across the room, severing the many steam lines that crisscrossed the overhead and bulkheads of the compartment. Nowell and most of his mates, just a few feet from the center of the blast, died instantly, their bodies shredded by shrapnel, wrenched and torn by "very severe concussion," and burned by "unbearable heat."[32] Lewis's party on the other side of the big compartment, fifteen or more feet away from the blast and protected by heavy metal objects, suffered only minor concussions. One-half of a handling party working a nearby bomb elevator survived; the half nearest the blast all died.

Pandemonium ensued as men struggled to their feet and tried to get out of the wrecked compartment. Electrician's Mate Tom Kuykendall was one of the few in Nowell's party to survive. As the deck heaved beneath him, Kuykendall sensed "expanding points of red-hot metal and the smell of burning explosives" all around. He recalled that the entire compartment filled with "flying debris and red hot air." Searing heat passed over his body, and he knew he had been badly burned, even though shock kept his nerves from transmitting pain. As the first shock passed, Kuykendall reached around for the sailors who had been lying next to him, but all were deathly still. He began crawling toward a nearby ladder that led out of the compartment. The space filled with steam from ruptured lines, adding to the surrealistic hell. But the moisture was actually a blessing, for it quickly dampened the fires that followed the explosion. Because ladders were twisted and still blazing hot from the blast and hatches were blown tightly shut, the only way out was through an escape hatch up to the hangar deck. For agonizing moments this metal, too, was unbearably hot to the touch, but the moisture helped cool it down, and soon the terribly injured Kuykendall and the others were on their way up to the hangar deck.[33]

The bomb cut a wide swath of destruction within the *Hornet.* The main electrical switchboard in the forward generator room was damaged, causing a loss of electrical power forward of the island area. Fires and smoke broke out elsewhere near where the bomb hit. The post office was destroyed, and the intakes to the forward three boiler rooms were so badly perforated that smoke from the decks above was sucked down into these compartments, rendering conditions almost intolerable. Smoke came through the ventilation system into damage control central, one deck down and several compartments away from the blast; even with the louvers closed, smoke seeped into the compartment. The automatic fire alarm system indicated numerous fires all over the ship, but Moran concluded that "no accurate information could be obtained from it since it was believed to be thrown out of order by the severe shock" of the bomb and the sudden decline in electrical power because of damage in the forward generator room. A minute after the bomb exploded there was a sound as if someone were trying to get into damage control central. Moran ordered the hatch opened, and Chief Machinist Duffy and several other enlisted men from the forward generator room staggered in. Their severe head and face burns were treated with tannic acid jelly from the first aid box. At first all the men could remember was a blinding flash. After further questioning, Duffy admitted that the men had been standing in the draft of a blower, trying to cool their faces and bodies in the sweltering heat below decks. When the bomb burst above, it sent a sheet of flame down the blower that seared the faces of everyone standing nearby and damaged the generator itself.[34]

The upward blast of the bomb tore through the small officers' coffee mess and adjacent wardroom one deck above. In an instant, McAteer remembered, everything was "blown to hell."[35] Bulkheads collapsed, chairs and tables became kindling, and McAteer was slammed around, suffering back and shrapnel injuries. As he slowly recovered his senses, the young doctor found himself completely disoriented. For months he had trained himself to walk in darkness from his battle station all the way out to the *Hornet's* fantail. He had practiced and practiced. But now all the familiar landmarks had been ripped away. Lights in the immediate area had gone out, and unlike the austere mess compartment below, the wardroom held comfortable, well-upholstered furnishings whose blasted remains quickly provided the fuel for a major fire. In the sudden, deathly quiet, McAteer found himself in the midst of suffocating smoke with every ladder twisted and broken. All about him his emergency medical team lay still.

Recovering his wits, McAteer removed a flashlight from the neck of a dead shipmate. Somewhere nearby there was a hatch to the wardroom and from there another hatch leading to the hangar deck. For several moments he painfully "struggled and bounced around in smoke and darkness and blasted furniture," trying to orient himself in a suddenly small world without walls. He knew that he should get down and crawl carefully around; there could be a hole anywhere in the deck, and he could fall far below and never get out. But somehow crawling did not seem human, so he remained upright, painfully groping through the smoke for some light, some landmark. By this time the ship was listing; McAteer thought it might have been torpedoed. The tilt added to his sense of urgency and unreality.

Up on the hangar deck a corpsman, violating regulations, opened a hatch leading down to the wardroom and yelled something. McAteer was never sure what, but he heard the voice and groped in the darkness and heat toward it. He finally saw light above through the smoke. It was the hatch leading to the hangar, but the ladder had been blasted away. Nothing remained but a hole. Painfully McAteer pulled his way up through it and crawled onto a ruined, flaming forward hangar deck. Behind, unknown to the doctor, Kuykendall followed the same route to salvation. Away from the fires there was finally unbelievably sweet, fresh air. For many minutes the doctor breathed it in deeply. Then he turned to see what he could do for the wounded lying around him.

As McAteer had been groping around in the dark, the *Hornet* received a final blow to her upper works. As one of the last enemy bombers dived toward the *Hornet*'s port side, the pilot realized that his angle of attack was faulty. Under a hail of shellfire, he overshot the carrier, corrected, came down her starboard side, reached the bow, turned again, and came up the port side along the foc's'le. Gunners on the starboard side and bow had covered the plane with fire, and as it turned, port-side pom-poms and machine guns did the same. But on the plane came, blazing back with its own machine guns. As the pilot reached a point just in front of the forward port-side 5-inch gun gallery, he sharply turned his Val right into the carrier. The wings sheared off as the aircraft hit the ship, but the fuselage, like a blunt, fiery spear, plowed 120 feet through bulkheads, deck braces, and cabins in officers' country, then smashed down onto the forward part of the hangar deck and came to rest athwart the forward elevator well directly over the ship's aviation gasoline supply. Burning furiously, its ammunition cooking off in dazzling rockets and pinwheels, the wreck turned deck plates above the gasoline tanks a glowing red.

The bodies of the Japanese pilot and bombardier could be seen writhing in the flames. Later their charred remains were retrieved, and remarkable rumors spread. According to one story, the pilot was carrying a map of either Costa Rica or the Panama Canal, presumably in a fireproof case. Another tale was that one of the dead Japanese airmen was actually a woman. The most grizzly report was that a *Hornet* crewman went down into the wreckage and cut off the pilot's ears, claiming that his uncle had offered him $500 apiece for that part of a Japanese body.[36]

Astoundingly, only two of the *Hornet*'s crew had been killed by the kamikaze, but the fire threatened to blow up the entire forward part of the ship. Fortunately the hangar deck's automatic sprinkler system functioned for about five minutes; it did not put out the blaze, but it dampened it and cooled off the hot deck plates below the burning plane.

The most serious blows, however, did not come from bombs or suicide planes but from torpedoes. As Seki's Vals completed their bombing runs, his Kates came racing in from either side. The pilots were superb. "I remember those things coming in," Foley recalled forty-three years later, "and they were so low over the water that they had to jump over the masts of the destroyers in the screen. They were down about, oh, I guess, 50, 70 feet from the water. They came over the horizon, so you couldn't see them, and came in full bore."[37] It was an unforgettable tableau: small, deadly flying machines racing in under fleecy, smoke-streaked skies to strike at great, gray-hulled warships that churned the sea to foam as they tried frantically to escape. As machine guns and cannons erupted, each participant in the sky and on the water was filled with a savage resolve to kill or be killed. Gunners who had been blasting upward found it impossible to shift their heavy weapons fast enough to fire on the new attack. And George Wrenn could not shoot down every enemy torpedo plane.

Eugene Blackmer had moved to the starboard catwalk just below the flight deck. Along with several hundred other men, he saw torpedoes coming in. And like them, he had the same thought: "Oh, oh, we're going to get it!"[38] Just as the last bombs crashed on and through the *Hornet*'s flight deck, two torpedoes ripped into the starboard side, one just below the after end of the island, at frame 110, the other roughly 175 feet astern.

Chuck Beck saw the Kates racing in and concluded that they were coming right at him. He left his catwalk shelter ahead of and below the

In this photo taken from the *Hornet* during the Battle of Santa Cruz, a Japanese torpedo plane ("Kate") is about to release its torpedo.

island and began crawling forward rapidly along the catwalk until he came to an emergency landing signal platform, where he rolled himself up into a tight ball and waited. When the torpedo hit, Beck felt the entire ship jump out of the water and to the left.[39]

Far below decks in the hot, noisy forward engine room Commander Creehan had been warned that an enemy torpedo attack "was pending." Seconds before the first enemy plane crashed onto the signal bridge far above, Mason sent down word through the voice phones to increase speed from twenty-seven knots to "all the engines could make." Creehan ordered fires lit under every boiler and then watched as the four big propeller shafts smoothly rotated at ever higher revolutions, finally reaching 292 rpm. The ship was rushing through the water at more than thirty-one knots, which Creehan found amazing in light of her badly fouled bottom. He worried about the chronically leaky tubes of his superheated boilers, but for the moment all seemed well.[40]

A few minutes later the engineers faintly heard and felt the bomb that destroyed the wardroom area. When the lights flickered and went out temporarily, they knew that the forward generator had been damaged or destroyed. All four shaft revolution indicators began gyrating wildly. Creehan had his talker, Chief Yeoman McGrath, inform the bridge that although the engines were "all right" the "counters" (propeller shaft revolution indicators) had gone out. Electrician's mates tried to restore them to normal operation, but forty to sixty seconds later everyone felt a heavy jar on the starboard bulkhead, obviously a torpedo hit. Cardon Ruchti, standing not far from Creehan, felt the ship jump, then "wiggle" a bit; that was all. But the shock raced through the *Hornet*'s large structure in an expanding wave. When it reached the island, Steve Jurika "felt as though the ship was a rat being shaken by a bull terrier, just literally shaken. My teeth rattled." He was thrown against a bulkhead so violently that he thought he had sustained severe internal injuries.[41]

Down in the forward engine room "all hell broke loose" when a hole at least four feet in diameter opened in the starboard bulkhead and "an avalanche of oil and sea water" poured in. An instant later the second torpedo struck the *Hornet* farther aft. A spray of oil carried over the turbines, drenching Creehan, his assistant engineering officer, and several enlisted men. The engine room began to fill with gas and smoke as further sprays of oil hit the superheated steam lines. Smoke from the wardroom fires began to roll in through the boiler intakes. Within seconds the forward engine room had become a death trap. Swiftly Creehan issued orders. Numbers one and four engine throttles were closed; Chief Machinist's Mate Kindlesparger got the bilge pumps and number four main circulator started. Then Creehan directed all hands to evacuate the area and told McGrath to pass the word to the bridge. Almost immediately the bridge confirmed the order to abandon not only the forward engine room but the entire ship. As he prepared to leave, Creehan swept his eyes over the gauges for the last time. Steam pressure was falling rapidly; the shaft revolution indicators that had just been restored indicated that number two and three shafts were rapidly slowing, undoubtedly because condensers had been damaged by the force of the torpedo hit. The ventilation system had failed, and the temperature was rising rapidly.[42]

As the last sailors and officers abandoned the forward engine room, Creehan found himself alone with a very young fireman whom he did not know. The sailor had remained behind to make sure his division officer got out. The engine room was flooding rapidly; oil was already frothing around the upper gratings. Together the two took a final quick walk around the empty space to make sure no one had been left behind. Then they left in a hurry. The sailor secured the watertight doors and hatches leading away from the forward engine room so tightly that flooding was confined to this space. His action allowed the ship to stay afloat with only a seven-degree starboard list.

While Creehan was reaching safety and learning about the second torpedo hit, Mason assessed the condition of his ship. The situation was grim. Within five minutes his big, elegant carrier had been reduced to a flaming, smoking wreck. Alexander Griffin described it as "a dim, infernal, sweltering place where grimy figures bent over the wounded and beat at burning gasoline with bare hands."[43] The captain had been rushing from one side of his narrow bridge to the other throughout Seki's deadly assault. He had seen and felt all five bomb and plane hits and had been jolted as strongly as anyone topside by the two torpedoes. Now, as the last of the Japanese Vals and Kates raced away, Mason felt his ship slowing. For several minutes momentum alone carried it through the water; its four big screws had stopped turning. Through the hatch to the steering compartment he called to his chief quartermaster: Was the *Hornet* responding to her helm? "No, sir. The rudder is jammed hard right."[44] Mason glanced at the inclinometer and saw that the ship had already achieved a ten-degree starboard list, although counterflooding of the port-side storage tanks would quickly reduce it to seven degrees.

The entire electrical system was shorting out, and all power to the undamaged engines aft, the sprinkler and fire hose systems, gun mounts, and damage control areas was being lost. All communications were down except for one voice-powered phone system. The *Hornet* was a drifting, helpless hulk on a sunlit sea. Below, Creehan had reached the third deck and learned by phone from Moran that the fire and trouble alarm systems in damage control central showed roughly twenty-five emergencies. All steering control from the bridge, battle two, and central control stations had been lost because of damaged cables. The firerooms threatened to become untenable because of smoke and fire. The steam damage control pump was inaccessible because of steam, smoke, and acrid fumes in the forward generator room. All high-pressure air had been lost because of ruptured lines. Even worse, when power died the rudder had been at a thirty-degree angle. If the ship were towed without any onboard power, she would constantly yaw in one direction, making it extremely difficult to keep her from turning in a continuous circle.

On the flight deck Blackmer watched a warrant officer whom he knew and admired suddenly go crazy. The man ran around waving a pistol until somebody tackled him and tied him up. Blackmer went below to the hangar to see if he could help.[45] It was no better there; panicky sailors from the engine and firerooms were spreading the word that the *Hornet* was to be abandoned at once. Down in damage control central Moran sadly concluded that there was no reason to stay at his post; with all power out there was nothing he could do to direct organized salvage efforts, and he would be more valuable on the bridge. He ordered damage control central and all adjacent compartments cleared, and more than one hundred cooks, engineers, and damage control personnel slowly climbed up one hundred feet through an escape hatch, a three-foot-wide tube, to the island, where they exited next to radar plot. Getting everybody up was a slow, nerve-wracking process accompanied by some outraged shouting and even a few panicky screams.[46]

Still, the ship might be saved. Creehan asked for volunteers to check out the firerooms. Lt. (jg) David Sword and several men soon returned to report that personnel there could carry on despite the smoke. That was one piece of good news. As Creehan proceeded to the hangar deck to muster his division, he received more encouraging information. The after generators had remained in operation until 1040, when the abandoned boilers ceased to generate steam. But the after boilers and diesel generator were undamaged; the damage inflicted by the second torpedo hit had been confined largely to supply and magazine spaces. If the boilers could be relit and the after generator started up, a limited amount of lighting and power could be made available to get the ship under way and the rudder back on center line. A key problem was the damaged electrical distribution boards. Power lines would have to be rerouted around these obstacles. It would take time, but it could be done.

As Creehan mustered his men amidships on the hangar, Mason canceled the abandon ship order. No one would take his command away without a fight! He told Soucek to leave Battle Station II at the rear of the island and go down onto the flight and hangar decks and supervise salvage operations. Soucek needed no prompting; he had been chafing to get to work. But so had hundreds of other men. They had suffered trauma as deep and shattering as anyone who had lived through a sudden automobile accident in which friends had been killed or terribly injured. But unlike civilians, these men had been taught and drilled to survive and react to emergencies if the right leadership was available. Now all those bitterly hot days on the boot camp "grinders" at Great

Santa Cruz: the *Hornet's* torn flight deck.

Lakes and San Diego, all the awed and habitual deference to petty officers, all those hours of incessant, unthinking drill, were about to pay off.

As the last Japanese attackers departed, Aviation Machinist's Mate Chuck Beck was roused from his cowering position against the forward landing signal platform by a bellowed order from the Air Group 8 line chief: "Fire crew! Fire crew! Get your asses out here!"[47] Beck rushed up on deck and joined a damage control party that was manning a hose to fight the fire near the island. But water power failed, and the hangar deck sprinkler system below cut out. Undaunted, sailors and officers rounded up hundreds of buckets from the undamaged areas throughout the ship and formed ad hoc water brigades to fight the stubborn fires on the flight deck, four decks below in the chiefs' quarters aft, in the forward elevator well, and in the gallery deck in and around Scouting 8's wrecked ready room.

While Soucek was making his way to the flight deck, Francis Foley was already busy on one of the bucket brigades. After the wrecked Val had fallen past him from the signal bridge to the flight deck, he had managed to send Air Group 8 instructions to head toward the *Enterprise* for landing. But the Big E herself was now being attacked as she, the *South Dakota*, and the rest of Task Force 16 emerged from the protection of the squall. The *Enterprise* was bombed several times, and her flight deck was put out of action temporarily. As soon as it could be made serviceable, the carrier began "madly refueling her own airplanes and flying them off to Guadalcanal and Espiritu Santo to make room for the *Hornet*'s airplanes."[48] Lt. Robin Lindsey, the Big E's landing signal officer, steadfastly ignored orders not to bring aboard any damaged aircraft that could conceivably crash and put out of commission the last available American flight deck in the South Pacific. Lindsey landed planes even in the midst of a second Japanese air raid, and his heroic efforts undoubtedly saved many pilots from fatal crashes at sea.[49]

As the pilots and gunners of Air Group 8 stepped out of their planes onto the Big E's flight deck, they saw a shocking signal chalked up on a hand-held blackboard that was being shown to every *Enterprise* pilot: "Proceed without 'Hornet.'"[50] By the end of the day *Hornet* and *Enterprise* air groups were totally mixed up both aboard the Big E and at island air bases around the area. Not until the *Enterprise* returned to Nouméa did the air groups finally sort themselves out.

After doing all he could to save the ship's air group, Foley had his teletype operator gather up about fifty feet of tape from the machine. It contained information about the *Hornet*'s position, course, and speed; the wind; and the relative position and estimated composition of the Japanese forces. Such intelligence could not be allowed to fall into Kondo's hands. When the tape was rolled up into a cylinder about two inches in diameter and ten inches long, Foley waterproofed it and stuck it inside his shirt. Suddenly one of the last planes from Air Group 8 appeared and circled overhead in the landing pattern, apparently preparing to ditch close aboard. Foley quickly had someone send a flashing signal to the pilot—"GO TO BIG E"—just as the antiaircraft cruiser *Juneau* came circling in on the same bearing. Those on the *Juneau* thought the message was for her, and both plane and cruiser promptly set off toward Task Force 16 on the horizon. Foley overheard Murray tell Mason, "Let her go. 'Big E' needs her more than we do." In hindsight it was a disastrous decision.[51] Foley then went out to the adjacent catwalk, climbed down a ladder to the flight deck, and joined the firefighters.

By this time long lines stretched from the edge of the flight deck to each fire. A score or more men in each line lowered buckets sixty feet over the side, hauled them up brimming with sea water, and passed them down the human chain to the fires. Just before each bucket was thrown at the flames, foamite powder was added to the water.

When Soucek reached the flight deck, he briefly joined the men in the bucket brigades. He later did the same thing in the hangar. The men never forgot this gesture of solidarity. Airdales Bob Taylor and Jack Medley, working on a brigade on the hangar, looked up to see their executive officer nearby, helping with the buckets. Although Soucek was a good-humored, easygoing gentleman, he had demanded an orderly and well-run ship, which meant numerous "field days" when cleanup was the primary order of business. Now, amid the stubborn fires, the torn-up deck plates, the bloody, smoke-blackened bulkheads, slippery foam, and gritty sand of the cavernous, acrid hangar deck, sweating crewmen relaxed the taut discipline of former days a bit and kidded their exec: "Hey, Commander, is it hot enough for you? . . . We'll sure as hell have a field day tomorrow, won't we?"[52]

At one point someone went down into the galley refrigerators, rapidly warming with the power out, and brought back big pails of melting ice cream. Scores of men took a moment or two to plunge filthy hands into the cool goo and bring it to mouths and throats parched by smoke and heat. A survival party from the engineering spaces got the same idea as they awaited orders to return below to make repairs. A burly, bearded fireman went down to the galleys and brought back not only ice cream but large cans of tomatoes, which he proceeded to open with a razor-sharp axe blade. Someone else found some bread, and men began munching on tomato sandwiches. Blackmer was there, still waiting for orders to do something. As he munched on his sandwich, the tomatoes reminded him of the bloodied bulkheads all around.[53]

While the crew toiled to save their badly damaged ship, the shattered medical department rallied to save badly wounded men. No other department on the ship had suffered so many serious casualties; it was as if Seki and his men had known exactly where to place their bombs. Battle Dressing Station I was located not far from Scouting 8's ready room on the gallery deck. It was "practically destroyed" by the crashing Val and the resulting fire. Unwounded medical personnel and their patients moved to the flight deck. Battle Dressing Station II was just behind the forward 5-inch gun gallery. When the suicide plane smashed through nearby, "lights failed, [and] smoke and fire started in this area." The sprinkler system came on, forcing evacuation of all personnel. Medical personnel and their patients were moved first to the forward gun gallery on the starboard side and later to the flight deck. Battle Dressing Station III was in the sick bay adjacent to the chiefs' quarters aft. Partially destroyed and with all lights out, it too was abandoned; most of the patients were moved to the after part of the hangar deck. Battle Dressing Stations IV and V were located near one another. Station IV, near the post office, was demolished. Dr. John Johnson and one pharmacist's mate were killed. The other medical personnel, who received severe flash burns on their faces and hands, reported to the flight deck. Number V was McAteer's station. He was not the only one to survive after all. Two pharmacist's mates followed him out of the destroyed compartment.[54]

Dr. E. H. Osterloh became acting medical officer. He worked on the flight deck, while McAteer took care of the wounded in the hangar. The job was difficult, for some badly wounded men like Electrician's Mate Kuykendall were so shocked and traumatized that they did not understand the extent of their injuries and joined bucket brigades or other damage control work until they dropped or their mates suddenly realized how badly hurt they were and summoned a pharmacist's mate.[55] Unable to stand without support, McAteer propped himself up against a bulkhead amid the hundreds of sweating, yelling men in the dark, cavernous bay and began his ministrations, aided by Chaplain Eddie Harp and members of the ship's band.

Harp and his bandsmen had begun the day at Battle Dressing Station I. When that was evacuated they moved to the hangar deck and began working as stretcher bearers. Once McAteer appeared they found a new task. Under his direction they stripped clothing from the wounded; then, as two of the bandsmen held McAteer up, he attended to burns, fractures, and shrapnel injuries. It was an agonizing business for a man with a wrenched back and a body full of small pieces of steel. McAteer examined minor wounds and told Harp how to apply bandages and tourniquets and administer morphine. Helped by the bandsmen, McAteer moved slowly down the hangar toward the stern, examining the wounded and either leaving them for Harp's treatment or ordering them taken to the fantail, where the most seriously injured could be evacuated with the least difficulty. McAteer wanted to get to the fantail himself, where there was more light to see and treat the injured.

As the day wore on, more medical personnel appeared at McAteer's side to help assess and treat the wounded. Emergency medical supplies stored in two large life jacket lockers near the rear of the hangar bay were broken out and moved to the stern. As the fires on the fourth deck aft were finally extinguished, several pharmacist's mates returned to sick bay to rescue what medical supplies they could. A full-fledged aid station was established on the fantail, just as McAteer had wished. He took command and kept working, still propped against a stanchion, while Harp had the dead brought out of the ship and prepared for burial. Throughout the entire ordeal not one man tried to cash in on the gifts he had earlier brought McAteer or the other doctors. All day seriously injured men insisted that shipmates be treated first. The exhilaration of battle and then the sense of camaraderie brought about by shared disaster seemed to ennoble almost everyone.

Buckets of foamite and water alone could not quench the *Hornet*'s fires, nor could those on the damaged carrier adequately treat their most severely injured crewmen. As soon as the last enemy plane departed, two destroyers, the *Morris* and *Russell*, despite the danger to themselves, came alongside the carrier's port and starboard sides to render assistance. At Midway the destroyer *Hamman* had gone down with the *Yorktown* when it was torpedoed alongside the carrier. But the destroyer skippers and crews did not hesitate when asked to assist the *Hornet*. Soon the *Mustin* joined her sisters alongside.

As the *Russell* approached close aboard on the port bow, a big swell slammed her against the *Hornet,* and the shock of contact released a lever controlling one of the destroyer's depth charge racks. A 600-pound depth charge dropped straight down off the tail. For several seconds men on the destroyer and carrier waited anxiously for the explosion that would certainly blow off the *Russell*'s stern and possibly inflict severe damage on the *Hornet.* But nothing happened, and the men went back to work.[56]

As stretcher bearers began to tenderly lift burned and blasted men from the carrier to the destroyers, the *Morris* passed over three big fire hoses connected to her own water pressure system. The first hose was laboriously hauled up to the signal bridge to finally quench the fire there. The other two hoses were passed across the flight deck to fight the gallery deck fires near Scouting 8's ready room. Next, fire hoses from the *Russell* and then the *Mustin* were dragged across the hangar and down two decks to combat the blaze around the chiefs' quarters and sick bay. By this time more than one thousand men were estimated to be battling the fires aboard the carrier. By 1100 all fires were under control, and the fierce conflagration around the forward elevator well had been extinguished. It would take hours to put out the fires near the chiefs' quarters and on the gallery deck, but the carrier was in no danger of being destroyed by flames alone.

The destroyers paid for their gallantry. Occasional swells that were

The destroyer *Russell* draws up alongside the badly damaged *Hornet*.

impossible to anticipate slammed the *Russell* and *Morris* repeatedly and heavily against the carrier. The *Russell* lost her starboard anchor, and both she and the *Morris* suffered heavy damage to their upper works.[57]

Mason now had three tasks. With enemy carriers and battleships possibly steaming hard in his direction, the first was to get the *Hornet* out of the area by any means possible. The second was to continue fighting the fires and evacuating the wounded and nonessential personnel to the nearby destroyers. The third was to repair the ship's power and electrical systems sufficiently to allow the *Hornet* to get under way once more. Murray on the flag bridge agreed completely. Kinkaid was not available for consultation; with the *Enterprise* fighting for her life under persistent, heavy enemy air attacks, he was concentrating on saving his own immediate command.

As soon as the fires were clearly under control, Murray ordered the cruiser *Northampton* to get in position to tow the *Hornet*. Soucek promptly left the fire brigade on the hangar deck and, with Foley, went forward to the foc's'le to take charge of towing operations. As the two men reached the port side of the foc's'le, the first thing they saw was a fused 250-pound bomb that had apparently been knocked off the wing of the Japanese suicide plane that had wound up in the forward elevator pit. Both men shared the same thought: "By God, we better get rid of that damn thing."[58] Although the *Hornet* was listing to starboard, the curvature of the ship's hull was such that the two men could wrestle the big bomb over the port side into the water. As it fell toward the sea, both men instinctively jumped back.

Henry Moran, numerous boatswain's mates, and about seven hundred men were on the foc's'le "doing everything humanly possible to hook up a few lines."[59] By the time Soucek and Foley arrived, the *Hornet* had put a light heaving line over the side and paid it out toward the *Northampton*. When the cruiser had difficulty maneuvering to pick up the line, an impatient young seaman from the carrier dove the sixty-odd feet into the water, caught the line, and swam with it to the *Northampton*. At 1105 the cruiser began paying out two hundred fathoms of $1\frac{1}{4}$-inch steel cable, which sweating, cursing crewmen hand-winched onto the *Hornet*'s foc's'le and prepared to make fast to the end of the port side anchor chain. Soucek and Foley stayed briefly to encourage the men but gave no orders. Satisfied that Moran had the situation under control, the two started back into the hangar deck and made their way toward the stern.

Just as the cable was about to be made fast on the *Hornet*'s foc's'le, a lone Val swept out of the clouds and headed straight for the bridge of the helpless carrier. Someone in the gun gallery sang out: "Here comes the Lone Ranger." No one laughed, but they appreciated the black humor. As the gunners opened up once more, every vessel around the *Hornet* cast off all lines and made emergency preparations to get under way. When the Val launched its bomb, the wit in the gun gallery added, "Yes, and here comes Silver, high-ho!"[60] Fortunately the pilot's angle of attack was slightly off, and his bomb landed twenty-five yards astern of the *Morris*, which was moving away from the starboard side of the *Hornet* abreast of her island.

Murray ordered the *Northampton* and the destroyers back alongside. Once again one of the *Hornet*'s sailors had to dive overboard to get a heaving line over to the cruiser's stern, but at 1134 the *Northampton* finally secured her cable to the damaged carrier. At 1223 Capt. Willard A. Kitts cautiously got the *Northampton* under way at one knot, then two. The towing cable became taut, and the two ships began to move slowly through the water.

The tow was frustrating from the start. The $1\frac{1}{4}$-inch steel cable was terribly strained as the 20,000-ton carrier, her rudder still jammed over at thirty degrees, constantly yawed out of alignment with the cruiser. Kitts had to make constant steering adjustments as he carefully brought the *Northampton* up to two, three, and then four knots. After just twenty minutes the towing cable snapped with a series of sharp reports that sounded like rifle shots.

Mason and his men refused to despair. The *Hornet*'s own towing cable, ten tons and two hundred fathoms of brand-new two-inch steel, the special pride and joy of Chief Boatswain Percy Bond of Lemon Grove, California, lay coiled and grease-coated in the carrier's number three elevator pit aft. Although slippery and hundreds of feet from the foc's'le, it was the ship's only hope. Moran ordered it heaved out of the pit. Hundreds of men, yelling and kidding, went to work. It took them two hours to haul the tons of greasy steel along five hundred feet of torn and twisted hangar deck, then along the port-side passage and up to the foc's'le. Another heaving line was paid out to the *Northampton*. At 1430 the new, heavier towline was secured. Once more Kitts carefully got his ship under way, and the new cable took the strain of the yawing carrier without difficulty. The *Hornet* began to move again.

Meanwhile, all wounded and unessential personnel, mostly from the air department, had been ordered to evacuate. Marcel Gouin was heartbroken. The *Hornet* was not sinking, only immobilized. When Keith Ban-

The futile attempt to tow the *Hornet* from the battle scene.

croft heard that the air group was departing, he rushed below to his dark berthing compartment. It was a foolish thing to do, he later realized, for in the gloom he could have fallen through a bomb hole. Grabbing a pillowcase from his bunk, Bancroft put in a tin of cigarettes, fresh underwear, socks, and his precious diary. Then he ran back up to the hangar and stood in line to go down a cargo net directly onto the deck of the *Russell*. He never got his feet wet.[61]

Others left too. McAteer was carefully lifted over the side. His work during this grim Monday morning and afternoon would earn him the Navy Cross and a commendation for "conspicuous gallantry" signed by both Halsey and Nimitz.[62] Charles McMurtry, whose huge burn blisters on his hands and face were now bursting, cautiously went down into the salty sea. Jimmy Walker went over the side and into the warm water. He took his shoes off, and when he got to the *Mustin*, he danced with pain on the scorching steel decks. Admiral Murray departed by small boat to the *Pensacola;* he could not direct the task force from a ship that had no essential communications.

On the fantail of the *Hornet* Blackmer and fifty other men helped Chaplain Harp reverently deal with bodies. After a certain number were stacked, Harp handed each man a small bottle of medicinal brandy.[63] Harp buried at sea seventy-five men in snow-white sheets. Then he went down a line into the warm water.

Francis Foley was also ordered to leave. He and Soucek had gone up to the bridge to tell Mason what was happening and what they had seen. Their report had prompted Mason's order to get nonessential personnel off as quickly as possible. Returning to the crowded stern, Foley discovered that he was the senior officer present. For the next several hours he oversaw the evacuation of four to five hundred men. It was a slow task.

Foley first ordered the rigging of abandon ship lines and made sure everyone had a life jacket. Then he directed the men to begin going over the side, while boatswain's mates broke out the several dozen large life rafts that had been stacked under the flight deck ramp. The rafts were brought to the fantail and dropped into the sea. The wind was near zero, perhaps three or four knots, and the water was as still as a millpond except for occasional gentle swells. Surely the big rubber tubes would stay where they landed. But they did not. Even the slightest amount of breeze caused them to drift. Some men panicked, jumping about thirty feet from the slightly slanting stern or letting go of abandon ship lines so they could drop into the water quickly enough to get to the nearest raft. As the rafts began to fill, some hysterical occupants refused to let anyone else aboard. Fortunately there were plenty of rafts and the faithful destroyers remained nearby.

Foley waited patiently until everyone was off the fantail. By 1540 seventy-five wounded and eight hundred nonessential personnel had been taken aboard the destroyers, which had been solicitously circling the stricken carrier "like Indians around a wagon train."[64] While gun crews searched the skies for more enemy planes, each tin can peeled off one at a time, came close aboard to pick up survivors, and then headed back to her screening station.

Below decks Creehan and his men had been working diligently and carefully to bring the *Hornet* back to life. For five hours, the engineering officer wrote in his after-action report, repeated efforts were made to raise steam in number one, two, and four boilers. Steam would be raised as high as 150 pounds per square inch; then spurts of water in the fuel oil lines would cause the fires to die. Because of blast damage it was impossible to route steam through either the main or auxiliary steam pipe systems. Around noon, after an hour of frustration, Creehan and Lieutenant Sword agreed that the best solution was to run a portable electrical lead from the undamaged after diesel generator to number four fireroom so the electrical fuel oil service pump and electrical blowers could be used. Once this tedious task was accomplished, suction was tried on various fuel tanks, but they had been contaminated with sea water from the torpedo hits. Finally a member of the repair party located an uncontaminated tank, and Creehan, using great caution, was able to raise steam to three hundred pounds on number four boiler. He routed this steam back through the generator line into the after generator room. Next Creehan's men removed a check valve in the cross connection to the auxiliary steam line, which permitted the saturated steam in this line to also enter the auxiliary line in the after generator room, where the stops were closed to isolate the system. With two rerouted systems providing steam, Creehan was able to begin warming up the after generator, and the repaired and rerouted electrical switching system was lined up in preparation for start-up.

Reviving power this way was risky. Running new electrical cables between the forward and aft engineering spaces required that numerous hatches remain open below the water line. To regain critically needed power Creehan and his men had to sacrifice watertight integrity.

With the last of the 875 evacuees gone and all major fires out, Mason became cautiously hopeful. For some time the *Hornet* had been moving ahead at three knots behind the *Northampton*'s careful tow. The cruiser's skillful ship handlers had figured out how to compensate for the carrier's jammed rudder, and what Mason termed the "continuous and valiant efforts" of the engineers "to get power on the ship" held out "a faint hope of success."[65] As the word passed along the flight and gallery decks that the *Hornet* might be soon steaming under her own power, hundreds of men cheered, and the gunners yelled to each other: "Hang on to your ammunition . . . we're going to save her."[66]

Two hundred miles to the northwest Gus Widhelm and George Stokely were drifting through the center of Kondo's task force. Hitting the water in their Dauntless was like crashing into a brick wall. As the aircraft came to a sudden stop, its nose went under. The seized-up engine was so hot that it boiled the water around it. The pin that held the cockpit hood open sheared off, and the hood slammed shut, locking Widhelm inside. He struggled to reopen the hood as the cockpit filled with water. Forcing his way out, he yelled at Stokely to get his parachute to use as a possible sail or protection against the sun; the rubber raft was already out and required a simple pull on the toggle to get it inflated. Within fifteen seconds of impact Widhelm, carrying parachute, maps, navigation chart, a pistol, and a knife, joined Stokely, and both men swam away from the sinking Dauntless, pushing their raft before them. Once aboard, Widhelm penciled their position on the side of the raft, and Stokely started cleaning their pistols.

The first enemy vessels they saw were two *Kongo*-class battleships coming up from the south. The airmen stowed their pistol parts in the raft's rubber pocket, tied everything else down securely, turned the raft over, and hid underneath. Soon the whole task force seemed to be around them—including Zeros, Vals, and Kates that were running out of gas with no flight decks on which to land. As the enemy planes went into the water, destroyers raced over to pick up those few pilots who were able to escape their sinking planes. As they watched, Widhelm and Stokely became aware of sharks around the raft. The two men boldly chased them off by splashing violently. Finally the battleships and destroyers sailed out of sight, and the Americans righted their raft and climbed back aboard.

Soon another formation of enemy vessels approached. Again Widhelm and Stokely overturned their raft and dived underneath. When they peered out, they thought the end had come. A Japanese destroyer was maneuvering to pick them up. They could see officers on the bridge frantically signaling to the deck below, where a sailor stood with a heaving line. Widhelm and Stokely quickly conferred and agreed to act as if they were trying to catch the line. Inexplicably, the destroyer steamed past them. Next a big cruiser, her upper decks torn and twisted from a recent bomb hit, appeared. This time the two fliers frantically jettisoned everything they could get their hands on, including rank and rating badges. Widhelm held his chart board over the side so he could let it go instantly if necessary. But the cruiser, too, slid by, and so did a destroyer just behind. "The enlisted crew waved and we waved back," Widhelm breezily told correspondent Stanley Johnston several weeks later. "They all had a nice set of teeth, we noticed when they grinned at us."[67] Apparently satisfied that the Americans would perish in the sun-baked tropical seas or would wash up on a Japanese-held island, Kondo's captains steamed away.

The fliers had emergency rations for thirty days and two canisters of fresh water. The food was packaged in small caviar tins. "It looked like fruit cake and tasted like fruit cake, and probably was fruit cake," Widhelm recalled. The men made a sail of the parachutes and tried to head south, but the wind was not cooperative. When Stokely asked where they might wind up if they just drifted, Widhelm suggested the Japanese bastion at Truk. "Boy, won't they be surprised when we try to take that base!" Stokely replied.[68] Later Gus teased George with the prospect of winding up somewhere in the Stewarts, which he claimed were filled with beautiful women. The second day they thought they heard a submarine beneath them. The airmen agreed that if it was Japanese, they would shoot the first man that came out.

Widhelm and Stokely were asleep in the hot sun on the third day when a PBY out of Espiritu Santo saw them, landed close to the raft, and hauled them in. O'Dowd, the rescue pilot, had been one of Widhelm's pupils at Pensacola. When Widhelm got to Espiritu, he promptly fell in with some B-17 fliers in a small crap game. As he pocketed $1,250 several hours later, one army man was heard to mutter: "We should have known you can't beat him." Gus felt immortal. "Widhelm is ready again!" was his favorite expression.[69]

As Widhelm and Stokely were dodging the Imperial Japanese Navy and Creehan was preparing to bring a portion of the *Hornet*'s electrical power back on line, Mason, still on the carrier's bridge, received an unidentified aircraft report from the circling destroyers over the battery-powered voice warning net. Twenty minutes later, at 1620, a group of five or six Kates was spotted on the starboard beam. They were coming down from about six thousand feet in a fast, weaving glide. They were part of the *Shokaku* and *Zuikaku* air groups launched from the *Junyo*. The *Northampton* cut the towline and turned hard to port as one or two of the torpedo planes headed toward her. The nimble cruiser, with antiaircraft guns raking the skies, avoided all torpedoes. The drifting *Hornet* was not so lucky.

The gunners did what they could, but without power all tracking of the heavy 5-inch guns and 1.1-inch pom-poms had to be done by hand against enemy planes that were racing in at well over 250 miles per hour. Once again sheets of flame erupted along the gun decks, and the skies filled with small, black explosions. But the Japanese kept coming. Al Fleming incautiously stood on the flight deck watching the action. With all power out he had closed down his fighter director office and the radar set. The *Enterprise* had taken over control of Task Force 61's air defense. Suddenly Fleming was struck in the head by a heavy piece of shrapnel

A Kate wings over the *Hornet*, dead in the water and listing to starboard. This was part of the afternoon attack at Santa Cruz.

from the *Hornet*'s own antiaircraft guns. He collapsed, writhing, with half of his face gone.

Glen Dock had spent the previous hours below in his hellishly hot fireroom, serving on several two-man teams that were trying to pump water out with hand-powered handy-billys. As the men cranked away the temperature passed 140 degrees. Everyone wore rags soaked in water around the face to keep going, and each man was periodically relieved so he could go topside and get some fresh air. About 1600 Dock went up to the O1 level to get some rest. Moments later he saw the Kates coming in and heard the guns opening up. One enemy plane went down far out. A second plane, already hit, launched its torpedo before cartwheeling into the sea; the torpedo fell end over end into the water and disappeared. The third plane came on. It launched its torpedo; then, badly hit, it skidded across the flight deck and fell over the other side. Dock watched the white bubbles of the torpedo wake streak toward him in the bright blue sea. He dropped to his knees as he had been trained to do. The torpedo seemed to take forever to get there; finally it hit just aft of where he was kneeling but failed to explode.[70] But as Dock started back down to the fireroom, another torpedo, which he did not see, headed straight for the starboard side.

Below, the toiling engineers heard the guns open up far above. Creehan was with a repair party on the third deck port side above the aviation storeroom when the third torpedo of the day struck the carrier just aft of where the first torpedo had crashed through the forward engine room that morning. About fifteen to twenty feet beyond where Creehan stood "a sickly green flash momentarily lighted the scullery compartment and seemed to run both forward" toward the repair party "and aft into the scullery compartment for a distance of about 50 feet." The flash had been preceded "by a thud so deceptive as to almost make one believe that the torpedo had struck the port side." It was accompanied by a hissing noise like escaping air and was immediately followed by a dull rumble. The deck beneath Creehan and his party seemed to crack open, and a geyser of fuel oil that rapidly reached a depth of two feet swept the men off their feet and flung them headlong down decks, which still sloped seven degrees. Gasping and choking in the lake of smelly goo, the men struggled to their feet and formed a hand chain to a nearby ladder and escape scuttle. Although the ladder had been smashed by the explosion, everyone managed to make it to the scuttle and the relative safety of the hangar two decks above. Moments later Electrician's Mate 3rd Class Tom Reese, still dazed from the explosion and subsequent cataract of water that flooded over him as he clung to a lifeline in the hangar bay, saw Creehan emerge and sag against a stanchion. He was covered with thick fuel oil from head to foot. The rest of the engineering gang escaped through fireroom intakes or through another escape hatch in the after generator room. Only one man was seriously injured: Lt. Kelsey broke his leg.[71]

In the after engine room, Lt. (jg) Buchan saw that the forward starboard corner bulkhead in the after engine room had ruptured, allowing hot oil to spurt through the access trunk. Both after engine room feed heaters had been knocked over at an angle, and the compartment itself was flooding rapidly. Steam pressure began to drop precipitously. With so many forward hatches open to the wall of water that was rushing into the ship from the torpedo hit, it was clear to all that the *Hornet* was doomed.

As the Kates departed and the *Hornet* took on an immediate fifteen-degree starboard list, five or six Vals suddenly emerged from the clouds.

Infuriated gunners aboard the carrier let loose with all they had. The daring enemy pilots, wing guns blazing, brought their planes right down on the ship, dropped their bombs, and thumbed their noses as they raced away. Some smashed into the sea.

Down on the hangar deck, Glen Dock saw Commander Soucek moving among a group of dead, collecting dog tags from bodies that were covered with mattresses or anything else that could shroud them. The living had fought magnificently; there was no reason to lower morale by allowing badly mangled bodies to lie in the open for all to see. Meanwhile, bullets from the Vals ripped through the flight and gallery decks. Glancing up, Dock saw puffs of aluminum silver paint drop off the overhead as the bullets zipped through into the hangar. While the young fireman dove into a small aviation machine shop on top of three or four shipmates already huddled there, Soucek continued his sad mission among the corpses.[72]

The *Hornet* suffered no major punishment from this latest assault, but it was time to leave. At 1650 Mason ordered everyone up from below and all the gunnery control personnel off the island; then he issued the order to abandon ship. As Mason went down to the flight deck to supervise the final evacuation, pay clerks, yeomen, and pharmacist's mates raced below to salvage payrolls, accounts, and health records. Quartermasters on the bridge took their notebooks and the ship's log and left. Oscar Dodson went down to the hangar and helped his communication people wrestle heavy bags of classified materials overboard. It took more than half an hour because the bags had to be heaved into the sea between the bobbing heads of sailors swimming toward the nearby destroyers. With his mission accomplished, Dodson returned to the flight deck to report to Mason. When the captain saw him, he yelled, "Damn it, Dodson, what are you doing still aboard? Get off the ship so I can!"[73]

But the communications officer had one more task to perform. He climbed up to flag plot, which was empty now that Murray had gone to the *Pensacola,* and found his briefcase with the coins and family mementos. It had been badly singed by the morning's fires in the nearby signal area but not seriously damaged. From the steeply slanting deck Dodson looked out over the sun-dappled sea, subtly changing color in the late afternoon light. Flag plot, the scene of so much bustle and action during the previous several months, was still. The ocean suddenly seemed immense, the destroyers far away, and the coin-filled case very heavy. "It was evident that a swimmer, carrying a briefcase, would never reach the nearest destroyer before darkness," Dodson decided.[74] Sadly he put the case back on the deck and went back down to the hangar and over the side.

"The ship was abandoned in a quiet and orderly manner," Mason wrote proudly in his after-action report. The rehearsals at Nouméa paid off. Boatswain's mates quickly lowered knotted lines to the water; life rafts were chopped down from the sides of the island and adjacent hull areas and thrown into the sea. The last of the wounded went first. Al Fleming was taken aboard a destroyer and several days later was on an operating table at Nouméa, where the hard but ultimately successful work of reconstructing his face began. After the wounded came the rest of the crew. "In dozens, then scores, then hundreds, the men went down the lines into the water. They wore life jackets as part of their battle dress. There was no confusion." About ten "non-swimmers" had to be coaxed into the sea, but most men went without a fuss.[75]

Back on the fantail, Foley finally prepared to leave. He had been ready to go an hour before, but before he could get to a line the Japanese had mounted their fatal torpedo attack; after that he felt he had to remain to oversee further evacuations from the stern. One of the senior doctors, Comdr. Emil Stelter, "a white haired man" and therefore to Foley at least "a little older," persistently held back until he and Foley were almost the only ones left. By this time it was very late in the afternoon, and the impatient destroyers were full of survivors. Stelter finally got on an abandon ship line but refused to go down. Foley pleaded with him. "I said, 'Please, doctor, go. You've got to go. I can't leave until you do.'" Slowly Stelter "eased on down" into the water. Foley followed him, a .45 in one hand, a whistle around his neck, and the waterproofed teletype tapes safely tucked in his uniform shirt.[76]

Henry Martin, the young communications officer, had wondered how he could keep his prized wristwatch dry in the sea. It was a distinctive Black Star and Gorham timepiece from one of the finest old jewelry stores in New York City. He found a condom, wrapped it around the watch, and put it in his shirt pocket. But when he got to the destroyer *Barton*, he discovered that the watch was gone. Days later, in New Caledonia, a sergeant from the *Hornet*'s marine detachment whom Martin knew well told him that one of the marine enlisted men might have found it. As he swam slowly toward a destroyer, the young man had pushed aside what he thought was a bit of seaweed, only to discover that it was a condom with a watch inside. A delighted Martin got his timepiece back.[77]

A few men felt no pain as they departed. Some of those preparing to evacuate from the fantail discovered the last little bottles of Eddie Harp's medicinal brandy amid the detritus of the makeshift dressing station and morgue. They left the *Hornet* happy sailors. One of them waved his small bottle in the air as he got close to the *Barton*, hoping it would be an inducement to be picked up.

Others struggling in the water remembered the important things in their lives. An engineering officer swimming carefully toward safety felt a hand on his shoulder. It was one of his young firemen, who reminded him respectfully that he had promised to give the boy his examination for third class electrician's mate the following week.

Foley, in the water now, was concerned about discipline. The caressing breeze and the occasional swells had blown life rafts away from the stern all afternoon, and marginal swimmers were desperate to get on the nearest rafts because they feared they would never reach the more distant ones. "I could see that I was virtually helpless. What the hell to do with all this fighting to get on the life rafts going on."[78]

A final enemy air attack solved his problem. At 1655, five minutes after Mason had left his bridge for the flight deck, a vee of six heavy bombers, probably from Rabaul, appeared at eight or nine thousand feet, barely visible through the gossamer cloud cover. Once again bombs rained down. Most of the few remaining crewmen on the carrier dashed for cover, but not all. Two 1.1-inch pom-poms and a .30-caliber machine gun opened fire. One gunner was an aviation radioman from the air group who had not been assigned a flight that day. He was about to abandon ship when the enemy came over. Glancing around, he saw an unmanned gun with ammunition around it. As he began firing he saw a fellow radioman running across the flight deck to help him. "Come on over, Pal," he yelled, gesturing toward unmanned machine guns nearby, "three shots for a quarter!"[79] Only one bomb struck the ship; it landed squarely on the after starboard-side 5-inch gun gallery and blew one of the guns completely off its mount and into the sea. The other bombs exploded in the water near the carrier.

Concussions from the detonations, carried through the water, could be deadly. But the sailors had been told what to do during innumerable safety classes aboard ship. If you floated on your stomach during a bombing attack, they were warned, "your belly will go through your asshole." But if you floated on your back, only a near miss could cause severe internal injury. Glen Dock, in the water with hundreds of others, felt the concussions kick him in the back like a mule. But he was uninjured, and so apparently was everyone else. The more experienced swimmers realized that the Japanese were performing an invaluable service: The uproar would keep sharks away for hours. As the water stopped shaking and heaving, Foley "kept blowing that damn whistle, yelling, 'Follow me!'" As he swam away from the ship, scores of sailors followed him to empty rafts or directly to the destroyers.[80]

Crew members on the waiting destroyers wondered about the mental state of the *Hornet*'s survivors. The men had taken a terrible beating all day. They had worked heroically and with humor and faith to save the Old Stinger, a piece of machinery that had become their home, office, club, workbench, restaurant, and gambling hall—in short, their life. And they had lost everything: their ship, their clothes, money, phonographs and records, books, letters from home, and many friends. Then and much later survivors would talk almost obsessively about how much cash they had left behind in the ship's safe. Once in the water, most had been bombed again. How could anyone survive such an ordeal unscathed? The *Barton*'s doctor later told Henry Martin that he thought all the survivors would be "psychos."

As the first raft approached the *Barton*, a boatswain's mate on the bow uneasily prepared to heave a line. "Hey, Boats," came a cheerful call from across the water, "betcha can't hit us the first time."[81] The *Barton*'s doctor turned away with relief. When a raft approached another destroyer, the crew was amazed to hear about a dozen men singing lustily and decidedly off key:

> East side, west side,
> All around the town . . .
> Boys and girls, together,
> Me and Mamie O'Rourke,
> We'll trip the light fantastic
> On the sidewalks of New York.

———

Careful footsteps echo down the slanting deck of the carrier's long, empty hangar bay. Mason has ordered a handful of pharmacist's mates to hurriedly check over as much of the vessel as they can to make sure that no one, wounded or able-bodied, has been overlooked. "Hey! Anyone here? Hey! It's abandon ship! Halloo, halloo! Anyone here? Abandon ship!" The cries reverberate through an empty hull that had been constantly filled with the sounds of men and machines from its birth. ("Pilots, pilots man your planes!" "Supper for the crew, supper for the crew." "Now lay before the mast all eight o'clock reports." "I'll call. Three whores and a pair of treys. Shit!" "Flight quarters! Flight quarters! All hands man your flight quarter stations." "Goddamn it! If I've told you once, I've told you a hundred times. . . .") "Halloo, halloo, it's abandon ship! Last call! Anybody here?" Only the dead inhabit the *Hornet* now, and perhaps the ghosts of Johnnie Waldron and the men of Torpedo 8 as well. "Halloo, halloo, we're goin' now, we're leavin'!" The pharmacist's mates rush to join Mason at the debarkation lines. The last voices fade away over the side. By 1727 everyone is gone, and the United States Ship *Hornet* (CV-8) passes forever from the navy lists. A hush falls over the big, abandoned hulk, which rolls gently in the soft swells of the tropical ocean.

The sun is setting rapidly, and Kinkaid is eager to be gone with the badly battered *Enterprise* and the wounded *South Dakota*. Japanese superiority in night fighting at sea is well established, and Kinkaid, a battleship admiral, has not commanded with particular distinction this day. One hundred fifty miles to the north Nagumo aboard his cruiser is cautiously optimistic that the battle has gone well. Kondo is already racing south with his battleships, determined to bring the small U.S. fleet under his guns and avenge Midway once and for all. He has dispatched a detachment of fast destroyers ahead to find the enemy. Halsey sends word to sink the *Hornet* to keep her from Japanese hands. In the captain's cabin of a destroyer Mason bows his head when he learns the news. As the small warships, crowded with *Hornet* survivors, race away, some men weep, watching their now flaming home disappear forever over the horizon.

As night falls the *Anderson* and the *Mustin* stand off the hulk and begin pumping shells and torpedoes into her. The wreck ignites in a dozen places and sinks lower. But in their excitement, the destroyers have sent their torpedoes not into the torn starboard side but into the undamaged port side. The hulk dips lower, comes to even keel, and refuses to go under. As the last stars appear in the heavens, the destroyers rush off with the remainder of the *Hornet* crew, satisfied that the derelict, an inferno now from stem to stern, will be of no use to the enemy. But, of course, it is. Kondo's destroyer sailors, hurrying into the area less than an hour after the Americans have departed, experience the profound satisfaction of watching the desecrator of Nippon blazing like a torch. Then they finally sink her with four twenty-four-inch lance torpedoes. Neither they nor their heartbroken enemies can know that the *Hornet* will be the last heavy carrier the United States will ever lose in battle.

Although most did not realize it, the men of the *Hornet*, scattered about three or four destroyers heading back to New Caledonia, were already experiencing what psychologists would later call group death. The physical entity that had bound them together during a year of desperate war was gone; their common identity was about to be progressively eroded. In his after-action report Mason pleaded that the 2,512 men who survived that final day form the crew of another carrier to be named *Hornet*. In his final report on the activities of the communications department, Dodson claimed that as two crewmen abandoned ship one asked the other if he would reenlist. "Goddamn yes," came the reply. "On the new *Hornet*."[82]

But the pressures and imperatives of war do not lend themselves to neat, happy endings. There would be a new carrier *Hornet*, to be sure, and another, the *Shangri-la*, named for that mythical place that President Roosevelt teasingly claimed had spawned Jimmy Doolittle and his daring raiders. But only a comparative few of the men of CV-8 would serve aboard these ships. The survivors were brought back to Nouméa and placed in a tent camp in the hills above the town. Almost immediately calls began to come for this key officer or that key enlisted man to fill a critical billet aboard ships in the harbor. Experienced and battle-hardened officers like Francis Foley were summoned home to new duties and new construction. After several weeks in the tent camp the enlisted men were lined up one morning to hear that most of those with rates would be going home also; the thousand or so nonrated men would stay where they were for reassignment within the Guadalcanal battle area. By this time the collective identity of CV-8 had almost disappeared.

Soon there came a call from Guadalcanal. Four hundred men were required to fill small-boat billets on both that island and Tulagi. The motor mechanics among the common seamen and airmen languishing in the hillside camp above Nouméa were natural recruits. They did not want to go. All believed they had earned the right to a ticket stateside. Comdr. Charles Melhorn, who had just come from a destroyer billet, took them "kicking and screaming" up to the grim islands. They arrived in mid-November, only hours before the great naval battles in Ironbottom Sound that finally ensured a U.S. victory in the Solomons.[83]

Jimmy Walker was one of those who were thrust right back into war. He spent eleven months on Guadalcanal. Forty-six years later he showed a picture of himself in those days: a twenty-two-year-old *Hornet* veteran with a long, black beard and eyes fixed in what James Jones, soldier, novelist, and historian, called the thousand-yard stare. The sailor off the *Yorktown* had been right when he told Jones so many months before in a Honolulu bar that it wasn't going to war once that got to you but the going back again and again and again.[84]

Epilogue

THE *Hornet* was gone, and with her 124 men who died aboard and another 9 who died of wounds on the destroyers. Nineteen members of the aircrew remained missing in action a week after the battle. Kinkaid was in retreat, and the Americans had apparently lost their third carrier battle of the year. Tokyo was jubilant. Imperial General Headquarters promptly labeled Santa Cruz the "South Pacific Sea Battle," and three days after the *Hornet* went down Yamamoto received an Imperial Rescript commending the Combined Fleet for its efforts. Twenty-four hours later Premier Hideki Tojo sent the admiral a telegram of congratulations.[1]

But appearances were deceiving. Fleet Headquarters at Truk understandably remained cautious. The victory at sea was glorious, but victory ashore was still beyond reach. Even as Kinkaid retreated, the latest Japanese offensive on Guadalcanal shattered against the guns of the U.S. Marines and Army. Moreover, Japanese intelligence suggested that the U.S. Navy was becoming stronger, not weaker. According to the Combined Fleet Summary Action Report, the enemy had mustered four carriers at Santa Cruz: one *Saratoga* type, one *Yorktown* type, and "two new type carriers." Although the Japanese believed the *Saratoga*- and *Yorktown*-class carriers had been sunk, "the enemy builds and christens second and third generations of carriers, as many as we destroy. No wonder they do not need to change the names."[2]

Although mistaken in its specifics, the report reflected an understanding of the critical ingredient in both American and Japanese naval strategy in 1942, which was never expressly stated but always present. It was time. The Americans possessed it; the Japanese did not. Over time the United States would simply outbuild and outman Japan, and both sides knew it. Japan somehow had to compel the United States to sue for peace before the summer of 1943 or face inevitable defeat when America's new navy reached the Pacific.

Nimitz and his men would have been delighted had they known of their enemy's hyperactive imagination and the impending sense of defeatism that it induced, for after Santa Cruz only the damaged *Enterprise* remained to ward off Nagumo's carrier fleet. The *Essex* and the first of her sisters were still several months away from commissioning on the East Coast. But if Yamamoto and his colleagues chose to think otherwise, so much the better.

The Japanese faced a major crisis of their own after Santa Cruz, which they managed to hide well. More than one hundred planes and irreplaceable veteran pilots had been lost. Exactly how many were downed by the *Hornet* and Air Group 8 will always be subject to conjecture. What is clear now, although it was not then, is that Santa Cruz destroyed the remnants of the splendid cadre of experienced and capable carrier pilots with which the Imperial Japanese Navy had entered the war. A handful had died over Pearl Harbor and more in the Coral Sea; the majority perished at Midway with four of the *Kido Butai*'s six frontline carriers. Nearly all the rest went down at Santa Cruz. And with the severe damage to *Shokaku* and *Zuiho*, Yamamoto could supply the Combined Fleet with only three flattops: *Zuikaku* and the light carriers *Junyo* and *Hiyo*.

Santa Cruz thus proved to be a partial American victory after all. Although Nagumo's fliers had destroyed a precious flattop and chased the Americans from the field, Kinkaid's pilots and gunners had so badly mauled the Japanese naval air arm that for the next twenty months no Japanese carrier fleet would dare to risk battle. In the interim Nimitz brought fifteen fleet and light carriers to the Pacific, and more would arrive every month. Nimitz immersed their air groups and ships' companies in battle after battle as the United States began its great march of conquest across the western Pacific. When Vice Adm. Jisaburo Ozawa finally sailed with nine carriers of his own to contest the American invasion of the Marianas, the inferiority of Japan's "second team" was unmistakable. More than four hundred Japanese aircraft were downed in a two-day battle with Marc Mitscher's far better fliers. It mattered little that Ozawa lost only two of his flattops—*Shokaku* and the splendid, new *Taiho*—and those to submarines, not naval aircraft. After June of 1944 Japan could muster only empty carriers to contest the inexorable U.S. advance across the Pacific. These vessels served as marvelous decoys to confuse and entice Halsey off Luzon during the battle for Leyte Gulf (the second Battle of the Philippine Sea), but they had no effect on the outcome. By this time American sea power had become so overwhelming in both size and efficiency that it could overcome the most egregious blunder of Halsey's career. Even if it had not, a Japanese victory at Leyte would simply have prolonged the war, not reversed it.

———

American admirals and captains did not fight their carriers with particular distinction in 1942. At best Fletcher won a draw with Vice Adm. Chuichi Hara in the Coral Sea. He and Spruance were incredibly lucky at Midway and almost squandered their good fortune. Mitscher came away from the battle disheartened by his own performance and that of his ship. Fletcher and Capt. Elliott Buckmaster, commanding officer of the *Yorktown,* were severely criticized for abandoning the stricken carrier prematurely, and Buckmaster never achieved significant higher command. Halsey was probably foolish to risk his tiny two-carrier fleet at Santa Cruz against Nagumo's four superb flattops, and Kinkaid performed without distinction, especially in the area of fleet air defense.[3] Yet two years later the U.S. carrier fleet was not only the largest and mightiest the world had ever seen but also the most efficient. What had happened?

The answer lies in American familiarity and expertise with complex technologies. As historian John Lundstrom has observed: "In war those commanders who happen to be among the first to fight, particularly when using new technology, are in a perilous position. Peacetime doctrine must be adapted to totally new situations. Often these trailblazers do not last long, leaving others to benefit from their accomplishments or learn from their inevitable errors. Those who must start on the defensive with inferior strength—especially after sudden, stunning defeats—face additional trials."[4] Japanese admirals had been operating carriers in combat, albeit against shore-based enemies only, for four years, and the Pearl Harbor raid had provided invaluable experience. On New Year's Day 1942 the Japanese were far ahead of their American enemies in carrier combat proficiency.

The U.S. carriers and those of the *Kido Butai* constituted a quantum leap in complexity from the battleships they replaced as queens of the sea. The CVs of 1942 were the most sophisticated and complex seaborne weapons employed up to that time. Each was a floating command post, airfield, gun platform, industrial assembly plant, and fueling station incorporated into one comparatively small hull. No other weapon system afloat, ashore, or aloft could match the breadth of their mission. Unlike the British carriers, which were largely confined to controlling the sea approaches to a continent, they fought each other for control of an enormous ocean empire. Only the finest crews could operate such complicated ships efficiently. The Japanese were patently superior in the weeks immediately after Pearl Harbor. But the Americans soon began to catch up.

Throughout the first ten months of 1942 the *Kido Butai*'s air departments remained as good as those aboard the best of the U.S. carriers. At Midway and the Eastern Solomons Nagumo was able to launch quickly large flights of aircraft from his carrier decks to assault targets on either land or sea. At Santa Cruz he beat Kinkaid to the punch and nearly obtained total victory.

Neither side had an obvious advantage in fleet air defense. American attack squadrons suffered significant casualties in the Coral Sea and catastrophic losses at Midway until McClusky and his mates exploited an incredible opportunity. At Santa Cruz, Gus Widhelm's squadron faced heavy opposition over the *Kido Butai*. Only in the first moments, as the American attack formed up, and in the last moments, when Moe Vose and his dive-bombers were inexplicably allowed to assume attack posture, did the Japanese combat air patrol falter. Although the Americans nearly destroyed the *Kido Butai* in 1942, their combat air patrols could not prevent Hara's pilots from fatally damaging the *Lexington* and Nagumo's fliers from so badly hurting the *Yorktown* that she was vulnerable to submarine attack. The *Enterprise* was nearly bombed to death in the Eastern Solomons. The loss of the *Hornet* at Santa Cruz must be charged to Kinkaid and his decision to rely on the new and untried fighter director team aboard the *Enterprise* rather than on Al Fleming's highly efficient people on the *Hornet*. Nonetheless, American air and surface defense did kill a large number of veteran enemy pilots in each of the four carrier battles of 1942. Certainly the deadly antiaircraft barrage mounted by the *South Dakota* at Santa Cruz helped destroy the remnants of Japan's "first team" and provided U.S. battleships with a new role as effective air defense vessels, a role that Japanese battleships never attained.

Japanese and American carrier crews proved equally adept at damage control. Many of the prewar carriers on both sides contained serious design flaws. The biggest vessels were converted battle cruisers, ships that in both world wars exhibited a distressing tendency to explode violently under mild punishment. The *Yorktown* class, with admitted deficiencies in machinery arrangement that concentrated propulsion and electrical systems too closely, was known to be vulnerable to one or two torpedo hits, which could disable a ship without necessarily sinking it. Many Japanese carriers were physically small for their type. So was the *Wasp.*

But a number of carriers survived incredible damage. The spectacular destruction of the *Akagi, Kaga, Soryu,* and *Wasp* and the unnecessary loss of the *Lexington* and perhaps the *Yorktown* obscure how well many carrier crews on both sides fought to save their ships. The *Enterprise* survived the Battle of the Eastern Solomons only because of superhuman efforts. The *Zuikaku* and *Shokaku* received terrible damage in the Coral Sea and at Santa Cruz, respectively, yet their crews managed to get both back to dockyards in the homeland for major repairs. And the *Hornet* was nearly saved. The Bureau of Ships noted in 1943 that:

> The improvement in damage control measures as the war progresses is notable. Although HORNET and YORKTOWN received about the same amount of damage, damage control and salvage measures were put into effect immediately on HORNET. The fires, which were more extensive than those on YORKTOWN, were brought under control in one hour and completely extinguished in two hours. Although power was lost on both ships, HORNET immediately flooded voids through the drain system reducing the list about 3 degrees. Although actual reduction in list was minor in this case, the psychological benefit to the crew must have been immediate in that it reduced anxiety that the ship might capsize. The last but most important improvement was in the immediate attempt to salvage the vessel. . . . at the time of the afternoon torpedo attack, . . . part of the propulsive machinery was almost ready for operation. Success was in sight when the afternoon torpedo attack destroyed all such possibility.[5]

Only a superb carrier crew could have come so close to saving their ship. The Japanese possessed such crews in 1942. So did the Americans. But after that year Japanese skills declined precipitately, while those of the Americans steadily improved.

Because of a rigid and above all elitist training and operations philosophy, Japan was unable after 1942 to produce a capable second generation of carrier sailors and pilots. At Pearl Harbor Japan's naval and aviation elite operated six splendid flattops and their air groups. But past that point the empire could not go. Japan possessed neither the imagination nor the flexibility, neither the industrial base nor the human resources, to conduct a protracted carrier war with its inevitable, heavy attrition of both ships and men. The first Japanese team of naval aviators, drawn overwhelmingly from the enlisted ranks, came to the fleet after a prolonged, brutal training course that could not be replicated—or efficiently reduced—during wartime. Japanese pilots were expected to fly until they died. The navy refused to shuffle experienced combat aviators back and forth between training schools and the fleet. Carrier captains were not expected to have a background in aviation; thus they seldom developed a sense of career-long identification with a novel, complex form of naval warfare or a commitment to prosecuting that warfare with imagination and initiative. The *Kido Butai* was the best that imperial Japan could produce. But once it was gone, Japan's status as a first-rate carrier power was gone.

The aircraft carrier proved to be a perfect weapon system for the United States, a large and dynamic nation whose genius for war included an unmatched "mastery of mobile warfare and the ability to improvise under the most difficult conditions."[6] Successful carrier operations demand simplicity, improvisation, initiative, ingenuity, and speed from all hands—not just the men in the air but also those in the hangar bays, machine shops, flight decks, and air offices.

The *Hornet* was one of the old navy's last gifts to the new fleet that began to appear in the Pacific in 1943. She and her sisters—*Enterprise, Lexington, Wasp,* and *Yorktown*—became the essential test beds for the development of wartime carrier operations. What was learned in 1942 aboard these few vessels laid the foundations for the operation of the great carrier task forces of 1944–45, which led the way to victory and determined the future course of seaborne air power.

In its six months of combat life the *Hornet* helped to define carrier capabilities and operations and to determine the nature of carrier warfare. Soucek and Marcel Gouin created an outstanding air department. Hangar deck officer Wayne Smith and Ed Osborn, his counterpart on the flight deck, developed and when necessary improvised enduring techniques for rapidly repairing, servicing, arming, spotting, launching, and landing modern naval warplanes. Francis Foley and his colleagues contributed substantially to the budding discipline of aviation battle intelligence and navigation. Al Fleming and his small but dedicated crew of radar operators helped transform fleet air defense from a guessing game to both an art and a science. Mike Sanchez and Gus Widhelm built an increasingly effective air group out of the wreckage and demoralization of Midway. They and George Formanek, Al Emerson, Red Hessel, Ed Stebbins, and the other members of Air Group 8 learned the skills and provided the examples of combat leadership and bravery that were essential in forging the spirit of America's huge second generation of wartime naval aviators, who almost effortlessly swept the enemy from the skies over the Marianas, the Philippines, the South China Sea, and finally the approaches to the home islands themselves.

Even in death the *Hornet* provided new lessons for carrier sailors. The ship was abandoned only because the sea was dominated by the enemy. When the United States owned the seas later in the war, no bomb-ravaged and gutted carrier would be abandoned as the *Hornet* had been. Damage control teams would operate with greater knowledge and efficiency, if with no greater dedication or skill, to accomplish what Pat Creehan, Apollo Soucek, Henry Moran, and their shipmates had been unable to do off Santa Cruz.

But in the end it was not just the captains, the pilots, and the officers but the ordinary seamen, firemen, gunner's mates, aviation "motor mechs," ordnancemen, electricians, and plane pushers who made the *Hornet* a ship to remember. The $36-a-month boys in their late teens and early twenties who came out of the boot camp grinders at Great Lakes and San Diego kept the engines running, the rations coming, the planes flying, and the guns firing on good days and bad. Without them the Mitschers and the Widhelms, the Masons and the Gouins, could have achieved nothing. Most of these youngsters eventually got home in 1942 or 1943; they took their battle-honed skills into training school classrooms or back out to the fleet. Wherever they went they helped a new service of raw recruits with two weeks of boot camp become the mightiest instrument of sea power ever formed.

––––––

The age of fighting sail lasted for two centuries, the battleship era for seventy-five years. Submarines have played a major, occasionally decisive role in naval warfare since their inception nine decades ago. "Many Navy men suspect that the golden age of carrier war is drawing to a close," Lt. Oliver Jensen wrote in early 1945. "There will be . . . perhaps no more sea battles to compare with those in the Philippine Sea."[7] The young naval journalist and historian was right. After Leyte Gulf, indeed after the Marianas "Turkey Shoot," carrier war was never again waged in the classic sense of a duel between two roughly equal fleets for control of the world. The age of carrier combat lasted only twenty-five months, from the Coral Sea in May 1942 to the Marianas in June 1944. During that period five classic battles were fought, four of them in the space of five months from the late spring to the mid-autumn of 1942. Those four conflicts—Coral Sea, Midway, the Eastern Solomons, and Santa Cruz—determined the course of the Pacific war and thus of the twentieth century. With carrier air power, empires that formerly could be lost in an afternoon could now be won or lost in minutes. The contending carrier fleets were not large, as befitted a young weapon system struggling to maturity. The small number of fleet carriers on each side was what made every battle so crucial. Thus throughout 1942 knowledgeable circles in both Washington and Tokyo rightly considered the loss of a single aircraft carrier a catastrophe. Each precious flattop, Japanese and American, wrote an important chapter in modern naval history.

The *Hornet* and her handful of prewar sisters thus occupy a unique and honored place in naval history. She and her crew helped pioneer a revolution in warfare at sea while holding the line against those who would destroy in the name of violence and revenge the hope and promise of a decent world.

Notes

Chapter 1. Birth

1. Francis Drake Foley, "Every Good Ship Has a Heart" (typescript provided by author, n.d.), 1.

2. Brent L. Gravatt, "On the Back of the Fleet," *Naval History* 4, no. 2 (1990): 18.

3. Stephen Jurika, interviewed by Paul B. Ryan, 4 March 1976, U.S. Naval Institute Oral History Transcripts, No. 14: 491–92, 502–3.

4. Ibid., 493.

5. Ibid., No. 12: 451.

6. Interview with Henry Martin, 41st *Hornet* Reunion, Norfolk, Va., 9–11 June 1989.

7. Francis D. Foley, interviewed by Paul Stillwell, 16 January 1985, U.S. Naval Institute Oral History Transcripts, No. 5: 394; Jurika oral history, No. 12: 454.

8. Tom Lea, "Aboard the U.S.S. *Hornet*," *Life*, 22 March 1943, 52.

9. Jurika oral history, No. 14: 494.

10. Alexander T. Griffin, *A Ship to Remember: The Saga of the* Hornet (New York: Howell, Soskin, 1943), 24.

11. Martin interview.

12. William Manchester, *The Glory and the Dream: A Narrative History of America, 1932–1972*, 2 vols. (Boston: Little, Brown, 1973, 1974), 1:300.

13. The operations plan and FDR are quoted in ibid., 284, 285.

14. Quoted in "11 on *Kearny* Died for Liberty, Knox Says at *Hornet* Ceremony," *Washington Post*, 21 October 1941; "Knox Praises Men Lost on the *Kearny*," *New York Times*, 21 October 1941.

15. Interview with Glen Dock, Port Orchard, Wash., 24 April 1994; interview with James Walker, 41st *Hornet* Reunion, Norfolk, Va., 9–11 June 1989.

16. Quoted in Griffin, *A Ship to Remember*, 19.

Chapter 2. Shakedown

1. Theodore Taylor, *The Magnificent Mitscher* (New York: Norton, 1954), 104.
2. Quoted in ibid., 105.
3. Interview with Gerald McAteer, Washington, D.C., 21 July 1989.
4. Walker interview.
5. Quoted in Griffin, *A Ship to Remember*, 37–38.
6. Interview with Cardon Ruchti, 41st *Hornet* Reunion, Norfolk, Va., 9–11 June 1989.
7. U.S.S. *Hornet* Deck Log, 27 December 1941, National Military Records Center, Record Group 24, National Archives, Washington, D.C. Hereafter cited as HDL.
8. Frederick Mears, *Carrier Combat* (Garden City, N.Y.: Doubleday, Doran, 1944), 16.
9. John B. Lundstrom, *The First Team: Pacific Naval Air Combat from Pearl Harbor to Midway* (Annapolis, Md.: Naval Institute Press, 1984), 142–43.
10. Alfred G. Ward, interviewed by John T. Mason, Jr., 27 August 1970, U.S. Naval Institute Oral History Transcripts, No. 2: 34.
11. Unless otherwise noted, the following account of shakedown, including quotations, is from Letter from Marc A. Mitscher to Admiral H. R. Stark, 30 January 1942, in U.S.S. *Hornet* (CV-8) War Diary, NRS 70: WWII History/Diary/Reports (microfilm), U.S. Navy Operational Archives Branch, Naval Historical Division, Washington Navy Yard, Washington, D.C., 1–5. Hereafter cited as HWD.
12. Griffin, *A Ship to Remember*, 30.
13. Glen Dock interview.
14. Mears, *Carrier Combat*, 21.
15. O. H. Dodson, "The Day the Coins Went Down," 35, from Francis D. Foley clipping file.
16. Mears, *Carrier Combat*, 22.
17. Interview with Eugene Blackmer, Everett, Wash., 3 May 1994.
18. HDL, 31 December 1941, 21 January 1942.
19. Chester Wilmot, *The Struggle for Europe* (London: Collins Clear-Type Press, 1952), 489, 491.
20. Ibid., 491.
21. Blackmer interview.
22. Wilmot, *The Struggle for Europe*, 491.
23. Masatake Okumiya, Jiro Horikoshi, and Martin Caidin, *Zero* (New York: Ballantine Books, 1956), 43.
24. Lundstrom, *The First Team*, 143.

Chapter 3. Preparing

1. Gilven M. Slonim, "A Flagship View of Command Decisions," *Naval Institute Proceedings* 84, no. 4 (1958): 82.
2. Quoted in Henry L. Miller, interviewed by John T. Mason, Jr., 24 March 1971, U.S. Naval Institute Oral History Transcripts, No. 1: 42. Miller, a navy lieutenant, trained the Doolittle raiders for carrier operations.

3. Donald B. Duncan, "Secret Planning for the Tokyo Raid," in *The Pacific War Remembered: An Oral History Collection*, ed. John T. Mason, Jr. (Annapolis, Md.: Naval Institute Press, 1986), 65, 67.

4. Jurika oral history, No. 13: 456; No. 14: 487.

5. Conversation quoted in Taylor, *The Magnificent Mitscher*, 112.

6. Griffin, *A Ship to Remember*, 45.

7. Quoted in ibid., 48; Taylor, *The Magnificent Mitscher*, 113.

8. Griffin, *A Ship to Remember*, 49.

9. Glen Dock interview.

10. U.S.S. *Hornet* Club, Inc., videotaped interviews with *Hornet* crew regarding the Doolittle raid, 1993. Hereafter cited as *Hornet* crew videotape.

11. Glen Dock interview.

12. Mears, *Carrier Combat*, 19.

13. Martin interview.

14. Lundstrom, *The First Team*, 140.

15. Clark G. Reynolds, *The Carrier War* (Alexandria, Va.: Time-Life Books, 1982), 79.

16. Mears, *Carrier Combat*, 20.

17. Ibid., 21.

18. Jurika oral history, No. 15: 510.

19. Except where noted, all of the following is from Mears, *Carrier Combat*, 21–28.

20. Taylor, *The Magnificent Mitscher*, 116.

Chapter 4. The Raid

1. Duncan, "Secret Planning," 67.

2. Ibid.

3. Ibid., 68.

4. Quoted in ibid., 69.

5. Ted W. Lawson, *Thirty Seconds over Tokyo*, ed. Robert Considine (New York: Random House, 1945), 23.

6. Slonim, "A Flagship View," 82.

7. Lawson, *Thirty Seconds over Tokyo*, 25.

8. Ibid.; HDL, 1 April 1942.

9. McAteer interview.

10. Ruchti interview.

11. McAteer interview.

12. *Hornet* crew videotape.

13. Conversation quoted in Miller oral history, No. 1: 37; and Henry L. Miller, "Training the Doolittle Fliers," in Mason, *The Pacific War Remembered*, 74.

14. Jurika oral history, No. 13: 458.

15. Stan Cohen, *Destination Tokyo: A Pictorial History of Doolittle's Tokyo Raid, April 18, 1942* (Missoula, Mont.: Pictorial Histories Publishing, 1983), 18.

16. Jurika oral history, No. 13: 457.

17. Ibid., 457, 459.

18. Ibid., 458; Martin interview.

19. Report of Action, 18 April 1942, in HWD, Serial 0015, 2.

20. Edward T. Layton, Roger Pineau, and John Costello, *"And I Was There": Pearl Harbor and Midway—Breaking the Secrets* (New York: William Morrow, 1985), 380–83.

21. Report of Action, 18 April 1942, 2.

22. *Hornet* crew videotape.

23. Jurika oral history, No. 13: 462.

24. Ibid., 473.

25. *Hornet* crew videotape.

26. Blackmer interview.

27. *Hornet* crew videotape; Report of Action, 18 April 1942, 4; Carroll V. Glines, "Launch Planes!" in *The United States Navy in World War II*, ed. S. E. Smith (New York: William Morrow, 1966), 215.

28. Slonim, "A Flagship View," 82–84.

29. Report of Action, 18 April 1942, 4.

30. Layton, Pineau, and Costello, *"And I Was There,"* 385; Mitsuo Fuchida and Masatake Okumiya, *Midway: The Battle That Doomed Japan*, ed. Clarke H. Kawakami and Roger Pineau (New York: Ballantine Books, 1955), 68–69.

31. Fuchida and Okumiya, *Midway*, 69.

32. Griffin, *A Ship to Remember*, 63.

33. Taylor, *The Magnificent Mitscher*, 119; Glines, "Launch Planes!" 214–15.

34. Griffin, *A Ship to Remember*, 66.

35. The Air Department Plan is quoted in Glines, "Launch Planes!" 217.

36. Ibid., 217–18; Martin interview.

37. Lawson, *Thirty Seconds over Tokyo*, 38.

38. Bost's story is in "Sailor Tells of *Hornet*'s Death; Tokyo Flyers [*sic*] Made Test Flight," from William J. Hill clipping file.

39. Lawson, *Thirty Seconds over Tokyo*, 38; Ruchti interview.

40. Lawson, *Thirty Seconds over Tokyo*, 39; McAteer interview.

41. Miller oral history, No. 1: 40.

42. Quoted in Cohen, *Destination Tokyo*, 40.

43. Martin interview; Lawson, *Thirty Seconds over Tokyo*, 43.

44. Report of Action, 18 April 1942, 4.

45. Cohen, *Destination Tokyo*, 41.

46. John Toland, *But Not in Shame: The Six Months after Pearl Harbor* (New York: Signet Books, 1962), 363; Griffin, *A Ship To Remember*, 66.

47. Donald M. Goldstein and Katherine V. Dillon, eds., *Fading Victory: The Diary of Admiral Matome Ugaki, 1941–1945*, trans. Masataka Chihaya (Pittsburgh: University of Pittsburgh Press, 1991), 111.

48. This and subsequent quotations from the *Hornet*'s deck log are from Cohen, *Destination Tokyo*, 41; see also HDL, 18 April 1942.

49. Cohen, *Destination Tokyo*, 41.

50. Quoted in Griffin, *A Ship to Remember*, 70.

51. Quoted in ibid., 71.

52. James Jones, *WW II: A Chronicle of Soldiering* (New York: Ballantine Books, 1976), 12.

Chapter 5. Sea Duty

1. James Jones briefly sketched wartime Honolulu in *WW II: A Chronicle of Soldiering*, 19; an even better visual account is John Ford's film *December 7th: The Movie*, made in 1942 but officially banned for the next half-century (a brief, censored 34-minute version was released in 1943). The entire film, digitally reprocessed, was released in 1991 by Kit Parker Video Films, Monterey, Calif.

2. Glen Dock interview.

3. Goldstein and Dillon, *Fading Victory*, 113, 115–16.

4. Griffin, *A Ship to Remember*, 72.

5. Ibid., 75.

6. Quoted in ibid., 74.

7. Ibid., 25.

8. Telephone interview with John B. Lundstrom, 11 January 1994.

9. Lundstrom, *The First Team*, 313.

10. Lundstrom telephone interview.

11. Interview with Francis D. Foley, Annapolis, Md., 7 July 1989; Lea, "Aboard the *Hornet*," 54.

12. Martin interview.

13. Griffin, *A Ship to Remember*, 27.

14. The following information on Torpedo 8 is from ibid., 36–39; Mears, *Carrier Combat*, 38–44; Martin interview; telephone interview with Henry Martin, 29 September 1994.

15. McAteer interview; Ruchti interview; HDL, 4 May 1942.

16. These incidents were recorded in the deck log at various times between January and July 1942.

17. Glen Dock interview.

18. Martin interview.

19. Glen Dock interview.

20. HDL, 21 May 1942; Blackmer interview.

21. Griffin, *A Ship to Remember*, 80–87.

22. Robert J. Casey, *Torpedo Junction: With the Pacific Fleet from Pearl Harbor to Midway* (Indianapolis: Bobbs-Merrill, 1942), 340, 342.

23. Quoted in ibid., 340.

Chapter 6. Mysteries at Midway

1. John Costello, *The Pacific War* (New York: Rawson, Wade Publishers, 1981), 279; Pat Frank and Joseph D. Harrington, *Rendezvous at Midway: USS Yorktown and the Japanese Carrier Fleet* (New York: John Day, 1967), 143.

2. Jack Sweetman, "50 Years Ago . . . Midway," *Naval Institute Proceedings* 118, no. 6 (1992): 74–75.

3. Richard B. Frank, *Guadalcanal* (New York: Random House, 1990), 24.

4. Sweetman, "50 Years Ago . . . Midway," 75.

5. Quoted in Frank, *Guadalcanal*, 24.

6. Fuchida and Okumiya, *Midway*, 72.

7. Goldstein and Dillon, *Fading Victory*, 114.

8. Ibid., 144.

9. Ibid., 143.

10. J. F. C. Fuller, *The Decisive Battles of the Western World and Their Influence upon History*, vol. 2, *1792–1944*, ed. John Terraine (London: Granada Publishing, 1970), 79.

11. Lundstrom, *The First Team*, 300.

12. Brent L. Gravatt, "On the Back of the Fleet," *Naval History* 4, no. 2 (1990): 18.

13. Quoted in ibid.

14. The following account of American tactical lessons and errors is derived from Lundstrom, *The First Team*, 301–3.

15. Quoted in ibid., 302.

16. Martin interview; Lundstrom, *The First Team*, 313.

17. John S. Thach, interviewed by Etta-Belle Kitchen, 6 November 1970, U.S. Naval Institute Oral History Transcripts, No. 3: 239.

18. Casey, *Torpedo Junction*, 361.

19. Joseph J. Rochefort, "Finding the *Kido Butai*," *Naval Institute Proceedings* 118, no. 6 (1992): 76.

20. Jones, *WW II: A Chronicle*, 20–21.

21. Quoted in Griffin, *A Ship to Remember*, 91. See also ibid., 90.

22. Quoted in ibid., 92.

23. Quoted in ibid., 95.

24. Casey, *Torpedo Junction*, 363.

25. Report of Action, 4–6 June 1942, in HWD, Serial 0018, 1.

26. Casey, *Torpedo Junction*, 363.

27. Report of Action, 4–6 June 1942, 1.

28. Ken Ringle, "The Code-Cracker & the Battle of Midway," *Washington Post*, 4 June 1992; Casey, *Torpedo Junction*, 364–67.

29. Mears, *Carrier Combat*, 44.

30. Report of Action, 4–6 June 1942, 1.

31. Ringle, "The Code Cracker"; Slonim, "A Flagship View," 85.

32. Quoted in Costello, *The Pacific War*, 280.

33. Raymond Spruance, "Forward," in Fuchida and Okumiya, *Midway*, 7.

34. Mears, *Carrier Combat*, 48–49.

35. Ibid., 46–47.

36. Interview with George Gay, Jacksonville, Fla., 12 October 1943, in Addendum to Report of Action, 4–6 June 1942, 2.

37. Martin telephone interview.

38. Quoted in Edward P. Stafford, *The Big E: The Story of the USS* Enterprise (New York: Dell Publishing, 1964), 88.

39. Ringle, "The Code Cracker."

40. Mears, *Carrier Combat*, 49; Griffin, *A Ship to Remember*, 120.

41. Quoted in Griffin, *A Ship to Remember*, 120–21.

42. Quoted in Mears, *Carrier Combat*, 52.

43. Peter Slavin, "Prange's Midway," *Naval Institute Proceedings* 118, no. 6 (1992): 79.

44. Malcolm A. LeCompte, "Radar and the Air Battles of Midway," *Naval History* 6, no. 2 (1992): 29, 31.

45. Quoted in Fuchida and Okumiya, *Midway*, 146.

46. Quoted in ibid., 149.

47. Gordon W. Prange, *Miracle at Midway* (New York: McGraw-Hill, 1982), 234.

48. Casey, *Torpedo Junction*, 373.

49. Gravatt, "On the Back of the Fleet," 18.

50. Report of Action, 4–6 June 1942, 2.

51. Casey, *Torpedo Junction*, 376.

52. Lundstrom, *The First Team*, 333.

53. Report of Action, 4–6 June 1942, Enclosure (C): Recommendations for Awards, 2.

54. Griffin, *A Ship to Remember*, 127.

55. Report of Action, 4–6 June 1942, 2; Lundstrom, *The First Team*, 334.

56. Blackmer interview.

57. Casey, *Torpedo Junction*, 376–77.

58. Report of Action, 4–6 June 1942, 3.

59. Martin telephone interview.

60. Prange, *Miracle at Midway*, 242–45.

61. Quoted in Report of Action, 4–6 June 1942, Enclosure (H): Statement of Leroy Quillen, 13 June 1942, 1.

62. Interview with Gay, in Addendum to Report of Action, 1–2.

63. Ibid., 2.

64. Defects Observed during the Action off Midway on 4 June 1942, in Air Operations Officer's Report, 12 June 1942, Addendum to Report of Action, 4–6 June 1942, 2.

65. Mears, *Carrier Combat*, 54.

66. Martin interview.

67. Prange, *Miracle at Midway*, 244; Slonim, "A Flagship View," 86; Lundstrom, *The First Team*, 348, 368.

68. Martin interview.

69. Casey, *Torpedo Junction*, 377; Mears, *Carrier Combat*, 55.

70. Griffin, *A Ship to Remember*, 139.

71. Quoted in ibid., 140.

72. Mears, *Carrier Combat*, 56.

73. Thach oral history, No. 3: 258.

74. Mears, *Carrier Combat*, 56–57.

75. Casey, *Torpedo Junction*, 380–81.

76. Mears, *Carrier Combat*, 58–59.

77. Oliver Jensen, *Carrier War* (New York: Simon and Schuster, 1945), 6–7.

78. Report of Action, 4–6 June 1942, 4.

79. Stanley Johnston's account of this attack in *The Grim Reapers* (New York: E. P. Dutton, 1942), 66–67, is incorrect regarding who led the *Hornet* assault team, the targets, and the results.

80. Griffin, *A Ship to Remember*, 143.

81. Report of Action, 4–6 June 1942, 5.

82. Martin interview; Martin telephone interview; HDL, 4 June 1942.

83. Interview with Keith Bancroft, Renton, Wash., 7 May 1994; Walker interview; Blackmer interview.

84. McAteer's recollections are from McAteer interview; Mears reported Mitscher's remarks in *Carrier Combat*, 57.

85. Griffin, *A Ship to Remember*, 138.

86. McAteer interview.

87. Martin interview.

88. Mears, *Carrier Combat*, 59; Report of Action, 4–6 June 1942, 4.

89. Layton, Pineau, and Costello, *"And I Was There,"* 447; Fuchida and Okumiya, *Midway*, 193–94.

90. Casey, *Torpedo Junction*, 390–91.

91. Report of Action, 4–6 June 1942, 5.

92. Mears, *Carrier Combat*, 62.

93. Report of Action, 4–6 June 1942, 5.

94. Ibid.

95. Mears, *Carrier Combat*, 63.

96. Quoted in Johnston, *The Grim Reapers*, 71–72; Griffin, *A Ship to Remember*, 152.

97. Quoted in Griffin, *A Ship to Remember*, 153.

98. Casey, *Torpedo Junction*, 408–44.

99. Air Operations Officer's Report, 7.

100. Frank Harvey, *Air War—Vietnam* (New York: Bantam Books, 1967), 4.

101. Walter Lord, *Incredible Victory* (New York: Harper & Row, 1967), 141.

102. Johnston, *The Grim Reapers*, 63.

103. Mears, *Carrier Combat*, 70–71.

104. Joseph Bryan III and Philip Reed, *Mission beyond Darkness* (New York: Duell, Sloan and Pearce, 1945).

105. Stafford, *The Big E*, 92.

106. Jurika oral history, No. 14: 505–7.

107. HDL, 9 June 1942; McAteer interview; Walker interview.

Chapter 7. Interregnum

1. Lundstrom, *The First Team*, 434.

2. Jurika oral history, No. 14: 507.

3. Casey, *Torpedo Junction*, 494–95. Although Japanese casualties at Midway are not precisely known, they probably numbered around three thousand men. For Japanese estimates see Fuchida and Okumiya, *Midway*, 162–66, 174, 213–14.

4. The following story is from McAteer interview.

5. Taylor, *The Magnificent Mitscher*, 138.

6. Martin interview; Martin telephone interview; List of Officers, 1–30 June 1942, in HDL.

7. Casey, *Torpedo Junction*, 413.

8. Goldstein and Dillon, *Fading Victory*, 164–74; the quotations are on 165.

9. Mears, *Carrier Combat*, 66.

10. Jones, *WWII: A Chronicle*, 25.

11. Lea, "Aboard the *Hornet*," 51.

12. Foley oral history, No. 4: 370.

13. Foley, "Every Good Ship," 5.

14. Lea, "Aboard the *Hornet*," 53.

15. Quoted in ibid.

16. Foley oral history, No. 4: 356–59; idem, "Every Good Ship," 5.

17. Lundstrom, *The First Team*, 235–40.

18. Griffin, *A Ship to Remember*, 161.

19. Lea, "Aboard the *Hornet*," 55.

20. Foley interview.

21. Blackmer interview; Bancroft interview.

22. Lea, "Aboard the *Hornet*," 56.

23. Quoted in ibid.

24. Bancroft interview.

25. The following discussion is based on data in James Fahey, *Ships and Aircraft of the U.S. Fleet: Victory Edition* (New York: Ships & Aircraft, 1945), 47, 49; and in *Jane's Fighting Aircraft of World War II* (New York: Military Press, 1989), 234.

26. Robert F. Sumrall, ed., *Warship's Battle Damage Report No. 1: USS Hornet (CV8)* (Missoula, Mont.: Pictorial Histories Publishing, 1985), rear cover photo caption.

27. Norman Friedman, *U.S. Aircraft Carriers: An Illustrated Design History*, ship plans by A. D. Baker III (Annapolis, Md.: Naval Institute Press, 1983), 97.

28. Foley oral history, No. 4: 358.

29. Quoted in Griffin, *A Ship to Remember*, 162–63.

30. Ibid.

31. Goldstein and Dillon, *Fading Victory*, 183.

32. Masanori Ito and Roger Pineau, *The End of the Imperial Japanese Navy*, trans. Andrew Y. Kuroda and Roger Pineau (New York: MacFadden Books, 1965; first published 1956), 61.

33. Richard Tregaskis, *Guadalcanal Diary* (New York: Random House, 1943), 84.

34. Ito and Pineau, *The End of the Imperial Japanese Navy*, 61–62.

35. Okumiya, Horikoshi, and Caidin, *Zero*, 149.

36. Quoted in ibid.

37. Jurika oral history, No. 15: 515, 516.

38. Glen Dock interview; Bancroft interview.

39. Foley, "Every Good Ship," 8.

40. Foley oral history, No. 4: 363; idem, "Every Good Ship," 6; Bancroft diary, provided by author, 17 August 1942; Bancroft interview.

41. Foley, "Every Good Ship," 7.

42. Bancroft diary, 17 August 1942.

Chapter 8. Harm's Way

1. Foley oral history, No. 4: 360–61.

2. Wilbur H. Morrison, *Above and Beyond, 1941–1945* (New York: St. Martin's Press, 1983), 119.

3. John B. Lundstrom, "Frank Jack Fletcher Got a Bum Rap, Part Two: Guadalcanal," *Naval History* 6, no. 3 (1992): 25.

4. Ibid., 24; Richard B. Frank, "'. . . Nailed the Colors to the Mast,'" *Naval History* 6, no. 4 (1992): 8.

5. Frank, "'. . . Nailed the Colors to the Mast,'" 8.

6. Ibid.

7. Foley oral history, No. 4: 359–60.

8. Lea, "Aboard the *Hornet*," 53.

9. Bancroft interview; Bancroft diary, 26 August 1942.

10. Griffin, *A Ship to Remember*, 167–69.

11. Goldstein and Dillon, *Fading Victory*, 191.

12. Ibid., 193.

13. Quoted in Griffin, *A Ship to Remember*, 175.

14. Bancroft diary.

15. Clay Blair, Jr., *Silent Victory: The U.S. Submarine War against Japan*, 2 vols. (Philadelphia: J. B. Lippincott, 1975), 1:221.

16. Griffin, *A Ship to Remember*, 177.

17. Quoted in Jensen, *Carrier War*, 5.

18. Jurika oral history, No. 14: 503.

19. Lea, "Aboard the *Hornet*," 50; Bancroft diary.

20. Jurika oral history, No. 15: 517–18.

21. Bancroft interview.

22. Bancroft diary; Eric Hammel, *Guadalcanal: The Carrier Battles* (New York: Crown Publishers, 1987), 257.

23. Mitchell's recollections are quoted in Ira Wolfert, *Battle for the Solomons* (Boston: Houghton Mifflin, 1943), 37–39; Durr's comments are quoted in Frank, *Guadalcanal*, 248.

24. Griffin, *A Ship to Remember*, 189.

25. Quoted in ibid., 190.

26. Ruchti interview.

27. Foley, "Every Good Ship," 11; McAteer interview.

28. Foley, "Every Good Ship," 11.

29. Quoted in Griffin, *A Ship to Remember*, 191.

30. Quoted in Foley, "Every Good Ship," 11.

31. McAteer interview.

32. The quotation is from Griffin, *A Ship to Remember*, 191. Other eyewitness accounts are from Foley, "Every Good Ship," 11; Bancroft interview.

33. Bancroft interview.

34. The most detailed account of the loss of the *Wasp* is in Hammel, *Guadalcanal: The Carrier Battles*, 261–77. See also Frank, *Guadalcanal*, 249; Fletcher Pratt, "Memorial of the *Wasp*," *Harpers Magazine*, May 1943, 555.

35. Hammel, *Guadalcanal: The Carrier Battles*, 279.

36. Ruchti interview; Bancroft interview; Foley interview.

37. The Ghormley message is quoted in Foley, "Every Good Ship," 12. The unease it inspired was mentioned by Ruchti in his interview.

38. Report on Performance in Battle, 7 October 1942, in HWD CV8/A9-8, 1.

39. Ibid., 1–2.

40. Ibid., 2.

41. Bancroft diary.

42. Bancroft diary; Anne Swenson, "'Hours of Hell' on *Hornet* Described by Navy Flyers," from Hill clipping file; Lea, "Aboard the *Hornet*," 57.

43. See, for example, J. Bryan III, *Aircraft Carrier* (New York: Ballantine Books, 1954).

44. For a classic statement of this view, see Max Hastings, *Overlord: D-Day and the Battle for Normandy* (New York: Simon and Schuster, 1984), 179.

45. Ruchti interview.

46. Joseph M. Worthington, interviewed by John T. Mason, Jr., 31 May 1972, U.S. Naval Institute Oral History Transcripts, No. 4: 193.

Chapter 9. Alone

1. Griffin, *A Ship to Remember*, 220.

2. Report of Performance in Battle, 7 October 1942, in HWD, CV8/A9-8, 3, 7.

3. Bancroft diary, 4 October 1942.

4. Report of Performance in Battle, 7 October 1942, 4.

5. Ibid.

6. Hammel, *Guadalcanal: The Carrier Battles*, 288.

7. Report of Action, 5 October 1942, in HWD, Serial 0023, 2.

8. Quoted in Griffin, *A Ship to Remember*, 210.

9. Report of Action, 5 October 1942, 2.

10. Ibid., 3.

11. Griffin, *A Ship to Remember*, 211–12.

12. Report of Action, 5 October 1942, 4.

13. Ibid.

14. Griffin, *A Ship to Remember*, 216.

15. Quoted in ibid., 214.

16. Blackmer interview.

17. Report of Action, 5 October 1942, 7.

18. Ibid.

19. Goldstein and Dillon, *Fading Victory*, 228.

20. Bancroft interview.

21. Quoted in Griffin, *A Ship to Remember*, 221 (italics added).

22. Report of Action, 12–13 October 1942, in HWD, Serial 085, Enclosure (A): Executive Officer's Report, 14 October 1942, 1.

23. Report of Action, 12–13 October 1942, Enclosure (C): C.O. VF-72 Action Report Form, 12 October 1942, 2.

24. Ibid., 3.

25. Executive Officer's Report, 14 October 1942, 2–3.

26. Quoted in Costello, *The Pacific War*, 353.

27. Quoted in Frank, *Guadalcanal*, 333.

28. Addenda to Report of Action, 16 October 1942, in HWD, Serial 090, Enclosure (A): C.O. VF-72 Action Report Form, 15 October 1942, 1.

29. Report of Action, 16 October 1942, in HWD, Serial 087, Enclosure (A): Executive Officer's Report, 17 October 1942, 2.

30. Report of Action, 16 October 1942, Enclosure (C): Scouting-Bombing Squadron 8 Report of Action, 17 October 1942, 1.

31. Ibid., Enclosure (C): Individual Pilot Reports, 1.

32. Report of Action, 16 October 1942, 1.

33. Foley, "Every Good Ship," 14.

34. Blackmer interview.

35. Harvey, *Air War—Vietnam*, 8.

36. Quoted in Foley, "Every Good Ship," 14.

37. Johnston, *The Grim Reapers*, 119.

38. Quoted in Costello, *The Pacific War*, 354.

39. Quoted in Layton, Pineau, and Costello, *"And I Was There,"* 462.

40. Ruchti interview.

41. Glen Dock interview.

42. Quoted in Griffin, *A Ship to Remember*, 236.

43. Ibid., 236–37.

Chapter 10. Death

1. Goldstein and Dillon, *Fading Victory*, 244.

2. Ibid., 245.

3. Ibid., 246.

4. Quoted in William F. Halsey and J. Bryan III, *Admiral Halsey's Story* (New York: McGraw-Hill, 1947), 121.

5. Don Eddy, "How We Lost a Gallant Lady: Interview with Charles P. Mason," *America*, November 1943, 32–33.

6. Martin interview; Griffin, *A Ship to Remember*, 238; Foley oral history, No. 5: 389; O. H. Dodson, "The Day the Coins Went Down," 36, from Foley clipping file.

7. Foley oral history, No. 5: 385.

8. Charles McMurtry, "6-Minute Attack by 70 Jap Planes Turns U.S. Carrier into Inferno," from Hill clipping file.

9. Except where otherwise noted, the following account of the air battle over and around Kondo's fleet on the morning of 26 October 1942 is derived from two sources: the immediate after-action interviews of Gus Widhelm and members of the Big E's Fighting 10 by Stanley Johnston, later published in *The Grim Reapers*, 129–40; and Eric Hammel's careful reconstruction forty-five years later in *Guadalcanal: The Carrier Battles*, 349–68.

10. Stafford, *The Big E*, 169.

11. Hammel, *Guadalcanal: The Carrier Battles*, 350–51.

12. Quoted in Johnston, *The Grim Reapers*, 133.

13. Hammel, *Guadalcanal: The Carrier Battles*, 363.

14. Quoted in Johnston, *The Grim Reapers*, 134.

15. Report of Action, 26 October 1942, in HWD, Serial 00100, 3.

16. Blackmer interview.

17. Report of Action, 26 October 1942, Enclosure (A): Executive Officer's Report, 30 October 1942, Excerpts from Pensacola Log of Fighter Director of Circuit, 26 October 1942, 1.

18. Hammel, *Guadalcanal: The Carrier Battles*, 378–81; George L. Wrenn, "A *Hornet* (CV-8) Fighter at Santa Cruz," in *The* Hornets *and Their Heroic Men*, ed. Kenneth M. Glass and Harold L. Buell (North Port, Fla.: U.S.S. *Hornet* Club, 1992), 8–9.

19. Quoted in Eddy, "How We Lost a Gallant Lady," 35.

20. Hammel, *Guadalcanal: The Carrier Battles*, 386.

21. Wrenn, "A *Hornet* Fighter at Santa Cruz," 9.

22. "*Hornet* Takes a Heavy Toll," 11, from Foley clipping file.

23. Quoted in ibid.

24. Quoted in "Oak Park Gunner on *Hornet* Tells Her Death Fight," from Hill clipping file.

25. Hammel, *Guadalcanal: The Carrier Battles*, 387.

26. McMurtry, "6-Minute Attack."

27. Tappan's account is provided in Anne Swenson, "'Hours of Hell' on *Hornet* Described by Navy Flyers [*sic*]," from Hill clipping file; Swope's account is in Hammel, *Guadalcanal: The Carrier Battles*, 391.

28. Tappan is quoted in Swenson, "'Hours of Hell'"; see also Ralph L. Cotton, "Recalling Santa Cruz," in Glass and Buell, *The* Hornets *and Their Heroic Men*, 10.

29. "'Disregard for His Own Life' Just Mechanical, Says Hero," from Hill clipping file.

30. Quoted in Eddy, "How We Lost a Gallant Lady," 103.

31. Quoted in ibid., 104; Griffin, *A Ship to Remember*, 259; Report of Action, 26 October 1942, Enclosure (H): Communication Officer's Report, 30 October 1942, 5.

32. Report of Action, 26 October 1942, Enclosure (F): First Lieutenant's Report, 30 October 1942, Report of Construction and Damage Control Organization, 6–7.

33. Report of Damage Sustained, in ibid., 2; Hammel, *Guadalcanal: The Carrier Battles*, 387–88.

34. First Lieutenant's Report, 30 October 1942, Report of Construction and Damage Control, 2.

35. The following account is from McAteer interview.

36. Glen Dock interview; Blackmer interview.

37. Foley oral history, No. 4: 371.

38. Blackmer interview.

39. Hammel, *Guadalcanal: The Carrier Battles*, 393.

40. Report of Action, 26 October 1942, Enclosure (E): Report of Engineer Officer, 30 October 1942, 1.

41. Jurika oral history, No. 15: 521.

42. Ruchti interview; Report of Engineer Officer, 1.

43. Griffin, *A Ship to Remember*, 258.

44. Quoted in Eddy, "How We Lost a Gallant Lady," 102.

45. Blackmer interview.

46. Hammel, *Guadalcanal: The Carrier Battles*, 404.

47. Quoted in ibid., 396.

48. Foley oral history, No. 4: 374.

49. Hammel, *Guadalcanal: The Carrier Battles*, 408.

50. "*Hornet* Takes a Heavy Toll," picture caption, 11.

51. Foley, "Every Good Ship," 18.

52. Interviews with Jack Medley and Robert Taylor, 41st *Hornet* Reunion, Norfolk, Va., 9–11 June 1989; the crewmen's remarks to Soucek are quoted in Eddy, "How We Lost a Gallant Lady," 104.

53. Walker interview; Glen Dock interview; Blackmer interview.

54. Report of Action, 26 October 1942, Enclosure (L): Medical Officer's Report, 30 October 1942, 1.

55. Hammel discusses a number of these cases in *Guadalcanal: The Carrier Battles*, 398–401, 457–58.

56. Ibid., 397.

57. Ibid., 397–98.

58. Foley oral history, No. 4: 375.

59. Ibid., 376.

60. "Oak Park Gunner."

61. Bancroft interview.

62. Gerald McAteer, "A Day to Remember," in Glass and Buell, *The* Hornets *and Their Heroic Men*, 7.

63. Blackmer interview.

64. Foley oral history, No. 4: 379.

65. Report of Action, 26 October 1942, 6.

66. Quoted in Griffin, *A Ship to Remember*, 263; see also McMurtry, "6-Minute Attack."

67. Quoted in Johnston, *The Grim Reapers*, 137.

68. Quoted in ibid.

69. Quoted in ibid., 137–38.

70. Glen Dock interview.

71. Report of Engineer Officer, 5; Hammel, *Guadalcanal: The Carrier Battles*, 463.

72. Glen Dock interview.

73. Quoted in Hammel, *Guadalcanal: The Carrier Battles*, 470.

74. Dodson, "The Day the Coins Went Down," 74.

75. Report of Action, 26 October 1942, 7; Eddy, "How We Lost a Gallant Lady," 105.

76. Foley oral history, No. 4: 378.

77. Martin telephone interview.

78. Foley oral history, No. 4: 379.

79. The incident was recounted by Oscar Dodson in Communication Officer's Report, 6. The radioman who urged his buddy to take the shots was probably Elmer Edwin Jackson; see Harold L. Buell, "A Hornet Airman," in Glass and Buell, *The* Hornets *and Their Heroic Men*, 9.

80. Glen Dock interview; Foley oral history, No. 4: 379.

81. Martin interview.

82. Quoted in Communication Officer's Report, 6.

83. Charles M. Melhorn, interviewed by Etta-Belle Kitchen, 15 February 1970, U.S. Naval Institute Oral History Transcripts, 93.

84. Jones, *WW II: A Chronicle*, 106.

Epilogue

1. Frank, *Guadalcanal*, 400; Goldstein and Dillon, *Fading Victory*, 255.
2. Goldstein and Dillon, *Fading Victory*, 252, 253.
3. John B. Lundstrom, "Frank Jack Fletcher Got a Bum Rap, Part One," *Naval History* 6, no. 2 (1992): 27. Lundstrom's article brings out some important new information. Certainly Fletcher was not the coward or the bumbling fool that critics such as Edwin Layton and Samuel Eliot Morison have maintained. But Lundstrom's argument does not overturn earlier verdicts concerning Fletcher's overall weakness as a carrier commander, especially before if not during the Battle of the Eastern Solomons.
4. Ibid.
5. Sumrall, *Warship's Battle Damage Report No. 1: USS* Hornet, 32.
6. Carlo D'Este, *Decision in Normandy* (New York: E. P. Dutton, 1983), 428.
7. Jensen, *Carrier War*, 172.

Bibliography

Unpublished Sources

Bancroft, Keith. Personal diary, June–October 1942. Provided by author.

Foley, Francis Drake. "Every Good Ship Has a Heart." Typescript provided by author, n.d.

U.S.S. *Hornet* Club, Inc. Videotaped interviews with *Hornet* crew regarding the Doolittle raid, 1993.

U.S.S. *Hornet* Deck Log, 20 October 1941–26 October 1942. National Military Records Center, Record Group 24, National Archives, Washington, D.C.

U.S.S. *Hornet* (CV-8) War Diary. NRS 70: WWII History/Diary/Reports. Microfilm. U.S. Navy Operational Archives Branch, Naval Historical Division, Washington Navy Yard, Washington, D.C.

Personal Interviews

41st *Hornet* Reunion, Norfolk, Va., 9–11 June 1989.

    Hill, William J.

    Martin, Henry.

    Medley, Jack.

    Ruchti, Cardon.

    Taylor, Robert.

    Walker, James.

Bancroft, Keith. Renton, Wash., 7 May 1994.

Blackmer, Eugene. Everett, Wash., 3 May 1994.

Dock, Glen. Port Orchard, Wash., 24 April 1994.

Foley, Francis. Annapolis, Md., 7 July 1989.

Kimpton, Roger. Telephone interview, 3 August 1994.

Lundstrom, John. Telephone interviews, 14 December 1993, 11 January 1994.

Martin, Henry. Telephone interview, 29 September 1994.

McAteer, Gerald. Washington, D.C., 21 July 1989.

Ruchti, Cardon. Telephone interview, 1 September 1994.

Slonim, Gilven. Telephone interview, 6 December 1993.

U.S. Naval Institute Oral History Transcripts

Foley, Francis D. Interviewed by Paul Stillwell, 16 January 1985.

Jurika, Stephen. Interviewed by Paul B. Ryan, 4 March 1976.

Melhorn, Charles M. Interviewed by Etta-Belle Kitchen, 15 February 1970.

Miller, Henry L. Interviewed by John T. Mason, Jr., 24 March 1971.

Stroop, Paul D. Interviewed by Etta-Belle Kitchen, 14 September 1969.

Thach, John S. Interviewed by Etta-Belle Kitchen, 6 November 1970.

Ward, Alfred G. Interviewed by John T. Mason, Jr., 27 August 1970.

Worthington, Joseph M. Interviewed by John T. Mason, Jr., 31 May 1972.

Published Sources

Blair, Clay, Jr. *Silent Victory: The U.S. Submarine War against Japan.* 2 vols. Philadelphia: J. B. Lippincott, 1975.

Bryan, J., III. *Aircraft Carrier.* New York: Ballantine Books, 1954.

Bryan, Joseph, III, and Philip Reed. *Mission beyond Darkness.* New York: Duell, Sloan and Pearce, 1945.

Casey, Robert J. *Torpedo Junction: With the Pacific Fleet from Pearl Harbor to Midway.* Indianapolis: Bobbs-Merrill, 1942.

Cohen, Stan. *Destination Tokyo: A Pictorial History of Doolittle's Tokyo Raid, April 18, 1942.* Missoula, Mont.: Pictorial Histories Publishing, 1983.

Costello, John. *The Pacific War.* New York: Rawson, Wade Publishers, 1981.

D'Este, Carlo. *Decision in Normandy.* New York: E. P. Dutton, 1983.

Eddy, Don. "How We Lost a Gallant Lady: Interview with Charles P. Mason." *America,* November 1943: 32–33, 102–8.

"11 on *Kearny* Died for Liberty, Knox Says at *Hornet* Ceremony." *Washington Post,* 21 October 1941.

Fahey, James. *Ships and Aircraft of the U.S. Fleet: Victory Edition.* New York: Ships & Aircraft, 1945.

Frank, Pat, and Joseph D. Harrington. *Rendezvous at Midway: USS Yorktown and the Japanese Carrier Fleet.* New York: John Day, 1967.

Frank, Richard B. *Guadalcanal.* New York: Random House, 1990.

———. "'. . . Nailed the Colors to the Mast.'" *Naval History* 6, no. 4 (1992): 6–12.

Friedman, Norman. *U.S. Aircraft Carriers: An Illustrated Design History*. Ship plans by A. D. Baker III. Annapolis, Md.: Naval Institute Press, 1983.

Fuchida, Mitsuo, and Masatake Okumiya. *Midway: The Battle That Doomed Japan*. Edited by Clarke H. Kawakami and Roger Pineau. New York: Ballantine Books, 1955.

Fuller, J. F. C. *The Decisive Battles of the Western World and Their Influence upon History*. Vol. 2, *1792–1944*. Edited by John Terraine. London: Granada Publishing, 1970.

Glass, Kenneth M., and Harold L. Buell, eds. *The Hornets and Their Heroic Men*. North Port, Fla.: U.S.S. *Hornet* Club, 1992.

Goldstein, Donald M., and Katherine V. Dillon, eds. *Fading Victory: The Diary of Admiral Matome Ugaki, 1941–1945*. Translated by Masataka Chihaya. Pittsburgh: University of Pittsburgh Press, 1991.

Gravatt, Brent L. "On the Back of the Fleet." *Naval History* 4, no. 2 (1990): 14–18.

Griffin, Alexander T. *A Ship to Remember: The Saga of the* Hornet. New York: Howell, Soskin, 1943.

Grosvenor, Melville Bell. "The New Queen of the Seas." *National Geographic Magazine* 87, no. 1 (1942): 1–30.

Halsey, William F., and J. Bryan III. *Admiral Halsey's Story*. New York: McGraw-Hill, 1947.

Hammel, Eric. *Guadalcanal: The Carrier Battles*. New York: Crown Publishers, 1987.

Harvey, Frank. *Air War—Vietnam*. New York: Bantam Books, 1967.

Hastings, Max. *Overlord: D-Day and the Battle for Normandy*. New York: Simon and Schuster, 1984.

"*Hornet*'s Last Day: Tom Lea Paints Death of a Great Carrier." *Life*, 2 August 1943, 42–49.

Hoyt, Edwin P. *Japan's War: The Great Pacific Conflict, 1853 to 1952*. New York: McGraw-Hill, 1986.

Ito, Masanori, and Roger Pineau. *The End of the Imperial Japanese Navy*. Translated by Andrew Y. Kuroda and Roger Pineau. New York: MacFadden Books, 1965; first published 1956.

Jane's Fighting Aircraft of World War II. New York: Military Press, 1989.

Jensen, Oliver. *Carrier War*. New York: Simon and Schuster, 1945.

Johnston, Stanley. *Queen of the Flat-tops*. New York: E. P. Dutton, 1942.

———. *The Grim Reapers*. New York: E. P. Dutton, 1943.

Jones, James. *WW II: A Chronicle of Soldiering*. New York: Ballantine Books, 1976.

"Knox Praises Men Lost on the *Kearny*." *New York Times*, 21 October 1941.

Lawson, Ted W. *Thirty Seconds over Tokyo*. Edited by Robert Considine. New York: Random House, 1945.

Layton, Edwin T., Roger Pineau, and John Costello. *"And I Was There": Pearl Harbor and Midway—Breaking the Secrets*. New York: William Morrow, 1985.

Lea, Tom. "Aboard the U.S.S. *Hornet*." *Life*, 22 March 1943, 49–58.

LeCompte, Malcolm A. "Radar and the Air Battles of Midway." *Naval History* 6, no. 2 (1992): 28–32.

Lord, Walter. *Incredible Victory*. New York: Harper & Row, 1967.

Lundstrom, John B. *The First Team: Pacific Naval Air Combat from Pearl Harbor to Midway*. Annapolis, Md.: Naval Institute Press, 1984.

———. "Frank Jack Fletcher Got a Bum Rap, Part One." *Naval History* 6, no. 2 (1992): 22–27.

———. "Frank Jack Fletcher Got a Bum Rap, Part Two: Guadalcanal." *Naval History* 6, no. 3 (1992): 22–28.

Manchester, William. *The Glory and the Dream: A Narrative History of America, 1932–1972*. 2 vols. Boston: Little, Brown, 1973, 1974.

Mason, John T., Jr., ed. *The Pacific War Remembered: An Oral History Collection*. Annapolis, Md.: Naval Institute Press, 1986.

Mears, Frederick. *Carrier Combat*. Garden City, N.Y.: Doubleday, Doran, 1944.

Morison, Samuel Eliot. *History of United States Naval Operations in World War II*. Vol. 1, *The Rising Sun in the Pacific, 1931–April 1942;* vol. 4, *Coral Sea, Midway and Submarine Actions, May 1942–August 1942;* vol. 5, *The Struggle for Guadalcanal, August 1942–February 1943*. Boston: Little, Brown, 1947–62.

Morrison, Wilbur H. *Above and Beyond, 1941–1945*. New York: St. Martin's Press, 1983.

Okumiya, Masatake, Jiro Horikoshi, and Martin Caidin. *Zero*. New York: Ballantine Books, 1956.

Prange, Gordon W. *Miracle at Midway*. New York: McGraw-Hill, 1982.

Pratt, Fletcher. "Memorial of the *Wasp*." *Harper's Magazine*, May 1943, 545–55.

Reynolds, Clark G. *The Carrier War*. Alexandria, Va.: Time-Life Books, 1982.

Ringle, Ken. "The Code-Cracker & the Battle of Midway." *Washington Post*, 4 June 1992.

Rochefort, Joseph J. "Finding the *Kido Butai*." *Naval Institute Proceedings* 118, no. 6 (1992): 76–78.

Slavin, Peter. "Prange's Midway." *Naval Institute Proceedings* 118, no. 6 (1992): 79.

Slonim, Gilven M. "A Flagship View of Command Decisions." *Naval Institute Proceedings* 84, no. 4 (1958): 80–89.

Smith, S. E., ed. *The United States Navy in World War II*. New York: William Morrow, 1966.

Smith, William Ward. *Midway: Turning Point of the Pacific*. New York: Thomas Y. Crowell, 1966.

Spector, Ronald H. *Eagle against the Sun: The American War with Japan*. New York: Free Press, 1985.

Stafford, Edward P. *The Big E: The Story of the USS* Enterprise. New York: Dell Publishing, 1964.

Sumrall, Robert F., ed. *Warship's Battle Damage Report No. 1: USS* Hornet *(CV8)*. Missoula, Mont.: Pictorial Histories Publishing, 1985.

Sweetman, Jack. "50 Years Ago . . . Midway." *Naval Institute Proceedings* 118, no. 6 (1992): 74–75.

Taylor, Theodore. *The Magnificent Mitscher*. New York: Norton, 1954.

Toland, John. *But Not in Shame: The Six Months after Pearl Harbor.* New York: Signet Books, 1962.

Tregaskis, Richard. *Guadalcanal Diary.* New York: Random House, 1943.

Wharton, Don. "He Stuck with the Wounded." *Look,* 24 August 1943: 26–27.

Willmott, H. P. *The Barrier and the Javelin: Japanese and Allied Pacific Strategies, February to June 1942.* Annapolis, Md.: Naval Institute Press, 1983.

Wilmot, Chester. *The Struggle for Europe.* London: Collins Clear-Type Press, 1952.

Wolfert, Ira. *Battle for the Solomons.* Boston: Houghton Mifflin, 1943.

In addition, *Hornet* veterans Francis D. Foley and William J. Hill permitted the use of their personal collections of contemporary newspaper and magazine clippings. Most clippings do not include source information.

Index

Midway, Battle of, (cont.)
in, 97–98, 111–12, 119, 120, 122–25,
132–41 passim, 145, 147–49; intelligence
operations during, 118–19, 127–28; U.S.
operations in, 118–49 passim, 154; U.S.
failures in, 149–54 passim, 226; results
of, 149, 274, 278, 286n3; Japanese failures in, 150, 153; assessments of, 156,
159; lessons of, 225
Midway Island: importance of, 80, 81, 98;
flight operations from, 121, 122, 123
Mikawa, Gunichi, 206
Mikuma, 147–49
Miles, Robert, 131
Miller, Frank, 222
Miller, Henry L., 49, 51, 52, 55–56, 68, 70
Mills, R. W., 89–90
Minneapolis, 183
Mitchell, John Jenks, 187–88
Mitchell, Samuel G. ("Pat"), 27, 32, 177;
background and character of, 85; at
Midway, 110, 117, 125, 126, 127, 129,
152; conduct of, 144; promotion of,
162
Mitchell, William ("Billy"), 2
Mitscher, Marc Andrew ("Pete"), 47, 78,
85, 92; background and character of, 5,
7, 153, 160, 183; as *Hornet* commanding
officer, 8–9, 10, 15, 20–21, 22–23, 25,
85, 158; and Pearl Harbor attack, 16,
18; and *Hornet* shakedown, 20–34 passim; training philosophy of, 30, 32–33;
and Air Group 8, 32, 33; and Doolittle
raid, 37–40 passim, 50, 52, 53, 57, 59,
60, 64, 66, 73, 76; promotion of, 107,
160; and preparations for Midway, 111,
112, 114; and relations with Waldron,
117, 126, 152–53; at Midway, 125–27,
128, 137, 138, 141, 144, 149, 273; recollections of, 142; relations with Ring,
142; after Midway, 154. *See also* Midway,
Battle of: U.S. failures in
Mitsubishi 97 (Japanese bomber), 203–4,
208, 209
Mogami, 147–49
Monssen, 90
Moore, Benny, 201
Moore, R. A. ("Moose"), 88, 120
Moore, "Whitey," 89, 120, 131
Moran, Henry: duties of, 92, 114; at Mid-
way, 114; and Guadalcanal campaign,
192, 194; at Santa Cruz, 222, 239, 240,
242, 247, 248, 255, 256, 277
Moran, W. J., 209
Morris, 253, 255, 256
Morrison, Wilbur H., 174
Muery, Louise John, 93–94

Murray, George, 207; at Midway, 150, 151,
183; as Task Force 17 commander, 171,
176, 178, 193, 197, 198, 199, 219, 221;
character of, 183–84; and Guadalcanal
campaign, 190, 211–15 passim; at Santa
Cruz, 222, 223, 225, 231, 250, 255, 257
Mustin, 253, 257, 268

Nagumo, Chuichi, 58; as *Kido Butai* commander, 49, 79, 103; and preparations
for Midway, 98, 99, 100, 112; at Midway, 120, 122–24, 127, 131, 133, 134,
136, 138, 144, 274; at Eastern Solomons,
179, 180, 274; and Guadalcanal campaign, 192; at Santa Cruz, 221–26 passim, 230, 268. *See also* Midway, Battle
of: Japanese failures in
Nashville, 40, 53, 66, 67, 70–73 passim
Nauru (island), 94, 95, 96
Nautilus, 127, 134, 182
Naval Expansion Act of 1938, 2
Nazi aggression, 1–2, 10, 14, 33, 48
New Hebrides Islands, 82, 179, 181, 193,
194
Newport News Shipbuilding and Drydock
Company, 1
Nimitz, Chester W., 30, 182; and Doolittle
raid, 37, 49, 50, 64; and cryptanalysis,
58; and Coral Sea, 82; and Midway,
95–96, 102, 109, 114, 115, 154; and
changes in Pacific Fleet, 160, 162, 164,
272; and Guadalcanal campaign, 173–
76 passim, 196–200 passim, 205, 210;
and conflicts with MacArthur, 174, 185;
background and character of, 183; com-
mand decisions of, 216. *See also* U.S.
Navy: strategies of
Nitto Maru, 66, 67, 71, 72, 101
Noa, 20, 28, 33
Noone, Bob, 240
Northampton, 198, 200, 208, 255, 256, 261
North Carolina, 3, 19–20, 166, 186, 188–91
passim
Nouméa, 94, 184, 185, 194, 196, 197, 204,
221, 250, 265, 269
Nowell, Lt. Comm., 240
Noyes, Leigh, 183, 184, 185, 187, 190

O'Brien, 189, 191
Ocean (island), 94, 95, 96
O'Dowd (pilot), 261
Oklahoma, 77
Operation MI. *See* Midway, Battle of
Osborn, Ed, 200, 276
Osterloh, E. H. ("Sam"), 112, 114, 252
Owens, Jimmie, 88, 120
Ozawa, Jisaburo, 272–73

Vandegrift, Alexander, 167, 176, 196, 197, 206, 210, 211, 217
Vaughn, Chief Petty Officer, 42
Vejtasa, Stanley, 221
VF-72: composition of, 163–64; at Santa Cruz, 226, 227, 228. *See also* Air Group 8
Vincennes, 40, 53, 59, 66
Vormstein, H., 64
Vose, James ("Moe"), 179, 192, 226, 229–30, 274

Waldron, John C., 28, 33, 82–83, 94, 95; background and character of, 86–87, 117; and relations with Ring, 107–8, 117; and preparations for Midway, 110, 112; at Midway, 116–18, 121, 126–27, 128, 129–30; death of, 131. *See also* Midway, Battle of: U.S. failures in
Walker, James, 11–12, 70, 143, 257, 270
Wall, Robert W., 70–71
Washington, 19–20, 186, 191, 206
Wasp, 15, 100–101, 102, 163, 179; commissioning of, 4; characteristics of, 40, 189, 275; and Guadalcanal campaign, 166, 174, 184, 186; loss of, 187–91, 192, 207, 275
Weimer, J. O., 209
White, K. B., 66, 68, 129–30, 229
White, T. H., 56, 68
Widhelm, William J. ("Gus"), 94, 166, 277; character of, 25, 86, 163; at Midway, 110, 120, 144, 147–49; promotion of, 163; and Guadalcanal campaign, 178, 179, 187, 192, 201, 212; at Santa Cruz, 223–29 passim, 231, 259–61, 274
Wilcox, John, 20, 33, 37
Wildcats. *See* F4F-3 Wildcat; F4F-4 Wildcat
Williman, R. D., 112

Wilmot, Chester, 30–31
Woodman, William, 193, 237
Woodson, J. D., 89
Worthington, Joe, 194
Wrenn, George, 232–33, 234–35, 244
Wright, 7, 8

Yamamoto, Isoroku, 31, 182; and Doolittle raid, 71–72, 75; at Midway, 95, 108–9, 119, 146, 149; and Guadalcanal campaign, 170, 180, 185, 196, 197, 203, 205, 210; and Eastern Solomons, 179; and Santa Cruz, 221, 271. *See also* Japanese navy: strategies of; Midway, Battle of: Japanese failures in
Yamato, 103, 112, 159
Yorktown, 3, 5, 15, 36, 85, 100, 101, 109, 273; sails to Pacific, 17; at Coral Sea, 81–82, 94, 95, 105; and preparations for Midway, 95–96, 97, 107, 110; at Midway, 118–20, 125, 133–41 passim; loss of, 137, 148, 190, 253, 274, 275. *See also* Air Group 3
Yorktown (class), 19, 21; development of, 3; design of, 4–5, 275

Zeke (Japanese warplane): characteristics of, 27, 65
Zero (Japanese warplane): characteristics of, 19, 27, 65, 105, 169
Zook, Earl, 186
Zuiho: at Midway, 145; and Guadalcanal campaign, 205; at Santa Cruz, 225, 229, 230, 231; damage to, 227, 272
Zuikaku, 101, 102, 142, 272; at Coral Sea, 81, 95, 105, 275; and Guadalcanal campaign, 180, 205, 210; at Santa Cruz, 223, 225, 231, 261

About the Author

AFTER A thirty-eight-month enlistment in the U.S. Navy, during which he sailed roughly fifty thousand miles on various small combatants and auxiliaries, Mr. Rose obtained a B.A. in history from the University of Illinois and a Ph.D. in American history from the University of California at Berkeley. He subsequently taught at the University of Nebraska, the University of Arizona, Carnegie-Mellon University, and Johns Hopkins University's School of Advanced International Studies.

In 1972 Dr. Rose joined the Historical Office of the State Department and transferred to its Bureau of Oceans and International Environmental and Scientific Affairs six years later. Until his retirement in 1989 he specialized in polar, oceans, and advanced technology affairs.

Among Dr. Rose's six published books are *The Long Shadow: Essays on the Second World War Era* (Greenwood, 1978) and *Assault on Eternity: Richard E. Byrd and the Exploration of Antarctica, 1946–47* (Naval Institute Press, 1980), which received a John Lyman Book Award Honorable Mention from the North American Society for Oceanic History.